To Austin, J.P., Levi, Loren and Matthew

The Economic Foundations of Property Rights

Selected Readings

Edited by

Svetozar Pejovich

Professor of Economics, Texas A & M University, USA

Edward Elgar

Cheltenham, UK • Lyme, US

Published by
Edward Elgar Publishing Limited
8 Lansdown Place
Cheltenham
Glos GL50 2HU
UK

Edward Elgar Publishing, Inc.
1 Pinnacle Hill Road
Lyme
NH 03768
US

A catalogue record for this book
is available from the British Library

Library of Congress Cataloguing-in-Publication Data
The economic foundations of property rights : selected readings /
    edited by Svetozar Pejovich.
        Includes bibliographical references
        1. Right of property—Economic aspects. I. Pejovich, Svetozar.
    HB701.E24 1997
    330.1'7—dc21   97–14361
                                                                        CIP

ISBN 1 85898 543 9

Printed and bound in Great Britain by
Hartnolls Limited, Bodmin, Cornwall

Contents

Acknowledgements

The publishers wish to thank the following who have kindly given permission for the use of copyright material.

Armen Alchian, Susan Woodward and the American Economic Association for article: 'The Firm is Dead: Long Live the Firm: A Review of Oliver E. Williamson's *The Economic Institutions of Capitalism*', *Journal of Economic Literature*, 1988, March, **XXVI**, 65–79.

Benjamin Klein and the American Economic Association for article: 'Transaction Cost Determinants of "Unfair" Contractual Arrangements', *American Economic Review*, 1980, May, **70**, 356–62.

Svetozar Pejovich and Cambridge University Press for articles: 'Property Rights and Technological Innovation' in E. Paul, F. Miller and J. Paul (eds), *Scientific Innovation, Philosophy and Public Policy*, 1996, 168–80 and 'Institutions, Nationalism, and the Transition Process in Eastern Europe' in Ellen Paul (ed.), *Liberalism and the Economic Order*, 1993, 65–78.

James A. Dorn and the Cato Institute for article: 'Pricing and Property: the Chinese Puzzle' in James A. Dorn and Wang Xi (eds), *Economic Reform in China: Problems and Prospects*, University of Chicago Press, 1990, 39–61, abridged.

Enrico Colombatto, Jonathan Macey and Economia Delle Scelte Pubbliche for article: 'A Public Choice View of Transition in Eastern Europe', *Economia delle Scelte Pubbliche*, 1994, **12**, 113–32, abridged.

Armen Alchian and Il Politico for article: 'How Should Prices be Set?', *Il Politico*, 1967, **XXXII**, 369–82.

Armen Alchian and Kluwer Academic Publishers for article: 'Some Implications of Recognition of Property Right Transactions Costs' in K. Brunner (ed.), *Economics and Social Institutions: Insights from the Conferences on Analysis and Ideology*, Martinus Nijhoff Publishing, 1977, 234–55.

Bruno Leoni and the Liberty Fund Inc for article: 'Freedom and the Rule of Law' in Bruno Leoni, *Freedom and the Law*, 1961, D. Van Nostrand Company Inc., 59–76 and 192.

Richard A. Posner and Little, Brown and Company for article: Extracts from 'Property' in Richard A. Posner, *Economic Analysis of Law*, 4th edition, 1992, 32–49.

Michael Walker and Douglass C. North for article: 'Institutions, Economic Growth and Freedom: An Historical Introduction' in M. Walker (ed.), *Freedom, Democracy and Economic Welfare*, Fraser Institute, 1988, 3–25.

Michael Walker and Lord Peter Bauer for article: 'Black Africa: Free or Oppressed?' in M. Walker (ed.), *Freedom, Democracy and Economic Welfare*, Fraser Institute, 1988, 213–23.

Terry L. Anderson, Peter J. Hall and the Southern Economic Journal for article: 'Privatizing the Commons: An Improvement?', *Southern Economic Journal*, 1983, **50**, 438–50.

Karl Brunner and Schweizerische Zeitschrift für Volkwirtschaft und Statistik for article: 'The Limits of Economic Policy', *Schweizerische Zeitschrift für Volkwirtschaft und Statistik*, 1985, **121**, 213–34, abridged.

James M. Buchanan and The University of Chicago for article: 'Politics, Property, and the Law: An Alternative Interpretation of Miller et al. v. Schoene', *Journal of Law and Economics*, 1972, October, **15**(2), 439–52.

Yoram Barzel and The University of Chicago for article: 'Measurement Costs and the Organization of Markets', *Journal of Law and Economics*, 1982, April, **XXV**(1), 27–48.

John Umbeck and the Western Economic Association for article: 'Might Makes Rights: A Theory of the Formation and Initial Distribution of Property Rights', *Economic Inquiry*, 1981, January, **XIX**, 38–59.

List of contributors

Armen Alchian, *Professor of Economics, University of California at Los Angeles, Los Angeles, California, US.*

Terry Anderson, *Professor of Economics, Montana State University, Bozeman, Montana, US.*

Yoram Barzel, *Professor of Economics, University of Washington, Seattle, Washington, US.*

Lord Peter Bauer, *Professor Emeritus, London School of Economics, London, England.*

Karl Brunner (deceased), *Professor of Economics, University of Rochester, Rochester, New York, US.*

James Buchanan, *Distinguished Professor of Economics, and Advisory-General Director, Center for the Study of Public Choice, George Mason University in Fairfax, Virginia, US. Nobel Laureate.*

Enrico Colombatto, *Professor of Economics, University of Turin, and Director, International Centre for Economic Research, Turin, Italy.*

James Dorn, *Vice-President for Academic Affairs, Cato Institute, and Professor of Economics, Towson State University, Baltimore, Maryland, US.*

Peter Hill, *Professor of Economics, Wheaton College, Wheaton, Illinois, US.*

Benjamin Klein, *Professor of Economics, University of California at Los Angeles, Los Angeles, California, US.*

Bruno Leoni (deceased), *Professor of Legal Theory and the Theory of the State, University of Pavia, Pavia, Italy.*

Jonathan Macey, *J. DuPratt White Professor of Law, Cornell University, Ithaca, New York, US.*

Douglass North, *Henry R. Luce Professor of Law and Liberty, Washington University, St. Louis, Missouri, US. Nobel Laureate.*

Svetozar Pejovich, *Professor of Economics, Texas A&M University, College Station, Texas, and Research Fellow, International Centre for Economic Research, Turin, Italy.*

Richard Posner, *Chief Judge, United States Court of Appeals for the Seventh Circuit and Senior Lecturer, University of Chicago Law School, US.*

John Umbreck, *Professor of Economics, Purdue University, Lafayette, Indiana, US.*

Susan Woodward, *Stanford, California, US.*

Foreword

In the past three decades the economics of property rights has often been considered almost as a part or a tool of 'law and economics'. To some extent this was justified. For most economists 'law and economics' was about the optimal allocation of property rights in a world where transaction costs are high, and where the temptation to assign them to the State tantalizing.

More recently, however, the very idea of property rights has come to the fore in its own right. More appropriately, law and economics is now regarded as one among the areas to which the property-right theory and methodology can be applied successfully. Other important domains are the economics of consumer and producer behaviour, of market structure and – of course – the economics of institutions.

In this light, today the property-right approach is gradually making its way to being acknowledged as far superior to its rival paradigms – the neoclassical and the real socialist. Although many would still accept neoclassical micro-economics as a useful teaching device, the shortcomings generated by the frictionless-economy assumption make its results doubtful from the positive viewpoint, utterly unacceptable from the normative side. Similarly, the real-socialist presumption of widespread and unavoidable market failure, although appealing at first glance, is not *per se* adequate to justify the absence of government failures, whereas its negative influence on technological progress seems beyond reasonable doubt. In short, the two orthodoxies of the twentieth century have led to useless economics and much too often to harmful policy making. The major event of the past fifty years – the fall of the Communist political and economics regimes in Eastern Europe – and the disappointment with the quick-and-successful transition recipes which followed, are the most obvious testimony. It goes to Professor Pejovich's credit to have emphasized these inadequacies long ago.

Instead, history clearly shows that technological progress is not only important as far as its direct consequences on growth are concerned, but also as regards its indirect effects, in that it makes it possible to internalize more and more externalities. In other words, a satisfactory property-right system makes deferred consumption viable. Investment in technology is enhanced, and technological progress in turn reduces market failures, raises growth and welfare.

This book is thus particularly important on two accounts. First, the papers it contains remind us of the roots of economic behaviour. Such roots are essentially the freedom to choose in a world of scarcity, where the rules of the game are determined by the nature of the property-right system, which should be designed to cut down transaction costs and to create the incentives to reduce such costs in the future (technological progress).

Moreover, these contributions allow us to realize that (normative) economics is not about 'how reality should be'. Rather, it is about identifying the borderline between enforcing the existing rules of the game (and thus eliminate uncertainty) and making such rules. Of course, such a borderline differs across countries and over time. In particular, this book explains that there cannot exist any ground for ethical state intervention. Similarly, there cannot exist a theory for neutral and amoral intervention, but just a general principle; nor would it be possible to conceive a theory for 'optimal' policy making. Hayek made this clear over fifty years ago. Pejovich today provides us with an updated and comprehensive development of Hayek's original insights – and with a lot of evidence, too.

In turn, the borderline question raises two sets of issues. One concerns the origins of the existing rules of the game. The other concerns the possibility that such rules may be prevented from evolving, even if desirable and desired by the majority of the individuals. The debate on these issues is in fact the core of three still rapidly-growing research agendas – institutional economics, public choice and rent-seeking. Quite appropriately, Pejovich has preferred to focus on the foundations of property-right economics, and introduce institutional matters so as to make the reader perceive the nature of the fundamental questions, as well as the tremendous potential distinctive of the property-right methodology. In fact, the property-right approach itself is about the mould of the institutional framework and about the ways the role of transaction costs can be shaped and possibly reduced. I believe this is the very central idea of this book. It is perhaps too simple a notion to be taken seriously by sophisticated formal economists; but surely too important to be dismissed or overlooked by social scientists, by policy makers, and by all those who want to understand the world we are all living in.

From this viewpoint, public choice and rent-seeking are of course important, but 'merely' instrumental to the attainment of further and deeper insights in the economics of institutions. As this book suggests, they deserve a separate treatment.

I feel that scholars and students of economics as a social science should be very grateful to Edward Elgar for having published this book. I am also very proud that the International Centre for Economic Research (ICER) was the place where a large part of this volume was conceived and worked through.

Enrico Colombatto
Director of ICER, and
Professor of Economics, University of Turin

Preface

In the early 1970s, Eirik Furubotn and I published a selection of readings in the economics of property rights. At that time, the economics of property rights was an outsider in our discipline, waiting to be recognized as a viable method for analysis of social issues. Twenty years later, the economics of property rights has its place under the sun. It has become an important and acceptable method of analysis of social issues.

I have selected readings for this book on the basis of three criteria. A primary objective is to give wider recognition to a number of pioneering works in the economics of property rights – works which, because they were outside 'mainstream' economics, were published in lesser known journals. Second, I aimed to include research that has helped either to form the basis of the economic theory of property rights or to emphasize its predictive abilities in place of research on specific issues. Finally, the selection reflects my own understanding of the economics of property rights. I do not pretend that my choices for this book reflect any broad consensus in the fields of property rights, new institutional economics and public choice.

I owe a large intellectual debt to Armen Alchian and G. Warren Nutter. My thinking about economic issues also reflects the substantial influence of James Buchanan, Douglass North and Richard Posner.

Over a period of many years, the Earhart Foundation has helped me to do what I wanted to do but could not and would not have accomplished without its generous support. I am forever in debt to David Kennedy, Anthony Sullivan and Richard Ware.

I would also like to acknowledge the influence of 'Dub' Hill and Charles King of the Liberty Fund, the financial support of the Bradley Foundation and an anonymous donor from Dallas, the friendship and academic encouragement of people such as professors John Moore and Jim Dorn, the importance of Professor Bruno Dallago's conference series at the University of Trento in Italy on my perceptions of the transition process in Eastern Europe, the loving patience of my wife Susan and my children Alexandra, Brenda, Mira and Philip. Finally, I must thank my students at the Academia Istropolitana in Bratislava and at Texas A&M University in College Station for their active and meaningful contributions to my thinking about the economics of property rights.

The readings included here were assembled during my tenure at the International Centre for Economic Research in Turin, Italy. By giving me time away from both my home and office, the Centre has kept outside shocks to a minimum and contributed greatly to this book.

Svetozar Pejovich
Turin, Italy

PART I

PROPERTY RIGHTS: DEFINITION AND ECONOMIC SIGNIFICANCE

[1]

Introduction to Chapters 2, 3, 4 and 5

A property right is a liberty or permit to enjoy benefits of wealth – in its broadest sense – while assuming the costs which those benefits entail.... It will be observed that property rights, unlike wealth and benefits, are not physical objects nor events, but are abstract social relations. A property right is not a thing. (Irving Fisher, *Elementary Principles of Economics*, New York: Macmillan, 1923, p. 27.)

Property rights are relations among individuals that arise from the existence of scarce goods and that pertain to their use. They are the norms of behavior that individuals must observe or bear the costs of violation. That is, property rights do not define the relationship between individuals and objects. Instead, they define the relationship among individuals with respect to all scarce goods. My right to vote defines my position *vis-à-vis* other members of the community with respect to the choice of government. My right to a computer in my office defines my position *vis-à–vis* other individuals with respect to the access to that computer. Both rights are property rights. People who assert that human rights and property rights are two different categories of rights are usually driven by ideological motives.

Roman law provided the most enduring (and complete) legal and philosophical foundations for property rights. Moreover, the borrowing from Roman law by English and American common law suggests that European legal tradition and common law have the same roots.

In *The Institute of Justinian* we find references to three categories of property rights that are very much with us today: private ownership, communal ownership, and public (state) ownership. To quote Justinian: 'Some things are by natural law common to all, some are public, some belong to a society or corporation, and some belong to no one. But most things belong to individuals, being acquired by various titles.'[1]

The right of ownership contains three elements; exclusivity of ownership, transferability of ownership, and constitutional guarantees of ownership. Exclusivity of ownership creates a strong marriage between one's right to choose how to use a good and bearing the consequences of that choice. By internalizing the costs of a decision, the right of ownership creates strong incentives for owners to seek (and to reduce the costs of seeking) the highest-valued uses for their goods. Transferability of ownership means that the owner has the right to transfer a good to others at mutually agreed upon terms. In a world of uncertainty and incomplete information, transferability of ownership provides incentives for goods to be transferred from a less optimistic to a more optimistic owner.[2] By protecting economic wealth from political power, the constitutional guarantee of ownership creates incentives for individuals to accumulate wealth via investments that have long-run consequences.[3] Professor Brunner wrote:

A competitive arrangement emerging from the diffusion of private property is however not a sufficient condition for human dignity. Still, it appears to be a necessary condition. In the absence of genuine alternatives a behavior reflecting fear, subservience and cautious servility dominates human patterns. . . . Successful survival in non-competitive organizational careers depends critically on a man's ability to anticipate his superior's whims and to please him with personal non-performance traits.[4]

We observe many examples of public ownership in the United States, such as Hoover Dam, the Tennessee Valley Authority, national parks, military bases, and postal services. However, the term *state* (or public) *ownership* is merely a facade of words hiding the true owner, which is the ruling political elite.

The decision-making group in government does not bear the entire cost of its decision about the use of public goods. The total costs of its decision is spread over all taxpayers.[5] Public decision makers do not capture the benefits of their decisions, either. No matter what the government charges for the use of public goods, no individual has a claim to the proceeds.

Public decision makers, then, have weak incentives to invest time and resources in identifying the highest-valued uses for state-owned goods they control, and strong incentives to invest time and resources seeking beneficial trade-offs (pecuniary as well as nonpecuniary) for themselves. An implication is that public decision makers' subjective perceptions of political reality explain the allocation of state-owned resources. Therein lies the problem with state ownership. Inefficiencies in government have less to do with the professionalism and work habits of public decision makers than with the penalty/reward system arising from state ownership in scarce goods.[6]

Communal ownership means that a well-defined group of people jointly hold a nontransferable asset. Ordinarily, members of the group have the right to decide how to use the asset and the right to allocate proceeds. But they have no right to sell those rights to others. The rights that members of the group have in nontransferable assets are acquired by joining the group and lost by leaving it.

Communal ownership in land was (and is) quite frequent in tribal communities, was known in old Rome, and is paralleled in modern times by various types of producers' cooperatives and labor-managed firms. Communal ownership has two important consequences affecting economic behavior. First, individual members of the group have incentives to overutilize assets. Second, since it is only through membership in the group that an individual can capture some benefits from resources held in common, communal ownership creates a bias against decisions that have long-term consequences.

In Chapter 2 Armen Alchian defines property rights, identifies some important categories of property rights, and discusses their behavioral implications. He also introduces the concept of transaction costs, which is discussed in more detail later in the book.

Chapter 3 offers Richard Posner's analysis of the relationship between law, property rights, and economic behavior. By making the rules of the game stable and credible, the legal system provides incentives for individuals to seek and exploit the most beneficial exchange opportunities regardless of their time horizons. As time goes by individuals learn how to adjust to the prevailing rules, identify exchange opportunities, create new choices, and exploit the most beneficial contracts.[7]

In Chapter 4 Bruno Leoni defines the rule of law and attributes its endurance in Western Europe and the United States to the British and continental legal traditions. The British tradition generalizes the principles of the constitution from specific decisions (precedents) entered by common law courts. As old precedents are dropped and new ones are added to the legal system, judge-made rules change the constitution incrementally. By implication, the state has a limited role in creating new laws, its main function being to maintain, protect, and enforce the prevailing rules of the game. The British tradition thus creates a stable, self-generating, and self-sustaining framework for human interactions.

The continental tradition, on the other hand, is not precedents driven. The principles of the constitution are written by experts, debated by citizens, and eventually adopted by democratically elected parliaments or constitutional assemblies. The rights of individuals are deduced from the general principles of the constitution. However, parliaments have the power, within well-defined constraints, to modify the prevailing constitution and even to replace it with another. Implications of those parliamentary powers are two-fold. First, rent seeking by political coalitions can bring about changes in the prevailing set of property rights. Second, the continental tradition provides more opportunities for the state to play an active role in creating and modifying the rules of the game.[8]

In Chapter 5, James Buchanan discusses the consequences of using different legal methods in assigning new property rights. His key point is that we must not forget that the word *constitution* must come before the word *democracy*. In a more recent monograph, Buchanan wrote:

> If individual liberty is to be protected, . . . constitutional limits must be in place prior to and separately from any exercise of democratic governance. . . . An understanding of priorities in this respect should, of course, offer the basis for an extension of constitutional constraints on majoritarian legislative processes in modern polities and notably with reference to potential monetary and fiscal exploitation, quite apart from the more obvious 'takings' activity that must everywhere be condemned.[9]

Notes

1. Quoted in R. Epstein, 'On the Optimal Mix of Private and Common Property', in *Property Rights* (E. Paul, ed.), Cambridge: Cambridge University Press, 1994, p. 24. Roman law defined a number of other types of property rights, many of which are present in our positive legal systems. Examples are *usus fructus* (the right to use a scarce good belonging to someone else or to rent it to others, but not to sell it or change its substance) and *usus* (the right to use a scarce good belonging to someone else, but not to rent it or sell it or change its substance).
2. In the neoclassical world, the transferability of onwership moves resources from a less productive to a more productive owner.
3. True, political power is not the exclusive road to wealth in socialism, and the separation of power from wealth in capitalism is not perfect, either. But, in general, the absence of private property rights tends to link political power and economic wealth, while the right of ownership tends to divorce them.
4. K. Brunner, 'Knowledge, Values and the Choice of Economic Organization', Kyklos, 23, 1970, p. 566.
5. One could say that decisions made by the managers of a large corporation are also spread over a vast number of shareholders. There is, however, an important difference. By buying a share of General Motors, I voluntarily accept the management's decisions that affect my wealth. I can also

avoid the consequences of the company's decisions by selling (or not buying) GM shares. As a taxpayer, I have no way of opting out short of voting with my feet, which is a costly choice.

6. An important difference between choices made by private owners and by public decision makers is as follows: state ownership provides public decision makers with incentives to produce what they think other people need. Private owners might also have their own ideas about what other people need. However, in order to survive, they have to produce what other people demand.

7. Rules that are neither stable nor credible raise the costs of contractual agreements that have long-term consequences. Jews in medieval Europe favored investments in jewelry and gold coins. In the 1990s, investors require shorter payoff periods in Russia than in Germany.

8. The United States has inherited the British tradition as evidenced by (i) the importance of judicial decisions in adjusting the principles of the constitution to changes in the political, social, and economic conditions of life, and (ii) a costly method for changing the constitution.

9. J. Buchanan, *Property as a Guarantor of Liberty*, Aldershot, England: Edward Elgar Publishing, 1993, p. 59.

Some Implications of Recognition of Property Right Transactions Costs*

The list of fields of economics in the Directory of the American Economic Association contains no references to transactions costs or to property, despite much recent interest and research in that area. Probably the paper in *recent* times that most stimulated progress was Coase's "The Problem of Social Costs."[1] It demonstrated that, with costless exchange transactions and well-defined and transferable property rights, resource uses—aside from wealth effects on relative consumption demands—are independent of initial rights assignments. This statement signifies that transactions costs —the *costs* attendant to transferring entitlements or rights— destroy the classic standard theorems on market exchange efficiency. It indicates that many so-called market failures are failures of *existence* of markets or, more accurately, are results of obstacles (costs) to transactions, agreements, contracts, or understandings about uses of resources. These costs arise because of difficulties of communication, information collation, contract stipulation, ambiguities of entitlements or rights that might be traded. A host of activities are encompassed by the rubric "transactions costs."

* Presented at the First Annual Interlaken Seminar on Analysis and Ideology, Switzerland, June, 1974.

1 Ronald H. Coase, *Journal of Law and Economics* 3 (1960): 1–5.

Transactions

An oral tradition (a euphemism for a rubric of terminology, conjectures, and plausible assertions) exists on the role of entitlement and transactions costs. The conception of transactions remains sufficiently indefinite to permit superficial reference to "transactions costs" as the key to any paradox, externality, public goods provision, etc.

The following activities seem to be worth noting in the transactions conception:

1. *Search* over society for *who* has what rights. The cost of this search is reduced by specialists—as for nearly all activity. For land or houses, there are real estate agents and for stocks, stockbrokers. Employment agencies, yellow pages, and advertising convey information about *who* has what rights available for transfer.

2. The investigation of *what rights* each person has in each case. Title search firms identify rights holders and their entitlements. Automobile registration gives clearer evidence. Retail merchants provide assurance that goods are not stolen or of bad title, and we can't forget lawyers.

3. Technological *attributes* of goods. Investigation of physical attributes is sometimes sufficiently expensive to interdict transactions. Advertising or display of a good or of evidence about its characteristics is often provided by specialist "middlemen" who trade in the good. Indeed, this is a major function of merchants. Should we (a) include only the costs of conveying information about attributes of the goods or (b) take the state of knowledge as exogenous and include only the costs of providing risk-sharing provisions, guarantees, assurances, or remedies—if attributes are not as represented? For the moment, we include both and dub the first "attribute determination" and the second "risk sharing." Means for providing attribute information are diverse as well as specialized; examples are brand names, franchises, warranties, guarantees, commitments of wealth to a long-run venture (a means of self-imposed losses for bad performance, which thus serves to inform potential customers of the greater loss the seller will incur for unreliable performance), free trials, advertising of attributes, and governmentally imposed standards.

4. *Price search* and *price predictability*. The discovery of

bid and offer prices is facilitated by essentially the same procedures as the search for rights holders. Centralized markets and quick public reporting of actual prices benefit those who create markets as well as the public. Stockbrokers specialize in "making" a predictable market for specific stocks. "Scalping" on the futures markets provides more price predictability. Specialists (retailers, wholesalers, brokers) who make a market or maintain inventories and contribute to price predictability thereby reduce costs of search and planning. Futures markets provide more predictability. If prices were revised instantly and unpredictably to constantly clear markets, their reduced predictability would make planning and optimizing more difficult and would induce more pretransaction search. For example, an architect can design a house more efficiently the more accurately he can predict the prices of alternative components at construction time. Predictability over time is of greater value where planning preparation costs are more sensitive to haste, where larger inventories are held, or where adjustment costs in switching to other sellers are greater.

A geographical—or temporal—distribution of potential prices with a higher mean, *but smaller variance,* can be efficient. For example, resale price maintenance over a set of retailers is, in some cases, a price-search economizing device, which is more economical for people whose search time is valuable and for purchases of low value relative to search-time costs—where the gains from marginal search per unit time are therefore low. Constancy of prices, despite queues of random length and timing, provide price predictability at the expense of unpredictability of queue times. Clearly, it seems inappropriate to expect fluctuating, instantaneously market-clearing prices, for that would induce more costly search and adjustment than would a combination of both greater predictability and queuing, depending upon costs of search relative to costs of queuing and the gains from predictability. Long-term constant (though lower) wages with secure employment is a means of providing predictability to employees.

5. *Contract stipulation.* The complexity of contract stipulations depends on the rights being transferred, objective predictability and measurability of performance, and the contingencies for which advance provision is made. Many

contingencies are met by ex post settlement in the way they would have been met if anticipated—using goodwill as a reward for mutually satisfactory settlements. Contract formation or stipulation includes specification of performance conditions and the allocation of risk resulting from the unpredictability of actual performance. These conditions are as significant as the price, since the price itself will depend upon those terms and conditions. (The activity referred to here is not that of *reaching agreement* on what to include in the conditions but that of making those conditions objectively testable, unambiguous, and measurable.)

If all contingencies could be stipulated unambiguously *and enforced costlessly,* then the quality attributes of any good could be left unknown to any or all parties, with payment being determined by actual subsequent performance. But "of course," since that stipulation and enforcement is not costless, the cost of discerning attributes of a good cannot be treated as unessential or unimportant. Some techniques for economizing on stipulative activity are the use of standard forms, or conventions, of explicit contract laws, and of agreements to submit to arbitration. Continued sales relations between the parties make satisfactory performance desirable to preserve the capital value of anticipated future sales. Undoubtedly, the vast majority of contracts contain incomplete specification of performance conditions, relying instead on the loss of goodwill wealth consequent to a termination of sales or purchases if performance deviates from the predicted performance.

Complex performance or a long-term performance will not necessarily be associated with long-term or complex contracts. If the performance, however complex, can be detected sequentially, payment can be provided sequentially in accord with performance. It is not so much the length of the activity to be agreed upon in a transaction as the costs of detecting the quality of continuing performance that seems to suggest the complex variety of detailed, contractual arrangements. For example, labor employment arrangements often contemplate a long-term relationship; yet no long-term contracts are formalized. Instead, the pay and termination conditions are *expressed* in short-term contracts, but the terms of pay and termination are those that would typify a long-term contract if such contracts were formalized. This view of employment contracts will go far to explain types of unemployment, layoffs, seniority, and relatively constant wages and pay patterns over time. One of the major efforts of this study proposal will be centered on employment transactions costs.[2]

6. *Contract performance.* Without monitors, controls, and ex post adjustments, incentives exist to shirk or neglect performance. Techniques for detecting or measuring performance and for providing payment in accord with performance will be varied and will be used only insofar as they are worth the costs. In some situations, failure to watch pay and performance will cause a loss of future contracts and impose a "goodwill" or "present value" loss on negligent parties. In other cases, a contractual system of rewards or payment procedures will be devised to monitor or facilitate mutual performance or appropriate revisions in subsequent exchange rates.

Some Categories of Property Rights

A transaction culminates in a rights or entitlements transfer. What is a "property right"? In the *rights* of a person to a resource we include the probability that his decision about demarcated uses of the resource will determine the use, in the sense that his decision dominates that of any other person. If my decisions about some use or condition of a car dominate those of all other persons—so that their decisions are ineffective in upsetting or attenuating my decisions—then I, rather than they, have a property right to the car. The decision class of demarcated uses or actions or conditions appurtenant to that resource identifies the *domain* of rights held in that resource, not the strength of the right. If the probability is one—certainty—that my decision will dominate, I have an "absolute" right with respect to the demarcated class of conditions or uses to which the rights apply. For example, I may have an "absolute" right to pick apples off a tree, but not to prune the tree. I may have an absolute right to drive an automobile, but not to have it repainted some other color. The domain or scope of demarcated uses or con-

2 See D. Gordon, "The Neo-Classical Theory of Keynesian Unemployment," *Economic Inquiry* 12 (1974): 431–459.

ditions of a good can be partitioned among several people. Call this *use-domain partitioning.*

Distinct from the partitions of the domain of uses of an entity is the *decision sharing* with other people with whom some rights over the same domain of uses are jointly held. A shared *decision process* states the procedure whereby those persons shall identify a decision to which all are bound. Majority vote is but one example whereby several joint holders identify or achieve a decision (which is not necessarily "agreement"). All engage in the *process* of selecting a decision even though not all may have preferred the resultant decision. Sharing a decision right with other people reduces the probability that any one sharer's preference will determine the decision, but it does not reduce the probability of a reached decision being effective. Though sharing of decision authority attenuates individual power to determine decisions with respect to some resource, that power often is thereby spread over a wider set of resources, as when a larger group shares a larger pooled set of assets.

In decision-shared rights we must consider the probability that one sharer's preference among potential decisions will be the selected decision, as determined by the decision-process arrangement, not by the personality or persuasive powers of the individual, however strong those might be. We are here referring, not to what determines each individual's preference ordering of decisions, but instead, to what role his preference (however influenced) has in determining the group's selected decision.

Related, but different, is the consequence sharing of the resulting use or saleable value of the resource. How these *consequences* are shared is not necessarily the same as for the *decision* sharing. One "vote" per head (or share of common stock) does not require that the consequences be shared equally per capita (or per share).

If we were to try to categorize or differentiate property rights, we would, we conjecture, do so on the basis of a vector of characteristics including at least: (1) the domain of activities or uses over which a decision may be assigned, (2) the process of reaching a decision for a group of sharing rights holders, (3) the rules for assigning consequences to sharing members, and (4) the transferability of each of these elements (entitlements) to other people.

A right will be said to be broader, the broader its decision domain. The less a potential domain is partitioned to others, the broader the property right. Authority to decide who will be allowed to rent "my" house and at what price is more partitioned by fair-housing and rent-control and zoning laws, which transfer to political processes some decision authority. The wider the set of possible uses that are collected into one domain or set of uses, the broader the domain of the property right. But what makes it more private?

We seem to use also the degree of decision sharing (number of sharers in the decision process) as a criterion. A private property right can refer to the fact that one person holds the decision rights alone, rather than severally with others. Or *private* can identify the indefinitely large domain of uses that are collected into one parcel of rights, so that we could set as a limiting form, *unlimited* indefinite domain of uses to be decided by *one* person. These *two* components—(a) *unlimited domain* and (b) *single*-person, unshared decision processes—seem to be characteristics of "private" property rights.

Ability to *transfer* (or alienate) decision authority to another is also an attribute characterizing private property rights. Another characteristic is *responsibility*, which means that the technological or exchange-value consequences of his decisions about his goods are to be borne by the decision maker. If the good changes value in use, or in exchange, the decision maker has that value of use or of exchange. No other person has to transfer some rights to him in order to compensate him for loss because of inappropriate decision, nor can others compel unilateral transfer of value from him. In sum, all persons are bound by the same class of rights in the goods in which they are said to possess rights. Thus, (1) indefiniteness of use domain, (2) nonsharing of decisions, (3) responsibility, and (4) transferability are elements heavily weighted in the *private* property conception.

If decisions are shared, the property could be corporate or partnership, although still characterized as "private" property. If the shares are not alienable, the term "private" property seems at odds with common usage.

Now let us contrast this rubric of private property with public property, in order to identify some differences.

Public and private property

Compare a privately owned with a publicly owned golf course (or auditorium, bus service, water service, garbage-collection service, airport, school, or even spaghetti factory). There are differences in their operation; at least anyone who has ever compared them will think so. Why do these differences occur?

Preliminary investigation suggests, for example, that the difference between a privately owned corporation with 1,000 owners and a state-owned entity in a democracy with 1,000 citizens is quite significant, because the 1,000 individuals are furthering their own individual interests in each entity under different systems of property rights. In economic jargon, "the opportunity sets differ." A desire to avoid, or suppress, the effects of the profit-making incentive is often a reason for resort to public property. The objectives sought via public property, however, cannot merely be announced to the managers or operators with the expectation that exhortation will be either sufficient or necessary to achieve the objective.

Public property entitlements and consequences must be borne by all members of the public; none can divest himself of any portion of that ownership. A person must move from one town to another to change his ownership in public property. But while one lives in any community with public property, he has rights in that community's property and cannot divest himself of that public entitlement; but, by definition, he can sell and shift private property rights without also having to leave the community.[3]

To see what difference is made by the right to transfer ownership shares, suppose public ownership could be sold. With capitalized profits or losses accruing to the owners, will incentives be any different?

---

3 It is tempting to emphasize the possibility, under public ownership, of someone joining the community and thereby acquiring a share of public ownership, without payment to any of the existing owners. This dilution of a person's share of ownership is presumably absent in private ownership. Of course, a community could close off immigration or require purchase of land, but public ownership would continue even if this dilution effect were important. Furthermore, many corporations issue new shares without preemptive rights to incumbents. Still, even if dilution of public ownership were eliminated by restriction of entry, the inability to sell one's share in public property rights remains a factor in the costs-reward system impinging on all members of the public and on the employees and administrators of the governmental institution.

An answer is suggested by two implications of the specialization of "ownership," which is similar to the familiar specialization of other kinds of skills or activities. The two are: rewards and costs are *more* strongly imposed on each person responsible for them (1) via (*a*) concentration of rights and (*b*) capitalization of future effects into present sales value and (2) via comparative-advantage effects of (*a*) specialized knowledge in control and (*b*) specialized risk bearing.

Concentration

Greater concentration of rewards and costs means that a person's wealth is more dependent upon his activities. The more he concentrates his wealth holding in particular resources, the larger is his wealth response to his own activities in those areas. For example, suppose there are 100 people in a community, with ten separate enterprises; and suppose each person, holding a 1 percent interest in each, could, by devoting one-tenth of his attention to some one enterprise, produce a saving or gain of $1,000. Since the individual is a one-hundredth part owner, he will acquire $10. If he does this for each of the ten different enterprises, his total wealth gain will be $100, with the rest of the wealth increment, $9,900, going to the other 99 people. Of course, if the other 99 people act in the same way, he will get from their activities an increase of wealth of $990,000/100 = $9,900, which gives him a total of $10,000. This is exactly equal to his own marginal product, most of which was spread over the other owners.

Let us now suppose a more concentrated holding; each person owns a one-tenth part of *one* enterprise only (which means that ownership has been reshuffled from pro rata equal shares in all ten enterprises to a concentration in one enterprise by each person. He will now be assumed to devote all his attention to one enterprise, so he again produces $10,000. Of this he gets $1,000. The remaining $9,000 goes to the other owners. The difference is that, now, $1,000 is dependent upon his own activities whereas formerly only $10 was. Or, more pertinently, the amount dependent upon the activities of other people is reduced from $9,900 to $9,000.

If we go to the extreme where the 10 enterprises are divided into 100, with each person as the sole owner of 1 enterprise, then all $10,000 of his year's wealth increase will be his to keep. The first of these three examples corresponds to "public property rights," the second to corporate joint private rights, and the third to sole proprietorship.

If public property rights were saleable, they would in effect become capitalizable private ownership rights, and there would be a movement toward concentration of ownership. Why? The wealth that a person can get or lose is more dependent upon his own activities. If, however, people prefer to collect a major portion of their wealth gain from other people's activities, the total wealth gain would decrease, since everyone would have less incentive to work. It suffices that there be at least one person who prefers to make himself less dependent upon other people's activities and who prefers at least some more wealth to some more leisure. He will then be prepared to buy up some property rights and pay a higher price for them than they are worth to some other people in their current forms of property.

Capitalization

Capitalization of values of future service into *present* exchange values of rights, and hence capitalization on the present wealth of rights owners, is more complete (i.e., less expensive to realize) for private than for public property rights. This means that, in making present decisions, foreseen future consequences are more fully heeded for private than for public property resources. The weaker impact on present values of marketable wealth reduces incentives to heed market values of both present and future consequences. One would therefore conjecture that privately owned resources will be used and priced differently from publicly owned insofar as these differences are differential responses to potential marketable values. Briefly, the wealth incentive is less strongly applicable for public property.

Comparative advantage in ownership: control

The preceding example did not involve differences of abilities, knowledge, beliefs, or attitudes toward risk. But if people differ in any of these respects, specialization in various tasks —including owning—will increase wealth. This is simply an extension of the logical theorem of gains from comparative advantage, which we shall not explain here.

The usual discussion of comparative advantage ignores "ownership" productivities. But people differ in their talents as owners—as monitors and decision makers. Owners bear the risk of value changes and make the decisions about how much to produce, how much to invest, how it shall be produced, and who shall be employed as laborers and managers.[4] Ownership ability includes attitude toward risk bearing, knowledge of and monitoring of different people's productive performance, foresight, and, of course, decision "judgment." These talents differ among people according to the particular industry, type of product, or productive resource associated with that industry. Differences in these skills make comparative advantage in property rights pertinent. If property rights are transferable, people will concentrate and use their property rights in those areas in which they believe they have a comparative advantage. Just as specialization in typing, music, or various types of labor is more productive, so is specialization in ownership. Some people specialize in electronics industry knowledge, some in airlines, some in dairies, some in retailing, etc. Private property owners can specialize in knowledge about electronics, devoting much of their effort and study to learning which electronic devices show promise, which are now most efficient in various uses, which should be produced in larger numbers, where investment should take place, what kinds of research and development to finance, etc. But public ownership reduces (by high transactions costs) specialization among owners—though not among employees in the publicly owned venture.

A person who is very knowledgeable about woodworking and cabinet or furniture building would have an advantage as an owner of a furniture company. He would, by being a stockholder, not necessarily make the company any better, but instead he would choose the better company—in terms of his knowledge—as one in which to own shares. The relative rise in the price of such companies enables the existing owners to issue new shares, borrow money more readily, and retain control. In this way the differences in knowledge enable people to specialize in the application of that knowledge

---

4 Armen A. Alchian and Harold Demsetz, "Production, Information Costs, and Economic Organization," *American Economic Review* 62 (1972): 777–793.

to the management and operation of the company—albeit, sometimes by indirect lines.

Comparative advantage in ownership: risk and beliefs

A second aspect of ownership specialization is risk bearing. If various ventures or resources represent different prospects of values, then exchange of ownership will enable a wealth-increasing reallocation of rights among people, leading to greater utility in the same sense that exchange of goods does. In addition, people differ in beliefs about the prospects of future values of the assets whose ownership can be transferred. Differences in "knowledge" can be used not only in an effort to be more productive but also as a means for distinguishing different prospect situations. For example, I may be the top administrator of the Carnation Milk Company, but I may hold stocks in some electronics company because I prefer the risk pattern provided by that combination rather than by holding Carnation stock also. In this way a person can separate the productivity of knowledge and effort (received as salary) from the risk bearing. I can, if I want, combine them by holding stock in a company in which I am active. This possibility of separating the *control* (effective administration or operation of the company—an activity that rewards comparative superiority in ability and knowledge) from *risk* and *beliefs* is, of course, regarded as an advantage by those who act as employed managers or administrators and by those who choose to act as corporate stockowners without also bothering to exercise their vote or worry about control. Yet it is often criticized as undesirable.

Not all of the stockholders have to exercise voting rights effectively to exert an influence on management. Most stockholders may go along simply because they believe the prospects for profits and losses are sufficiently promising relative to other assets they could own. If losses eventuate, their pertinent alternative is to sell out. To whom? To other buyers who, because of the reduced profit prospects, will offer only a lower price. These "nonactive" owners perform a function in that, at least, they provide the willingness to bear some of the value consequences. So long as scarce resources *exist*, value changes *will* occur. The question left is, then, who is to bear the reduced value; someone has to.

Often it is said that joint ownership in the modern corporation has separated ownership and control. What this means is that risk bearing and management are more independent. This is correct in the sense that each stockholder does not have the same kind of control as does a sole owner. But it is a long normative leap to decrying this. Specialization in risk bearing and in managerial decision making about uses of resources in now possible. Complete separation of the two does not exist for *every* joint stockholder, for to the extent that some share owners are inactive or indifferent to alternative choices or management problems, other stockholders (joint owners) will be more influential. In effect, the "passive" owners are betting on the decisions of "active" owners —"betting" in the sense that they are prepared to pay for any losses produced by these "activists" and in turn collect some of the profits, if any. In the absence of any right to buy and sell shared rights, everyone would have to bet on the activists as a group (the case of public property). The right to sell concentrates this betting on those who are prepared to pay the most (or demand the least) for the right to do so. And it concentrates the control or management with those who believe they are relatively most able at that task—with the less able being eliminated more surely in private, transferable rights than in public because: (1) evidence of poor management and the opportunity to capture profits by eliminating it is revealed to outsiders by the lower selling price of the ownership rights; (2) the specialization of ownership functions is facilitated; and (3) the possibility of concentrating one's wealth in certain areas permits greater correlation of personal interest and effort in line with wealth holdings.

We conjecture: *Under public community rights the consequences of any decision are less fully thrust upon the decision maker than under private property.* They are *less* fully borne than if the same action were taken in a private property institution, with a similar number of owners. One would expect that public agencies would, in order to offset or counterbalance this reduced cost bearing, impose special constraints on public employees or agents. Public agents who are authorized to spend public funds will be more severely constrained with extra restrictions because costs of their actions are less effectively thrust upon them.

Some Suggested Analytical Interpretations

Transactions costs and their relationship to property rights suggest several ramifications that may merit some attention.

1. It is often said that someone who pollutes the air—or disturbs the peace and quiet—should not do so or should buy rights for doing so. Why? Because he is presumed not to own the resource being abused. The tacit assumption is that air is owned by nondrivers of autos, that rights to the use of land are owned by residents on the land and not by those who put noise or smoke on it. This is a sheer presumption about where rights "should" be assigned. Commentators have jumped to the conclusion that, because no one now is explicitly assigned those rights, the rights belong to those who have no reason to change the prior existing state of resources or that the rights should be assigned to political agents. If auto drivers owned the air, so that people who wanted less smog or cleaner air had to buy the air rights (to cleaner air) from drivers, the results would be no different from the results if rights were initially assigned the opposite way— *absent transactions costs!* Since smoke and smog are produced in the act of increasing someone's utility, the reduction of clean air is no different from the reduction of my leisure when I work for the university rather than relaxing on the golf course, contemplating the path of my golf ball. So I contend that the university imposes pollution on me.

Clearly, the growing concern about various forms of "pollution" and environmental law—and even torts—indicates the value of developing an understanding of the factors contributing to "transactions costs" and of the institutions and means for adapting to or reducing them.

2. Because the world is not characterized by costlessly "well-defined" property rights and costless transactions activity, some resources appear to be used wastefully or inappropriately. Apparently some desirable revisions of resource use are apparent (to observers) and, if brought about, would produce gains beyond the sacrificed values of current uses—if only the people could be made aware of and *responsive* to these potentialities, as could be done if the costs of reaching a contract and enforcing it were not so high. Coase illustrated ways in which these potential gains, if not achieved by voluntary contracts among the parties, were

often achieved by judicial settlements or by direction of law. Jurists often enforce the highest-valued uses by assigning disputed entitlements or rights to the persons whose interest it was to use resources in that way (or whose interest it would have been to buy those use rights had the market been sufficiently well organized and rights sufficiently well defined to permit transferability).

An explicit conjecture is that over decades, judicial evolution is toward well-defined rights in the sense of making them more definite, secure, and cheaply transferable. The conjecture is that this would tend toward *private* property rights. But this conjecture remains to be evaluated.

3. The well-known Modigliani-Miller theorem that the value of an enterprise is independent of its form of financing is a special application of the Coase theorem; absent transactions costs, rights will be partitioned in their highest-valued ways and thereby have the highest values.[5] So long as entitlements are well defined, partitionable, and transferable, under the motive of enhanced wealth they will be revised and used in the maximum-valued ways—if transactions costs are absent. Their initial sale value will be capitalized to reflect those values.

In fact, of course, rights are not costlessly transferable or revisable. Therefore, what forms of rights are most appropriately issued initially by, say, a new corporation? Bonds, common stocks, preferreds, convertibles, warrants? Are there any factors that would explain the optimal initial mix, given transactions costs of subsequent revisions or transfers? We conjecture that differences in beliefs by investors about the potential performance of the enterprise can account for differences in appropriate initial mixes—given transactions costs that are not insignificant.

4. A remaining vestige of confusion about the meaning of the propositions about effects of transactions costs arises from "blackmail" or nuisance liability problems. Smith would threaten to impose larger damages on Jones at trivial cost to Smith—say by cheaply creating smoke or by revealing secret, malign information about Jones. Similarly, the low cost of creating smoke to extract preventive payment from

---

5 Franco Modigliani and Merton Miller, "The Cost of Capital, Corporation Finance and the Theory of Investment," *American Economic Review* 48 (1958): 268-297.

the threatened party was believed, erroneously, to upset the "costless" transactions analysis. What the blackmail or nuisance threats do, however, is simply reveal that rights to the land's condition are not held by the threatened party but are instead *distributed* among many other people no *one* of whom can by agreement with the threatened party and the others exclude other parties from creating smoke. (From every other party, the rights would have to be purchased by one agent who could exercise or transfer exclusive authority.) There exists the problem of assembling all the dispersed entitlements from the various holders into one general exclusion right. Thus, if there were many neighbors of my land, each of whom had a nonexclusive entitlement to dump smoke on my land (i.e., could not prevent others from doing so), and if the sum of values to each person of dumping his smoke was less than the damage to me, it would pay me to buy and consolidate the rights from all the neighbors (the rest of the society).

If it be thought that each would have an incentive to hold out for the total value and thereby obstruct agreement, it should be recognized that this so-called blackmail is really "bargaining." Each party tries to obtain most of the value of the land use—whether by threatening to withhold agreement or, in so-called blackmail cases, by threatening to destroy potential use value by dumping smoke. But this really is only the classic bilateral monopoly bargaining problem, common in many other areas. It does not depend on the rights assignments; it instead reflects an obstacle to achieving an agreed-upon price. The parties are "bargaining" over the exchange rate for transfer of rights. With "pure" competition on both sides, the exchange rate would be uniquely determined by rivalry of alternative bidders and sellers. But otherwise, there is a *range* of mutually beneficial exchange prices. When threatening to quit while bargaining over my salary I am imposing a bargaining cost and trying to obtain more of the transactions surplus. When I threaten not to accept an offer, I am "blackmailing" my employer (given that I would have accepted his initial offer if I knew for sure that there was no possibility of getting more from that employer). *This* so-called blackmail becomes merely the costs of bilateral monopoly-monopsony bargaining.

But there is another kind of problem that should not be

confused with "the" blackmail problem. Suppose rights to privacy were deemed to exist and to be held by the person himself but were inadequately guarded by state legal action, with less than adequate compensation for invasion of privacy (even though the revealers were punished). Since state punishment does not guarantee complete deterrence, some whose privacy is threatened will add private action. Society may deem some of such private action *improper* because of its perverse effects of *inducing* activity designed to penetrate privacy. For example, suppose thieves could resell stolen goods to victims (at a price less than the owner's costs of going to the state for protection and recovery). Such private actions would undermine the punitive state-provided system of deterrence and protection. In a collusive agreement of protected people, although it pays individuals to break the agreement privately, it pays even more for the group not to. Lacking a theory of government and social norms, we can only call attention to the differences between the monopoly-monopsony bargaining case and this blackmail undermining of state-enforced deterrence. Do not confuse the two.

5. Another consequence of the entitlements–transactions costs analysis has been to aid the *formal* economic analysis of liability rules. Is the producer liable or is the consumer? The employer or the employee? The driver of this car or that car or neither? Unfortunately, the term *liability* is ambiguous. If the consumer is liable, does it mean that in the absence of contracts to the contrary he is presumed to bear the losses of contingent events? Does it mean that he cannot legally contract with a seller about the risks of consequences of future performance? If the former, it merely identifies a presumed contractual condition *in the absence of specific contract terms* to the contrary. It presumably is an approximation to terms that a majority of contracts would contain and thereby reduces contract stipulation costs.

If, on the other hand, *liability* means stipulation of conditions that *must* be included in any contract, does the imposed liability rule make a difference? In what effects? Other terms of the contract, as when employer liability for accidents is imposed, can be altered to reduce wages that compensated for self-insurance against accidents. What is changed is only the *system* of insurance for accidents. Employees now must purchase group insurance via lower wages, whereas formerly they could accept higher wages and *either* pay for group insurance *or* self-insure. To *impose* a mandatory contract stipulation in all employee-employer contracts is to impose prohibitively high transactions cost for some contract revisions. Employees must buy employer-administered group insurance. Only if transactions costs (*including* legal restrictions on rights transfers) are absent, are *initial* assignments of liabilities irrelevant, for they can be renegotiated. With costs of renegotiation, initial rights allocation does alter the end result. In sum, since "bearing the liability" is merely another way to say something about who starts with what rights, the *rule* of liability is a negotiable, initial provision in a contract.

If (*a*) it is a negotiable, initial suggestion that will hold only in the absence of explicit provisions to the contrary, nothing is changed if there are no costs of making contracts. If (*b*) the specified liability is not negotiable and *must* be included in all *new* contracts, then other negotiable conditions will offset the imposed conditions so as to more closely, though not completely, achieve the results that would have been achieved in the absence of the imposed stipulations. If (*c*) new stipulations are imposed on *existing* contracts without any permissible revisions in the continuing contract, the rule of liability matters (at least) for the duration of the contract. With transactions costs present, as they always are, *imposed* rules of liabilities or rights make a difference in who takes what kind of, more, or less preventive or precautionary action.

6. Another major clarification consequent to the analysis of the costs of transfer of rights was that of "externalities," which are now explained or interpreted as consequences of poorly defined, poorly assured property rights, which implies high transactions costs. It became clear also that the Pigou tradition of "externalities" as something to be handled by taxes, subsidies, or government activity was inappropriate. It is neither obvious nor demonstrable that all government processes would induce a "better" allocation than had been achieved already. Furthermore, an alternative to *that* kind of governmental action is making the property rights better defined, transferable, and secure and easier to enforce at law. This second facet attracted significant empirical study beyond that being given to other political means of meeting

the problem of "externalities." The implications for basic reinterpretation of the tort laws are wide ranging.

The concept of externalities is bankrupt because of its ambiguity. Buchanan and Stubblebine restructured the term *externalities* in such a way as to permit its graceful abandonment—via the route of adding adjectives, adverbs, and other modifiers to distinguish the various subconcepts and thereby exposing the many inconsistent meanings of *externality*.[6] In one sense, almost all human actions have externalities in that one person's acts affect other people. Sometimes only those acts that affect the technological production function of other people are called externalities—though Viner was considerate enough to call these "technological external diseconomies"[7]—a conception that is well worth retaining. Sometimes *externalities* has been used to describe only unheeded effects on other people. Whatever the terminology, it is worth distinguishing the case in which someone else would benefit from my actions, but by less than the cost to me, from those cases in which the marginal effects on others have a value in excess of the value to me, but in which there are costs of communicating or negotiating an enforceable agreement between the interacting parties. In this case, it seems the issue is usefully describable, not as one of "externalities," but as one of communication, contracting, or property rights costs, all mingled in the term *transactions costs*.

7. The above suggests a new question: What institutional arrangements have evolved to reduce the costs of communicating information, of contracting, and of defining and enforcing property rights so as to induce potentially mutually beneficial resource uses and activity? (The question is *not*, What if, miraculously, all those costs were absent? This latter query is equivalent to asking for zero costs of steel, cloth, and food. We would be richer, obviously.)

We have analytically explored one facet of this pertinent question with a proposition that what is known as a firm is essentially a contractual arrangement for reducing the costs

6 James Buchanan and Craig Stubblebine, "Externality," *Economica* 29 (1962): 371–384.

7 Jacob Viner, "Cost Curves and Supply Curves," *Zeitschrift für Nationalokonomie* 3 (1931): 23–46.

of detecting and monitoring (adjusting rewards appropriately) joint production performance. This explanation, though not inconsistent with the elements contained in the interpretations of Knight and Coase,[8] does provide refutable implications. It does so by moving beyond the idea that transactions costs are obstacles to the pure market economy's assigning every resource use via pairwise market contracting. Also, a definition of a firm is provided. And implications are derived about whom the control monitor is responsible to, who will receive the residual, the assets that will be owned by that firm's owner, the types of activities that will be more likely managed by partnerships, and some differences among profit sharing, nonprofit, corporate, socialist, cooperative, and governmentally owned firms.

And of course, we need not emphasize the problems into which socialists have been led. The Czechoslovaks were moving toward a market system—as some Russians would like to do—but the Czechs faced up to the issue more bluntly and with less political opposition and perceived that more private rights are necessary for a market pricing system to work as desired. Younger plant managers were pushing in that direction for efficiency incentives. Power would be transferred from the political authorities to individual businessmen. A continuation of that trend would weaken the socialist party control. That handwriting on the wall clearly predicted, and "justified," the Russian invasion. In Yugoslavia, property rights in resources are persistently being privatized—that is, removed from political agents. In every Communist country, there will develop a conflict between the new aspiring plant managers who see ways to improve operations and increase their wealth if only they could reap more of the harvests of their increased output. The necessity for rights to be transferable if the market is to be used is the dilemma the Russian economists are slowly discerning. The conflict between a potential rising entrepreneurial class and the political authorities is inevitable. And it is pathetic to observe Russian economists in their agonizing, awakening awareness of this dependence of an "efficient" market system on a system of transferable private property rights. They

8 Frank H. Knight, "Fallacies in the Interpretation of Social Costs," *Quarterly Journal of Economics* 38 (1924): 524-606; Ronald H. Coase, "The Nature of the Firm," *Economica* 4 (1937): 368-405.

struggle to avoid the term *property rights*, just as they avoid the term *interest;* but they have accepted the latter under the name of *efficiency index*—which is, admittedly, a pretty good name. What will they call the private property rights in productive assets in Russia?

8. Another clarification stemming from a formal analysis of property rights and their transfer costs pertains to the public-good *analytic* concept. If heavy goods involved greater transactions costs than lighter goods, market forces would have less influence on the use of heavy goods; if animate services had higher transactions costs, they would be allocated less by individual exchange in private markets. For any goods with higher transactions costs, the same would follow. The implication is that a public-private goods *technological* distinction provides in itself *no implications whatsoever* about efficient or "appropriate means of disposition, production, or control of public and private goods." Literally, nothing makes the public-versus-private good *technological* attribute an appropriate criterion for political or market control—despite articles by the "high" and "low" to that effect— unless that technological characteristic is merely a name for high transactions costs.

A technological characteristic is relevant if and only if it correlates with—and then only as a proxy for—transactions costs. Wild animals, airplane airspace, underground oil and gas, all have relatively high cost components in the transactions rubric, and that makes them more fit for group or nonmarket control. Some technologically public goods involve lower property rights and transactions costs than some private goods; the consequence should not be missed for analysis of procedures of control.

Many policies about problems of "free riders" or of reaching agreements about production and uses of public goods presume that government activities provide superior methods of overcoming these questions. As yet, no clear theory of government behavior has been established on the basis of which to derive such presumptions. The private sector does have much that serves to meet many so-called free riders and the problem of reaching agreements. Direct attention to transactions costs under various forms of property rights will avoid at least the technological fallacy.

9. Taking a lesson from the public goods–private goods misclassification, we can ask if there is any significance to the private *property*–public *property* distinction. Is there any reason to believe the incidence of the private-public good characteristic is correlated with transactions costs? We think so. And if it is correlated with transactions costs, we should expect to be able to derive contrasting implications about behavior and uses of resources under public and private property rights.

[3]

§3.1 The Economic Theory of Property Rights: Static and Dynamic Aspects

To understand the economics of property rights, it is first necessary to grasp the economist's distinction between *static* and *dynamic* analysis. Static analysis suppresses the time dimension of economic activity: All adjustments to change are assumed to occur instantaneously. The assumption is unrealistic but often fruitful; the attentive reader of Chapter 1 will not be too disturbed by a lack of realism in assumptions.

Dynamic analysis, in which the assumption of instantaneous adjustment to change is relaxed, is usually more complex than static analysis. So it is surprising that the economic basis of property rights was first perceived in dynamic terms. Imagine a society in which all property rights have been abolished. A farmer plants corn, fertilizes it, and erects scarecrows, but when the corn is ripe his neighbor reaps it and takes it away for his own use. The farmer has no legal remedy against his neighbor's conduct since he owns neither the land that he sowed nor the crop. Unless defensive measures are feasible (and let us assume for the moment that they are not), after a few such incidents the cultivation of land will be abandoned and society will shift to methods of subsistence (such as hunting) that involve less preparatory investment.

As this example suggests, legal protection of property rights creates incentives to use resources efficiently. Although the value of the crop in our example, as measured by consumers' willingness to pay, may have greatly exceeded its cost in labor, materials, and forgone alternative uses of the land, without property rights there is no incentive to incur these costs because there is no reasonably assured reward for incurring them. The proper incentives are created by parceling out mutually exclusive rights to the use of particular resources among the members of society. If every piece of land is owned by someone—if there is always someone who can exclude all others from access to any given area—then individuals will endeavor by cultivation or other improvements to maximize the value of land. Of course, land is just an example. The principle applies to all valuable resources.

All this has been well known for hundreds of years.[1] In contrast, the

§3.1   1. See, e.g., 2 William Blackstone, Commentaries on the Laws of England 4, 7

static analysis of property rights is little more than 50 years old.[2] Imagine
that a number of farmers own a pasture in common; that is, none has the
right to exclude any of the others and hence none can charge the others
for the use of the pasture. We can abstract from the dynamic aspects of
the problem by assuming that the pasture is a natural (uncultivated) one.
Even so, pasturing additional cows will impose a cost on all the farmers.
The cows will have to graze more in order to eat the same amount of
grass, and this will reduce their weight. But because none of the farmers
pays for the use of the pasture, none will take this cost into account in
deciding how many additional cows to pasture, with the result that more
cows will be pastured than would be efficient. (Can you see an analogy to
highway congestion?)

The problem would disappear if someone owned the pasture and
charged each farmer for its use (for purposes of this analysis, disregard
the cost of levying such a charge). The charge to each farmer would include
the cost he imposes on the other farmers by pasturing additional cows,
because that cost reduces the value of the pasture to the other farmers
and hence the price they are willing to pay the owner for the right to
graze.

The creation of exclusive rights is a necessary rather than a sufficient
condition for the efficient use of resources: The rights must be transferable. Suppose the farmer in our first example owns the land that he sows
but is a bad farmer; his land would be more productive in someone else's
hands. Efficiency requires a mechanism by which the farmer can be induced
to transfer the property to someone who can work it more productively.
A transferable property right is such a mechanism. Suppose Farmer A
owns a piece of land that he anticipates will yield him $100 a year above
his labor and other costs, indefinitely. Just as the price of a share of
common stock is equal to the present value of the anticipated earnings to
which the shareholder will be entitled, so the present value of a parcel of
land that is expected to yield an annual net income of $100 can be cal-

---

(1766). And property-rights systems are prehistoric in their origins. Vernon L. Smith, The
Primitive Hunter Culture, Pleistocene Extinction, and the Rise of Agriculture, 83 J. Pol.
Econ. 727 (1975).

The proposition that enforcing property rights will lead to a greater output is questioned
by Frank I. Michelman in Ethics, Economics, and the Law of Property, 24 Nomos 3, 25
(1982). He suggests that the farmer who knows that half his crop will be stolen may just
plant twice as much. This suggestion overlooks

   (1) the added incentive to theft that will be created by planting a larger crop and the
       resulting likelihood that more than one-half of the larger crop will be stolen;
   (2) the unlikelihood that farming would be so much more profitable than substitute
       activities not entailing preparatory investment as to keep people in farming; and
   (3) the likelihood that the farmer, if he remained in farming, would divert some of his
       resources from growing crops to protecting them with walls, guards, etc.

   2. See Frank H. Knight, Some Fallacies in the Interpretation of Social Cost, 38 Q.J. Econ.
582 (1924).

culated and is the minimum price that A will accept in exchange for his property right.[3] Suppose Farmer B believes that he can use A's land more productively than A. The present value of B's expected earnings stream will therefore exceed the present value calculated by A. Suppose the present value calculated by A is $1,000 and by B $1,500. Then at any price between $1,000 and $1,500 both A and B will be made better off by a sale. Thus there are strong incentives for a voluntary exchange of A's land for B's money.

This discussion implies that if every valuable (meaning scarce as well as desired) resource were owned by someone (the criterion of universality), ownership connoted the unqualified power to exclude everybody else from using the resource (exclusivity) as well as to use it oneself, and ownership rights were freely transferable, or as lawyers say alienable (transferability), value would be maximized. This leaves out of account, however, the costs of a property-rights system, both the obvious and the subtle ones. Those costs are a particular focus of this chapter.

An example will illustrate a subtle cost of exclusivity. Suppose our farmer estimates that he can raise a hog with a market value of $100 at a cost of only $50 in labor and materials and that no alternative use of the land would yield a greater net value—in the next best use, his income from the land would be only $20. He will want to raise the hog. But now suppose his property right is qualified in two respects: He has no right to prevent an adjacent railroad from accidentally emitting engine sparks that may set fire to the hog's pen, killing the hog prematurely; and a court may decide that his raising a hog on this land is a nuisance, in which event he will have to sell the hog at disadvantageous (why disadvantageous?) terms before it is grown. In light of these contingencies he must reevaluate the yield of his land: He must discount the $100 to reflect the probability that the yield may be much less, perhaps zero. Suppose that, after this discounting, the expected revenue from raising the hog (market value times the probability that it will reach the market) is only $60. He will not raise the hog. He will put the land to another use, which we said was less valuable;[4] the value of the land will fall.

But the analysis is incomplete. Removing the hog may increase the value of surrounding residential land by more than the fall in the value of the farmer's parcel; or the cost of preventing the emission of engine sparks may exceed the reduction in the value of the farmer's land when he switches from raising hogs to growing, say, fireproof radishes. But, the alert reader may interject, if the increase in value to others from a different

---

3. Discounting to present value is discussed in greater detail in §6.13 *infra*.

The certainty with which A anticipates continuing to receive this return, the prevailing interest rate, his preference for or aversion to risk, and other factors will enter into his valuation of the property. Cf. §4.5 *infra*. We can ignore these refinements for now.

4. The anticipated profit from raising the hog is now only $10 (the farmer's costs are $50). The next best use, we said, would yield a profit of $20.

use of the farmer's land exceeds the decrease to him, let them buy his right: The railroad can purchase an easement to emit sparks; the surrounding homeowners can purchase a covenant from the farmer not to raise hogs; there is no need to limit the farmer's property right. But as we shall see (in §3.8 *infra*), the costs of effecting a transfer of rights — transaction costs—are often prohibitive, and when this is so, giving someone the exclusive right to a resource may reduce rather than increase efficiency.

We could, of course, preserve exclusivity in a purely notional sense by regarding the property right in a given thing as a bundle of distinct rights, each exclusive; that is in fact the legal position. The economic point however is that the nominal property owner will rarely have exclusive power over his property.

§3.2   Problems in the Creation and Enforcement of Property Rights

Property rights are not only less exclusive but less universal than they would be if they were not costly to enforce. Imagine a primitive society in which the principal use of land is for grazing. The population of the society is small relative to the amount of land, and its flocks are small too. No technology exists for increasing the value of the land by fertilizer, irrigation, or other techniques. The cost of wood or other materials for fencing is very high and, the society being illiterate, a system for publicly recording land ownership is out of the question. In these circumstances the costs of enforcing property rights might well exceed the benefits. The costs would be the costs of fencing to keep out other people's grazing animals, and would be substantial. The benefits might be zero. Since there is no crowding problem, property rights would confer no static benefits, and since there is no way of improving the land, there would be no dynamic benefits either. It is therefore not surprising that property rights are less extensive in primitive than in advanced societies and that the pattern by which property rights emerge and grow in a society is related to increases in the ratio of the benefits of property rights to their costs.[1]

§3.2   1. There is a surprisingly extensive economic literature on the historical development of property-rights systems: for example, in the prehistoric, primitive, and ancient world (see, e.g., Smith article in §3.1 *supra*, note 1; D. Bruce Johnsen, The Formation and Protection of Property Rights Among the Southern Kwakiutl Indians, 15 J. Leg. Stud. 41 (1986); David E. Ault & Gilbert L. Rutman, Land Scarcity, Economic Efficiency, and African Common Law, 12 Research in Law & Econ. 33 (1989)); in the middle ages (see, e.g., Carl J. Dahlman, The Open Field System and Beyond: A Property Rights Analysis of an Economic Institution (1980)); and in the nineteenth-century American West (see, e.g., Terry L. Anderson & Peter J. Hill, The Race for Property Rights, 33 J. Law & Econ. 177 (1990); John R. Umbeck, A Theory of Property Rights, With Application to the California Gold Rush (1981)).

The common law distinction between domestic and wild animals illustrates the general point. Domestic animals are owned like any other personal property; wild animals are not owned until killed or put under actual restraint (as in a zoo). Thus, if your cow wanders off your land, it is still your cow; but if a gopher whose burrow is on your land wanders off, he is not your property, and anyone who wants can capture or kill him, unless he is tame—unless he has an *animus revertendi* (the habit of returning to your land). (Can you think of an economic argument for the doctrine of *animus revertendi*?)

The reason for the difference in legal treatment between domestic and wild animals is that it would be both difficult to enforce a property right in a wild animal and pretty useless; most wild animals, as in our gopher illustration, are not valuable, so there is nothing to be gained from creating incentives to invest in them. But suppose the animals are valuable. If there are no property rights in valuable fur-bearing animals such as sable and beaver, hunters will hunt them down to extinction, even though the present value of the resource will be diminished by doing so. The hunter who spares a mother beaver so that it can reproduce knows that the beavers born to her will almost certainly be caught by someone other than him (so long as there are many hunters), and he will not forgo a present benefit to confer a future benefit on someone else. Property rights would be desirable in these circumstances but it is hard to imagine a feasible scheme for giving the hunter who decided to spare the mother beaver a property right in her unborn litter. The costs of enforcing such a property right would still exceed the benefits, though the benefits would now be substantial.

There are two possible solutions. The more common is to use the regulatory powers of the state to reduce hunting to the approximate level it would be at if the animals were hunted at an optimal rate; this is an example of how regulation can be a substitute for property rights in correcting a divergence between private and social costs or benefits. The other solution is for one person to buy up the entire habitat of the animals; he will then regulate hunting on his property optimally because he will obtain all the gains from doing so.[2]

Another example of the correlation between property rights and scarcity is the difference in the water law systems of the eastern and western states of the United States. In the eastern states, where water is plentiful, water rights are communalized to a significant extent, the basic rule being that riparian owners (i.e., the owners of the shore of a body of water) are each entitled to make reasonable use of the water—a use that does not interfere

2. On the economics of the fur trade, see Harold Demsetz, Toward a Theory of Property Rights, 57 Am. Econ. Rev. Papers & Proceedings 347, 351-353 (May 1967), one of the pathbreaking articles in the "new" law and economics. See also Dean Lueck, The Economic Nature of Wildlife Law, 18 J. Leg. Stud. 291 (1989).

unduly with the uses of the other riparians. In the western states, where water is scarce, exclusive rights can be obtained, by appropriation (use).

Now consider the example of things, often very valuable things such as the treasure in a shipwreck, which were once owned but have been abandoned. Here the general rule is finders keepers. In a sense this is the same rule as for wild animals and for water in western states. Ownership of the thing is obtained by reducing it to actual possession. Until then the thing is unowned (the unborn beavers, the abandoned ship), and it is this gap in ownership—this interval when no one has a property right—that is the source of the economic problem.

But the problem is slightly different in the animal and treasure cases. In the case of wild animals the problem is too rapid exploitation; in the case of abandoned property it is too costly exploitation. Suppose the treasure in the shipwreck is worth $1 million and it will cost $250,000 to hire a team of divers to salvage it. Because the expected profit of the venture is so high, someone else may decide to hire his own team and try to beat the first team to it. A third and even a fourth may try, too, for if each one has the same chance (25 percent) of reaching the treasure first, then the expected value of the venture to each one ($1 million $\times$ .25) will still cover each one's expected cost. If four try, however, the cost of obtaining the treasure, $1 million, will be four times what it would have been if only one had tried.[3] Actually the net social loss from this competition will be less than $750,000, because the competition probably will result in the treasure's being found sooner (thus increasing its present value) than if only one were trying. But the gain in time may be modest and not worth the additional expenditures that accelerated the search.

There would be no problem of excessive cost if the treasure had not been abandoned; for then the owner would simply have hired one of the four salvagers for $250,000. But when we call property abandoned in the legal sense, we mean that the cost of revesting the property in the original owner is prohibitive, either because he cannot be found at reasonable cost or he considers the property (perhaps incorrectly) to be worth less than the cost of finding or using it. The problem of too costly exploitation of a valuable resource, like the problem of too rapid exploitation, is rooted ultimately in the sometimes prohibitive costs of enforcing property rights.

The law can do something about the abandonment problem and to some extent has done so. The common law sometimes gives the first committed searcher for abandoned property a right to prevent others from searching so long as his search is conscientiously pursued. Another common law rule makes abandoned treasure trove (currency and bullion), if

---

3. The tendency of an expected gain to be translated into costs through competitive efforts is called rent-seeking, recurs many times in this book, and is the subject of a growing literature. See essays collected in Toward a Theory of the Rent-Seeking Society (James Buchanan, Robert Tollison & Gordon Tullock eds. 1980). The journal Public Choice publishes many articles on rent-seeking.

found, escheat to the government rather than becoming the property of the finder. This rule reduces the investment in finding to whatever level the government thinks proper; the government determines that level by determining how much reward to give the finder. In the case of currency (as distinct from treasure that has historical, aesthetic, or collectors' value), the optimal level is very low, perhaps zero. Finding money does not increase the wealth of society; it just enables the finder to have more of society's goods than someone else. The optimal reward may therefore be very low — maybe zero. The trend in the common law is to expand the escheat principle of treasure trove into other areas of found property and thus give the finder a reward rather than the property itself; this makes economic sense.

It might appear that nothing could be more remote from sunken treasure than patented inventions, and yet the economic problem created by patents is remarkably like that of abandoned property. Ideas are in a sense created but in another sense found. Suppose that whoever invents the widget will, if allowed to exclude others from its use by being granted a patent, be able to sell the patent to a manufacturer for $1 million. And suppose that the cost of invention is $250,000. Others will try to be first to invent the widget. This competition will cause it to be invented sooner. But suppose it is invented only one day sooner; the value of having the widget a day earlier will be less than the cost of duplicating the entire investment in invention.

§3.3   Intellectual Property

As the preceding paragraph illustrates, the economist experiences no sense of discontinuity in moving from physical to intellectual property. In particular, the dynamic rationale for property rights is readily applied to the useful ideas that we call inventions. Suppose that it costs $10 million to invent a new type of food blender, the marginal cost of producing and selling the blender once it is invented is $50 (why is the $10 million not a marginal cost?), and the estimated demand is for 1 million of the blenders (we can for present purposes ignore the fact that demand will vary with the blender's price). Unless the manufacturer can charge $60 per blender, he will not recoup his costs of invention. But if other manufacturers face the same marginal cost as he, competition will (in the absence of patents) bid the price down to $50, the effort at recoupment will fail, and anticipating this the manufacturer will not make the invention in the first place; he will not sow if he won't be able to reap. Moreover, in a world without patents, such inventive activity as did occur would be heavily biased toward inventions that could be kept secret, in just the same way that a complete absence of property rights would bias production toward things that involve minimum preparatory investment (as we saw in §3.1 *supra*). So we have patents; but the law uses several devices to try to minimize the costs of duplicating inventive activity that, as we saw in the preceding section, a patent system invites. Here are four of them:

1. A patent expires after 17 years, rather than being perpetual. This reduces the value of the patent to the owner and hence the amount of resources that will be devoted to obtaining patents.

2. Inventions are not patentable if they are "obvious." The functional meaning of obviousness is discoverable at low cost.[1] The lower the cost of discovery, the less necessary patent protection is to induce the discovery to be made, and the greater is the danger of overinvestment if patent protection is allowed. If an idea worth $1 million costs $1 rather than $250,000 to discover, the amount of wasteful duplication to get a patent will be greater, perhaps $249,999 greater.

3. Patents are granted early—before an invention has been carried to the point of commercial feasibility—in order to head off costly duplication of expensive development work.[2]

4. Fundamental ideas (the laws of physics, for example) are not patentable, despite their great value. Until the advent of costly atomic-particle accelerators, basic research did not entail substantial expenditure, and patent protection might therefore have led to too much basic research. By confining patentability to "useful" inventions in rather a narrow sense, the patent law identifies (though only crudely) inventions likely to require costly development before they can be brought to market. The nonpatentability of basic discoveries, like the limited term of patents, reflects more than just a concern with costs of acquiring patents, however; there are also serious identification problems, as in the case of wild animals. An idea does not have a stable physical locus, like a piece of land. With the passage of time it becomes increasingly difficult to identify the products in which a particular idea is embodied; and it is also difficult to identify the products in which a basic idea, having many and varied applications, is embodied. Here then is another example of how the costs of property rights limit their extent.

The costs of the patent system include (besides inducing potentially excessive investment in inventing) driving a wedge between price and marginal cost, with results explored in Part III of this book. Once an invention is made, its costs are sunk; in economic terms, they are zero. Hence a price that includes a royalty to the inventor will exceed the opportunity

§3.3   1. Edmund W. Kitch, Graham v. John Deere Co.: New Standards for Patents, 1966 S. Ct. Rev. 293; Roberts v. Sears, Roebuck & Co., 723 F.2d 1324, 1344 (7th Cir. 1983) *(en banc)* (concurring and dissenting opinion).

2. Edmund W. Kitch, The Nature and Function of the Patent System, 20 J. Law & Econ. 265 (1977). Notice the analogy to the "committed searcher" principle mentioned in the preceding section.

cost of the product in which the invention is embodied. This wedge, however, is analytically the same as the cost of a fence to demarcate a property right in land; it is an indispensable cost of using the property rights system to allocate resources.

Intellectual property furnishes many other interesting examples of the economics of property law. Only a few can be discussed here. Let us begin with trade secrecy,[3] because it is frequently an alternative to patenting: A manufacturer who is confident that he can keep his manufacturing process a secret for longer than the period for which he could protect it by a patent may decide to rely on trade secrecy law and forgo seeking a patent. He will save the costs and avoid the uncertainties of the patent route; and he will not have to disclose the process, as he would in a patent application, thereby enabling his competitors to duplicate it once the patent expires.

There is no time limit on a trade secret—and this despite the fact that the holder of the secret need not prove that it meets patent law's criteria of novelty, nonobviousness, and the rest. The result may seem a loophole in patent law as well as an invitation to devote excessive resources to maintaining secrecy, until we realize that a trade secret is a severely limited right. For the most part, all that trade secrecy law prevents is the wrongful appropriation (e.g., by tort or breach of contract) of the secret; competitors are free to duplicate it by independent discovery or even by reverse engineering of the secret holder's product, as well as to take advantage of any accidental disclosure of the secret by its holder. In effect, competition is substituted for patent law's proof requirements and durational limitation as a check on excessive investments, whether in maintaining or in unmasking trade secrets. For if the secret is readily discoverable by independent inventive efforts, the holder of the secret will have little to gain from expending resources on keeping it a secret, while if the secret is so original and ingenious that it could not be discovered by independent effort within the period of patent protection, the longer protection that trade secrecy will confer in such a case provides an appropriately enhanced reward for extraordinary creativity.

Of course, there is some risk of duplication of inventive efforts, but perhaps not much. If the secret is easily unmasked, by minimal independent efforts, the secret holder will have little incentive to keep it a secret, as we have noted; but in any event the waste of resources in duplication will be slight. If the secret can be unmasked only by a substantial investment, but the expense would be worthwhile given the expected benefits, the secret holder will have to worry that if he does not patent his secret product or process a competitor will. For after the expiration of the one-year grace period for applying for a patent on an invention that the inventor has already begun to use, the inventor can neither patent the

3. See David D. Friedman, William M. Landes & Richard A. Posner, Some Economics of Trade Secret Law, 5 J. Econ. Perspectives 61 (Winter 1991).

invention himself nor (if he has kept it secret) prevent an independent discoverer from patenting it. So we can expect a secret holder to expend substantial resources on keeping his secret only in those rare cases where a competitor is unlikely, even at great expense, to be able to discover it independently — and if the futility of the endeavor is obvious, the competitor will not incur the expense, and there will be no waste of resources.

Copyright law[4] resembles patent law in granting time-limited rights, but resembles trade secret law in allowing independent discovery. The reason for the latter feature may be that patents protect only inventions, which can be and are indexed in the Patent Office, while copyrights protect an infinitude of sentences, musical phrases, details of architectural blueprints, and other minutiae of expression, making it impossible to search the entire body of pertinent copyrighted materials in order to make sure that one is not infringing; some amount of inadvertent copying is thus inevitable.

The durational limitation on copyrights is now so generous (the author's life plus 50 years) that one may wonder why the law doesn't go the whole hog and grant perpetual copyrights. The danger of attracting excessive resources into the production of copyrighted works cannot be the explanation; as a result of discounting to present value (see §6.11 *infra*), the knowledge that you may be entitled to a royalty on your book 50 to 100 years after you publish it is unlikely to affect your behavior today. Property rights in land are perpetual; why not in books? One reason is that it is more inefficient to have unowned land lying around (say, as the result of the expiration of a time-limited property right) than to have unowned intellectual property. Ideally, *all* land should be owned by someone, to prevent the congestion externalities that we discussed in connection with the natural pasture from arising. But, with an important exception to be noted shortly, there is no parallel problem concerning information and expression. A's use of some piece of information will not make it more costly for B to use the same information.

Second, while it is natural to suppose that the scope (including duration) of intellectual property rights represents the striking of a balance between the interests of the creators and of the users of intellectual property, the creators themselves may benefit from the limiting of those rights. Most poems, novels, plays, musical compositions, movies, and other creative works (including inventions) build heavily on earlier creative works—borrowing plot details, stock characters, metaphors, chord progressions, camera angles, and so forth from the earlier works. The greater the scope of copyright protection of the earlier works, the higher the cost of creating the subsequent works. So while an increase in the scope of copyright protection will enhance an author's expected revenues from the sale or

4. See William M. Landes & Richard A. Posner, An Economic Analysis of Copyright Law, 18 J. Leg. Stud. 325 (1989); Wendy J. Gordon, Fair Use as a Market Failure: A Structural and Economic Analysis of the Betamax Case and Its Procedure, 82 Colum. L. Rev. 1600 (1982).

licensing of his own copyrights, it will also increase his cost of creating the works that he copyrights. The tradeoff favors a durational limitation because, while the increment in present value from an increase in revenues in the distant future is, as we said, apt to be negligible, the increase in an author's cost could be great if, because of perpetual copyright, no earlier works were in the public domain, and thus available to be used in the creation of new works without copyright expense.

Here is another example of how limiting a copyright owner's rights can actually increase the value of the copyright. The fair use doctrine of copyright law allows a book reviewer to quote passages from the book without getting the copyright holder's permission. This reduces the cost of book reviews and hence increases the number of reviews, and authors as a group benefit, since book reviews are free advertising. Even unfavorable reviews stimulate sales, at least when the alternative would be no review at all. But most reviews are favorable.

Book reviews are particularly *credible* advertising, moreover, because they are not controlled by the advertiser (i.e., the publisher of the book). If authors could censor the reviews of their books by denying permission to quote from them, book reviews would be no more credible than paid advertising. Authors as a group thus would suffer from a rejection of fair use for book reviews, even if an occasional author gained.

When a book review does reduce the sales of a book, it does so not because, like a routine copyright infringement, it supplies the demand for the book—rarely is a book review a close substitute for the book being reviewed—but because it points out flaws in the book and thus provides valuable information without undermining the rewards for creating *worthwhile* intellectual property. The harm to an author that comes from drawing attention to the *lack* of value of the intellectual property he has created is not the kind of harm that a law intended to encourage the production of intellectual property should seek to prevent.

The Supreme Court has held that the fair use doctrine allows the sale of video recorders for use in recording television programs, even though no royalty was paid to the copyright owners for the privilege of recording.[5] Many people use their video recorders to record programs that are being shown at an inconvenient time or that they want to watch more than once. Such uses benefit the copyright owner even though no royalty is paid. Most programs are bought by advertisers, who pay more the more viewers they reach; by enlarging the effective audience for a program, a video recorder enables the copyright owner to charge more to the advertisers. However, since the evidence was compiled on which the Supreme Court based its decision, devices have come on the market that make it easy for

5. Sony Corp. of America v. University City Studios, Inc., 464 U.S. 417 (1984). The defendants were the companies who made the recorders; they were sued as "contributory infringers." The people who bought the recorders at retail would have been "direct infringers." What is the economic rationale of the doctrine of contributory infringement?

the owner of a video recorder to erase the commercials in a program he records before he watches it. What does this imply about the current economic validity of the Court's decision?

An offbeat example of a property right in intangibles is the right of privacy, usually discussed as a branch of tort law, but functionally a brand of property law.[6] The earliest judicial recognition of an explicit right of privacy came in a case where the defendant had used the plaintiff's name and picture in an advertisement without the plaintiff's consent. Paradoxically, this branch of the right of privacy is most often invoked by celebrities avid for publicity (and therefore is sometimes called the "right of publicity"); they just want to make sure they get the highest possible price for the use of their name and picture in advertising. It might seem that creating a property right in such use would not lead to any socially worthwhile investment but would simply enrich already wealthy celebrities. However, whatever information value a celebrity's endorsement has to consumers will be lost if every advertiser can use the celebrity's name and picture. Just as in the grazing case, the value of associating the celebrity's name with a particular product will be diminished if others are permitted to use the name in association with their products.

The existence of a congestion externality provides an argument that rights of publicity should be perpetual and thus inheritable (a matter of legal controversy today). We don't want this form of information or expression to be in the public domain, because it will be less valuable there, whether the celebrity is dead or alive.

From an economic standpoint, rights of publicity are similar to trademarks; both involve property rights in information used to identify and promote a product or service. Trademarks involve a host of interesting economic issues,[7] some of which are deferred to later sections of this chapter and to the discussion of consumer protection in Chapter 13. The economic function of trademarks is, by giving assurance of uniform quality, to economize on consumer search costs. Strictly speaking, all a trademark does is identify the *source* of a particular product or service—for example, the General Electric trademark identifies General Electric as the producer of the goods to which the trademark is affixed. But this means the consumer knows whom to blame if his light bulb doesn't work, so trademark law gives producers an incentive to maintain quality, which in turn reduces the need for the consumer to shop as carefully as he would otherwise have to do. Even if the nominal price of a trademarked item is higher because of the producer's investment in advertising and enforcing his mark, the total cost (sometimes economists call this the "full price," to distinguish it from the nominal price, i.e., the price charged by the seller) to the

---

6. See Richard A. Posner, The Economics of Justice, chs. 9-10 (1981).
7. See William M. Landes & Richard A. Posner, Trademark Law: An Economic Perspective, 30 J. Law & Econ. 265 (1987); Landes & Posner, The Economics of Trademark Law, 78 Trademark Rptr. 267 (1988).

consumer may be less because the trademark conveys information about quality that the consumer might find it costly to obtain otherwise.

The great challenge for trademark law is to enable each producer to identify his own brand without increasing the costs to other producers of identifying and marketing their brands. The best trademark from this standpoint is the fanciful mark, such as Kodak — an invented word, as distinct from one taken from the language. The number of possible combinations of letters to form new words is infinite, so there is no danger that a fanciful mark will increase the cost to another producer of finding words to identify and market his product. Much trickier is a "descriptive" mark; allowing someone to use "word processor" as his trademark would make it costly for competing producers of word processors to market their brands, because they could not use a compact description. So the law protects descriptive marks only if the mark has acquired "secondary meaning," which means that the consumer has come to identify the term with a particular brand, rather than with the product as a whole. (An example is "Holiday Inn.")

Often when a trademarked good begins life as a patent or other monopoly, the trademark comes to denote the good itself, rather than the source, and when that happens the trademark is termed "generic" and trademark protection is stripped away. Examples of trademarks to which this has happened are "aspirin," "cellophane," and "yo-yo." If the trademark owner were allowed to exclude competitors from using the generic term to describe their brands, he would be imposing costs on them. This would be fine if society wanted to give trademark owners a form of monopoly power the better to encourage people to think up catchy marks, but the costs of inventing trademarks, as distinct from the cost of inventing useful products or processes or of writing books, are too low to justify so extensive a property right.

A trademark is not time-limited, nor should it be. Were there a time limit and it expired before the producer had ceased making the trademarked item, he would have to rename the product, and consumers would be confused. Because, as we shall see (in §3.11 *infra*), a trademark cannot be sold or otherwise transferred apart from the product that it designates, a trademark automatically expires when the product is discontinued.

We have seen that the legal and economic concepts of property do not always coincide (the next section discusses this question further). Here is one more example. An issue in privacy is whether a person should have a right to conceal embarrassing facts about himself—for example that he is an ex-convict. There is some, but not much, judicial support for such a right. The economist sees a parallel to the efforts of sellers to conceal hidden defects in their products. A person "sells" himself by trying to persuade potential transacting partners—an employer, a fiancée, even a casual acquaintance—that he has good qualities. Should he be encouraged to deceive these people, by being given a right to sue anyone who unmasks his hidden "defects"? At least on economic grounds, the answer seems to be no. It would be different if what was "unmasked" was not an embarrassing fact but a superb dinner recipe. We would then be in the realm of the trade secret, broadly defined, where secrecy is a method of enforcing an informal property right and encourages an investment in a socially valuable idea. Concealing discreditable facts about a private individual, a firm, or a product does not. The significance of this proposition for the crime of blackmail is examined in Chapter 6.

§3.4   Property Rights in Law and in Economics: The Case of Broadcast Frequencies

Thus far we have hewn pretty closely to the lawyer's idea of a property right (except with regard to the right, if any, to conceal embarrassing facts), but often the legal and economic conceptions of property rights diverge. Here is an example from broadcasting.[1]

In the early days of radio, before comprehensive federal regulation, there was some judicial support for the proposition that the right to broadcast on a particular frequency in a particular area without interference from other users was a property right that could be protected by injunction. With the creation in 1928 of the Federal Radio Commission (forerunner of the Federal Communications Commission), Congress took a different tack. Licenses authorizing the use of particular frequencies in particular areas were to be granted at nominal charge for renewable three-year terms to applicants who persuaded the commission that licensing them would promote the public interest. Congress expressly provided that licensees were to have no property rights in the use of the frequencies assigned them; the purpose of this provision was to foreclose any claim to compensation by a licensee whose license was not renewed at the end of the three-year term.

Some of the objections that were advanced to the recognition of property rights in frequencies have an odd ring in an economist's ear. For example, it was said that if broadcasting rights could be bought and sold like other property, the broadcast media would come under the control of the wealthy. This confuses willingness to pay with ability to pay. The possession of money does not dictate the objects that will be purchased. The poor frequently bid goods away from the rich by being willing to pay more in the aggregate.

§3.4   1. See Ronald H. Coase, The Federal Communications Commission, 2 J. Law & Econ. 1 (1959); Jora R. Minasian, Property Rights in Radiation: An Alternative Approach to Radio Frequency Allocation, 18 J. Law & Econ. 221 (1975); Thomas W. Hazlett, The Rationality of U.S. Regulation of the Broadcast Spectrum, 33 J. Law & Econ. 133 (1990).

In the actual administration of the federal regulatory scheme for broad-casting, willingness to pay has played a decisive role and a system of de facto property rights has emerged. The desirable radio and television li-censes have been awarded in comparative proceedings in which, much as in a system of property rights, willingness to pay—not for the license as such but for the legal representation and political influence that may de-termine the outcome—has decided in many cases who would control the resource at stake. This method of initially assigning broadcast rights is, however, less efficient than an auction or other sale. There is a good deal of uncertainty in the political regulatory process, so the applicant who pays his lawyers, lobbyists, etc., the most money—thereby indicating that he attaches the greatest value to obtaining the right—will often not receive it. Moreover, the social costs of this method of allocation are much greater than the costs of allocation through the market (how about the private costs?). Competition to obtain a license could dissipate the expected value of the license in legal, lobbying, and related expenses. (Where have we seen this problem before?) Participation in an auction of broadcast fre-quencies would not require costly legal and lobbying services, at least if rigging the auction can be prevented at low cost.

The failure to assign the right to the applicant who values it the most is only a transitory inefficiency. Once broadcast rights have been obtained in a licensing proceeding, they can be sold as an incident to the sale of the physical assets of the radio or television station. When a television station having a transmitter and other physical properties worth only a few hundred thousand dollars is sold for $50 million, one can be confident that the major part of the purchase price is payment for the right to use the frequency. Thus broadcast rights usually end up in the hands of those who are willing to pay the most money for them, even if the initial "auc-tion" may not have allocated the rights efficiently.

The willingness of broadcasters to pay tens of millions of dollars for a right terminable after three years may seem peculiar. But broadcast licenses have been terminated only for serious misconduct, in much the same way that one can lose one's land for nonpayment of real estate taxes.

So in economic, although not in formal legal, terms there are property rights in broadcast frequencies. The right is obtained initially in a com-petition in which willingness to pay plays an influential, and quite possibly a decisive, role. Once obtained, the right is transferable, though imper-fectly so, as we shall see in §3.11 infra. It is exclusive (interference with a licensee's use of his frequency will be enjoined). And it is for all practical purposes perpetual. The holder of the right is subject to various regulatory constraints but less so than a public utility, the principal assets of which are private property in the formal legal sense.

The concept of a de facto property right is of broad applicability. Some economists, indeed, use the term property right to describe virtually every device—public or private, common law or regulatory, contractual or governmental, formal or informal—by which divergences between private and social costs or benefits are reduced.[2] In a book on law, this usage can be confusing, so we shall generally confine our use of the term to formal property rights, recognizing however that they are just a subset of property rights in a broader economic sense.

§3.5   Rights to Future Use

The rights system in broadcasting is not only costly and *sub rosa* but also incomplete in important respects. One is the difficulty of obtaining rights for future use, a problem we have already encountered in connection with shipwrecks and wild animals. To purchase vacant land with the intention of holding it for future development is a common type of transaction, while to disclose in an application for a broadcast license an intention to indefinitely defer starting to broadcast would guarantee denial. The same thing is true of water rights under the appropriation system that prevails in the western states. One acquires property rights in water by the actual diversion and use of a stream, and the right embraces only the amount of water actually used; a right may not be obtained for exercise at a later date. But both the broadcast and water limitations are circumvented to some extent, in the case of broadcasting by deferring actual construction after the license has been obtained, in the case of water by obtaining a preliminary permit that establishes the applicant's prior right even though the construction of diversion works and the use of the diverted water are postponed.

The hostility to recognizing rights for future use may be related to the apparent "windfall" element that is present in both the broadcasting and water contexts. In both the right is awarded without charge although the applicant may have gone to great expense to obtain it, and it often can be resold immediately at a considerable profit. This need not be evidence of a true windfall; applicants as a group may just break even. The windfall, however, would appear even larger if the profit were obtained by someone who appeared not to be providing any service.

A related hostility, reflected in many corners of the law, is to speculation, the purchase of a good not to use but to hold in the hope that it will appreciate in value.[1] Speculation performs a valuable economic function by helping make prices accurately reflect the conditions of supply and

2. For illustrations, see Armen A. Alchian & Harold Demsetz, The Property Right Paradigm, 33 J. Econ. Hist. 16 (1973), and essays in The Economics of Property Rights (Eirik G. Furubotn & Svetozar Pejovich eds. 1974).
  §3.5 1. Or the sale of a good in the expectation that its value will decline, as in short selling of stock. An example is given in this paragraph.

demand (see also §4.9 *infra*). Speculation has both a static function — bringing prices into line with current demand and supply, i.e., avoiding present shortages or gluts — and a dynamic one. A futures market (for example, a market in which you can buy at a fixed price wheat for delivery not today but a year from now) can smooth consumption over time, canceling the effects of gluts and shortages. If, for example, a shortage is anticipated, speculators will step up their futures purchases (because they expect the market price to be higher next year); the futures price will therefore rise; and the rise will induce sellers to hold back a portion of the current supply, or to charge a higher price to current buyers — but that is the same thing (why?)—in order to take advantage of the anticipated higher price in the future. The resulting expansion in future supply will, in turn, moderate that price; in this way speculation can, contrary to myth, reduce price swings.

It is easy to see how, in the case of land, water, and broadcast frequencies —all of which can at different times be in either insufficient or excessive supply—speculation, if permitted, could optimize the use of resources over time, just as in our wheat example. But purchases for future use need not be speculative; they can be the opposite of speculative—hedging. A farmer may know that he will need more water for irrigation in a few years, and rather than take the risk of changes in the price of water he may decide to sign a contract now, at a fixed price, for future delivery of a specified quantity of the water. (Hence the seller will be speculating on future changes in the price of water — speculation facilitates hedging!) If such sales are forbidden, the farmer may decide to use more water now than he really needs, just to be sure of having a right to the water in the future when he will need it. The main effect of forbidding purchases of water or broadcast frequencies or oyster beds for future use is to encourage uneconomical uses, uses not to meet a demand but to stake a claim.

The problem of premature use is analytically similar to that of excessive investment in finding buried treasure or in obtaining a patent (see §3.2 *supra*). To acquire a valuable right, people may invest resources beyond the point at which those resources confer a net social benefit. Homesteading is a good example.[2] If land is given away without pecuniary charge, but the gift is conditioned (as it was) on the homesteader's actually occupying and working the land, the homesteader will work it to the point where the last dollar's worth of effort yields a dollar of benefit in securing his claim, even if less than a dollar's worth of agricultural output is produced. Of course, if the government *wants* the lands occupied as soon as

---

2. See, e.g., Terry L. Anderson & Peter J. Hill, The Race for Property Rights, 33 J. Law & Econ. 177 (1990). See generally David D. Haddock, First Possession Versus Optimal Timing: Limiting the Dissipation of Economic Value, 64 Wash. U.L.Q. 775 (1986).

possible for political or military purposes, a homestead law may be an efficient method of achieving this purpose.[3]

As the last point shows, it is not always inefficient to condition a property right on use; and recall the discussion of wild animals. Trademark law provides an interesting example. The legal protection of a trademark depends on the trademark holder's actually selling the product or service that the trademark designates. You cannot just dream up names for products that you or someone else might someday want to sell and register the names in the Trademark Office and thereby obtain a right to exclude others from using them. Allowing such "banking" of trademarks might draw excessive resources into the activity of thinking up trademarks. The trademark registry might become clogged with millions of marks, making it costly for sellers to search the registry in order to avoid infringing a registered mark.

3. Douglas W. Allen, Homesteading and Property Rights; or, "How the West Was Really Won," 34 J. Law & Econ. 1 (1991).

[4]

Freedom and the Rule of Law

It is not easy to state what English-speaking people mean by the expression "the rule of law." The meaning of these words has changed in the last seventy or even fifty years, and the phrase itself has acquired rather an obsolete sound in England as well as in America. Nevertheless, it once corresponded to an idea that (as Professor Hayek pointed out in his first lecture on freedom and the rule of law given at the National Bank of Egypt in 1955) "had fully conquered the minds if not the practice of all the Western nations," so that "few people doubted that it was destined soon to rule the world." [1]

The complete story of this change cannot be written yet, since the process is still going on. Moreover, it is a story to a certain extent complicated, fragmentary, tedious, and, above all, hidden from people who read only newspapers, magazines, or fiction and who have no special taste for legal matters or for such technicalities as, say, the delegation of judicative authority and legislative powers. But it is a story that concerns all the countries of the West that had and still have a share not only in the juridical ideal denoted by the expression "the rule of law," but also in the political ideal designated by the word "freedom."

I would not go so far as to say, as Professor Hayek does in the above-mentioned lecture, that "it is in the technical discussion concerning administrative law that the fate of our liberty is being decided." I would prefer to say that this fate is also being decided in many other places—in parliaments, on the streets, in the homes, and, in the last analysis, in the minds of menial workers and of well-educated men like scientists and university professors. I agree with Professor Hayek that we are confronted in this respect with a sort of silent revolution. But I would not say with him or with Professor Ripert of France that this is a revolution—nay, a *coup d'état*—promoted only, or even chiefly, by technicians like lawyers or the officials of ministries or of departments of state. In other words, the continuous and creeping change in the meaning of "the rule of law" is not the result of a "managerial" revolution, to use Burnham's apt expression. It is a much broader phenomenon connected with many events and situations the real features and significance of which are not easily ascertainable and to which historians refer by such phrases as "the general trend of our times." The process by which the word "freedom" began to assume several different and incompatible meanings in the last hundred years involved, as we have seen, a semantic confusion. Another semantic confusion, less obvious, but no less important, is revealing itself to those patient enough to study the silent revolution in the use of the expression "the rule of law."

Continental European scholars, notwithstanding their wisdom, their learning, and their admiration for the British political system, from the times of Montesquieu and Voltaire have not been able to understand the proper meaning of the British constitution. Montesquieu is probably the most famous of those who are open to this criticism, particularly as far as his celebrated interpretation of the division of powers in England is concerned, in spite of the fact that his interpretation (many people would say his misinterpretation) had, in its turn, an enormous influence in the English-speaking countries themselves. Eminent English scholars, in their turn, suffered a similar criticism because of their interpretations of European Continental constitutions. The most famous of these scholars is probably Dicey, whose misunderstandings of the French *droit administratif* have been considered by another well-known English scholar, Sir Carleton Kemp Allen, a "fundamental mistake" and one of the main reasons why the rule of law has evolved in the English-speaking countries of the present day in the way that it has. The fact is that the powers of government were never actually separated in England as Montesquieu believed in his day, nor was the *droit administratif* in France or, for that matter, the Italian *diritto amministrativo* or the German *Verwaltungsrecht* actually identifiable with the "administrative law" that Sir Carleton Kemp Allen and the generality of contemporary English scholars are thinking of when they speak of the recent changes in the respective functions of the judiciary and of the executive in the United Kingdom.

After long reflection on this subject, I am inclined to conclude that even more fundamental than the misinterpretations of Dicey, on the one hand, and of Montesquieu, on the other, have been those of the scholars and ordinary people who have tried to adopt, on the European Continent, the British "rule of law" and have imagined that the Continental imitation of the English or the American system (say, for instance, the German *Rechtsstaat* or the French *état de droit* or the Italian *stato di diritto*) is really something very similar to the English "rule of law." Dicey himself, who had a lucid view of some very important differences in this respect and who several thinkers believe was rather prejudiced against the French and generally against the constitutions of the European Continent, actually thought that at the beginning of the present century there was not a great deal of difference between the English or the American "rule of law" and the Continental constitutions:

If we confine our observation to the Europe of the twentieth century, we might well say that in most European countries the rule of law is now nearly as well established as in England and that private individuals at any rate who do not meddle in politics have little to fear as long as they keep the law, either from the government or from anyone else.[2]

On the other hand, some Continental scholars—e.g., the great French *garantistes* like Guizot and Benjamin Constant and the German theorists of the *Rechtsstaat* like Karl von Rotteck, K. Welcker, Robert von Mohl, and Otto von Gierke—supposed (I would say, wrongly) that they were describing and recommending to their fellow citizens a type of state very similar to that of England. In our day Professor Hayek has tried to demonstrate that the German doctrine of the *Rechtsstaat,* before its corruption by the historicist and positivist *reactionnaires* at the end of the nineteenth century, contributed a great deal, in theory if not in practice, to the ideal of "the rule of law."

This ideal and that of the *Rechtsstaat* before its corruption did indeed have much in common. Almost all the features that Dicey described so brilliantly in the above-quoted book in order to explain what the English "rule of law" was, are traceable also in the Continental constitutions from the French constitution of 1789 to those of the present day.

The *supremacy of the law* was the chief characteristic cited in Dicey's analysis. He quoted the old law of the English courts: "La ley est la plus haute inheritance, que le roi had; car par la ley il même et toutes ses sujets sont rulés, et si la ley ne fuit, nul roi et nul inheritance sera" ("the law is the highest estate to which the king succeeds, for both he and all his subjects are ruled by it, and without it there would be neither king nor realm"). According to Dicey, the supremacy of the law was, in its turn, a principle that corresponded to three other concepts and therefore implied three different and concomitant meanings of the phrase "the rule of law": (1) the absence of arbitrary power on the part of the government to punish citizens or to commit acts against life or property; (2) the subjection of every man, whatever his rank or condition, to the ordinary law of the realm and to the jurisdiction of the ordinary tribunals; and (3) a predominance of the legal spirit in English institutions, because of which, as Dicey explains, "the general principles of the English constitution (as, for example, the right to personal liberty or the right to public assembly) are the result of judicial decisions . . . . ; whereas under many foreign constitutions the security given to the rights of individuals results or appears to result from the general (abstract) principles of the constitution." [3]

Americans may wonder whether or not Dicey considered the American system in the same class as the Continental systems of

Europe. Americans derive or appear to derive their individual rights from the general principles laid down in their Constitution and in the first ten amendments. As a matter of fact, Dicey considered the United States a typical instance of a country living under "the rule of law" because she had inherited the English traditions. He was right, as one sees when one recalls, on the one hand, the fact that a written bill of rights was not considered necessary at first by the Founding Fathers—who did not even include it in the text of the Constitution itself—and, on the other hand, the importance that judicial decisions on the part of ordinary tribunals had and still have in the political system of the United States as far as the rights of individuals are concerned.

Professor Hayek, among more recent eminent theorists of "the rule of law," takes into consideration four features of it that correspond to a certain extent, although not entirely, to Dicey's description. According to Professor Hayek, the *generality*, the *equality*, and the *certainty* of the law, as well as the fact that administrative discretion in coercive action, i.e., in interfering with the person and the property of the private citizen, *must always be subject to review* by independent courts, are "really the crux of the matter, the decisive point on which it depends whether the Rule of Law prevails or not." [4]

Apparently, the theories of Professor Hayek and of Dicey coincide except for some minor details. Professor Hayek, it is true, emphasizes the difference between laws and orders in connection with the "generality" of the law and points out that the law must never concern particular individuals or be enacted when, at the moment of enactment, it can be predicted which particular individuals it will help or damage. But this may simply be considered as a special development of Dicey's idea that the "rule of law" means the absence of arbitrary power on the part of the government. *Equality*, in its turn, is an idea embodied in the Dicean description of the second characteristic of the rule of law, that is, that every man, whatever his rank or condition, is subject to the ordinary law of the realm.

In this connection we must notice a difference between Dicey's

and Hayek's interpretations of equality or at least of its application in some respects. Professor Hayek agrees with Sir Carleton
Kemp Allen in reproaching Dicey for a "fundamental mistake"
relating to the interpretation of the French *droit administratif*.
Dicey, according to Sir Carleton and Professor Hayek, was wrong
in believing that the French and generally the Continental *droit
administratif*, at least in its mature stage, was a sort of arbitrary
law because it was not administered by ordinary tribunals. According to Dicey, only ordinary courts, in England as well as in
France, could really protect citizens by applying the ordinary law
of the land. The fact that special jurisdictions, like that of the
conseil d'état in France, were given the power of judging in cases
where private citizens litigated with officials employed in the
service of the state, appeared in the eyes of Dicey as a proof that
the equality of the law towards all citizens was not actually
respected on the Continent. Officials, when litigating in their
official capacity with ordinary citizens, were "to some extent
exempted from the ordinary law of the land." Professor Hayek
charges Dicey with having contributed a great deal to preventing
or to delaying the growth of institutions capable of controlling,
through independent courts, the new bureaucratic machinery in
England because of a false idea that separate administrative
tribunals would always constitute a denial of the ordinary law
of the land and therefore a denial of "the rule of law." The fact
is that the *conseil d'état* provides ordinary citizens in France as
well as in most countries of Western Europe with a fairly unbiased
and efficient protection against what Shakespeare would have
called "the insolence of office."

Is it fair, however, to hold Dicey responsible for the fact that
a process similar to that of the formation and functioning of the
conseil d'état has not yet taken place in the United Kingdom?
Perhaps what has hindered the development of an adminstrative
court of appeals in England (which would correspond to the
French *conseil d'état* or to the Italian *consiglio di stato*) is the
fact, noticed by Allen, that in England "at the very mention of a
'new-found halliday' not a few hands are at once thrown up in

horror at a 'foreign importation.' " [5] In fact, hostility toward
un-British types of law and judicature is an old characteristic
of the English people. The present inhabitants of the British Isles
are, after all, the descendants of those who proudly proclaimed,
many centuries ago, "nolumus leges Angliae mutari" ("we do not
want any changes made in the laws of the Anglo-Saxons"). Dicey's
role in the resistance to the importation of Continental forms of
law into England was a comparatively small one. Allen himself,
while cautiously suggesting how to adopt new means to protect
citizens against British bureaucracy, hastily adds that "nobody in
his right mind proposes to imitate in England the *conseil d'état*"
and that people who still believe that " 'administrative law' (if
they will even permit the term) is the same thing as *droit administratif* are living in an age long past." [6]

Incidentally, the amusing thing in this peroration by Sir
Carleton is that he seems to imply here that "administrative law"
is something much better than the foreign *droit administratif,*
while at the beginning of his work he had reproached poor Dicey
for his "complacent comparison with French administrative law,"
that is, with "that remarkable jurisprudence, at all events in its
modern developments," and had charged Dicey with having "left
the British public under the impression that the effect of administrative law in France was to place officials in a special privileged
position rather than (as is the fact) to give the subject a large
measure of protection against illegal state action." [7] One might
add that this is a protection that the present English administrative law does not offer at all to the subjects of the British Crown
because, as was pointed out recently by another English scholar,
Ernest F. Row,

whereas the French administrative courts are courts and administer a
perfect code of law by a perfectly definite procedure akin to that of
the other courts, the new English system [that is, that bestowal on the
executive of judicial functions that the former Lord Chief Justice of
England used to qualify as "administrative lawlessness" and as the
"new despotism"] is nothing of the kind, for by it these disputes

between individuals and the government are settled by the government, itself a party to the dispute, in a purely arbitrary manner, according to no regular and recognized principles and by no clearly defined legal procedure.[8]

Dicey and Hayek apparently differ only slightly in their respective interpretations of equality as a characteristic of the rule of law. Both maintain that independent courts are essential in order to grant to the citizens equality before the law. A minor difference between the two interpretations of the functions of the courts seems to be that while Dicey does not admit the existence of two different judiciary orders, one to settle disputes between ordinary citizens only and one to settle disputes between ordinary citizens, on the one hand, and state officials, on the other, Hayek thinks that the existence of two different judiciary orders is not objectionable in itself, provided that both orders are actually independent of the executive.

Things are probably not so simple as Professor Hayek's conclusion seems to imply. Of course, independent administrative tribunals are better than the simple bestowal of judiciary power on the executive in administrative matters, such as occurs in England today and, to a certain extent, in the United States as well. But the very presence of "administrative tribunals" gives added point to the fact (which Dicey disliked) that there is not one law for everybody in the country and therefore the equality of all citizens before the law is really not respected as it would be if there were only one law of the land and not also an administrative law side by side with the common law.

Dean Roscoe Pound pointed out in an essay cited by Professor Hayek [9] that contemporary tendencies in the exposition of public law subordinate the interests "of the individual to those of the public official" by allowing the latter to "to identify one side of the controversy with the public interest and so give it a great value and ignore the others." This applies more or less to all kinds of administrative laws, whether they are administered by independent courts or not. A general principle that underlies all relations between private citizens and government officials acting in their official capacity is what the Continental theorists (like, for example, the German Jellinek or the French Hauriou or the Italian Romano) would call the *status subjectionis* of the individual in regard to the administration, and, correspondingly, the "supremacy" of the latter over the individual. State officials, as representatives of the public administration, are regarded as people having *eminentia jura* (pre-eminent rights) over other citizens. Thus, officials are entitled, for instance, to enforce their orders without any prior control whatever on the part of a judge over the legitimacy of these orders, whereas such a control would be prescribed if a private citizen demanded anything of another private citizen. It is true that Continental theorists admit as well that individuals have a right to personal liberty that limits the *eminentia jura* or, as they also say, the *supremacy* of the administration. But the principle of the supremacy of the administration is something that today qualifies the administrative law of all countries in Continental Europe and, to some extent, of all countries in the world.

It is exactly this principle that administrative tribunals take into account in judging controversies between private citizens and officials, whereas ordinary judges would consider all the private parties involved in a case as exactly on the same level. This fact, which has in itself nothing to do with the extent to which the administrative tribunals are independent of the executive or of state officials, is at the base of the existence of administrative tribunals as separate courts of judicature. Now, if we admit, with Dicey, that the only law to be taken into consideration in judging controversies between citizens (whether they are state officials or not) is one that is in accordance with the rule of law as Dicey conceives of it, his conclusion that a system of administrative courts (whether they are independent of the government or not) is to be avoided and that only ordinary courts are to be accepted is perfectly consistent.

Dicey's conclusion may or may not be applicable to present circumstances, but it is a consequence of the principle of equality

before the law, that is, of one of the principles implied by both
his and Professor Hayek's interpretation of the meaning of "the
rule of law."

In England, Dicey wrote,

the idea of legal equality, or of the universal subjection of all classes
to one law administered by the ordinary courts, has been pushed to its
utmost limit. With us every official, from the Prime Minister down
to a constable or a collector of taxes, is under the same responsibility
for every act done without legal justification as any other citizen. The
reports abound with cases in which officials have been brought before
the courts and made, in their personal capacity, liable to punishment
or to the payment of damages for acts done in their official character
but in excess of their lawful authority. A colonial governor, a secretary
of state, a military officer, and all subordinates, though carrying out
the commands of their official superiors, are as responsible for any act
which the law does not authorize as is any private and unofficial
person.[10]

The situation described by Dicey in 1885 is certainly not that
which prevails at the present time, for a typical feature of the new
"administrative law" in England is the removal from the jurisdiction of the ordinary courts of many cases in which the executive is or may be itself one of the parties to the dispute.

Dicey cannot be justly criticized for his condemnation of administrative tribunals on the basis of a principle he has so clearly
enunciated, viz., the universal subjection of all classes to one law.
Otherwise we ought to conclude that while all men are equal
before the law, some men are "more equal than others."

In fact, we now know how far the interpretation of the principle of equality before the law can go in political systems in which
the principle of the purely formal—nay, of the ceremonial—
legality of any rule whatever, regardless of its content, has been
substituted for the principle of the *Rechtsstaat* and, correspondingly, of "the rule of law" in its early meaning.

We can form as many categories of people as we want in order
to apply the same laws to them. Within each category people
will all be "equal" before the particular law that applies to them,

regardless of the fact that other people, grouped in other categories, will be treated quite differently by other laws. Thus, we can create an "administrative law" before which all people grouped in a certain category defined in the law will be treated in the same way by administrative tribunals, and side by side with it we can recognize a "common law" under which people, grouped in other categories, will be no less equally treated by the ordinary courts. Thus, by a slight change in the meaning of the principle of "equality," we can pretend to have preserved it. Instead of "equality before the law," all that we shall have will then be *equality before each of the two systems of law enacted in the same country,* or, if we want to use the language of the Dicean formula, we shall have *two laws of the land instead of one.* Of course, we can, in the same way, have three or four or thousands of laws of the land—one for landlords, one for tenants, one for employers, one for employees, etc. This is exactly what is happening today in many Western countries where lip service is still paid to the principle of "the rule of law" and hence of "equality before the law."

We can also imagine that the same courts are entitled to apply all these laws of the land equally to all those included in the categories concerned. This may still be called approximately "equality before the law." But it is obvious that in such a case not everybody will receive equal treatment under the law of the land considered as a whole. For instance, in Italy, the third article of the constitution states that "all citizens are equal before the law." In fact, however, there are laws that constrain landlords to keep tenants at a very low rent, notwithstanding previous agreements to the contrary, whereas other categories of people, who entered into contracts in other capacities than those of landlords or of tenants, are not interfered with by any special law and still may—nay, must—keep the agreements that they have made. We also have in my country other laws that constrain people to give away a part of their land for a compensation fixed by the government itself and which the proprietors think in many cases to be ridiculously low when compared with the market price of the land. Other people—for instance, owners of buildings, of business firms, or of securities—are still left free to do what they want with their property. The Italian Constitutional Court has held valid in a recent decision a law that entitles the government to pay a nominal price to proprietors expropriated by the land reform laws, on the ground that this price was fixed with regard to the common interest of the country (and, of course, it is very difficult to ascertain what the "common interest" is). Theorists could probably elaborate a series of principles to explain all this and speak, for instance, of a *jus subjectionis* of the landlords or of *jura eminentia* or *supremacy* on the part of the tenants and the government officials who fix the amount to be paid to the expropriated landlords. But things remain as they are: people are not equally treated by the law of the land considered as a whole in the sense intended by Dicey in his famous book.

The possibility of several laws valid at the same time for different classes of citizens in the same country, but treating them differently (the most common example is that of progressive taxation according to the citizens' income, which has already become a general feature of the fiscal policy of all Western countries) is related in its turn to the principle of the *generality of the law*. Indeed, it is not easy to establish what renders one law *general* in comparison with another. There are many "genera" under which "general" laws may be contrived, and many "species" which it is possible to take into consideration within the same "genus."

Dicey considered "the legal spirit" a special attribute of English institutions. The whole British political system was based, according to him, on general principles resulting "from judicial decisions determining the rights of private persons in particular cases brought before the courts." He contrasted this with what happens on the Continent (and, he might have said, in the United States as well), where "the security given to the rights of individuals results or appears to result from the general principles of the constitution," emerging in its turn from a legislative act. Dicey explained with his usual lucidity what he meant by this:

If it be allowable to apply the formulae of logic to questions of law, the difference in this matter between the constitution of Belgium and the English constitution may be described by the statement that in Belgium individual rights are deductions drawn from the principles of the constitution, whilst in England the so-called principles of the constitution are inductions or generalizations based upon particular decisions pronounced by the courts as to the rights of given individuals.[11]

Dicey also stated that, although "this was, of course, a formal difference" of no moment in itself, great practical differences had been revealed by historical evidence relating, for instance to the French Constitution of 1791, which proclaimed a series of rights, while "there never was a period in the recorded annals of mankind when each and all of these rights were so insecure, one might almost say completely nonexistent, as at the height of the French Revolution." The reason for these differences between the English and the Continental systems was, according to Dicey, the lack of legal skill on the part of the legislators (and here Dicey seems to echo the well-known impatience of the English judges with the work of legislatures) required to contrive remedies to secure the exercise of rights on the part of the citizens. Dicey did not think that this skill was incompatible with written constitutions as such and declared with admiration that "the statesmen of America have shown unrivaled skill in providing means for giving legal security to the rights declared by the American constitutions," so that "the rule of law was as marked a feature of the United States as of England." [12] According to Dicey, the exercise of the rights of the individual under the English constitution was more *certain* than the exercise of similar rights under Continental constitutions; and this "certainty" was mainly due to greater legal skill on the part of the English-speaking people in contriving remedies connected with these rights.

Certainty is a feature that Professor Hayek also emphasizes in his recent analysis of the ideal of "the rule of law." He conceives it in a way that is only apparently different from that of Dicey, although this difference may be very important in some respects.

According to Professor Hayek,[13] the certainty of the law is probably the most important requirement for the economic activities of society and has contributed much to the greater prosperity of the Western world as compared with the Orient, where the certainty of the law was not so early achieved. But he does not analyze what the term "certainty" properly means when referred to the law. This is a point that needs to be dealt with very accurately in a theory of "the rule of law," although neither Dicey nor Professor Hayek nor, for that matter, most other scholars enter very much into this matter. Different meanings of the expression "the certainty of the law" may be at the very foundation of most of the misunderstandings between Continental and English scholars relating to the rule of law and to apparently similar concepts like those of written constitutions, *Rechtsstaaten,* etc. Dicey did not have a completely clear conception of what the "certainty" of the law meant for him when he described the main features of the rule of law. Apparently, this fact is connected with the absence of written—and therefore, in a way, of *certain*—rules in the English traditional common law, including constitutional law. If certainty were connected only with written rules, neither the common law nor that part of it that can be called constitutional law would be certain at all. In fact, many of the recent attacks on the "uncertainty" of case law on the part of English-speaking and particularly of American lawyers and political scientists belonging to the so-called "realistic school" are based on a meaning of the term "certainty" that implies the existence of a definitely written formula the words of which ought not to be changed at will by the reader. This impatience with unwritten law is an outgrowth of the increasing number of statutes in contemporary legal and political systems and of the increasing weight that has been given to statutory law as compared with case law (that is, with the unwritten law) in England as well as in other countries of the British Commonwealth and in the United States of America.

The certainty of the law is connected with the idea of definitely written formulae, like those that the Germans would call *Rechtssaetze,* also in the meaning Professor Hayek gives to the word "certainty" in his lectures on the rule of law. He declares that even "the delegation of rule-making to some kind of non-elective authority need not be contrary to the rule of law so long as this authority is bound to state and publish the rules in advance of their application. . . ." He adds that "the trouble with the widespread modern use of delegation is not that the power of making general rules is delegated, but that authorities are in effect given power to wield coercion without rule, because no general rule can be formulated for the exercise of the powers in question." [14]

There is a sort of parallelism between what, according to Professor Hayek, is immaterial in relation to administrative law or administrative courts and what is really essential for him in the concept of "certainty." What matters for him is that administrative law be administered by *independent* courts, regardless of the fact that there is something peculiar called "administrative law" and no matter whether the courts administering it are special courts or not. In a similar way, Professor Hayek believes that no serious inconvenience can arise from the fact that rules are issued by parliaments or by some delegated authority, provided only that those rules be general, clearly stated, and published in advance.

General regulations laid down in due time and made known to all citizens make it possible for them to foresee what will happen on the legal stage as a consequence of their behavior, or, to use the words of Professor Hayek: "as a general rule, circumstances which are beyond his [the individual's] field of vision must not be made a ground for his coercion."

This is surely a classic interpretation of the certainty of the law. One can also add that it is probably the most famous one, for it has received many celebrated formulations since the days of ancient Greek civilization, as some quotations from the *Politics* and the *Rhetoric* of Aristotle could easily prove. When that philosopher praises the government of laws, he very probably has in mind those general rules, known in advance to all citizens, which were written in his day on the walls of public buildings or on special pieces of wood or stone, like the *kurbeis* that the Athenians used for that purpose. The ideal of a written law, generally conceived and knowable by every citizen of the small and glorious towns scattered all along the coasts of the Mediterranean Sea and inhabited by people of Greek descent, is one of the most precious gifts that the fathers of Western civilization have bequeathed to their posterity. Aristotle knew well the harm that an arbitrary, contingent, and unpredictable rule (whether a decree approved by the mob in the Athenian *agora* or the capricious order of a tyrant in Sicily) could cause to ordinary people in his day. Thus, he considered laws, that is, general rules laid down in terms that were precise and knowable to everybody, as an indispensable institution for citizens who were to be called "free," and Cicero echoed this Aristotelian conception in his famous dictum in the *oratio pro Cluentio:* "omnes legum servi sumus ut liberi esse possimus" ("we must all obey the law if we are to remain free").

This ideal of certainty has been implanted and reinforced in the European Continent through a long series of events. Justinian's *Corpus Juris Civilis* was for several centuries the very book in which the ideal of the certainty of the law, understood as the certainty of a *written law,* appeared to be embodied, in the Latin as well as in the German countries. This ideal was not repudiated, but was even emphasized, in the seventeenth and eighteenth centuries in Continental Europe, when the absolutistic governments, as the late Professor Ehrlich has pointed out in his brilliant essay on legal reasoning (*Juristische Logik*), wanted to make sure that their judges did not alter the meaning of their rules. Everybody knows what happened in the nineteenth century in Continental Europe. All the European countries adopted written codes and written constitutions, accepting the idea that precisely worded formulae could protect people from the encroachments of all possible kinds of tyrants. Governments as well as courts accepted this interpretation of the idea of the certainty of the law as the precision of a written formula laid down by legislatures. This was not the only reason why Continental Europe adopted codes and constitutions, but it was at least one of the main reasons. In brief, the Continental idea of the certainty of the law was equivalent to the idea of a precisely worded, written formula. This idea of certainty was to a great extent conceived as *precision*.

Whether this is actually the notion that the English people had of the certainty of the law and whether this idea was actually implied in their ideal of "the rule of law" is not clear at first sight. We shall return to this question a little later.

The Greek or Continental notion of the certainty of the law actually corresponds to the ideal of individual liberty formulated by the Greek authors who speak of government by the laws. There is no doubt that government by the laws is preferable to government by decrees of tyrants or of the mob. General laws are always more predictable than particular and sudden orders, and if the predictability of the consequences is one of the unavoidable premises of human decisions, it is necessary to conclude that the more that general rules render predictable, at least on the legal plane, the consequences of individual actions, the more these actions can be called "free" from interference on the part of other people, including the authorities.

From this point of view, we cannot help admitting that general rules, precisely worded (as they can be when written laws are adopted), are an improvement over the sudden orders and unpredictable decrees of tyrants. But unfortunately, all this is no assurance that we shall be actually "free" from interference by the authorities. We can set aside for the moment the questions arising from the fact that rules may be perfectly "certain" in the sense we have described, that is to say, precisely formulated, and be at the same time so tyrannical that nobody can be said to be "free" by behaving according to them. But there is another inconvenience that also results from adopting such general written laws, even when they do allow us considerable "freedom" in our individual behavior. The usual process of law-making in such cases is by way of legislation. But the legislative process is not something that happens once and for all. It takes place every day and is continually going on.

This is particularly true in our time. In my country the legislative process now means about two thousand statutes every year, and each of them may consist of several articles. Sometimes we find dozens or even hundreds of articles in the same statute. Quite frequently one statute conflicts with another. We have a general rule in my country that when two particular rules are mutually incompatible because of their contradictory content, the more recent rule abrogates the old one. But, according to our system, nobody can tell whether a rule may be only one year or one month or one day old when it will be abrogated by a new rule. All these rules are precisely worded in written formulae that readers or interpreters cannot change at their will. Nevertheless, all of them may go as soon and as abruptly as they came. The result is that, if we leave out of the picture the ambiguities of the text, we are always "certain" as far as the literal content of each rule is concerned at any given moment, but we are *never certain* that tomorrow we shall still have the rules we have today.

This is "the certainty of the law" in the Greek or Continental sense. Now I would not go so far as to say that this is "certainty" in the sense that one requires in order to foresee that the result of legal actions taken today will be free from legal interference tomorrow. This kind of "certainty," so much praised by Aristotle and by Cicero, has, in the last analysis, nothing to do with the certainty we should need to be actually "free" in the sense meant by these old and glorious representatives of our Western civilization.

However, this is not the only meaning of the expression "the certainty of the law" as used and understood in the West. There is another meaning that is much more in accord with the ideal of "the rule of law" as it was conceived by the English as well as the American people, at least in the times when "the rule of law" was an ideal undoubtedly connected with individual freedom understood as freedom from interference on the part of everybody, including the authorities.

192

NOTES

1. F. A. Hayek, *The Political Ideal of the Rule of Law* (Cairo: Fiftieth Anniversary Commemoration Lectures, National Bank of Egypt, 1955), p. 2. Virtually the entire substance of this book has been republished in *The Constitution of Liberty* by the same author.
2. Albert Venn Dicey, *Introduction to the Study of the Law of the Constitution* (8th ed.; London: Macmillan, 1915), p. 185.
3. *Ibid.*, p. 191.
4. F. A. Hayek, *op. cit.*, p. 45.
5. Carleton Kemp Allen, *Law and Orders* (London: Stevens & Sons, 1956 ed.), p. 396.
6. *Ibid.*, p. 396.
7. *Ibid.*, p. 32.
8. Ernest F. Row, *How States Are Governed* (London: Pitman & Sons, 1950), p. 70. For the situation in the United States, *see* Walter Gellhorn, *Individual Freedom and Governmental Restraints* (Baton Rouge: Louisiana State University Press, 1956) and Leslie Grey, "The Administrative Agency Colossus," *The Freeman* (October, 1958), p. 31.
9. F. A. Hayek, *op. cit.*, p. 57.
10. Dicey, *op. cit.*, p. 189.
11. *Loc. cit.*
12. *Ibid.*, p. 195.
13. F. A. Hayek, *op. cit.*, p. 36.
14. *Ibid.*, p. 38.

[5]

POLITICS, PROPERTY, AND THE LAW: AN ALTERNATIVE INTERPRETATION OF MILLER ET AL. v. SCHOENE*

JAMES M. BUCHANAN
Virginia Polytechnic Institute and State University

W ARREN Samuels has used the fascinating case of *Miller et al. v. Schoene*[1] as a vehicle for presenting his conception of the interrelationships between politico-legal and economic processes.[2] I share with Samuels the methodological conviction that only by moving beyond the narrowly-conceived limits of economic theory and into the examination of the political, legal, and social constraints within which economic actions are bounded can we hope to unravel much of the confusion that currently describes the discussion of concrete policy issues. I differ profoundly with Samuels, however, on the theory of politics, property, and law that his interpretation implies. The arguments in *Miller et al. v. Schoene* may be examined from a different conception of the functional role of judicial process, of legislation in democracy, and of the appropriate means through which tolerable efficiency can be attained in a regime of economic interdependency.

Classificatory labels are subject to oversimplification, but for purposes of casual identification, my approach is that of the political economist who interprets Paretian criteria in essentially Wicksellian terms and who can be described, somewhat more broadly, as falling within what has been called the "Virginia school."[3] By contrast, Samuels' approach is more consistent with post-Pigovian welfare economics, and notably with reliance on "social welfare functions" to provide guidance to the governmental authorities, treated as independent from the citizenry.

* I am indebted to Professors Roland N. McKean, W. Craig Stubblebine, and Gordon Tullock for helpful comments on an earlier draft.

[1] 276 U.S. 272 (1928).

[2] Warren J. Samuels, Interrelations Between Legal and Economic Processes, 14 J. Law & Econ. 435 (1971). For a more comprehensive statement of Samuels' methodological position, see his Welfare Economics, Power, and Property, 1971 (mimeographed, Mich. St. Univ.).

[3] *Cf.* Mancur Olson & Christopher Clague, Dissent in Economics, in 38 Social Research 753 (Winter, 1971).

I.

The following excerpts from Samuels' paper summarize the facts:

Miller et al. v. Schoene is a case which involves red cedar and apple trees and their respective owners; and cedar rust, a plant disease whose first phase is spent while the fungus resides upon its host, the chiefly ornamental red cedar tree, which is not harmed by the cedar rust. The fungus does have a severely adverse effect upon the apple tree during a second phase, attacking its leaves and fruit. The legislature of the state of Virginia in 1914 passed a statute which empowered the state entomologist to investigate and, if necessary, condemn and destroy without compensation certain red cedar trees within a two-mile radius of an apple orchard.[4] *Miller et al.*, plaintiffs in error in the instant case, unsucessfully brought suit in state courts, and sued to reverse the decision of the Supreme Court of Appeals in Virginia. The arguments for the plaintiffs in error were basically simple and direct, as well as of profound heuristic value. Their main contention was that the legislature was, unconstitutionally in their view, attempting to take or destroy their property to the advantage of the apple orchard owners.[5]

In Samuels' interpretation, the Virginia legislature, and, ultimately, the Supreme Court "had to make a judgment as to which owner would be visited with injury and which protected."[6]

The legislature chose to favor the apple growers and to penalize the owners of the red cedar groves. The courts upheld the legislature in this action. According to Samuels, the result was an "effective new law of property."[7] An unforeseen and unpredicted natural event, the emergence of red cedar rust, necessitated State intervention and State decision, one way or the other. When previously-existing rights to property are challenged by any party, the State, acting through its legislative-cum-judicial arms and agencies, must, willy-nilly, make a choice among conflicting claimants. Presumably, the State will be guided in its deliberations and in its decision by the relative pressure of divergent economic interests responsibly exerted. Samuels places his trust in the emergence of the measurably-superior benefit even without the necessity of compensation. This approach offers a significant role for the cost-benefit analyst who may, presumably, measure relative monetary values independently of distributional consequences, and whose results will be, or should be, used by the legislator-cum-judge in his attempt at reaching a "correct" decision.

---

[4] Warren J. Samuels, *supra* note 2, at 436.

[5] *Id.* at 436-37.

[6] *Id.* at 438-39.

[7] *Id.*

II.

My quarrel with Samuels is more fundamental, however, than that which is inherent in reconciling outcomes of a collective decision-making process with those that might be classified as "efficient" by some idealized economic observer. Samuels appeals too readily to state decision-making which, in its very nature, forestalls the exchange or market-like pressures toward internalizing the interdependencies that may arise as exogenous elements to modify the overall social environment. There is, of course, no guarantee that the State will select that alternative which maximizes the values of the social product, and, even when this concern is dropped, there is nothing in the Samuels' model which allows for the mutuality of gains that is part-and-parcel of an economic approach to social interaction.

The owners of adjoining plots of land coexisted peaceably before the onset of red cedar rust, a natural event that was not foreseen. There was no explicit economic interdependence between persons growing apple trees and those growing red cedar trees, and, with reference to this subset of the population, the system was on the Pareto efficiency frontier. That is to say, before the fungus there existed no potential trades or agreements among the apple growers and the cedar growers that remained unexploited. A natural event then occurred. The new fungus which did not damage the cedar trees on which it grew, did threaten severe damage to the apple trees. Between the owners of apple orchards and the owners of red cedar lands a new interdependence emerged. Potential gains-from-trade should have existed that would have allowed this interdependence to be eliminated. Before such "trade" could be undertaken, however, individual participants would have had to be certain as to their property rights. Presumably, in the case at hand, the structure of rights in existence did not allow the apple grower to destroy diseased cedar trees on neighboring lands. The set of "previously existing rights" allowed the red cedar owners to grow diseased trees safe from molestation by damaged apple growers. This was acknowledged by all parties.[8]

This description of the historical setting should not, however, imply that there was here, or ever is, a unique means of delineating property rights. It could have been that the rights of cedar growers extended only to the nur-

---

[8] One caveat must be introduced at this point. The evidence for the acknowledged acceptance of previously existing rights lies in the absence of legal claims made by single apple growers against cedar landowners. If the conditions outlined in Part III, below, should have been present, however, no single apple grower might have been willing to make the investment required to initiate legal action, which, had it been taken, might have resulted in a modified definition of existing rights. For purposes of the more general purposes of my discussion in this paper, it seems best to assume that such a modified definition would not have been forthcoming.

ture of undiseased trees, and/or, conversely, the rights of apple growers could have been defined in terms of the nurture of healthy trees, which might have included the right to eliminate all neighborhood interferences. The principle to be emphasized, however, is that *some* structure, *any* structure, of well-defined rights is a necessary starting point for the potential "trades" that are required to remove the newly-emergent interdependence. When an unpredicted environmental change occurs, the structure of rights may, of course, contain ambiguities and possibly alternative definitions. In such case, it becomes an appropriate and necessary task for the courts to lay down the precise limits of allowable actions by the parties in question. In this behavior, however, the courts are "locating the limits" that exist in "the law"; they are not, and they must not be seen to be, defining *new* limits or changing pre-existing ones. The courts clarify ambiguities; they lend precision; they draw black and white lines in gray areas. Once they have done so, the ground is laid for the emergence of those agreements which can serve to internalize the interdependence. If there should have been some confusion over the rights of the apple growers and the cedar growers under the "previously-existing law," the courts, but *not* the legislative arm of the Commonwealth of Virginia, should have been called upon for resolution. No dispute arose at this level, however; all parties were agreed on the precise structure of rights inherent in "the law" as it stood.

The model can be clarified if we think initially of the interaction between a single apple grower and a single cedar landowner. Once cedar rust was recognized to exist, it was to the apparent advantage of the orchard owner to initiate possible action to purchase or to lease the adjacent cedar land, to purchase the standing cedar, or to compensate the cedar grower for cutting his trees. A region of potential mutual gain existed, and bargains might have been struck which would have moved the solution toward the efficiency surface, possibly forestalled only by recalcitrant bargaining strategy on the part of one or both of the parties. In the trading process, of course, both parties would have secured gains over and above those secured in the post-fungus disequilibrium. Mutual agreement should have signaled mutual gain.

Consider the contrast between this procedure and that which is implicit in Samuels' discussion. Here the apple grower appealed directly to the State, and the State decided just which one of the two claims was to be favored. The issue became strictly one of *either/or*. The informational requirements for decision immediately arise. How could the damage to the apple crop be estimated as against the damage to the value of cedar trees from premature cutting? In this instance, the "expert," the Virginia entomologist, was called upon to make a determination. This tends to prejudice the general argument in Samuels' favor. In most economic interdependencies, there are no "experts," and there are likely to be major errors in any cost-benefit estimates. More importantly, even if the testimony of expert witnesses be introduced, who can claim that the collective decision-makers will, or should, follow their advice?

Note that, when the parties are allowed freely to bargain and to reach mutually satisfactory agreements, the apple grower's *own* assessment of probable damage to his crop becomes the measure of his own maximum payment to secure the elimination of the danger. On the other side, the cedar grower's *own* estimate of the value of his standing trees over and above their value as cut trees becomes the basis for his possible willingness to accept or to reject proferred compensations. The equity or inequity of compensation is irrelevant; what is relevant is the necessary place of compensation in the trading process between the two parties. Only when transfers are actually made can relative values be measured by those whose interests are directly involved.

If the number of apple orchard owners in every fungus area was small, there should have been no action taken by the collectivity so long as the previously-existing structure of rights was well-defined. The efficient solution could have been depended on to emerge from the interaction between the parties in each interdependence. In the tradition of classical political economy, the forces of self-interest could have been relied on to generate an outcome that would tend to maximize the value of social product. There is no means of determining whether this would have resulted in a cutting of the red cedar groves or the continued infestation of apple trees by cedar rust.[9]

III.

If, however, the numbers on the apple-grower side of the interactions in question should have been large, or beyond critical "small-number" limits, the familiar free-rider obstructions to voluntarily negotiated solutions might have arisen. In this situation, there might have remained a functional role for collective action. The legislative arm of the collectivity might have intervened, and it is possible for us to interpret the actual events of *Miller et al. v. Schoene* in this, quite different framework.

If, for example, there should have been *n* apple-orchard owners involved in an interdependence with a single red cedar landowner, there might have been no voluntary agreement reached, despite the possibly relatively superior value of an undiseased apple yield. It might not have been to the economic

---

[9] In this small-number setting, the same result should have been predicted to emerge, regardless of the existent structure of rights. On this, see R. H. Coase, The Problem of Social Cost, 3 J. Law & Econ. 1 (1960).

advantage of any single grower to initiate agreements with the cedar land-owner, or to make unilateral payments to this landowner in exchange for usage of the land. There would have been no means, in this case, through which the single orchardman could have *excluded* his fellows from the enjoyment of the disease reduction that his own action might procure from the cedar landowner. Reduction in cedar rust would have been, in this situation, a purely "public good," in the modern usage of this term, to the community of apple growers involved in the particular interaction. Resort to collective or joint action might have been dictated.[10] The possible reason lies in the dual interdependencies that this setting involved; one, that between each apple grower and the cedarman or men, and, two, that among the separate apple growers themselves. The first of these interdependencies could have been removed by freely negotiated trades in the absence of the second. The presence of the second or public-goods interdependence, however, might well have prohibited the negotiation of a solution to the former.[11]

The failure of negotiated settlements to emerge, however, would have been consistent with continuing inefficiency only under a particular assumption about the land ownership pattern among apple growers. Only if this pattern was invariant would the public-goods dilemma have inhibited negotiated internalization. That is to say, if in each interaction there should have been a number of apple growers sufficient to have created a potential public-goods barrier to negotiated voluntary settlements, some assumptions must be made to the effect that this number was unchangeable within certain limits. If such a restriction is not imposed on the model, mutual gains from trade

---

[10] Individual adjustment equilibria may be inefficient in all cases where there are large numbers of apple growers in a single interaction, regardless of the structure of property rights. A change in the distribution of rights will, however, change the direction of the allocative bias. To show this, assume that the cedar landowner had no right to grow diseased trees, and that destruction of such trees was enforceable on petition to the courts. In this instance, petition by any single apple grower would have been sufficient to initiate action. Each apple grower would, therefore, have been placed in a highly favorable strategic bargaining position vis-a-vis the cedar landowner. The cedars would probably have been destroyed under these legal arrangements even if their premature cutting involved damages considerably in excess of that to the apple crops. For an extended general discussion related also to the content of note 11, *infra*, see James M. Buchanan, The Institutional Structure of Externality (Va. Polytechnic Inst. & St. Univ. Research Paper 808231-1-6, Jan., 1971).

[11] It is also useful to note that the existence of large numbers on the other side of the interaction need not have been obstructive in the reaching of voluntarily negotiated settlements. Consider a model in which there was only a single orchardman, affected adversely by the cedar rust on land owned by *n* separate cedar growers. So long as the amount of apple damage was related continuously to the amount of cedar rust, that is, so long as there was not a discrete all-or-none solution indicated, the single orchardman could have worked out agreements with the separate cedar growers separately and unilaterally. There would have been no interdependencies among the cedar tree growers.

would have existed among the separate orchardmen, and individual owners of apple-land parcels would have had incentives to merge land holdings into units sufficiently large to remove or to reduce substantially the free-rider motivation that might otherwise have inhibited direct negotiation of agreements with the owner or owners of cedar lands. The interdependencies would have been, in a nonrestricted model, removed or internalized in a two-stage process of trading agreement. In the first, the many separate land parcels devoted to apples that were simultaneously affected by the cedar rust from a plot of trees would have been consolidated or merged into a single ownership entity. In the second, this entity would have negotiated an agreement with the cedar landowner or owners concerning the elimination of the diseased trees.

This model is fully applicable, however, only when transactions costs are negligible. "Transactions costs" offers a generalized rubric within which many of the barriers to negotiated settlements may be placed. The point is that the interaction among the separate apple growers generated by the cedar rust might have been only one, albeit a new, dimension that had economic content. These might have been many other variables that were relevant for land consolidation. If, for example, apples should have been a significant but not the exclusive source of external income for a large number of family-sized farms simultaneously affected by the cedar rust from a nearby plot of cedar trees, the opportunity costs of land-parcel consolidation directed at this interdependence alone might well have exceeded the benefits, while, at the same time, the damage to the apple crop exceeded the differential value of standing over cut cedar trees.

IV.

The analysis suggests that there might have been an efficiency basis for resort to collective or state action in the apple-cedar interaction under discussion here, but that this basis required the presence of certain narrowly-defined conditions. If there were large numbers of apple growers involved in each interaction, and if transactions costs were such that voluntary agreement on land consolidation could not have been predicted to emerge, the community of all apple growers might have called on the State to resolve the alleged dilemma in which they found themselves.[12] Interestingly enough, the Virginia Cedar Rust Act required the petition of *at least ten* freeholders before the State entomologist was empowered to act. This suggests that the

---

[12] In so doing, those who request state intervention are advancing a personal judgment or hypothesis concerning the inefficiency of the existing state of affairs. They cannot, of course, determine unilaterally whether or not the alleged inefficiency is, in fact, real.

large-number condition might have been recognized to be necessary for State action by the framers of the legislation. Samuels' discussion, however, nowhere suggests that these conditions are necessary for collective intervention to be justified.

It will be useful to examine the appropriate form of collective action, however, on the assumption that these required justifications were, indeed, present. The State might have responded to the issue by granting to appropriate-sized apple-growers' cooperatives some powers of coercion over members. Normally, however, we should have expected the legislative arm of the State to consider more direct action. The State may be conceived, therefore, as offering to supply a public good, one that will be made available to all members of the large community if it is made available to any one member. The standard and familiar requirements for efficiency in the provision of such a good or service can be readily defined. Total benefits must exceed total costs, and the summed marginal evaluations over all members of the community affected must be equated with the marginal cost of provision.

The question then becomes one of implementing this set of efficiency norms through the political process. If the conditions for justifying collective interference are held to be present, how can collective action be organized so as to insure that the net result involves a shift toward rather than away from society's efficiency surface? It is here that Knut Wicksell offers guiding principles.[13]

We may first consider the collective decision in question as an isolated independent event. Since there is no way of assessing the intensities of individual interests except through the revealed choice behavior of individuals themselves, a group-decision rule of unanimity was suggested by Wicksell. If so much as one person in the community is harmed, there is no insurance that the damage he suffers may not outweigh the benefits or gains to all other persons in the group. The rule of unanimity is the Wicksellian equivalent of a Pareto move, and the impossibility of securing unanimous consent for any change becomes the Wicksellian criterion for classifying an attained position as Pareto optimal. The ideal-type collective decision process is, therefore, an effective unanimity rule with all members of the community participating in the choice.

Cost considerations dictate departures from this ideal in several respects. Representation of individual or subgroup interests through the instrument of legislative bodies are accepted as a necessary practicable substitute for the fully participatory town-meeting type institutional structure. Again in some

---

[13] *Cf.* Knut Wicksell, A New Principle of Just Taxation, in Classics in the Theory of Public Finance, 72 (Richard A. Musgrave & Alan T. Peacock eds., 1958).

quasi-ideal limits, the members of the legislative assembly or assemblies represent, and hence act in the interests of, all citizens. The first stage in the practical implementation of the Wicksell scheme is, therefore, the application of an effective rule of unanimity in an appropriately-selected legislative assembly.

With particular reference to the historical Virginia decision under discussion, we should note that collective action via the legislative body did offer an institutional means for internalizing the possible public-goods interdependence among the apple growers and for implementing the possible "trades" with the cedarmen. The legislative process is the instrument for reconciling the separate interests, for effecting some compromise and agreed-on solution. The legislative process, interpreted in this light, is functionally quite distinct from the judicial process. There is no role for the judiciary in the decision relating to the supply and financing of a public good. A categorical distinction must be made here, one that Samuel's treatment tends to blur over if not to disregard entirely.

Strict adherence to a rule of unanimity in a legislative body is not practicable. Wicksell himself recognized that the opportunities for strategic bargaining were too great here, and that these opportunities worked to make decision-making costs excessive. Such considerations aside, however, it will be useful to examine the type of legislative action that might have been expected to emerge under the operation of a unanimity rule in the Virginia legislature in 1914. In order to do this, simply assume that members of the legislative assembly did, in fact, genuinely represent all interests, and notably those of both the apple growers and the cedarmen, and, further, that each legislator voted strictly in terms of the estimated interests of his constituents, untainted by the strategic bargaining possibilities offered by the operation of the rule itself.

In such a setting, the representatives for the damaged apple growers might have proposed State action ordering the cutting of diseased trees near apple orchards. Those legislators representing the cedar landowners would, of course, have opposed any such proposals unless compensations were paid to their own constituents. In order to meet these objections, the apple-interest legislators would have then put forward alternative schemes which would have necessarily included taxes levied on their own constituents as the means of financing the compensations required to secure the acquiescence of the cedar tree growers, or, in this situation, their legislative representatives. The required compensations become, in this instance, and under the existing set of property rights, the cost of providing the collective or public good, defined as the reduction or elimination of cedar rust damage to the apple crops. As Wicksell emphasized, some such combined proposal (taxes and compensation payments) must have commanded the assent of all members of the assembly if the apple damage exceeded the damage from premature cutting of cedar. This provides the *only* test for efficiency that can be institutionalized politically. If the efficiency gains should have been significant, there might have been, of course, many possible sets of taxes and compensation payments which could have secured unanimous support in the legislature. The particular proposal adopted would have depended, in part, on the simple order of presentation of the alternatives, which may, of course, have been quite arbitrarily determined.

Considered as an isolated political decision, therefore, the action of the Virginia legislature in allowing the condemnation of diseased cedar trees, *without* compensation, and hence without taxes imposed on the prospective beneficiaries, the apple growers, violated the Wicksellian-Paretian precepts. In no way could such legislative action be interpreted as a surrogate for a voluntarily negotiated settlement among the parties at issue, with the collectivization made necessary only by the free-rider, transactions-cost considerations noted. There is no means of determining, from the historical record, whether the action was or was not efficient.

V.

Our interpretation of *Miller et al. v. Schoene* is not complete, however, precisely because the action of the Virginia legislature cannot be considered as an isolated political event, nor can it be evaluated as such. Political choice takes place over many time periods and over several sets of alternatives in each period, covering widely divergent subject matter. Many "public goods" are supplied and financed; many proposals for collective supply and financing are rejected. As we noted above, any strict requirement of unanimity in legislative decision-making would generate costly delays in reaching agreement on anything, if indeed, agreement is reached at all. Historical evidence suggests that unanimity is the exception rather that "the rule" and legislative bodies are constitutionally empowered to act on less-than-unanimity rules, often under some version of majority voting as embedded in a complex structure of procedure and often with certain rights of executive veto. Any departure from strict unanimity provides an opportunity for collective choices that fail to meet the Pareto efficiency criterion. This must be acknowledged. Nonetheless, at some "constitutional" stage of decision on the structure of collective decision rules themselves, the prospective inefficiencies generated by less-than-unanimity voting may be less than those predicted to be generated by the decision-making inefficiencies which the more restrictive voting rule would insure.[14]

[14] For a general discussion of the theory of rule-making, see, James M. Buchanan & Gordon Tullock, The Calculus of Consent (1962).

In this more realistic setting for legislative decision-making, however, any evaluation of a single choice action becomes much more difficult. In the Virginia case discussed, the absence of compensation to the owners of red cedar trees cannot, in itself, now be taken as clear evidence that the political process did not serve as an indirect and complex surrogate for the negotiation and settlement process among the parties. In a constitutional sense, we might think of both apple and cedar growers as having acquiesced in the continuing operation of a legislative process embodying constrained majority voting in the recognition that, on occasion, the economic interests of any particular subgroup in the community might be damaged, and perhaps severely. In this broader conception of collective decision-making, the deliberations and choices made in a democratically selected and representative assembly may be interpreted as the only practicable institutional means of reconciling differences, or implementing "bargains" or "trades," in the presence of those conditions that are requisite for collective action. The interests potentially damaged, in our case those of the cedarmen, could have exercised their voting power on issues about which they were relatively indifferent in order to register their intensity of opposition to the tree-cutting statute. If, in fact, the damage to red cedars should have exceeded those of apple-crop infestation significantly, logrolling interaction in the Virginia legislature might have insured against passage of the statute in question.

As we know, however, the statute was enacted, and the cedar owners appealed to the courts, first at the state and then at the federal level. In this setting, the only role of the judiciary should have been one of determining whether or not the decision taken by the legislature was made constitutionally. This should have involved, first, an examination of the decision rule itself, about which there was apparently no issue. Secondly, the decision might have been evaluated in terms of the precepts of the "fiscal constitution" that were implicitly if not explicitly in being.

The taxing powers of the State allow the taking of private property for public or general purposes. If we interpret the statute that allows the condemnation of trees without compensation as a tax-in-kind on owners of such trees, in disregard of the offsetting side of the budget account, there might have been plausible grounds for the courts to uphold the legislative action. The critical element here should have concerned the nondiscriminatory nature of the tax. Formally, however, since the "tax" was imposed on all owners of red cedar trees in two-mile radii of apple orchards, an argument could have been made that such action was nondiscriminatory over a sufficiently broad class of persons. In this context, such a "tax" on the owners of red cedar trees, on the landowners, might have been legally interpreted as no different from a tax on the owners of pool tables, playing cards, or any other of the many narrowly-specified bases observed in the real world.

If the offsetting or balancing side of the budget account should have been treated in isolation, the courts might have also found legitimate grounds for upholding the legislation. Representative assemblies have been empowered, constitutionally, to provide benefits to specific subgroups in the community, whether these be occupationally, geographically, industrially, or otherwise classified. Indeed, the nondiscriminatory or uniformity requirements generally held applicable to the tax side of the budget have never been applied to the public spending side.[15] Interpreted, therefore, as a specific subsidy to apple growers whose trees had been diseased, the "outlay" could have been held constitutionally valid.

On the other hand, if the two sides of the conceptualized fiscal account should have been joined in the court's deliberations, the constitutionality of the Virginia legislature's action might have proved highly questionable. In this light, the action seems similar in many respects to that which evoked the Supreme Court rejection of the original Agricultural Adjustment Administration on constitutional grounds. In *United States v. Butler* (1936), the Court held that the levy of a specific tax for the specific benefits of one subgroup was not a valid exercise of state power.[16]

Regardless of the Court's verdict in *Miller et al. v. Schoene*, Samuels' interpretation of the Court's action seems contrary to that which would seem appropriate under the alternative approach that I have tried to develop. It would have been illegitimate for the "Court, as part of the state, . . . (to) make a judgment as to which owner would be visited with injury and which protected"[17], or "decide which party would have what capacity to coerce another." The judicial role should have been limited strictly to a determination as to the constitutionality of legislative action, and this should not have included any attempt at making a judgment as to the economic efficiency or inefficiency or to the equity or inequity of the legislative choice actually made.

In its actual judgment, it is not clear that the Court exceeded the bounds

---

[15] Recent court decisions with respect to educational spending differences among differing communities within states indicate some change in legal interpretation. For a thorough discussion of the historical asymmetry in legal treatment here, see David Tuerck, Constitutional Asymmetry, in 2 Papers on Non-Market Decision-Making 27 (1967); for a more comprehensive treatment, see Tuerck's Uniformity in Taxation, Discrimination in Benefits: An Essay in Law and Economics, 1966 (unpublished Ph.D. dissertation in Alderman Library, Univ. of Va.).

[16] 297 U.S. 1 (1936). Consider the hypothetical case in which cedar rust proved beneficial to apple crops, but in which the rust required investment on the part of cedar tree owners. Would the Court have upheld legislation that required that such investment be made without compensation? Presumably not, yet, analytically the setting seems identical with that which prevailed.

[17] Warren J. Samuels, *supra* note 2, at 438-39.

of judicial propriety. The Court said that "the state does not exceed its constitutional powers by deciding upon the destruction of one class of property in order to save another which, *in the judgment of the legislature*, is of greater value to the public."[18] In this statement, the Court does not seem to have considered itself to be doing what Samuels' interpretation suggests; it apparently did not attempt to inject its own standards of value measurement in determining the constitutionality of the legislation. The Court's decision may have been in error in terms of consistent constitutional principles, but the error did not necessarily lie in the Court's misconception of its own functional role in a democratic governmental process.

VI.

Old arguments are important only if they shed light on matters of modern relevance. Disagreements between Warren Samuels and James Buchanan on the interpretation of *Miller et al. v. Schoene* might be privately but not publicly interesting if comparable conflicts are anticipated infrequently and/or those that arise are economically insignificant. The major thrust of Samuels' paper, however, concerns the continuing ubiquitousness of such conflicts along with their economic importance. In the vision of collective action that I have imputed to him, Samuels envisages an activist State, ever ready to intervene when existing rights to property are challenged, ever willing to grasp the nettle and define rights anew, which once defined, immediately become vulnerable to still further challenges. This projects an awesome role for the State in an environment that is subjected continuously, and necessarily, to the exogenous shocks resulting from natural phenomena, from technological change, from growth itself. Broadly conceived, something akin to cedar rust must appear every day, and, in Samuels' paradigm, the State must never rest. The structure of rights, as of any moment, is subjected to question, and away goes the "white knight" to decide whose claim shall be favored and whose rejected.

What if Mr. A simply does not like long-haired men? The presence of such men in the community harms him just as much as cedar rust harmed the apple growers. Is Mr. A then empowered to challenge the existing structure of rights that allows men to wear hair as they please? It matters not that "reasonable legislative-cum-judicial authorities" should always or nearly always decide in favor of the long-haired defendants. In Samuels' model, the challenge itself must be appropriately processed, and each instance resolved on its own merits, with no apparent prejudice in favor of the "previously existing rights."

18 Miller *et al.* v. Schoene, 276 U.S. 272, 279 (1928).

My own approach is sharply different. There is an explicit prejudice in favor of previously existing rights, not because this structure possesses some intrinsic ethical attributes, and not because change itself is undesirable, but for the much more elementary reason that only such a prejudice offers incentives for the emergence of voluntarily negotiated settlements among the parties themselves. Indirectly, therefore, this prejudice guarantees that resort to the authority of the State is effectively minimized. It insures that an efficiency basis for collective action emerges only when a genuine public-goods externality arises and persists. Furthermore, this prejudice allows for a distinct and categorical separation between the legislative and judicial roles, something that is strangely absent in Samuels' vision.

Unfortunately, the theory of politics, property, and the law that is implied in Samuels' interpretation of *Miller et al. v. Schoene* reflects the conventional wisdom of our time. This makes the number of bills passed the criterion of legislative excellence, a criterion that is implanted in the spirit of every aspiring politician. Much more seriously, this wisdom also involves an activist Federal judiciary, a judiciary that is now acknowledged to legislate, and which accepts, and is seen to accept, this role as such. Indeed, in Samuels' argument we may locate an apologia for the omnipresent hand of the State in all our lives, an omnipresence required by the necessary uncertainty of legal rights in a world subject to exogenous shocks. The State must adjudicate all conflicting claims, must take on all challenges to this and that, and, in the process achieve the "unknown passing through the strange," a politico-legal setting that itself contributes to "future shock."

PART II

HOW AND WHY DO PROPERTY RIGHTS DEVELOP?

Introduction to Chapters 7, 8 and 9

History matters. It matters not just because we can learn from the past, but because the present and the future are connected to the past by the continuity of a society's institutions. (Douglass North, *Institutions, Institutional Change and Economic Performance*, Cambridge: Cambridge University Press, 1990, p. vii.)

Look at what happened to the buffalo and the whale; look at what is happening to publicly owned forests and many rivers. Human greed is destroying our universe. We hear these and similar arguments almost daily. Environmentalists, ecologists, and sociologists among others love to use those arguments to justify governmental controls over the use of scarce goods. Yet blaming human greed for the destruction of resources is quickly refuted by evidence. We observe that the same greedy humans have also chosen to preserve cattle, young trees in privately owned forests, clean water in privately owned lakes, and many other scarce resources.

A theory that blames our self-interest for destruction of some resources is empty because it fails to explain why our self-interest protects many other resources such as private lakes, private forests, and private golf courses. Clearly, analysis should try to identify the factors capable of explaining why some resources are being overused while others are not. Research and evidence have demonstrated that property rights are one such factor.

For example, consider a non-owned (i.e., free for all) tree that is one year old. Suppose that the value of lumber in that tree is $100. I can capture the benefits from that tree only by taking it into my physical possession; that is, by cutting it now, selling lumber to a lumber yard, and investing (or consuming) the proceeds at the prevailing rate of interest. My opportunity costs plus the prorated value of the tools I need to cut that tree are my private costs of taking the tree into my possession. If my private costs of cutting the tree are less than $100, I will cut it. If I choose (for whatever reasons) not to cut that tree, someone else will. The prevailing property rights in the tree provide no incentives for individuals to include in their costs calculations the fact that the value of lumber in the live tree (at cutting time) might be growing at a rate higher than the prevailing rate of interest.

Suppose now that I own the tree. I have incentives to keep it alive as a long as the rate of growth in the value of lumber exceeds the market rate of interest. Suppose I cut the tree at the age of three and sell the lumber for $300. In a year, $300 invested at the going rate of interest, say 15 per cent, would grow to about $345. My alternative use for the same resource is to leave it alone. Suppose that in that case the value of lumber in the live tree would have increased in one year from $300 to $400. I certainly would choose to preserve the tree. In fact, I would have incentives to keep the tree standing until the market rate of interest approximates (or exceeds) the rate of growth in the value of lumber in the live tree.[1] That is, the right of ownership creates incentives for the tree to be cut when private and social costs are about equal. And a policy that would keep the tree standing after the rate of interest exceeds the rate of growth of lumber in the live tree would only serve to satisfy some groups' preferences at the expense of the production of more wealth.

In the first case, my choice of cutting the non-owned tree does not take into account its social costs. Thus, externality is clearly present. In the second case, no externality is present because my choice of cutting the tree takes into account its social costs. Incentives specific to alternative property rights explain why some resources are overused while others are well protected. Clearly, blaming human greed for destroying some resources offers no useful basis for public policy.

In a world of uncertainty and incomplete knowledge, individuals then have incentives to change or modify the prevailing property rights in a good whenever their private benefits from making the bundles of rights more complete are expected to exceed their private costs of policing and enforcing those changes. More complete property rights in scarce goods in turn internalize some externalities. The more property rights we hold in a good, the smaller is going to be the gap between private and social costs. Indeed, most externalities in the private-property, free-market economy can be attributed either to high costs of defining the right of private ownership (e.g., of rivers) or to the absence of the right of private ownership (e.g., in public housing).

Incentives specific to the right of ownership – which arise from the marriage between one's right to choose how to use a good and bearing the consequences of that choice, the right to transfer the good to a more optimistic owner, and the constitutional protection of the right of ownership – tend to eliminate the differences between private and social costs as well as between short-term and long-term decisions.

By demonstrating that systematic two-way relations exist between changes in the bundle of property rights in scarce goods and economic choices, chapters by Douglass North, Terry Anderson and Peter Hill, and John Umbeck have made a significant contribution to the economic theory of property rights. Douglass North's analysis of the differences in economic development in Spain and England is especially instructive. These chapters represent a large body of research which demonstrates that property rights affect the economic game in specific and predictable ways and that, in turn, new property rights develop in response to innovations, new knowledge, new markets, new sources of supplies, and changes in relative prices. An implication is that property rights are not exogenous constraints of neoclassical economics.

It is interesting to note that the economic theory of property rights supports Marx's early vision that economic forces at work within the prevailing system are responsible for changes in the rules of the game. I use the word *vision* because Marx's analysis was quite primitive, ideology driven, and its propositions were not verifiable.[2] Yet, Marx deserves credit for being the first social scientist to try to endogenize changes in property rights.

Finally, we must note that human history is also full of examples of governments using their political and police powers to change the prevailing property rights by fiat. Some exogenous changes in property rights might be justifiable. However, most property rights that are imposed exogenously are either perceived as theft or create incentives to reduce the production of wealth. An extended quotation from Armen Alchian and William Allen is warranted because it also reflects on the process of creating property rights in many East European countries since 1989.

An excellent example is provided by the Enclosure Movement in England about 500 years ago. Farmers had rights to use particular portions of land in common with other people but not the right to sell this right. If the rights had been legally salable it would have paid a person to sell his use rights to the person who could make the most valuable use of the land. One would think that the law would have been modified, so that each holder of a right to use could be identified and allowed to sell his right to someone. . . . However, the common-use right holders were not allowed to sell their rights; they simply were denied the right, and some lucky (politically powerful) person was declared to be in control of the sole right. This method of creating private property has no bearing on how the system will operate thereafter, but to the people of the time, the operation of a system of private property (capitalism) was identified . . . with expropriation of common-use rights. Tenants who lost their rights regarded private property as theft.[3]

Notes
1. It is reasonable to assume that the amount of lumber in the live tree increases at a decreasing rate as the tree gets older.
2. Marx's line of reasoning can be summarized as follows: in primitive societies, people are totally dependent for their economic survival on an alien and hostile nature. Triggered by their survival instinct, people seek to lessen their dependence on nature. Human history is, then, a continuous struggle of man against nature; the ultimate purpose of this struggle being to reverse the original relationship between human beings and nature. The critical vehicle in the human struggle against nature is economic development. Each time a person creates a new tool (primitive hammer or modern computer), mankind takes a small step to reduce dependence on nature (or to reverse the initial relationship). However, Marx said, as people learn how to produce and use goods, they have to decide who has what access to those goods. That is, property rights develop spontaneously and within the prevailing economic system.
3. A. Alchian and W. Allen, *University Economics*, Belmont: Wadsworth, 1966, second edition, p. 474.

[7]

Institutions, Economic Growth and Freedom:
An Historical Introduction

Douglass C. North

This essay* uses an exploratory analytical framework to examine the origins of modern economic growth in the Western world. This growth was inextricably involved with the emergence not only of secure property rights but of political, religious, and "civil" freedoms. Because the Western world evolved in two widely divergent directions, I wish to explore both the "successful" story of Britain (and the Netherlands) and the unsuccessful story of Spain (and Portugal). My objective is not simply to demonstrate that the freedoms were mutually reinforcing aspects of the pattern of successful countries; but, more important, to explore the dynamics of long-run societal change in terms of the evolution of contrasting institutional environments. One story takes us to British North America, the thirteen colonies, independence, and the growth of the United States; the other, to Spanish imperial policy in the Indies, Latin American colonial development, independence, and the subsequent relative failure of Latin American countries.

In the sections that follow, I explore the issues that are involved in the history (I); the nature of institutions (II); the sources of institutional change (III); the initial historical conditions in England and Spain (IV); English development (V); Spanish development (VI). In the final section, I briefly examine the consequences in the New World. Of necessity, the historical sections are little more than outlines, illustrating the framework developed in Sections II and III.

---

* I wish to thank Elizabeth Case for improving this essay.

4 Douglass C. North

I.   HISTORY

I shall not tarry long over the definition of freedom. While a lengthy analysis should go into the complexities of this issue, here I simply assert that the freedoms I am concerned with are uniformly applied rules with respect to the security of persons and property over a range of civil, political, religious, and economic activities. They include freedom of religious and political expression; protection against arbitrary imprisonment; the right to bailment; protection against impairment of the right to use, derive income from, or alienate property. None of these freedoms is absolute; nor are they ever perfectly enforced. At the margin they can lead to anarchy, or tyranny, or a reduction in the choices of others. Hence, they are always relative to their consequences upon others.

Their connection to economic growth is straightforward. The more secure are these freedoms, the lower the costs of transacting; and declining transaction costs are (given relatively non-controversial behavioural assumptions) a critical historical source of economic growth. The implications of this assertion are that one can understand neither the nature of freedom nor economic growth in a traditional neo-classical framework, since this framework is devoid of institutions; and that institutions are at the heart of a meaningful understanding of freedom and determine transaction costs in a society.[1]

II.   THE NATURE OF INSTITUTIONS

Institutions are rules, enforcement characteristics of rules, and norms of behaviour that structure repeated human interaction. Hence, they limit and define the choice set of neo-classical theory. We are interested not in the institutions per se, but in their consequences for the choices individuals actually make.

Constitutions, statute and common laws, contracts specify in formal terms the rules of the game, from the most general constitutional cones to specific terms of exchange. Rules (and their enforcement) are constrained by the costliness of measuring the characteristics or attributes of what constitutes rule-compliance or violation. Hence, the technology of measurement of all the dimensions (sight, sound, taste, etc.) of the human senses has played a critical role in our ability to define property rights and other types of rules. Moreover, since we receive utility from the various attributes of goods and services rather than from the entities themselves, it is the costliness of measuring the separable dimensions that is critical in this study.[2] The relationship between the benefits derived from rule-specification and the costs of measurement not only has been critical in the history of property rights (common property vs. private property) but is at the heart of many of the issues related to the structure and effectiveness of enforcement.

If it were costless to measure the performance of agents or the attributes of goods and services as well as the terms of exchange, then enforcement would not be a problem. We would be back in the neo-classical world of the instantaneous exchange of a unidimensional good or service. But because measurement is costly and the parties to exchange stand to gain by receiving the benefits without incurring all of the costs of exchange, not only is enforcement typically imperfect, but the structure of the enforcement process will affect outcomes and hence choices. Let me elaborate both points.

Enforcement is typically imperfect for two reasons: 1) measurement is costly; and 2) the interests of principals and agents are not identical. The costliness of measurement implies that at the margin the benefits from additional monitoring or policing will be balanced against the incremental costs. Moreover, as I shall discuss below, the marginal benefits and costs of policing will be weighed against those of investing at the margin in ideological persuasion. Rules are enforced by agents (police, foremen, judges, juries, etc.), and therefore the standard problems of agency theory obtain. It is important to stress here that both the structure of the enforcement mechanism and the degree of imperfection of enforcement are important in the choices that are made.[3]

Rules and their (imperfect) enforcement are not the complete story. If they were, the modeling of institutions and hence the costs of transacting could be made, at this stage of our knowledge, much more precise. But norms of behaviour also matter; and we know very little about them.

As a first approximation, norms are informal constraints on behaviour that are in part derivative from formal rules; that is they are extensions of such rules and apply to specific issues. These informal procedures, deriving as they do from formal organizational structures and agendas, are important but still relatively easy to analyze.[4] Much more important, norms are codes of conduct, taboos, standards of behaviour, that are in part derived from perceptions that all individuals form both to explain and to evaluate the world around them. Some of these perceptions are shaped and molded by organized ideologies (religions, social and political values, etc.). Others are honed by experience, which leads to the re-affirmation or rejection of earlier norms.

However they are formed, and however they evolve, norms play a critical role in constraining the choice set at a moment of time and in the evolution of institutions through time. They are important at a moment of

6 Douglass C. North

time precisely because of the costliness of measurement and the imperfect enforcement of rules. To the degree that individuals believe in the rules, contracts, property rights, etc., of a society, they will be willing to forego opportunities to cheat, steal or engage in opportunistic behaviour. In short, they live up to the terms of contracts. Conversely, to the degree that individuals do not believe in the rules, regard them as unjust, or simply live up to the standard wealth maximizing behavioural assumption we typically employ in neo-classical economics, the costs of contracting, that is transactions costs, will also increase. Empirical evidence suggests the price we are willing to pay for our convictions is a negatively sloped function, so that ideological attitudes are less important as the price increases; but both the slope of the function and shifts in the functions are subjects about which we know very little.[5]

The foregoing paragraphs suggest that ideas and value matter at a moment of time. They do so because of "slack in the system," "agency costs," "consumption on the job," etc., all of which result from the costliness of measurement and enforcement. But how do they change through time? Certainly fundamental changes in relative prices lead not only to rule (and enforcement) changes; but to changes in ideas and values, and the rate of these two kinds of change may be markedly different. This subject will be explored below, but first let me raise some specific issues about institutions, transaction costs, and the consequent choices of the "players" which bear on the subject of this essay.

Let me start with a quotation from Bill Riker.

> ...Every time I convince myself that I have found an instance in which constitutional forms do make a difference for liberty, my discovery comes apart in my hands...Professor Ostrom believes that at least part of the reason we believe we are a free people is that we have certain constitutional forms, but it may just as easily be the case that the reason we have these constitutional forms is that we are a free people.[6]

Now let me quote Bill Riker again, a decade later.

> The Constitution was in a formal sense a necessary condition for the achievement, that is had the Articles [of Confederation] survived, the nation would not have flourished. To see this, note the Constitution was, in a formal sense, necessary for political unity and the consequent political dominance of the United States, first in America and its expansion westward, then in the western hemisphere by restraining European empirical expansion and finally in the world, helping to destroy in two world wars Western European monarchies and empires and later in countering the Soviet empire. All this depended on political unity. Yet without the

Constitution, North America might very well have been as Balkanized as South America.[7]

Rules themselves are not a sufficient condition for determining outcomes even though they are, on occasion, critical. Indeed, the second quotation is from an extraordinarily insightful analysis of the formation of the Constitution, in which Riker makes the convincing case that its creation results from a rather unique concatenation of events that, as the quote implies, changed the destiny of the thirteen confederated states. But it is important to remember that a number of Latin American countries patterned their constitutions after that of the United States with radically different results.

It may be a slight exaggeration to assert that enforcement is always imperfect, but this statement focuses our attention on a critical and neglected aspect of economic history: the essential role of third party enforcement of contracts for human economic progress. There is a large literature in the new industrial organization on self-enforcing contracts, etc.; but as with so much of modern economics, it misses the larger issues involved in exchange in a specialized world. Personal exchange solves the problems of contract fulfillment by repeat dealings and a dense network of social interaction. But the key to the high-income societies of the western world is still the one that Adam Smith propounded more than two hundred years ago. And increasing specialization and division of labour necessitates the development of institutional structures that permit individuals to take actions involving complex relationships with other individuals far removed from personal knowledge and extending over long periods of time.

The essential institutional reliability means that we have confidence in outcomes increasingly remote from our personal knowledge. As the network of interdependence widens, the institutional requirements necessary to realizing the productivity gains arising from specialization are efficient factor and product markets and a medium of exchange with reliable features. The establishment and enforcement of property rights conducive to the creation of such markets would then allow individuals in highly complex, interdependent situations to have confidence in their dealings with individuals with whom they have no reciprocal and ongoing exchange relationships. This is only possibly as a result of a third party to exchange, government, which specifies property rights and enforces contracts.

Let me emphasize that while third party enforcement is far from perfect, there are vast differences in the relative certainty and effectiveness of contract enforcement, temporally over the past five centuries in the Western world, and more currently between modern Western and third world countries. The evolution of government from its medieval mafia-like character to that embodying modern legal institutions and instruments is a

8 Douglass C. North

major part of the history of freedom. It is a part that tends to be obscured or ignored because of the myopic vision of many economists, who persist in modeling government as nothing more than a gigantic form of theft and income redistribution.

In a recent paper, Robert Axelrod tells the story of Alexander Hamilton writing, on the last night of his life, all of the reasons why he should not engage in a duel with Aaron Burr.[8] They were rational and overwhelmingly convincing reasons but in the end not sufficient to overcome the dishonour that he perceived would result from a code of conduct that required such a solution of disputes amongst gentlemen. Axelrod's purpose in telling this story was to illustrate that norms of behaviour, which are not legal rules, are enforced by the attitudes and behaviour of others in the society.

But this is surely only part of that complex of ideas, customs, dogmas, values, ethical standards, etc., which make up our understanding of the world around us, establish our normative standards, and help define the choices we make. While some norms are externally enforced, others are internally enforced codes of conduct, like honesty, integrity, etc. It would be an immense contribution to have a testable general theory of the sociology of knowledge and therefore an understanding of the way overall ideologies emerge and evolve.[9] In the absence of such a theory, we can still derive an important and potentially testable implication about norms at a more specific micro-level of analysis, which is derived from an understanding of institutions. Specifically, the structure of rules and their enforcement help define the costs we bear for ideologically determined choices; the lower the costs, the more will ideas and ideologies matter. Let me provide three illustrations.

A basic paradox of public choice is that individual votes don't matter, but lots of people still vote. Brennan and Buchanan point out this dilemma in a recent paper but do not satisfactorily resolve it.[10] Surely one of the things voters are doing is expressing strongly held convictions at low cost to themselves. Moreover, in the aggregate votes do of course matter. The expression "putting your money where your mouth is" characterizes neither voters nor for that matter academics. Both can afford to be in the literal sense, "irresponsible."

Recently a large volume of literature has grown up around agency theory applied to legislators, with the voter as principal and the legislator as agent. Empirical work suggests that legislators frequently vote their own conviction rather than principals' interests.[11] Other empirical work suggests that the institutional structure of Congress permits legislators to engage in strategic voting behaviour that effectively conceals their true objectives.[12]

Finally, judges with lifetime tenure can and do vote their own convictions, as even the most casual study of courts in general and the Supreme Court in particular testifies. Moreover, this is not an accident. The constitutional provisions, as interpreted by the Marshall Court (1801-1835), were deliberately designed to remove judges from interest group pressures.[13]

It is one thing to be able to show that ideas matter; but as noted above, it is much more difficult to trace the way they have evolved. For example, the demise of slavery, one of the landmarks in the history of freedom, is simply not explicable in an interest group model. Surely the micro argument described above is important to understanding its end. That is, most of those who voted for its elimination, either directly or indirectly, paid little or no costs; they could simply express their abhorrence of one human being owning another. There was no institutional way for the slave owner to buy off the voters. On the other hand, the *way* in which the anti-slavery movement grew (and frequently was used by interest groups) so that it could lead to these votes is a much more complex story.

It's time we took stock. The neo-classical model describes the output of an economy as a function of the quantity and costs of a set of inputs of land, labour, capital, and entrepreneurship, given some production function derived from the state of technological knowledge. But this formulation is, if not incorrect, largely misleading, since if that were all there were to the output of societies, they would all be rich (given again some rather non-controversial behavioural assumptions). If we make the story more complex by introducing transportation costs as an obstacle to realizing the gains from trade, then we should observe with the decline in those transportation costs, which has been going on for several thousand years, a corresponding growth in wealth and income. As a matter of fact, at the time of the Roman Empire in the first two centuries A.D., there was a Mediterranean-wide market, which disappeared with the empire's demise after the Fifth Century A.D. Here, transportation costs had not risen; rather, the costs of transacting had risen with the disappearance of a unified political system of rules and laws (at least partially) enforced over the Mediterranean world. Restated more usefully, the costs of production are a function of the costs of the traditional inputs listed above and the costs of transacting.

It is important to stress that economic growth can and has occurred as a consequence of increasing productivity associated with either decline in production costs or decline in transaction costs. But while falling production costs are a result of technological change or economies of scale, reduced transaction costs are a consequence of the development of more efficient institutions;[14] and since political institutions are the source of the specification and enforcement of property rights, our examination must encompass both political and economic institutions.

The measurement of transaction costs is beset with all of the problems of measurement in traditional national income accounting. To the extent that transactions occur in the market economy, they can be measured.[15] However, costs of transacting arising from queuing, waiting, rationing, bribery, etc., which are substantial in all economies but particularly in Third World and socialistic economies, are unmeasured.

In considering historical measurement we must remember that the costs of transacting have frequently been so high that no production or exchange occurred. The lack of institutions and instruments to facilitate production and exchange in factor and product markets (as well as the existence of institutions designed to raise the costs of transacting) resulted in predominantly personalized (and localized) production and trade. The development of institutions to facilitate transacting is marked not only by expansion of production and exchange in particular factor markets, but by a subsequent decline in transaction costs as the institutions develop. The dramatic decline in real interest rates in 17th Century Netherlands and early 18th Century Britain followed the development of capital market institutions; it is probably the best quantitative measure (and the most critical indicator) of improving productivity in the transactions sector.

The foregoing discussion profiles transactions costs in a growing economy. The emergence of political institutions that specify "efficient" property rights and provide increasingly effective enforcement should show up in terms of the development of economic institutions to facilitate market exchanges. As a result, costs per transaction will be falling; but the size of the transaction sector in the aggregate will be a growing proportion of GNP, as increasing specialization and division of labour multiplies the aggregate volume of exchanges. This is precisely the pattern for the United States, where the measured size of the transaction sector in 1870 is about one-quarter of GNP and in 1970 is almost one-half.

III. THE SOURCES OF INSTITUTIONAL CHANGE

There are two issues I wish to address on institutional change: 1) What causes the change; and 2) what determines its path. In neither case have I a completely satisfactory answer.

Before we turn to these two issues, we must examine the role institutions play in reducing uncertainty in human interaction, since it is this stabilizing role of institutions which separates clearly the framework of analysis being developed here from the traditional neo-classical approach. We can most readily understand the difference if we have ever visited a foreign country and attempted to "do business" with them. We will find that of necessity we must learn their "way of doing things." The structural forms of human interaction that characterize societies are a combination of rules, enforcement features, and norms of behaviour. Until we learn what these are, the costs of transacting are high. Once we understand them, we can effectively communicate and engage in varieties of social, political, and economic exchange. The function of institutions is to provide certainty in human interaction, and this is accomplished by the inherent features of rules and norms. Rules are typically nested in a hierarchical structure, each more costly to change. But even in the absence of the hierarchical institutional structure, the status quo typically has an advantage over changes in a variety of political structures, as a consequence of agenda control and committee structure.

However, it is norms of behaviour that probably provide the most important sources of stability in human interaction. They are extensions, elaborations, and qualifications of rules that have tenacious survival ability, because they become an integral part of habitual behaviour. The reduction of uncertainty, in consequence, makes possible regular human interaction; but it in no way implies that the institutions are efficient, only that they dampen the consequences of relative price changes.

But institutions do change, and fundamental changes in relative prices do lead to institutional change. Historically population change has been the single most important source of relative price changes, though technological change (including and importantly, changes in military technology) and changes in the costs of information have also been major sources. Moreover, as briefly noted in the previous section, changes in norms of behaviour, while certainly influenced by relative price changes, are also influenced by the evolution of ideas and ideologies.

A stylized characterization of the process of institutional change could proceed as follows: As a result of a relative price change, one or both parties to an exchange (political or economic) perceives that he (they) could do better with an altered agreement (contract). Depending on his relative (and presumably changed) bargaining power, he will, as a consequence of the changed prices, re-negotiate the contract. However, contracts are nested in a hierarchy of rules. If the re-negotiation involves alteration of a more fundamental rule, he (or they) may find it worthwhile to devote resources to changing it; or gradually, over time, the rule or custom may simply become ignored and/or unenforced. Agenda power, free-rider problems, and norms of behaviour will add meat (and lots of complications) to this skeletal outline.

An important distinction in this argument is made between absolute bargaining power and changes at the margin. To illustrate this distinction, I turn to the medieval world. The "agreement" between lord and serf on the medieval manor reflected the overwhelming power of the lord vis-a-vis the serf. But changes at the margin, as a consequence of 14th Century population decline, altered the opportunity costs, increased the relative bargaining power of serfs, and led to the gradual evolution of copyhold.[16]

While institutional evolution may proceed in the above manner, without explicit intent or design, dramatic changes in the rules (or their enforcement) occur as well. The gathering in Philadelphia in 1787 is a clear example. Riker, in the essay referred to above, makes clear that the instigators of the convention were Federalists and that their opposition both misunderstood and misjudged their ability to write and ratify a new constitution. Indeed, it was the promised addition of the Bill of Rights as the first order of business under the new constitution that made ratification possible (Riker, forthcoming). Perhaps it is worth noting that the writers were "gentlemen" and that their promise was both believed and carried out.

A special note should be made of the role of military technology in institutional change. Not only have changes in military technology resulted in different, efficient (survival) sizes of political units, but, as in the story that follows, they have consequently induced fundamental changes in other institutions, so that fiscal revenues essential to survival could be realized.

The second issue of institutional change is what determines the direction of change. From what must have been quite common origins several million years ago or even as recently as the hunting and gathering societies that predate the "agricultural revolution" in the 8th millennium B.C., we have evolved in radically different directions (and at radically different rates). How have we evolved such divergent patterns of social, political, and economic organization? To consider a specific example, as I will do in the subsequent sections of this paper, how do we explain the divergent paths of British and Spanish development, both at home and in the contrasting histories of North and South America?

I believe the answer lies in the way that institutional structures evolve. The closest (although by no means perfect) analogy is the way we perceive that the common law evolved. It is precedent-based law: Past decisions become embedded in the structure of rules, which marginally change as cases arise involving some new or, at least in the terms of past cases, unforeseen issue, which when decided becomes, in turn, a part of the legal framework. However, I don't intend to imply by this analogy that the result is "efficient." In fact, as we shall see, Spanish institutional evolution moved in the direction of stagnation.

Let me illustrate institutional evolution by reference to a specific act, which was almost as important as the Constitution in United States history. This was the Northwest Ordinance, passed by the Congress (when it was under the Articles of Confederation) in 1787, at the very time that the Constitutional Convention was meeting in Philadelphia. It was the third act dealing with the issues that arose with respect to the settlement, governance, and integration of the vast lands to the west in the new nation. Where did the rules incorporated in these acts come from and how were they arrived at?

The Ordinance is quite simple and brief. It provided for rules of inheritance and fee-simple ownership of land; it set up the basic structure of the territorial governments and provided for the mechanisms by which territories gradually became self-governing. Additionally, it made provisions for when a territory could be admitted as a state. Then there were a series of Articles of Compact, in effect a bill of rights for the territories (i.e., provisions for religious freedom, the writ of habeas corpus, trial by jury, bailment, enforcement of contract and compensation for property). There were additional provisions about good faith to the Indians, free navigation on the Mississippi and the St. Lawrence, public debt, land disposal, the number of states that could be divided up within the Northwest Territory, and finally a provision prohibiting slavery (though the return of run-away slaves was provided for) in the territories.

It is easy to trace most of the provisions. They had evolved and become a part of the rules of political units of the colonies during the previous 150 years (described in more detail below). These included inheritance laws, fee simple ownership of land, and many of the provisions of the Bill of Rights. Some, however, were precedent-based but had become controversial because of new issues. This was particularly true of the size and the conditions for admittance of new states. The precedence base derived from the original provisions of charters and the Articles of Confederation. Controversies arose from the implications of changing political power with the new government. One of the rules, the prohibition of slavery, appears to have been the result of vote-trading between the authors of the Northwest Ordinance and the writers of the Constitution; slavery was prohibited in the former bill in return for counting slaves as 3/5 of a person in the Constitution, which increased the representation of Southern slave states in Congress (a major issue of the period).[17]

The Northwest Ordinance provided the basic framework dictating the pattern of expansion of the American nation over the next century. While its provisions were at times modified by new issues and controversies, it provided a clear, "path-dependent" pattern of institutional evolution. It is only understandable in terms of precedent, new issues, and the bargaining strength of the parties. It is essential to note that precedent not only defined and determined many of the provisions but also dictated the existing agenda, decision rules, and method of resolution. the larger point of this illustration is that we can only understand historical change by modeling the way institutions evolved through time. That brings us to the following brief outline of English and Spanish institutional change, from the 1500s to the 19th Century in North America and Latin America.

IV. THE INITIAL HISTORICAL CONDITIONS
IN ENGLAND AND SPAIN

Despite the similarities between England and Spain (discussed below) at the beginning of the Sixteenth century, the two countries had evolved very differently. Spain had just emerged from seven centuries of Moorish domination of the peninsula. It was not really a unified country. Although the marriage of Ferdinand and Isabella brought Castile and Aragon together, they continued to maintain separate rules, Cortes, and policies. England, in contrast, had developed a relatively centralized feudalism, as a result of the Norman conquest, and had recently established the Tudors with the Battle of Bosworth (1485).

Yet, in common with the rest of the emerging european nation states, they each faced a problem with far-reaching consequences. That is, that a ruler required additional revenue to survive. The tradition was that a king was supposed to live on his own, which meant that the income from his estates, together with the traditional feudal dues, were his total revenue. The changes in military technology associated with the effective use of the cross-bow, long-bow, pike, and gun powder enormously increased the cost of warfare and led to a fiscal crisis first described by Joseph Schumpter (1919). In order to get more revenue, the king had somehow to make a bargain with constituents. In both countries this initially led to the development of some form of representation on the part of the constituents in return for revenue. In both countries, the wool trade became a major source of crown revenue; but thereafter their stories diverge. We can better appreciate these divergent stories in the framework of a very simple model of the state, consistent with the framework developed int he previous sections of this essay.[18]

The king acts like a discriminating monopolist, offering to different groups of constituents "protection and justice," or at least the reduction of internal disorder and the protection of property rights, in return for tax revenue. Since different constituent groups have different opportunity costs and bargaining power with the ruler, there result different bargains. But there are also economies of scale in the provision of these (semi) public goods of law and enforcement. Hence, total revenue is increased, but the division of the incremental gains between ruler and constituents depends on their relative bargaining power; changes at the margin in either the "violence" potential of the ruler or the opportunity costs of the constituents will result in re-divisions of the incremental revenues. Moreover, the rulers' gross and net revenues differ significantly as a result of the necessity of developing agents (a bureaucracy) to monitor, meter, and collect the revenue; and all the inherent consequences of agency theory obtain here. The initial institutional structure that emerged in order to solve the fiscal crisis therefore looked similar in all the emerging nation states of Europe. A representative body (or bodies) or constituents, designed to facilitate exchanges between the two parties, was created. To the ruler it meant the development of a hierarchical structure of agents, which was a major transformation from the simple (if extensive) management of the king's household and estates to a bureaucracy monitoring the wealth and/or income of the king's constituents. Let us see how this initial institutional framework evolved in the two cases.

V.   ENGLISH DEVELOPMENT

The tension between rulers and constituents (although that would hardly describe the situation at Runnymede in 1215) surfaces with the Magna Carta; but the fiscal crises come to a head with Edward I and Edward III during the Hundred Years War. Stubbs in his *The Constitutional History of England* summarizes the consequences.

> The admission of the right of parliament to legislate, to inquire into abuses, and to share in the guidance of national policy, was practically purchased by the monies granted to Edward I and Edward III.

A logical consequence was that in the 16th Century under the Tudors the structure of Tudor government was revolutionized, as Geoffrey Elton has described in *The Tudor Revolution in Government*. This revolution transformed the government from an elaborate household structure to a bureaucracy increasingly concerned with overseeing and regulating the economy. It had early on been the wool trade which had served as the basis for a good deal of tax revenue; and, as told by Eileen Powers (1941), the wool trade involved a three-way relationship between the exporters, the wool growers as represented in Parliament, and the Crown. In this agreement, the Merchants of the Staple achieved a monopoly of the export trade and a depot in Calais. Parliament received the right to set the tax and the

Crown obtained the revenue. In England the combined mix of the growth of the wool trade, the development of fee-simple ownership in land, and the development of arable lands and new crops imported from the Dutch all contributed to an expansion of agriculture. At the same time, in the non-agricultural sector the economy became increasingly diversified. Although the Tudors continued to attempt to control the economy and to freeze the structure of economic activity into guilds and monopolistic activities, their efforts were relatively ineffective. They were ineffective because 1) the statutes only covered existing industries, so that new industries escaped rule; 2) despite opposition by town guilds, industries moved to the countryside and effectively escaped guild control; 3) the control of wages and labourers in the Statute of Artificers of 1563 was only partially and sporadically enforced; 4) enforcement in the countryside was typically in the hands of unpaid justices of the peace who had little incentive to enforce the law.

The cloth trade therefore grew in the countryside. The interplay between the expansion of diverse economic activities escaping from guild restrictions and the pressures for the development of parliamentary control over the sovereign came to a head with the Stuarts, with the fumbling efforts of James I, the continuing fiscal crises that occurred under Charles I, and the articulate opposition of Coke and others. It was Coke who insisted that the common law was the supreme law of the land, and who repeatedly incurred the anger of James I. It was Coke who led the parliamentary opposition in the 1620s, which established common law control over commercial law. By the end of Elizabeth's reign a changing benefit cost pattern of economic activity was emerging with the widening of domestic and foreign markets; the result was the expansion of voluntary organizations in the form of joint stock companies, and growing resentment against the crown sponsored monopolies which excluded private companies from many of these growing markets. *Darcy vs. Allein* was only the most celebrated case reflecting this ongoing struggle to create a set of rights that would be outside the control of the monarchy. Passing the Statute of Monopolies was just another step in the ongoing process.

Yet the issue of the supremacy of Parliament hung in the balance for much of the 17th Century; and as the struggle continued, Parliament not only attempted to wrest from the King's control the granting of monopolies (as in the Statute of Monopolies), but also to protect itself from the King's wrath by establishing religious, civil, and political freedoms as well (such as the Petition of Right in 1629). It distorts the story, however, to think of it as a clear-cut struggle between an absolutist "oriented" king and a unified Parliament concerned with economic, civil, and political liberties.[19] As the Civil War attests, a complex of religious, economic, and political interests coalesced into armed caps. Moreover, the winning coalition one day could be in the minority the next day. Hence, there was persistent interest and concern with broadly based and impersonally guarded rights.

Sixteen eighty-nine produced the final triumph of Parliament, and in rapid consequence came a set of economic institutions reflecting the relatively increasing security of property rights. The creation of the Bank of England (1694) and the development of new financial instruments led to a dramatic decline in the cost of transacting and has been described as the English financial revolution. Both institutions and consequent falling transaction costs reflect increased security of the time dimension of property rights, a dimension critical to both the long-term capital market and to economic growth itself.

In terms of the very simple political model outlined in Section II, the original trade of certain rights to Parliament in return for revenues was a product of the fiscal crises of the One Hundred Years War. In the 17th Century the Tudors' tripartite arrangement between the Crown, Parliament, and merchants granted further rights to Parliament in return for tax revenues (and still further rights were granted to the Commons by Henry VIII for support in his controversial seizure of church properties). In consequence, the Tudors required an organized bureaucracy to oversee tax collection and to regulate other parts of the economy. The triumph of Parliament in 1689 simply shifted the locus of decision-making to Parliament, which raises the issue of why Parliament would not then proceed to act just like the King. Tollison and Ekelund argue:

> Higher costs due to uncertainty and growing private returns reduced industry demands for regulation and control in England. All this strengthened the emergent Constitutional democracy, which created conditions making rent-seeking activity on the art of both monarch and merchant more costly. When the locus of power to rent-seeking shifted from the monarch to Parliament...the costs of supply and regulation through legislative enactment rose, for reasons suggested by the theory of public choice.[20]

The framework of institutional evolution I have described suggests a somewhat more complicated story than Ekelund and Tollison provide. They assert, "While it is flattering to think that intellectuals affect public policy—surely they do to some extent—it seems completely out of character for economists to think that intellectual arguments could affect real magnitudes so strongly."[21] But the embedding of economic and political freedoms in the law, the interests of principals (merchants, etc.) in greater degrees of freedom, and the ideological considerations that swept England in the 17th Century combined to play a role in institutional change.

VI. SPANISH DEVELOPMENT

While the major steps in Spanish institutional evolution are not in question, nor is the final result, I do not believe that the specific steps along the way have been as clearly delineated as in the English story. [It should be emphasized that I am not nearly as familiar with the Spanish literature as with the English; but it is my impression that an explicit analysis of the evolution of property rights and their political origins has not been a focus of Spanish economic history.] However, some sketch is possible.

Prior to the union of Ferdinand and Isabella the kingdom of Aragon (comprising approximately Valencia, Aragon, and Catalonia) had a very different character than Castile. Aragon had been reconquered from the Arabs in the last half of the 13th Century nd had become a major commercial empire extending into Sardinia, Sicily, and part of Greece. The Cortes, reflecting the interests of merchants, "had already secured the power to legislate and even to limit the king's power to issue legislation under certain conditions" (Veliz, 1980, p. 34). In contrast Castile was continually engaged in warfare, either against the Moors or in internal strife. While the Cortes existed, it was seldom summoned,

> and as nobility and clergy were exempt from financial exactions that could conceivably join them with representatives of the town in resisting additional levies by the Crown, they did not pose (that is the towns did not pose) a credible challenge...(Veliz, 1980, p. 35).

In the fifteen years after their union, Isabella succeeded in gaining control not only over the unruly war-like barons but over church policy in Castile as well. The result was a centralized monarchy in Castile; and it was Castile that defined the institutional evolution of both Spain and Latin America.

A major source of fiscal revenues was the Mesta (the sheepherders guild), which in return for the right to migrate with their sheep across Castile provided the Crown with a secure source of revenue, but also with consequences adverse to the development of arable agriculture and the security of property rights, as well as with soil erosion.[22]

Within Castile the other chief source of revenue was the alcaba, a sales tax. But as the Spanish empire grew to become the greatest empire since Roman times, its major sources of revenue were increasingly external, derived from Sicily, Naples, the low countries, and the New World. Control internally over the economy and externally over the far-flung empire entailed a large and elaborate hierarchy of bureaucrats armed with an immense out-pouring of royal edicts. [Over 400,000 decrees had been issued concerning the governance and economy of the Indies by 1635, an average of 2,500 a year since Columbus sailed first to the Indies (Veliz, 1980, p. 43)]. Designed to provide minute regulation of the economy, guilds also provided a vehicle for internal economic regulation. Price ceilings were imposed on grain and state-owned trading companies, and monopolistic grants provided control of external trade.

As the military costs of controlling the empire outstripped revenues (which declined with the revolt of the Netherlands and the gradual decrease in receipts of treasure), the Crown raised the internal tax (alcaba) from 1.2 percent to 10 percent and repeatedly went into bankruptcy, which it resolved through the seizure of properties and financial assets. The consequence was the decline of the Spanish economy and economic stagnation.[23]

In terms of the foregoing model of the polity, the bargaining position of the Crown, vis-a-vis the Cortes, shifted in favour of the Crown and consequently resulted in the decline of the Cortes. The governance structure then became a large and elaborate bureaucracy and there were endless efforts by the Crown to control its far-flung agents. Indeed, the history of the control of the Indies is an elaborate story in agency theory, beginning as early as Isabella's recision of Columbus' policies towards the Indians in 1502. Distance magnified the immense problem of monitoring agents in the New World; but despite the dissipation of rent at every level of the hierarchical structure, the Crown maintained effective control over the polity and over the economy of the New World.[24]

VII. CONSEQUENCES IN THE NEW WORLD

It is likewise much easier to trace the institutional evolution of the English North American colonies than their Latin American counterpart. The initial conditions are in striking contrast. English America was formed in the very century when the struggle between Parliament and the Crown was coming to a head. Religious diversity, as well as political diversity in the mother country, was paralleled in the colonies. In the Spanish Indies, conquest came at the precise time that the influence of the Castilian Cortes was declining. The conquerors imposed a uniform religion and a uniform bureaucratic administration on an already existing agricultural society.[25]

In the English colonies there was substantial diversity in the political structure of crown proprietary and charter colonies. But the general development in the direction of local political control and the growth of assemblies was clear and unambiguous. Similarly, the Navigation Acts placed the colonies within the framework of overall British imperial policy, and within that broad framework the colonists were free to develop the economy. Indeed, the colonists themselves frequently imposed more restrictions on property rights than did the mother country. (The exception was the effort of proprietors to obtain quit-rents from settlers in proprietary colonies, such as that of Lord Penn. The problem of enforcement and collection in the context of the availability of land resulted in very indifferent success.)

In the Spanish Indies, a bureaucracy detailed political and economic policy.

> ...the 'residencia' was the principal means employed by the king to keep viceroys and other functionaries under control. On the expiration of their term of office, all officials had to undergo the official investigation of their conduct. The fear of the residencia was frequently an incentive to serve the monarch well; it also limited any autonomous inclination of ambitious civil servants in the periphery of the empire. [Veliz (1980), p. 73.]

As for the economy, the Marquis of Pombal, who was the Secretary of State for Foreign Affairs and War and "ruled like a virtual dictator" Portugal and its empire from 1755-1777, is said to have stated:

> I find it absolutely necessary to bring all the commerce of this kingdom and its colonies into companies, then all merchants will be obliged to enter them, or else desist from trading, for they certainly may be assured that I know their interests better than they do themselves and the interest of the whole kingdom. [Veliz (1980), pp. 108-109.]

Some merchants and the Lisbon Chamber of Commerce protested.

> Pombal properly dissolved the chamber and had several of its leading members imprisoned; the rest were regrouped under direct government supervision into a 'Juntado Commercio' that dutifully approved all the minister's decisions. [Veliz (1980), p. 109.]

The French and Indian War (1755-63) is the familiar breaking point in American history. British efforts to impose (very modest) taxes on colonial subjects, as well as to curb westward migration, produced a violent reaction that led through a sequence of steps to the Revolution, the Declaration of Independence, the Articles of Confederation, the Northwest Ordinance, and the Constitution: a sequence of institutional expressions that formed a consistent evolutionary institutional pattern, despite the precariousness of the process.

In the Spanish Indies the recurrent crises were over the efficiency and control of the bureaucratic machinery. The decline under the Hapsburgs and the revival efforts under the Bourbons led to restructuring of the bureaucracy and even some liberalization of trade (under the Bourbons) within the empire. But the control of agents was a persistent problem, compounded by efforts of the Creoles to take over the bureaucracy in order to pursue their own interests. To whatever degree the wars of independence in Latin America were a struggle between colonial control (of the bureaucracy and consequent polity and economy) and imperial control, the struggle was imbued with the ideological overtones that stemmed from the American and French revolutions. Independence brought United States inspired constitutions, but with radically different consequences. In contrast to the United States, in Latin America, "The imaginative federal schemes and courageous attempts at decentralization had one thing in common after the first few years of republican independence: they were all tried but none worked. Some were disastrous; none survived."[26]

The contrasting histories of North and South America is perhaps the best comparative case that we have of the consequences of divergent institutional paths for political and economic performance. We are only just beginning to extend economic and political theory to the study of institutions.[27] I hope this "Historical Introduction" gives some indication of the promise of this approach for the study of economic growth and the history of freedom.

22

NOTES

1. In a neo-classical world, economic growth is a function of the growth of the capital stock, broadly conceived to include not only physical and human capital, but the stock of resources, technology, and pure knowledge. Moreover, in this frictionless world one would equalize the rate of return at the margin by investing in whatever part of the capital stock yielded the highest return. Hence, there is not a fixed factor and diminishing returns as in the classical economic result. In this world the rate of growth is a function of the savings rate and the rate of growth per capita is a function of that rate over the rate of growth of population. In this neo-classical world growth is not a very interesting problem, and the distance between that formulation and the economic history of the world is vast and is determined by the cost of transacting.

2. See Lancaster (1966) and Becker (1965) for the origination of this consumer theory argument. It has been extended into the transaction cost framework by Cheung (1074), North (1981) and Barzel (1982).

3. Oliver Williamson's approach is basically deficient for several reasons, but principally because he takes imperfect enforcement as a given (otherwise opportunism would never pay) rather than recognize that both the characteristics of the enforcement process and the degree of imperfection are essential in modeling institutions and to the costs of transacting.

4. See for example Kenneth Shepsle and Barry Weingast, "The Institutional Foundations of Committee Power," 1986.

5. See Kalt and Zupan (1984) for discussion of these issues.

6. *Public Choice*, 1976.

7. "The Lessons of 1787," *Public Choice*, forthcoming.

8. Robert Axelrod (1985).

9. The immense literature on the subject from Marx and Mannheim to Merton is not very convincing, although Robert Herton's chapters written in 1949 are still a good summary of the state of the art.

10. Brennan and Buchanan (1983).

11. Kalt and Zuppan (1984).

12. Denzau, Riker and Shepsle (1985).

13. Landes and Posner (1975) provide an interest group model of the Supreme Court, but the evidence simply does not support such an argument. See Buchanan (1975) and North (1978).

14. For an analysis of the contribution of falling transactions costs on productivity growth in ocean transportation between 1600 and 1850, see North (1968).

15. See North and Wallis (1987) for a lengthy discussion of the issues and measurement of the transaction sector in the American economy between 1870 and 1970.

16. See North and Thomas (1973) for a description of this process.

16. For an elaboration of these issues, see "The Northwest Ordinance in Historical Perspective," North (forthcoming).

17. This simple "neo-classical theory of the state" is elaborated in North (1981), Chapter 3.

18. Moreover it should be noted that the rights that Parliament had in mind were those of the nobility and the gentry.

19. Ekelund and Tollison (1981), page 149.

20. Ekelund and Tollison (1981), page 151.

21. The history of the Mesta (Klein, 1920) is an exception to my assertion that the history of Spanish property rights has not been told. For a summary of the effects of the Mesta on the development of property rights in Spain, see North and Thomas (1973), Chapter 10.

22. For a more detailed account and sources, see North and Thomas (1973), Chapter 10.

23. For a more detailed account, see Veliz (1980), Chapter Three, "The Regalist Indies."

24. "The Indian population was subdued and subordinated by the new ruling class of Encomenderos. But the Encomendero class itself was the target of a royal program that reduced its political significance by installing a class of state office holders" (Lang, 1975, p. 220).

25. Veliz (1980), p. 151. Veliz provides a country-by-country summary account of the decline of democratic government and the revival of the "centralist" bureaucratic structure and tradition in Latin America (Chapter 7).

26. See North (1986) for an analysis of the "New Institutional Economics."

24

BIBLIOGRAPHY

Axelrod, Robert (1985) "Modeling the Evolution of Norms," Working Paper.

Barzel, Yoram (1982) "Measurement and the Organization of Markets," *Journal of Law and Economics*.

Becker, Gary (1965) "A Theory of the Allocation of Time," *Economic Journal*.

Brennan, Geoffrey and James Buchanan (1982) "Voter Choice and the Evolution of Political Alternatives: A Critique of Public Choice," Center for the Study of Public Choice: mimeo.

Buchanan, James (1975) "Comment on the Independent Judiciary in an Interest group Perspective," *The Journal of Law and Economics*.

Cheung, Stephen (1974) "A Theory of Price Control," *Journal of Law and Economics*.

Denzau, Art, William Riker, and Kenneth Shepsle (1985) "Farquharson and Fenno: Sophisticated Voting and Homestyle," *American Political Science Review*.

Ekelund, Robert and Robert Tollison (1981) *Mercantilism as a Rent Seeking Society*, College Station: Texas A & M Press.

Elton, Geoffrey (1953) *The Tudor Revolution in Government*, Cambridge: The University Press.

Kalt, Joseph and Mark Zuppan (1984) "Capture and Ideology in the Economic Theory of Politics," *American Economic Review*.

Klein, Julius (1920) *The mesta*, Cambridge: Harvard University Press.

Lancaster, Kelvin (1966) "A New Approach to Consumer Theory," *Journal of Political Economy*.

Landes, William and Richard Posner (1975) "The Independent Judiciary in an Interest Group Perspective," *The Journal of Law and Economics*.

Lang, James (1975) *Conquest and Commerce: Spain and England in America*, New York: Academic Press.

North, Douglass (1968) "Sources of Productivity Change in Ocean Shipping, 1600-1850," *Journal of Political Economy*.

North, Douglass and Robert Thomas (1973) *The Rise of the Western World*, Cambridge: The University Press.

North, Douglass (1978) "Structure and Performance: The Task of Economic History," *Journal of Economic Literature*.

North, Douglass (1981) *Structure and Change in Economic History*, New York: W.W. Norton.

North, Douglass (1986) "The New Institutional Economics," *Journal of Institutional and Theoretical Economics* (March).

North, Douglass and John Wallis (1987) "Measuring the Transaction Sector in the American Economy, 1870-1970," in *Long-Term Factors in American Economic Growth*, Volume 51 of the Income and Wealth Series, Stanley L. Engerman and Robert E. Gallman, eds., University of Chicago Press.

Powers, Eileen (1941) *The Wood Trade in English Medieval History*, London: The Clarendon Press.

Riker, William (1976) "Comment on Vincent Ostrom," *Public Choice*.

Riker, William (1986) "1787 and Beyond," *Public Choice*.

Shepsle, Kenneth and Barry Weingast (1986) "The Institutional foundations of Committee Power," Washington University: Political Economy Working Paper #105.

Stubbs, William (1896) *The Constitutional History of England*, London: The Clarendon Press.

Veliz, Claudio (1980) *The Centralist Tradition of Latin America*, Princeton University Press.

[8]

Privatizing the Commons: An Improvement?*

TERRY L. ANDERSON
PETER J. HILL
Montana State University
Bozeman, Montana

I. Introduction

Recent years have seen political economists turning to an institutional paradigm wherein the extent to which property rights are defined and enforced is an important determinant of human action [12]. The institutional or property rights approach has become an important component of explanations of both economic growth and economic inefficiency. The institutional environment now holds a prominent place in explanations of differential growth rates among political units and over time.[1] The property rights approach has also become commonplace in the analysis of the environmental crisis where the lack of well-defined property rights is seen as the cause of environmental problems and movement toward a more complete specification of those rights as the solution. Even bureaucratic inefficiencies have been analyzed in the context of property rights [17].

If one had to characterize all of the above literature in terms of one brief policy conclusion, it would be to "establish property rights." Such establishment would provide incentives for efficiency by internalizing social costs and benefits. In this way the market could promote economic growth, achieve optimal levels of pollution, and generally reduce inefficiency. Convincing evidence substantiating the important role of private property rights continues to be mustered, making it difficult to disagree with this policy conclusion.

The purpose of this paper is not to disagree with the importance of establishing property rights, but to point out and emphasize that the definition and enforcement process may preclude whatever gains might have been realized by the establishment of rights. We hypothesize that under certain institutional arrangements, the establishment of private rights to resources can leave a society no better off than when rights were held in common. In other words, the "tragedy of the commons" may be no worse than the rent dissipation that can result in the process of private property establishment. In what follows we will develop this theory more fully. The first applications are to the American frontier, which provides one of the best opportunities to compare alternative methods of defining and enforcing private rights. More current applications suggest that less centralization of definition and enforcement may improve efficiency.

* Helpful comments were received from Tom Borcherding, Jon Christianson, David Friedman, Ronald Johnson, and Steve Littlechild.
    1. See for example North and Thomas [19].

II. The Economics of Property Rights Production

In 1972 Professors Alchian and Demsetz provided us with an innovative method for analyzing the firm which relied upon the nature of contractual obligations [1]. In their framework the firm is viewed as a form of team production wherein multilateral contracts are replaced by a set of bilateral contracts between a residual claimant and the owners of inputs used in joint production. The result of their model is a series of testable implications suggesting that a set of bilateral contracts provides an efficient system for monitoring and rewarding inputs. The firm evolves as an efficient market which promotes competition in the form of "the *revelation and exchange* of knowledge or information . . ."[1, 795]. When the benefits of this "revelation and exchange" can be captured by the owner in the form of a residual claim, the incentives for efficiency are obvious.

There are also institutional innovations that have efficiency advantages over alternative institutions when valuable resources are being used in the joint production of private property rights. We have pointed out elsewhere that "establishing and protecting property rights is very much a productive activity toward which resources can be devoted"[2, 165]. The efficiency of this productive process will depend upon whether the gains (rents) from having private rights accrue to a residual claimant or to a common pool. *Our hypothesis, which follows from the Alchian-Demsetz interpretation, is that when the methods of defining and enforcing private rights are devised through residual claimant action there is a greater incentive to conserve on resources used in the process than when that process is imposed exogenously by non-claimants.* The definition of property rights generates rents to resources which would otherwise be dissipated under communal ownership. Considerable attention has been paid to the necessity of defining and enforcing rights in order to prevent this rent dissipation. However, there appear to be few efforts to apply this framework to property rights definition in order that we might predict how different definition processes impact on efficiency.[2]

As illustrated in Figure 1, the first owner of labor will equate the wage rate with the value of his marginal product and therefore allocate L_1 units of labor to resource exploitation, in this case let us say farming. The area $OVWU$ will represent the rent to the resource that is captured by the owner of the labor.

Since there are no exclusive rights to the resource and assuming no collusion among potential laborers, "rent becomes a residual, with every decision-making unit. . . . maximizing the portion left behind by others"[8, 59]. Thus, as Cheung has shown, all of the rents to resources will be dissipated through increased effort when institutions governing the use of resources are not developed. In the limit, L_2 total units of labor will be committed to farming, and this results in economic waste since the marginal product at L_2 is less than the opportunity costs from alternative occupations. It is even possible for the marginal product to be negative. The inefficiency generated by the over-commitment of effort to the fixed resource is shown by triangle WXY, the area where MC lies above VMP. This inefficiency is just equal to the rent which would have existed had L_1 units of effort been expended, i.e., triangle WXY equals triangle VZW equals rectangle $OVWU$.

Of course the situation represented in Figure 1 is not a stable one because there are gains to be had through institutional innovation. Social output would rise by the amount

2. Exceptions are [6], [11], and [24].

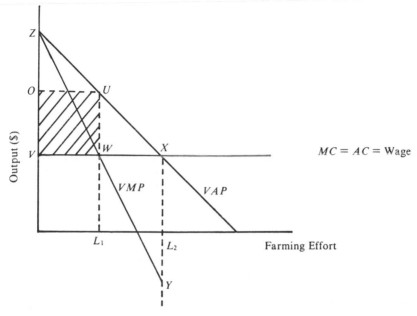

Figure 1. Rent Dissipation in the Common Pool

of rents to natural resources if fewer units of labor were devoted to farming. The size of the efficiency loss can be reduced, and thereby rents increased if farming effort is reduced. Professor Cheung expressed it this way in his example of a fishery:

> . . . there exists incentives to fishermen to restrict the *number* of decision units who have access to the fishing right. That is, even if each decision unit is free to commit the amount of fishing effort, the "rent" captured by each will be larger the smaller the number of decision units [8, 63].

Potential rents to resources are valuable and, therefore, will attract efforts to claim them. When the method of claiming rents is through increased fishing effort, rent dissipation and inefficiency are the result.

Another method of claiming the rents is through the definition and enforcement of exclusive rights to use the resource without actually harvesting it. Establishing and protecting property rights can be as fruitful to the individual as increased fishing or farming effort. It follows then that as the potential rents from resources rise, as the value of the resource increases, more efforts will be devoted to definition and enforcement activity. The worth of perfectly defined and enforced rights is represented by the net present value of the rents and individuals would be willing to spend up to that amount to obtain these rights. If the rents can be obtained for less than this amount, net rents will be positive and society's output will be greater. The point which has been missed in the property rights literature is that even though inefficiency from too much farming effort may be reduced through the assignment of private rights, the gains from such assignment can be lost in the efforts to define and enforce private rights. This says that while private property rights are a necessary condition for efficient market allocation, they are not a sufficient condition. The definition and enforcement process can simply shift the inefficient allocation of resources from the resource commons to the property rights commons and on net, society may be no better off with private property rights.

Returning to Figure 1 allows a comparison of the two types of inefficiencies. L_2 units of farming effort generate inefficiency of $WXY = OVWU$. The farming effort in excess of L_1 can be characterized as the rent dissipation effort. If property rights to land could be established, rents $OVWU$ would go to the owner since farming effort would be reduced from L_2 to L_1. Our point is that the process of determining who gets rent $OVWU$ can also attract resources. Individuals would be willing to expend up to the expected value of capturing the rents in the definition and enforcement of private rights, and under certain gaming conditions they might even expend more.[3] If the expenditure for well-defined and enforced rights is in the form of ownership claims to other assets, the transaction is merely an exchange of wealth. The exchange may be between the new "owner" and the collective (society) as in the case of a government auction of rights, or it may be between the new "owner" and a politician/bureaucrat as in the case of bribes.[4] On the other hand, if the expenditure is in the form of real resources for "lobbying," the transaction becomes net social waste and, in the limit, will equal the common pool inefficiency of WXY.[5]

Whether or not rents will be dissipated by definition and enforcement activity, therefore, depends upon the process whereby rights evolve. The Alchian-Demsetz framework of a residual claimant provides interesting insights into the efficiency of different processes. Consider two individuals faced with the problem of defining rights to an unclaimed acre of land. They have an incentive to establish ownership in the cheapest manner, since they bear the cost of the resources consumed in the property rights production. Of course, one person could capture all the rents if he were able to get to the land first, but since each has this opportunity, competition between them would tend to dissipate at least some of the rents. Squatter sovereignty will result in a race wherein each would be willing to expand up to the expected value of getting the land in attempting to win the race. If, however, they could agree to reduce expenditures on the race, the residual for each would increase.

As long as those bargaining for the property rights are free to choose their own definition process, there is an incentive to reduce definition costs since they are residual claimants. This is not to say that they will always resolve the issue and define property rights at the lowest cost. The prisoners' dilemma problem, in fact, may result in full dissipation. Consider a piece of land with rent of $200 when property rights are well defined and enforced. Suppose that, if the two parties agree to walk to the parcel and to divide it equally, each will expend $10 worth of resources. The residual for each becomes $90 as shown in Cell I of Figure 2. If on the way to the land, however, one potential claimant can get the jump on the other insuring an earlier arrival and ownership of the entire acre, he can spend up to $110 worth of resources in the race and still be better off. Potential claimant B, of course, faces the same possibility. The results of these two actions

---

3. This is true only if the VAP curve is linear. With nonlinearity it is possible to have $OVWU$ either greater or less than WXY. If $OVWU$ is greater than WXY, rent dissipation can be worse than common pool inefficiency.

4. For an elaboration on these differences see Buchanan [6].

5. To conclude that this expenditure represents net social waste necessitates the standard assumption of the rent-seeking literature than "the costs incurred .... have no socially valuable by-products" [22, 809].

Individual *B*

	Walk	Run
Walk	90,90	0,95
Run	95,0	0,0

(Individual *A* — rows: Walk, Run)

Figure 2. Rents with the Prisoners' Dilemma

are shown in Cells II and III. If both decide to run, however, rent dissipation is the result and the pair find themselves in Cell IV. In this simplified two-person world, James Buchanan has noted that

> it is surely plausible to suggest that rationality precepts will direct each person to adhere to the initial contractual terms. Each person will recognize that unilateral defection cannot succeed and that any attempt to accomplish this would plunge the system back into a position that is less desirable for everyone than that which is attained from adherence to contract [5, 65].

The "rationality" to which Buchanan refers is related to the fact that the two parties have a claim on the resources saved through adherence to the initial process and that the cost of detecting a rule-breaker is relatively low. As the number of participants in the game increases, the prisoner's dilemma problem becomes more acute because the share of the residual declines while the cost of detection rises.

In the limit the share of the residual is zero and the incentive for reducing the amount of resources consumed in the definition process will be the same. This is in fact exactly what happens when the person determining the process is a governmental official who has no claim on the residual rent but whose only claim is on power within the bureaucracy. Returning to the example of land worth $200, suppose a third party chooses the process for deciding the division. Allocating the property to whichever individual arrives at the location first might seem "fair," but many resources can be wasted in the process. This assumes that participants could not rig the race by agreeing beforehand that one person would walk to the property while the other waited at the starting line and that they would later split the property 50-50. In fact, without collusion each would be willing to spend up to the expected value of the rent to win the race. With probabilities of success accurately estimated, all of the potential rents would be dissipated. As the number of entrants to the race increases, the likelihood of collusion declines, and the potential for rent dissipation rises. In this case we insure the worst solution to the prisoner's dilemma. However, this resource waste costs the third party nothing since he had no claim on the rents anyway.

Our prediction that rent dissipation results when the property rights definition process is designed by a non-residual claimant is likely to be even stronger given the nature of modern bureaucracies. Since decision makers legally cannot claim a share of rents derived from increased efficiency, they must seek alternative forms of payment. Corruption is one possibility, but this may simply be one way of collecting a portion of the rents. Another possibility is that the bureaucrat can gain power and command over political resources if the definition process necessitates an even larger bureaucracy. Thus the controlling authority may require activities that dissipate rents in order that it can be given command over some political resources. Competing claimants to common property resources may have to prove themselves "worthy" of having rights bestowed upon them, with, of course, the bureaucrat needing considerable allocation of funds in order to make judgements of "worthiness." Or the bureaucrats may find that they can require activities that produce positive utility for bureaucrats. Hence, rather than there being no incentive to reduce resources expended in the definition of property rights, there may actually be an incentive to increase such expenditures.

The ability of the bureaucracy to induce this type of rent-seeking activity, of course, will be constrained by the number of alternative "firms" which can establish rights without causing rent dissipation. Other agents can "organize opposition and attract supporters from among the constituents by offering a better division of the existing rents" [18, 256]. Residual claimant types of organizations offer one possibility for a "better division" by eliminating rent dissipation activities.[6]

In summary, the major implications of our model are:

1. Rent dissipation can occur in the *process* of establishing private rights to a common property resource as well as in the use of a common property resource.

2. The rent dissipation from the process of establishing rights to a resource can be every bit as large as the rent dissipation from exploitation of the resource under common property rules.

3. When the process of establishing rights is determined by residual claimants (potential owners of the rents) there is a greater incentive to conserve on the resources used in that process than when the procedure is determined by non-claimants.

III. Alternative Processes in the American West

We now turn to the American West to examine cases of property rights definition and enforcement. Our theory predicts that early efforts at establishing rights to land, where those involved in the definition and enforcement procedure were clearly the residual

---

6. There is the possibility that competition to become a member of the residual claimant organization will occur and that rent dissipation will occur at this level. In this case one can imagine an infinite regress such that *no* gains are *ever* possible from *any* establishment and/or definition of property rights. All gains from the possession of such rights would be competed away at one level or another. However, if one allows for heterogeneous claimants, some will be among the first to perceive opportunities for rents to be created from establishing rights to common property resources. Thus these perceptive entrepreneurs, as the individuals with a comparative advantage in "rights production," will be the first to become involved and will likely see the advantages of contracting with other similar entrepreneurs to limit rent dissipation. Without the assumption that information is imperfect and that all potential claimants to resources are not homogenous in their abilities and perception, the property rights argument becomes an empty one. We should never concern ourselves with alternative property rights arrangements because all the gains from more efficient institutions will be dissipated at some margin.

claimants, would have been considerably different than definition and enforcement activity under the Homestead Acts, where the rules were established by those who had little or no claim to residual rents.

The American frontier has long been noted as a place where extralegal institutions for defining and enforcing property rights arose. Since the frontiersmen were aware of the rent dissipation which accompanies common ownership these institutions represented their efforts to eliminate that dissipation by defining private rights.[7] These institutional innovations occurred in the absence of formal government and took the form of land clubs or claims associations, cattlemen's associations, mining camps, and wagon trains. Rights were established to land, water, timber, minerals, livestock, and personal property. The actual methods used for establishing private rights varied from case to case, but, if the above theory is correct, we should observe an effort in all cases to conserve upon the real resources consumed in the definition and enforcement process. Evidence from the land claims clubs, mining camps, and livestock associations suggests that this was the case.

Much of the land in the West was settled before it was formally opened by the federal government to legal ownership. In the absence of pre-established methods for determining ownership rights, claims associations sprang up. Their primary purpose was to register the settlers' claims to land and to insure those claims would be honored when the federal rules were put into effect. Clubs could establish whatever rules they wanted; they adopted their own constitutions and bylaws, elected officers, and established rules for adjudicating disputes and procedures for the registration of claims.[8] If lands were surveyed, such registration was relatively simple and was carried out through the range, township, and quarter section of the claim. In the absence of a government survey, the claims clerk was provided a physical description of the claim, including landmarks and the names of surrounding claimants. The club provided coercive power, if necessary, to enforce the members' rights. The association also attempted to insure that the squatters could buy the land at the minimum price when it was put up for sale by the government.

In addition to providing private ownership for members, another alleged purpose was to protect the farmers from "speculators," and much of the historical research on the clubs has debated whether in fact they accomplished this task [4]. An alternative explanation of their efforts to limit land ownership to those actually on the scene is that they clearly understood that the larger the number of users of the common pool resource, the greater the likelihood of rent dissipation. Thus the purposes of claims clubs can be seen as twofold: first, to reduce the claimants on the resource, and secondly, to find low cost methods of defining and enforcing rights to the resource. The evidence indicates that the associations had a reasonable amount of success in doing both.

As predicted by our theory, the definition process of land claims clubs followed a relatively low-cost method, and the available evidence on enforcement activity is also consistent with the hypothesis that residual claimant associations will discourage rent dissipation. Of between 25 and 100 claims associations in Iowa,[9] only three show any evidence of requiring rent-seeking activity. In his study of "The Iowa Claim Clubs: Symbol or Substance," Allan Bogue concludes that "regulations prescribing the degree to which the member must improve his claim appear in the manuscript records of Poweshiek,

7. For a discussion of some of these institutions see Anderson and Hill [2].
8. For an example of a constitution of a claims club see Shambaugh [23].
9. Shambaugh [23] says there were 100 associations in Iowa while Bogue [4] says there were only 25.

Johnson, and Webster county associations, but *not* in the selections of the club laws printed in the histories of other counties."[10] When resource investments were required, they did not approach the requirements of the Homestead Acts. For example, in Webster County claimants had to expend labor worth $10 for each month after the first month, while Poweshiek County required labor worth $30 during the first six months and $30 for each succeeding six months. In Johnson County resident members were not required to invest any resources into their land until they so desired. Non-residents did have to expend $50 worth of labor for each six months the claim was held [4, 51]. It should be emphasized that these expenditures were specified in terms of labor, allowing the farmer a great deal of latitude with his investment. In this way the claimant could count effort which would have been expended regardless of the club rules. This is in sharp contrast to the Homestead Acts which specified the investments in terms of cabin size, irrigation ditches, and planted trees, most of which were unnecessary.

The rules in the gold mining camps of California provide similar evidence consistent with our hypothesis. John Umbeck [26] examined the contracts formed by miners for the purpose of defining and enforcing rights. His evidence shows that the contracts did require miners to work their claims for a certain number of days each week because their presence was an effective means of enforcing rights. At the same time, however, the contracts did not specify what constituted working a claim. In this way the miner organizations were able to minimize typical dissipation due to common property as well as dissipation in the definition and enforcement process.

Another example of residual claimant effort to define and enforce property rights is the cattlemen and livestock associations that existed throughout the West. These groups also acted in ways which conserved upon the resources devoted to definition and enforcement activity. Louis Pelzer summarizes, in his book *The Cattlemen's Frontier*, the role these groups played on the frontier:

> From successive frontiers of our American history have developed needed customs, laws, and organizations. The era of fur-trading produced its hunters, its barter, and the great fur companies; on the mining frontier came the staked claims and the vigilance committees; the camp meeting and the circuit rider were heard on the religious outposts; on the margins of settlement the claim clubs protected the rights of the squatter farmers; on the ranchmen's frontier the millions of cattle, the vast ranges, the ranches, and the cattle companies produced pools and local, district, territorial, and national cattle associations [21, 87].

The problem of unrestricted entry was clearly understood by the settlers, and these associations were designed to restrict that entry. Granville Stuart, an early rancher said, "The business was a fascinating one and profitable so long as the ranges were not overstocked" [25, II, 185]. The lure of free grass sounded attractive, but those who came to use it soon discovered that others also came until all rents to the common resource were dissipated.[11]

The cattlemen's associations, members of which were residual claimants, devised two methods of restricting entry and establishing rights which discouraged rent dissipation. The first was squatter sovereignty or prior use which was as old as the frontier itself. Members of associations simply had to announce their squatter claims as shown by the following newspaper advertisement:

10. [4, 51] emphasis added.
11. For a detailed discussion of the theory of common property as it applies to the open range problem in the West, see Dennen [10].

> I, the undersigned, do hereby notify the public that I claim the valley, branching off
> the Glendive Creek, four miles east of Allard, and extending to its source on the South
> side of the Northern Pacific Railroad as a stock range. Chas. S. Johnson [20, 183].

Such a definition process required almost no investment of resources, though enforcement was not without cost. Such a claim was not enforceable in any court of law, but had to be enforced through the local cattlemen's associations. Such groups also used the local newspapers to announce their intentions to enforce the "accustomed range."

> We, the undersigned, stock growers of the above described range, hereby give notice
> that we consider said range already overstocked; therefore we positively decline allow-
> ing any outside parties or any parties locating herds upon this range the use of our
> corrals, nor will they be permitted to join us in any roundup on said range from and
> after this date [10, 427].

The last portion of this advertisement points out the other way that cattlemen's associations were able to reduce wasteful rent dissipation. The normal operation of a cattle ranch on the frontier necessitated cooperation among neighbors, especially in the case of the twice yearly roundups. The ranchers in an area would work together in the late spring to brand the year's calf crop and again in the fall to gather cattle for marketing. Given the high costs of fencing and the redundancy of each rancher gathering cattle with independent roundups, cooperation provided a way of minimizing costs. The organization of this joint effort was through the cattlemen's associations which in turn could restrict entry by excluding entrants from the roundup. As a special agent of the U.S. General Land Office put it, "This mode of controlling the public lands is quite as effective as if the parties referred to had gone to the expense of fencing the entire tracts" [10, 427]. Since the roundup was already something which was necessary for production, using it as a means of defining and enforcing range rights required little or no additional resource expenditure.

As our theory suggests, attempts by the claims clubs, mining camps, and the cattlemen's associations to establish rights over scarce resources were through processes which conserved upon resources expended in the definition and enforcement activity. Although there are a few cases when claims clubs required improvements upon the land to insure ownership, in the others the simple filing of a claim was sufficient. In establishing range rights some resources were expended to prevent rent dissipation through common ownership. However, the fact that the stockmen accepted newspaper claim advertisements and that they tied establishment efforts to other ranch activities, such as the roundup and the drive, suggests that as residual claimants of the rents they did attempt to conserve on definition and enforcement activity. There is no evidence that they required the construction of unnecessary buildings or the utilization of inappropriate ranching techniques in order to determine ownership. They were well aware that such requirements would have consumed valuable resources for which they had alternative uses.

Of course this is not to argue that property rights were "perfectly" enforced. Within the groups there were those who broke the rules, attempting to capture more of the rents. Furthermore, as more people migrated to the frontier, the existing residual claimant groups had to increase their expenditures on definition and enforcement.[12] In some cases this was accomplished through fencing, in others through range wars, and in others through government intervention.

12. For a more detailed discussion see Libecap [15, 15-20].

In contrast, the definition and enforcement processes of the federal land distribution system following the Civil War suggest that non-residual claimants did encourage rent dissipation. The history of land policy in the United States is one which saw land either awarded to squatters, sold, granted to encourage production of certain goods or services, or given to those willing to make certain investments in the land. But these federal requirements for distribution of the public domain never seemed to suit the frontiersmen. From the Ordinance of 1785 to the Homestead Act of 1862, complaints ranged from prices which were too high to size limitations which were too low. The Easterner had a different frame of reference and different set of goals, but perhaps more important for our analysis, the lawmakers who had the authority to set the rules for definition and enforcement of property rights did not have the incentive to reduce wasteful rent dissipation.[13]

Were there any more efficient methods by which the public domain could have been converted to private ownership? One that is clearly superior to those used is an auction system. Although the highest bidder has to give up claims to resources in order to get ownership, the advantage lies in that these resources are merely transferred to another owner, in this case the government, rather than dissipated in the enforcement process. As Taylor Dennen expresses it:

> Under the auction system, settlers will exchange money, that is, a command over resources, for a land title. However, with the price of land set at zero, individuals will use up real resources to get to the land at the moment when its present value turns from negative to zero. . . . The problem is fully analogous to the dissipation of consumers' surplus under price controls or rationing by waiting. That is, where prices are inhibited in their role of allocating commodities, consumers will use up valuable resources such as capital equipment or labor time in order to obtain commodities. From the point of view of those interested in maximizing the value of output, such resource expenditure is pure waste [11, 729-30].

Some of the early land laws approached this system in that they disposed of the land by auction with the provision that a minimum price be paid. As long as the actual present value of the land exceeded the minimum price, no resources were wasted. However, in many cases the minimum price did exceed the present value and thus encouraged squatting. To the extent that claims associations were successful in establishing private rights to the land without resource waste and to the extent that preemption rights were allowed, the disposal policy during the first half of the nineteenth century was relatively efficient. Moreover, the Graduation Act of 1854 provided for successive reductions in the minimum price at which unsold public lands would be offered. Though the Act was only in effect for eight years, it did approach the simple auction.

With the Homestead Act of 1862 there was a significant shift in the land disposition policy, one which encouraged much more waste of resources. This Act and those which have followed explicitly required expenditures of labor and capital in order to establish ownership. Under the Homestead Act of 1862, property rights could be established to 160 acres through five years of residence. However, under this first act, land could be preempted by the payment of a $1.25 fee per acre after six months of residence. The original act was revised and expanded in 1873 with the Timber and Culture Act, followed by the Timber and Stone Act in 1878, the Desert Land Act in 1877, the Enlarged Homestead Act in 1909, and finally the Stockraising Homestead Act in 1916.

---

13. See Dennen [11] and Higgs [14] for specific discussions of the Homestead Acts.

In all of these rent dissipation occurred in two major ways. First, since the allowable size of holdings was far below that which was economically most efficient, too many people lived on the land. As with any common pool resource entrants were willing to continue homesteading as long as rents were available. Second, rent dissipation occurred because unnecessary resources had to be invested. Land was irrigated that otherwise would not have been, trees were planted when they would not have been, and, in much of the West, plowing was required on land that was more suited for grazing. Stories abound of resources employed in land rushes.

> For example, considerable time was spent simply waiting, or jockeying for an advantageous position at the starting line. On occasion special vehicles were constructed which would presumably speed more quickly over the land to a claim site. Supposedly in one instance an individual who had a right to enter the unsettled territory spent considerable time training a pony to race to a particularly good claim [11, 730].

The exact extent to which the government's means of public domain disposal wasted resources must await further research, but there is evidence that it did encourage substantial rent-seeking activity. When prices entered into the process, such activity was reduced. For example, the Timber and Stone Act and the Preemption Act provided that $2.50 and $1.25 per acre, respectively, be paid for land. In addition, however, other rent-seeking activities were encouraged and required. For the Timber and Stone Act and the Preemption Act, Professors Libecap and Johnson have estimated that "expenditures attributable to Federal restrictions and which involved real resources: agent payment, development costs, and miscellaneous expenditures," amounted to between 60 percent (Timber and Stone) and 80 percent (Preemption) of the total land value [16, 137]. When one considers that 27 percent of over one billion acres disposed of by the federal government passed through this type of disposal system and that of these, 285 million acres were taken up more than once, the potential for waste becomes staggering. As Dennen concludes, "There is no reason to believe that the impact of the federal land-disposition system on the national economy was insignificant" [11, 736].

IV. Modern Applications

Examples of residual claimant groups active in definition and enforcement are difficult to find outside the frontier setting. On the other hand, examples abound of rent dissipation in the process of privatizing rights. In the case of oil, problems associated with unitizing common pools have brought bureaucracies into the allocation process. Though one can conceive of a collective means for establishing rights to all pools, these means have not been adopted. As Robert Haveman points out, "public regulatory bodies have been established and elaborate rules have been designed to control the behavior of users of the resource. Rule setting, behavior monitoring, and rule enforcement is the standard pattern" [13, 870]. When rights to oil on public lands are defined the "work effort bidding" method is often used. In 1977 the House and Senate debated amendments to the Outer Continental Shelf Land Act that were designed to reduce the "unfair advantage" of cash bidding by forcing parts of the bid to be in the form of work effort [27, 10-15; 28, 9-13]. Just as the Homestead Act generated too many cabins on the American Frontier, exploration requirements on the outer continental shelf generate an excessive amount of drilling activity. This has been particularly true under the British and Norwegian rules for drilling in the North Sea. Kenneth Dam summarizes the impact of the British Ministry of Power's effort to establish rights there:

> More significant, however, was the Ministry's request for a statement of each company's work programme for the blocks for which it was still in the running. It came to be known that the Ministry expected much more active drilling programmes in areas which were widely sought after than in the least coveted area. Indeed, by a process which is none too clear to the outsider looking in after the fact, a "going price" came to be known for each area. This going price was denominated in such things as holes drilled and exploration work undertaken. He who is unwilling to pay the going price could not expect to be awarded a licence [9, 59-60].

Another familiar example illustrates simple rent dissipation through the assignment process. The methods used by the Federal Communication Commission to assign rights to radio and television frequencies forced applicants to prove their "worthiness." As Ronald Coase put it, "when rights, worth millions of dollars, are awarded to one businessman and denied to others, it is no wonder some applicants become over anxious and attempt to use whatever influence they have (political or otherwise), particularly as they can never be sure what pressure the other applicants may be exerting" [7, 26]. The fact that WFTV, Orlando, Florida, a television station estimated to be worth $40 million, has been in front of regulatory commissions and courts for 27 years trying to obtain its license suggests that rents are being dissipated through the licensing process. In the end someone will obtain control of the station, but in the meantime considerable rents will be dissipated through resource expenditure.

V. Conclusion

We have argued in this paper that the rules for defining and enforcing rights are much more likely to promote rent dissipation when the rule makers are not potential residual claimants. On the American frontier residual claimant organizations systematically reduced rent seeking in the definition and enforcement process; on the other hand, the Homestead Act which followed these groups promoted dissipation. The bureaucratic struggle for power and budget builds in an incentive for rule makers to encourage rent seeking. This conclusion is extremely relevant today when privatization of public land and other resources is being considered. Selling public land at auction will generate revenue for the Treasury, itself a common pool [3], but if our theory is correct, we can predict efforts on the part of agencies to resist such an auction. The current process for assigning rights to public land ensures that agencies such as the Forest Service and the Bureau of Land Management retain power and budget. If those agencies could auction off land and retain the proceeds, they might have an incentive to do so. However, if the proceeds become a common pool, the bureaucratic incentive is to maintain rent dissipating policies. The important conclusion to remember is that removing the inefficiency of open access through privatization or other entry restrictions can simply shift rent dissipation to another arena.

References

1. Alchian, Armen A. and Harold Demsetz, "Production, Information Costs, and Economic Organization." *American Economic Review*, December 1972, 777-95.
2. Anderson, Terry L. and P. J. Hill, "The Evolution of Property Rights: A Study of the American West." *The Journal of Law and Economics*, April 1975, 163-79.
3. Baden, John and Rodney D. Fort, "Natural Resources and Bureaucratic Predators." *Policy Review*, Winter 1980, 69-81.
4. Bogue, Allan G. "The Iowa Claim Clubs: Symbol and Substance," in *The Public Lands*, edited by Vernon Carstensen. Madison: University of Wisconsin Press, 1963.
5. Buchanan, James M. *The Limits of Liberty*. Chicago: University of Chicago Press, 1975.
6. _____. "Rent Seeking Under External Diseconomies," in *Towards a Theory of a Rent Seeking Society*, edited by James M. Buchanan, Robert Tollison, and Gordon Tullock. College Station: Texas A & M Press, 1980.
7. Coase, Ronald H., "The Federal Communications Commissions." *The Journal of Law and Economics*, October 1959, 1-40.
8. Cheung, Steven N. S., "The Structure of a Contract and the Theory of a Non-Exclusive Resource." *The Journal of Law and Economics*, April 1970, 49-70.
9. Dam, Kenneth, "Oil and Gas Licensing in the North Sea." *Journal of Law and Economics*, October 1965, 51-75.
10. Dennen, R. Taylor, "Cattlemen's Associations and Property Rights in the American West." *Explorations in Economic History*, October 1976, 423-36.
11. _____, "Some Efficiency Effects of Nineteenth-Century Federal Land Policy: A Dynamic Analysis." *Agricultural History*, October 1977, 718-36.
12. Furubotn, Eirik and Svetozar Pejovich, "Property Rights and Economic Theory: A Survey of Recent Literature." *Journal of Economic Literature*, December 1972, 1137-62.
13. Haveman, Robert H., "Efficiency and Equity in Natural Resource and Environmental Policy." *American Journal of Agricultural Economics*, December 1973, 868-78.
14. Higgs, Robert. *The Transformation of the American Economy, 1865-1914*. New York: John Wiley and Sons, Inc., 1971.
15. Libecap, Gary D. *Locking Up The Range*. San Francisco: Pacific Institute for Policy Studies, 1981.
16. _____ and Ronald N. Johnson, "Property Rights, Nineteenth-Century Federal Timber Policy, and the Conservation Movement." *The Journal of Economic History*, March 1979, 129-42.
17. McKean, Roland N., "The Unseen Hand in Government." *American Economic Review*, June 1965, 496-505.
18. North, Douglass C., "A Framework for Analyzing the State in Economic History." *Explorations in Economic History*, July 1979, 249-59.
19. _____ and Robert Paul Thomas, *The Rise of the Western World*. London: Cambridge University Press, 1972.
20. Osgood, Ernest Staples. *The Day of the Cattleman*. Minneapolis: University of Minnesota Press, 1929.
21. Pelzer, Louis. *The Cattlemen's Frontier*. Glendale, Calif.: Arthur H. Clark Co., 1936.
22. Posner, Richard A., "The Social Costs of Monopoly and Regulation." *Journal of Political Economy*, August 1975, 807-27.
23. Shambaugh, Benjamin F., "Frontier Land Clubs, or Claim Associations." *Annual Report of the American Historical Association*, Vol. 1, 1900, 67-84.
24. Southey, Clive, "The Staple Thesis, Common Property, and Homesteading." *Canadian Journal of Economics*, August 1978, 547-559.
25. Stuart, Granville. *Forty Years on the Frontier*, edited by Paul C. Philips, 2 Vols. Cleveland: The Arthur H. Clark Company, 1925.
26. Umbeck, John, "The California Gold Rush: A Study of Emerging Property Rights." *Explorations in Economic History*, July 1977, 197-226.
27. United States House Report No. 95-590, 1977.
28. United States Senate Report No. 95-284, 1977.

[9]

MIGHT MAKES RIGHTS: A THEORY OF THE
FORMATION AND INITIAL DISTRIBUTION OF PROPERTY RIGHTS

JOHN UMBECK*

This paper is a theoretical and empirical investigation into the formation and initial distribution of property rights. Violence is singled out as a major constraint on this formation process. Its role is explicitly modeled in a choice theoretic framework and some of the implications are tested using data collected from contracts written during the California gold rush of 1848.

At the present time there is no general economic theory of the formation and initial distribution of property rights. With the possible exception of the externality literature, most economic models assume that the rights to all scarce resources are clearly defined and have been rationed out to individuals according to some unexplained initial endowment process. While these assumptions, once posited, allow the economist to concentrate on those market forces which affect the quantities of property rights exchanged and the prices which emerge through transactions, they completely ignore the question of how rights emerge and are initially allocated.[1]

The purpose of this paper is to use the orthodox theory of competition to explain the formation and distribution of property rights among individuals. In part II, a relatively simple theory will be developed which, when the relevant competitive constraints are identified, is capable of predicting how newly formed rights to property will be initially distributed. In part III, I will describe the setting of a unique empirical test of my hypothesis: the California gold discovery of 1848. Finally, in part IV, some of the theoretical implications will be tested against the backdrop of the ensuing gold rush.

I. INTRODUCTION

In the most general sense, ownership rights are "the expectations a person has that his decision about the uses of certain resources will be

*Purdue University. I want to thank Steve Cheung for first suggesting that I examine the California gold rush period and Yoram Barzel and Chris Hall for their helpful comments on earlier drafts. Thanks must also go to the National Science Foundation, the Foundation for Research in Economics and Education at U.C.L.A. and the Krannert Graduate School at Purdue University, all of whom assisted financially. This paper is part of a larger study of property rights and contracts soon to be published as *A Theory of Property Rights* by the Iowa State University Press.

1. Notice that our inability to explain the initial distribution of wealth severely limits our ability to explain differences in personal income. Yet, while there have been numerous attempts to explain relative incomes, economists have been deficient in their attempts to explain the initial distribution of the stock from which all income flows.

38

effective."[2] Interpreted in this manner, ownership can emerge from a variety of circumstances. For example, a person may acquire rights in coconuts simply because he is the only one who can climb a tree. Similarly, an individual may have rights to fish because he alone knows where to catch them. Or, a pretty woman may have the rights to a seat on a crowded bus because she is pretty. Notice, however, that even in these cases the individuals can be deprived of their rights by other individuals. Non-tree climbers can cut the coconut tree down, the fisherman can be continually watched and followed until his private fishing spot is discovered, and the pretty woman can be thrown from her bus seat or made physically unattractive. In other words, ownership rights to property can exist only as long as other people agree to respect them or as long as the owner can forcefully exclude those who do not agree.

If the individuals agree to respect each other's ownership rights, they may do so either implicitly, in which case they are usually called customs or traditions, or explicitly through contract, in which case they are called laws or rules. Included in the former group would be such things as not "cutting in" to a line of waiting people or asking if a seat is already taken in a theater. Casual empiricism suggests that the rights to relatively valuable resources are usually assigned explicitly through contract and not left to custom. It is the contractually agreed upon distribution of newly formed rights that this paper is trying to explain.

However, even if all individuals enter into an explicit agreement to assign and respect each other's ownership rights, some force or threat of force will still be required. This follows from the postulate of individual maximization. If one person can violate the terms of the agreement and deprive another of his assigned rights he will do so if the gains exceed the costs. Therefore, the contracting group must agree to impose costs upon anyone who would take someone else's property. This will involve the forceful exclusion of would-be violators. *Ultimately all ownership rights are based on the abilities of individuals, or groups of individuals, to forcefully maintain exclusivity.*

Force also underlies all allocative systems. To see why, imagine any rationing device. This could include a race, with the person coming in first getting some percent of the stock of wealth and the person coming in second getting some lesser amount and so on. It could include a beauty contest, with the one judged most beautiful getting a larger share of the wealth than the others. It could even include offers of exchange, with an appointed auctioneer selling the wealth to the ones making the highest bid. However, notice that all of these rationing devices require agreement. If some individual, relatively proficient in the use of force, received less of the wealth through the race (or the beauty contest or the auction) than he could have gained through the use of forceful persuasion, he will disregard

2. Alchian and Allen (1969, p. 158).

the outcome and take his share from the other victors. In other words, all of these allocative systems require agreement; all except force. It is this characteristic which sets it apart from other rationing systems.

It is important to note that nothing said so far implies that force or even the threat of force will be the actual rationing system used by individuals. However, potential force is the relevant constraint underlying any initial agreements (and subsequent agreements) which allocate wealth among competitors. It is relevant in the sense that the agreement, regardless of the competitive criterion used, must ration to each individual at least as much wealth as he could have through the use of his own force or there will be no agreement.

Under certain conditions, the constraint of violence may generate precise and testable implications. For example, assume that the costs of acquiring and maintaining exclusivity with personal force are not significantly different from the costs of assigning and enforcing ownership rights through contract. Assume also that if a contract is formed all the individuals who held property with force are party to the initial agreement. Because the formation of the contract itself does not create any additional property or significant cost savings and because no wealth maximizer would accept less wealth than he could have through the use of his personal force, *the agreed upon contract must initially endow each individual with the same amount of wealth as that which they could have had through violence.* With this in mind, let us now set up a model of the distribution of rights under the constraint of competition through violence.

II. THE MODEL[3]

Assume there is a group of people on an island containing only one scarce resource, gold, which is buried in the land. There is no government or state and there are no laws or law enforcement agencies to constrain the behavior of the individuals as they pursue their own self-interest. In resolving the competition which arises because of the scarcity of gold land, I will assume initially that the costs of entering into any contractual arrangement are prohibitive. In other words, it is not economical for two or more individuals to agree on anything. Personal violence is the only remaining alternative by which a person can exclude others from the land he is claiming for his own.

The concept of violence, or the use of physical force on another individual, is ambiguous. It could include the actual use of guns, knives or fists, or merely the threat of their use. It could also include the building of a fort or other protective structures. To clarify the concept as it will be

---

3. The methodology for developing theories of non-price rationing which generates refutable implications is described in Cheung (1974). The only other attempt to formulate an economic theory of anarchy that I know of was by Winston Bush (1972).

used here, and to simplify the analysis, violence will be defined as the labor time allocated to excluding other individuals from a piece of land.

The outcome of any competition between two miners over the same land will depend upon the amount of time each is willing to allocate and their relative abilities in the use of violence. For example, if two miners are equal in their ability to use violence, any conflict between them will be resolved according to the amount of labor time each allocates to fighting. If they each allocate two units of labor time, the outcome will be a draw. If one uses more labor time, he will be the winner. Similarly, if one miner is twice as proficient in the use of violence compared to another, he will have to use only half as much labor time as the other to achieve a draw.

To further simplify the analysis, assume that each miner can costlessly determine how much labor other miners are willing and able to allocate to a particular conflict. This assumption allows the resolution of a conflict without the actual use of scarce resources (labor time) in violence because no one would fight if the outcome were already known in advance. To illustrate, suppose two miners both want the exclusive rights to mine a given piece of land. If they are equal in their abilities to use violence, the rights to the land will go to the one who is willing and able to allocate the most labor to fighting. No fight will actually take place. The loser, knowing that he will lose, will just give up his claim to the land. This assumption has the added advantage of avoiding the theoretical problems of strategies, since each miner knows precisely how much violence the other is willing to use.

Finally, in order to concentrate attention on just one non-exclusive resource, I will assume that the exclusive rights to a miner's labor and the gold he extracts from the ground belong to him and are costlessly enforced private property. This assumes away anarchy in the most general sense and, as a result, the model proposed here can not explain how one individual could capture the rights to another's labor. This is not to say that a generalized theory of violence could not explain slavery. In fact, I am quite certain that personal force would be the most relevant constraint in any theory of slavery. Note however that the nature of the traditional economic model places an interesting constraint on the selection of assumptions. *We must assume initially that each individual has the right to some resource.* Without this assumption, the individual's decisions could not affect the allocation of anything and there would be no behavior to explain. This suggests that economic theory will never be able to examine anarchy as a state in which no one has the rights to anything. Furthermore, because the rights to one's labor are a prerequisite for implementing any decisions over non-human capital, we must assume the individual has some rights to his own labor. I have chosen the extreme form and assumed these labor rights are costlessly enforced.

A. The Initial Distribution of Homogeneous Land. To begin with,

FIGURE 1

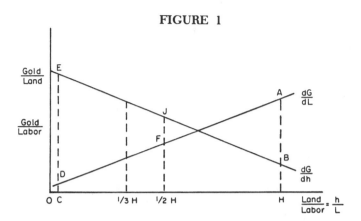

assume that there are two miners with identical production functions for gold mining and equal abilities in the use of violence. They are competing for the exclusive rights to work a limited amount of gold bearing land. With the aid of Figure 1, it is possible to demonstrate the equilibrium quantity of land going to each individual.

In this graph, the horizontal axis measures the ratio of land to labor (h/L) as inputs in the mining process. The vertical axis measures the marginal gold product of land ($\partial G/\partial h$) and labor ($\partial G/\partial L$). By assumption, the curves measuring marginal products are the same for both miners (X and Y) and diminishing returns are assumed for both inputs, land and labor. To further simplify the analysis, I shall assume that there is no aversion to the use of violence by either miner[4] and there are no work-leisure tradeoffs, so that each miner has a fixed amount of labor ($\overline{L}$) which he is willing to allocate to mining in this time period.

If miner Y were not present, X would claim exclusive rights to additional land as long as its marginal product was greater than zero. In this case, X is limited to the amount of land available which, by assumption, is OH. With OH land and $\overline{L}$ labor, the marginal product of land is equal to HB and the marginal product of labor is HA. The ratio HB/HA is the marginal rate of substitution between land and labor in the production of gold and gives us a measure of how much labor X is willing to allocate to maintain the exclusivity of his marginal unit of land. For example, if HB/HA equals $1/2$, the maximum labor units X would use in violence to protect the Hth land unit would be $1/2$.

Miner Y now enters the scene. To exclude X from one unit of land would require that he be willing to use at least $1/2$ units of labor in vio-

---

4. With this assumption the total cost of using force is the value of the gold which could have been mined with the time allocated to violence.

lence. To Y, with no land, the first unit would have a marginal product of CE while his marginal product of labor would be only CD. The ratio CE/CD is greater than HB/HA implying that Y is willing to use more labor than X in any conflict over the marginal land unit. From my previous assumptions, it follows that Y will acquire his first unit of land. Notice that this land was taken from X without the actual use of labor in violence. The threat of force was sufficient.

Because labor was never used in the acquisition of exclusive mining rights, each miner still has $\bar{L}$ labor to allocate to gold production. However, as long as Y values an additional unit of land (in terms of labor) more than X, land rights will be transferred from X to Y. Equilibrium will occur when the land is distributed in such a way that the marginal rates of substitution between land and labor for both X and Y are equal. Given the assumptions, this will be at 1/2H, where the land is divided evenly between the two miners.

This equilibrium can easily be generalized to a case with three or more miners. To demonstrate this, assume that X and Y each have 1/2H land when another identical miner (Z) enters. Z is now in the same position as Y was in the last example. With no land, he is willing to allocate CE/CD units of land to exclude X or Y from one unit of their land. Since this is more than either X or Y is willing to use to protect their marginal land, Z will acquire his first unit. This process will continue until each miner has 1/3H land. Here, they will each have the same marginal rate of substitution and further conflicts would result in a draw. More generally, with N homogeneous miners, the equilibrium would occur where each individual had 1/N units of land. *The theory implies that the total amount of homogeneous mining land will always be divided evenly among the competing miners.*

Before examining the equilibrium conditions for non-homogeneous inputs, two comments should be made concerning this model. First, I have made no distinction between the initial acquisition of land and the continued maintenance of exclusivity. While this distinction may be important, for now the threat of violence to exclude others is assumed to be a once and for all threat sufficient to maintain exclusivity throughout the time period underlying the production function. Second, it is assumed that the miner has the choice of using labor only in mining or violence. He has no other alternatives available. A more general theory, for example, may give him the option of allocating some of his labor time to improving his abilities to use violence. In effect, I am assuming that the cost of substituting at other margins is prohibitive.

   B. The Initial Distribution of Non-homogeneous Land. Assume miners X, Y, and Z are identical in their abilities to mine and to use violence. Based on their expectations of land productivity, they have initially distributed the mining rights evenly, with each getting 1/3H as shown in Figure 2. Because the curves here are the same as those in Figure 1, each miner has the same marginal rate of substitution and the equilibrium condition is satisfied.

Z unexpectedly discovers that his land is more productive than that of X or Y. Graphically, this would appear as a shift upward in $\partial G/\partial h$ for the land held by Z.[5] Even with this increase in the productivity of his land, Z is still in equilibrium because his willingness to use labor in violence to acquire additional (less productive) land has not changed.[6] However, Z's total gold yield, $ORK1/3H$, is now larger than the gold yield of X or Y so the other miners would be willing to give up their own land for the land Z is working. To simplify the analysis, assume that the decision to acquire rights to lands with different productivities is an all-or-nothing decision. No longer is it possible for X or Y to take marginal units of land from Z while keeping their original holdings.[7] If they want Z's land, they

FIGURE 2

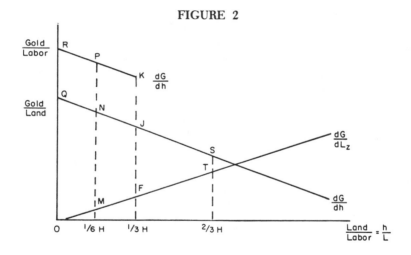

5. In Figure 2, the line representing Z's marginal product of labor ($\partial G/\partial L$) would also shift upward because as Z's land becomes more productive incremental labor units would add more to the total gold yield. However, there is assumed to be a change in the *relative* productivity of Z's land compared to that of labor so $\partial G/\partial h$ shifts more than $\partial G/\partial L$. (In terms of an isoquant mapping, the slope of the isoquant would now be different at each point). Since the horizontal axis in Figure 2 measures the ratio of land to labor, only the relative position of the marginal product curves is relevant, not the absolute position.

6. This is because the additional land units which he could take from the other miners have not increased in productivity. Therefore, his decision at the margin will remain unchanged. Note again that this shift in the marginal product curve is a relative shift as discussed in note 5 above.

7. This assumption is not as ad hoc as it appears. As I will show in the next section, it is dictated by the conditions which existed during the California gold rush. In the gold fields, lands with similar gold content were generally clustered together. This meant that the miners could acquire additional land without having to incur significant travel costs to actually mine their marginal acquisitions. Lands with measurably different gold content were usually separated by enough distance that it was not practical to acquire and mine lands of varying productivity. In this model, the all-or-nothing assumption is merely a proxy for prohibitive costs of moving between land holdings of different gold content.

have to give up all their prior claims to property and then use threats of violence to acquire some of the more productive land. Suppose Y decides to leave his land to threaten Z with violence. This will have two effects. First, this will leave X with the land vacated by Y, thus increasing his holdings to $2/3H$ and his gold yield to $OQS\ 2/3H$. Second, since Y and Z have the same capacity for mining and fighting, they will each get equal shares of Z's land or $1/6H$. Y and Z will each produce $ORP\ 1/6H$ units of gold, which I shall assume is equal to the total output of X. With this distribution of land, no individual has any incentive to move. Y and Z both would like extra units of the more productive land; but, since they are both willing to use the same amount of labor to exclude the other, any conflict would result in a draw. Furthermore, neither Y nor Z would leave their more productive land to get some of X's, because that would result in a decline in their total gold yield. This is an equilibrium[8] in which *individuals holding more productive land will get less land than others whose holdings are not so productive.*

Up to this point I have argued that the relevant constraint upon the initial distribution of property is violence. If individuals can not agree, they are left with only one alternative — the use of force. Any contractual arrangement entered into by wealth maximizers must assign to each individual the rights to at least as much property as they could get with personal force. Using the model developed under this constraint, it was possible to derive the amount of land to which any miner could claim exclusive rights. It follows from the above reasoning that if these miners form a contract which explicitly assigns land rights, the contractual distribution must conform to the following: more productive gold lands will be distributed in smaller parcels than land which is less productive; lands of equal productivity will be divided equally.

C. The Contract. While the distribution under anarchy places an important constraint on the initial endowment process, a closer examination of the contracting process itself is worthwhile. Like all contracts, the contract by which ownership rights are assigned is merely an instrument to facilitate some kind of exchange. In this case, one individual gives up any claim he might have made (through force) on other parcels of land in exchange for the agreement that other individuals will not exercise (through force) any claims on his assigned land. In negotiating the terms of this exchange, each miner will attempt to maximize the share of land he will be assigned, but he will be constrained by the competition of other miners. The assumption that the miners are homogeneous in their abilities

---

8. Notice that this equilibrium does not satisfy the same marginal conditions as earlier models. The miners now have different marginal rates of substitution because of the all-or-nothing assumption. The relevant decision margin is no longer one extra unit of land but the extra gold yield. To attack Y or Z, X must sacrifice his entire gold yield. He would do this only if his expected share of the more productive land would yield more gold than his current land. In other words, miners would leave their land to threaten Y and Z as long as their share of the more productive land yields a gold output in excess of what can be earned elsewhere.

to extract gold implies that each will be *willing* to pay the same price (in terms of the claims to other land which the potential owner must give up) for the rights to any given parcel of land. This is because the present value of the land will be the same for each miner. The assumption that they are homogeneous in their abilities to forcefully exclude others implies that each miner will be *able* to pay the same price for any given parcel. This is because each has an equal claim to any parcel. Together, they imply that the outcome of bargaining for the ownership rights will be such that homogeneous land will have the same price and thus, be evenly distributed among the contracting parties. Richer lands, because they will command a higher price (in terms of the claims to other poorer land which the bidder must forego), will be held in smaller parcels.[9]

To this point I have argued that the initial distribution of ownership rights among individuals can be derived from a traditional economic model. These rights are assigned to individuals through contract and the precise allocation is determined by competition. In this contract each miner is given, by the other miners, the exclusive rights to a parcel of land. In exchange, this miner must give up any claims he may have on remaining land and agree to respect the exclusive rights of the other miners. The assumptions made here imply *that contracts which stipulate original endowments will provide a distribution of ownership rights such that there is an inverse relationship between the value (per unit) of the land and the size of the parcel allowed any one individual.*

Before concluding this section, it might be of some value to examine the role of force in this model. Perhaps the study of violence is misleading or, at best, redundant. After all, the implication that homogeneous miners would, in equilibrium, have equal shares of land could just as easily be derived from the general constraint of competition. Under this constraint miners would eliminate any excess earnings until everyone was receiving a normal return. Since all income, in my model, is derived from mineral land, the equilibrium condition would be for everyone to have equal shares of homogeneous land. Granting that this is correct, what is gained by the study of violence?

Competition, in the most general sense, exists whenever two or more individuals are trying to get something which only one can have. Any action which generates net benefits greater than that of any alternative will be extended, by wealth maximizers, until the excess is eliminated. If all of the inputs required for this activity are homogeneous, then the income will be divided evenly among competitors. However, when this implication is tested against the real world, a problem arises. No two individuals are identical in all respects. The same is true of land, machines or any other set of inputs. If a theory is to be useful it must specify the

9. Notice that this analysis also suggests that 1) individuals who have a comparative advantage in the use of force will be endowed with more land than other individuals and 2) individuals who have a comparative advantage in mining will be endowed with less land than other miners.

conditions under which it can be tested. In this case, it should indicate what characteristics within any input set should be similar or approximately homogeneous. For example, if resources are to be allocated according to the order in which one finishes a long distance run, the relevant characteristics for predicting who gets how much would be speed and stamina. On the other hand, if competition is to take place on a billiard table, speed and stamina are probably irrelevant. In the absence of any contractual agreements, competition for scarce goods must take the form of individual violence, or the use of force, to exclude potential claimants from property. Given the point in time, the relevant characteristics can be determined and implications derived and tested. As I already pointed out, the theory developed here also allows us to make predictions about the distribution of rights when individuals are not equal in their abilities to use force. Unfortunately, in the California gold rush period, which I shall describe in detail later, I could find no evidence indicating any significant variance between miners in their violence capabilities. Therefore, the test which I will be using could be viewed as a test of a more general theory of competition with the individuals' potential for force serving as an explicit test condition.

   D. Coalitions, Prior Wealth and the Test Conditions. Previously, it was assumed that the costs of acquiring and maintaining exclusivity with personal force are not significantly different from the costs of assigning and enforcing rights through contract. This made it possible to ignore the problem of coalitions. To illustrate the nature of this problem, assume that there are ten homogeneous miners negotiating for the distribution of one hundred homogeneous units of land. The hypothesis presented here implies that if all ten miners negotiate simultaneously for the land, each will get ten units. However, what if nine of the miners enter into a coalition and agree to reduce the land allotment to the tenth miner? They could try to reduce his holdings to zero but, if transaction costs are insignificant, the tenth miner can successfully negotiate for a parcel of land equal in value to the costs which the coalition must incur to exclude him. If, as I assumed, the agreement among the nine colluding miners does not significantly reduce their costs of excluding, then the tenth miner can still claim for himself the same amount of land as he could if there had been no coalition. [10]

   There is one final consideration before examining the empirical test. Would the initial contractual allocation of land be different if one indi-

---

   10. This assumption is identical to merely assuming away any gains from forming a coalition contract. On closer examination, this problem is more general than it might first appear. Any time an exchange takes place between two maximizers it must be because there are net gains. How will these net gains be distributed between the trading parties? Typically, we employ a Walrasian auctioneer, or his counterpart "perfect competition," to generate a determinate distribution of the gains from exchange. More recently the theories of the core, theories of game strategy and theories of bargaining have emerged. The variety of assumptions included in these models sometimes constrain the negotiation process such that a single solution derives. To avoid making this paper much longer than it already is, I have chosen this much simpler assumption. I could just as easily have assumed a Walrasian auctioneer and achieved the same results.

vidual came into the mining area with some previously acquired wealth and used it to buy either specialists in the use of force (hired guns) or labor to mine his land? While the answer to this question is probably yes, it will not be considered in this paper because the model proposed here assumes that each miner comes into the gold fields with nothing except his own labor. We are trying to explain how he then acquires wealth in the form of gold land. The existence of prior wealth violates one of the assumptions of the model. Of course, by assuming this possibility away, we are placing an additional constraint on the empirical test conditions. However, as I will show in the next section, this is not a problem in the California gold rush.

In testing the implications derived in this section, it is necessary to find a situation which conforms in essential aspects to the assumed constraints of the hypothesis. For example, we must find a piece of land to which no individuals have the enforcible rights to exclude others. The use of this land must be unconstrained by any prior contractual arrangements, including private contract or government law. Any agreement which the group does form must explicitly assign exclusive land rights to each individual in a manner which is measurable for testing. The individuals must be relatively homogeneous with respect to their abilities to produce from the land the finished product and their abilities to forcefully exclude others from the land. Finally, the constraints must be such that no individual purchases other labor units for mining or enforcement purposes. When these conditions are met, the hypothesis is testable.

In the next section, I will show that in the California gold rush of 1848 the actual state of affairs came remarkably close to satisfying the theoretical constraints. In fact, it came so close that one might think me guilty of ad hoc theorizing. In actuality, I did construct the theory with some knowledge of the conditions in California during the gold rush. I deliberately made assumptions which closely conformed with those conditions. For example, the assumptions about no prior wealth, no slavery and the all-or-nothing decision on claims of differing productivity were made knowing that they roughly approximated the real events. In this sense the theory is ad hoc. However, *the theory was formalized and the implications derived before I had acquired any of the actual contracts. In other words, the data obtained from the miners' contracts could have refuted the theory and in this sense was not ad hoc.*

III. TEST CONDITIONS[11]

A. *The Laws Regarding the Acquisition of Mining Rights.* The lands now included in the state of California belonged to Mexico until 1846 when United States troops took over and declared military rule. The

---

11. This section contains only an abbreviated account of the events leading up to the establishment of private ownership rights to California gold land. For the reader who is interested in a much more detailed description of these events see Umbeck (1977).

peace treaty which ended this Mexican-American conflict in 1848 gave all non-privately owned property to the U.S. federal government. While this new territory included almost all of what was soon to be one of the richest gold fields in the world, there were no federal laws regulating the private acquisition of exclusive rights to mineral lands.[12]

The discovery which started the famous gold rush was made on January 24, 1848, nine days before the signing of the peace treaty. Shortly thereafter, the U.S. military governor of California decreed "From and after this date, the Mexican laws and customs now prevailing in California relative to [the acquisition of private mining rights on public lands] are hereby abolished." No alternatives were offered.[13]

There were no federal laws constraining an individual in the use of gold land until 1866 when the U.S. Congress passed a bill allowing miners to claim exclusive rights which would be recognized and enforced by the federal government.[14] However, even had there been prior legal constraints, they probably could not have been enforced during the early gold rush years because most of the local and federal law enforcers in California deserted to the gold fields. The military governor wrote:

> . . . If sedition and rebellion should arise, where is my force to meet it? Two companies of regulars, every day diminishing by desertions, that cannot be prevented, will soon be the only military force in California . . . In the meantime, however, should the people refuse to obey the existing authorities . . . my force is inadequate to compel obedience.[15]

As information concerning the discovery spread, the population in the gold fields increased. By the end of August, 1848, the number of miners was estimated at somewhere between 5 and 10 thousand. One year later, after the famous rush of 1849 which brought people from nearly every country in the world, the population was thought to be over one hundred thousand and, within two more years this figure reached a quarter of a million.[16]

Immediately following the discovery, the first miners worked independently of one another. They would travel and live in small groups, but the actual mining was done on an individual basis. These first miners found gold bearing land to exist over an area three hundred miles long

12. Gregory Yale (1867, pp. 325-354). See also the *American Law of Mining*, Vol. 1, Cumulative Supplement (1973, pp. 17-39).

13. Yale (1867, p. 17).

14. Lindley (1903).

15. Letter from the military governor to the adjutant general on August 19, 1848, in Williams (1921, p. 61).

16. A complete discussion of population estimates through immigration reports, election returns and census reports will be found in Langley and Mathews, (1859, pp. 119-122, 184-189).

and one hundred miles wide along the western foothills of the Sierra Mountains. Throughout 1848, with the relatively abundant gold land and the relatively small number of miners, there were no indications that anyone explicitly claimed exclusive rights to a particular piece of land. Most of the miners carried guns, yet the reports of violence during the early period are remarkably scarce.[17] Apparently, it was less costly to move to new land than to fight.

With the huge population increase of 1849, gold land became relatively scarce and the potential for conflict increased. However, instead of violence, the miners chose to enter into explicit contractual arrangements with all those present at a particular gold deposit. In these contracts, it was provided that each individual was to get a parcel of land of specified size. As long as the miner worked this parcel, called a "claim," at stipulated intervals, he had exclusive rights to the land and all the gold contained. The following account is fairly representative of the actual allocation process.

> The first workers on the bar had taken up claims of a generous size, and soon the whole bar was occupied. The region was full of miners and they came pouring down upon the river, attracted by the reports of a rich strike, until their tents and campfires presented the appearance of a vast army. Those without claims far exceeded in number the fortunate ones. A miners' meeting was called to make laws. Majority ruled in a mining camp in those days, and it was voted to cut down the size of claims to forty feet. The claim owners were powerless to resist, but had to admit to the fiat of the majority. The miners were then registered in the order of the date of their arrival upon the bar, and in that order were allowed to select claims until all were taken. Even then there was a great crowd of disappointed ones.[18]

While it was usually stipulated that the group would help enforce each others rights, the individual miner would frequently stake out his claim with wooden posts and to these attach a written notice identifying himself as the claimant and warning others to stay away. For example,

> All and everybody, this is my claim, fifty feet on the gulch, cordin to Clear Creek District Law, backed up by shotgun amendments.[19]
> ... any person found trespassing on this claim will be persecuted to the full extent of the law. This is no monkey tale butt I will assert my rites at the pint of the sicks shirter if leagally necessary so taik head and good warnin.[20]

17. See the letter from the military governor in which he reports his observations concerning law and order in Bryant (1876, pp. 458-462). Most of the writers from this period agree that this was a relatively peaceful time in California history. Of course, this does not mean violence was not used. The loser in a violent confrontation would not be around to complain.

18. Farriss and Smith (1971, p. 287).

19. Shinn (1884, p. 558).

20. Shinn (1884, p. 559).

The land claimed by the groups of miners came to be known as mining districts. Each time a new deposit was discovered, a group of miners would rush to the site and form a new district through explicit contract. It is estimated that between 1848 and 1866 there were nearly five hundred independent mining districts established, each with its own unique distribution of land among the contracting parties. Copies of many of these original contracts are still available and provide the data necessary for testing my hypothesis.

B. *The Technology of Force.* The types of weapons available in 1848, while simple in comparison to modern nuclear arms, would still take some time to describe. Fortunately, this is not necessary because the theory developed in Part II suggests that it was the individual's *relative* ability to use force that was important. The conclusion derived here, that miners' relative abilities in the use of force did not differ significantly, is based on two observations. First, weapons such as cannons or rockets were not used in the gold fields. Walls were not constructed around claims nor were jails built. The pistol, which nearly every miner wore,[21] was the primary instrument for maintaining exclusivity. While some men probably could use the gun with greater accuracy or speed than others, I suspect that the variance in ability was not large. The six shooter was not called "the equalizer" for nothing. Second, this conclusion is further substantiated by the observation that the miners did not hire specialists in force to help them maintain their exclusive land rights.[22] In order for specialization to occur, an individual must have a comparative advantage at least large enough to offset the transaction costs associated with specialization: that specialization was not observed indicates that little if any such advantage existed. From these two observations, I would conclude that any variance in the miners' abilities to use force was not significant.

C. *The Technology of Mining.* From 1848 until the mid 1860's, the vast majority of mining operations in California were in placer deposits. These deposits were superficial accumulations of gold dust and small nuggets which had been eroded away from a gold vein by the action of moving water. The gold particles were then carried down from the Sierras by the streams and rivers and eventually, when the current slowed, came to rest on a sand bar or along the banks.[23]

Prior to 1850, the mining technology was limited to the pan and the cradle. The former was a shallow dish, usually made out of tin, about 18 inches in diameter and 3 inches deep with gently sloping sides. Gold bearing soil or "paydirt" was dug out of the ground with a pick and

21. This fact is testified to by nearly every observer during this period. See Hittell (1898, p. 46); Mansfield (1918, p. 103); Marryat, (1855, p. 123).

22. In not one account, by either miner or historian, can I find any mention of a specialist in violence. Many districts appointed mayors or Alcaldes who served as judges in determining whether or not district laws had been violated, but these men never served to enforce the law by themselves. For a detailed account of these men, see Shinn, (1885, pp. 78-117, 167-190).

23. Hittell, (1861).

shovel, placed in the pan and submerged under slowly moving water. By applying a circular motion to the pan, the lighter dirt was washed away leaving only the heavier gold flakes. The latter was a wooden box about forty inches long, twenty inches wide and four inches deep. This rested on rockers, like a child's cradle, with the head of the box elevated above the lower end. At the head was placed another box, called a riddle box, which had a bottom made of sheet iron perforated with holes about one-half inch in diameter. Dirt was thrown into the riddle box and water added while the cradle was rocked. The smaller sized rocks, sand, dirt and gold fell through the perforations to the floor of the cradle where there was fastened a set of cleats. The water washed the dirt out the lower end, leaving the heavier gold and sand trapped behind the cleats. Two or three times a day the cleats were cleaned with a spoon. This residual was then washed in a pan to separate the gold from the remaining impurities. In 1850 it was discovered that by lengthening the cradle the rocking motion was no longer required. This longer, stationary trough became known as a "sluice" and greatly reduced the costs of extracting gold. Because the rockers were not necessary, the sluice could be made much larger to facilitate the processing of huge quantities of paydirt. With this invention, the primary constraints on the production of gold were getting enough water and dirt to the sluice. Water was brought to the sluice by way of wooden troughs, and dirt was moved with the shovel, bucket, wagon and a lot of sweat until 1852 when hydraulic mining was discovered. Very simply, hydraulic mining involved directing a high pressure stream of water from a hose against the side of a hill containing paydirt. The water washed the dirt directly into the sluice, over the cleats and out the lower end, thus combining all of the operations into one.[24]

The apparent simplicity of the mining process is confirmed by numerous accounts from the miners themselves. They claimed that just a couple of hours practice with the pan or cradle could make anyone proficient in its use. However, while a high I.Q. or the coordination of an acrobat might not have been a prerequisite for survival in the mining business, certainly endurance was. Using a pick and shovel in temperatures approaching 100 degrees, washing dirt in rivers formed from melting glaciers, subsisting on a diet of questionable nutritional content and living in unsanitary conditions quickly destroyed the weak and the sickly. In fact, just the rigors of the voyage to California, whether by boat or foot, killed many potential miners before they reached the gold fields, eliminating all but the strongest.[25] When combined with a relatively simple mining technology, hard work and disease had the effect of reducing the variance in the abilities of the individuals to mine gold.

The theoretical implications derived in part I were based upon the

24. Probably the best non-technical description of the various mining techniques is found in Hittell (1863).

25. Moerenhout (1885) and Howe (1923).

assumption that individuals were homogeneous with respect to mining skills. This assumption appears to have been closely approximated in the California gold rush. However, the theory also assumed that no individual had significant prior wealth such that he could hire additional miners and possibly alter the derived implications. This condition was also satisfied in the time period under investigation. Two observations support this conclusion. First, several wealthy individuals residing on the east coast financed mining companies to go to California. On average, these companies consisted of forty to fifty persons who were to mine gold as a group and share it with their financial backers remaining in the states. Well documented accounts of these companies reveal that most did not survive as a group long enough to reach California. Those that did, soon disbanded, forsaking their original agreement and each individual worked for himself.[26] Enforcement costs being prohibitively high, the east coast financiers did little to recoup their losses. Second, in all of the available records from the gold fields, there are only a few accounts of contracts in which one miner hired another to work for him.[27] Actually, these few contracts involved the hiring of local Indians to search for gold. The gold they found was then purchased from them in exchange for blankets, pans, beads, etc. These observations suggest that there is little reason to suppose that prior wealth had any significant impact on the initial distribution of land in the California gold rush.

IV. EMPIRICAL TESTS

While individuals did not appear to differ significantly in their abilities to mine or to use force, the gold yield per square foot of land reportedly had a large variance throughout the gold fields.[28] Given these observations, if the hypothesis is correct, we should observe that any mining contract which assigned individuals the exclusive rights to mine a particular piece of land would have specified an inverse relationship between the productivity of the land and the claim size initially allowed each miner. Furthermore, where land in a district was equally productive, the allowed claim size would have been the same for everyone. If these relationships are not observed, the theory is refuted. However, before presenting the data obtained from the mining contracts, there is one additional point which requires some discussion.

Because the gold was usually found below the surface soil, the gold yield of a piece of land could have been determined only by actual mining operations. Before mining began, however, the land had to be divided up

---

26. Moerenhout (1885); Howe (1923); Hughes (1937).

27. Coy (1948, p. 42); Hittell (1899, p. 129); Mansfield (1918, pp. 43,46); Bryant (1876, pp. 454, 461); Bancroft (1888, p. 92 and note 14); Buffum (1859, pp. 93-94, 128, 129).

28. Numerous reports from the miners themselves indicate that it was not unusual for one miner to discover thousands of dollars worth of gold within a space of ten feet square while his neighbor, working the adjacent land found nothing. Many of these reports can be found in Bancroft (1888).

among competing miners. Therefore, the size of the claim, as provided in contract, would have depended on the *expected* yield and not the actual yield after mining. While expectations are not observable, the theory may still be testable if we can identify some observable variable which would have a predictable effect on the miners' expectations. Fortunately, an examination of the mining technology and the geological process by which the placer deposits were formed reveals such a variable: the distance separating a claim from a source of water.

Previously it was noted that most of the placer deposits were formed by the actions of moving water. The miners soon discovered that the richest deposits lay near the beds of rivers. There were exceptions to this. Over time, some of the prehistoric rivers had considerably altered course after depositing their gold so that a few very rich gold fields were found in dry areas. However, as a rule, these would not have been as productive as those with water. This is because gold is heavier than most of the surrounding elements and has a tendency to settle over time, working its way into the surface soil until it comes to rest on the bedrock. The continued action of water would have eroded away much of the topsoil and laid bare the bedrock, thus reducing the work required to obtain the gold. Miners working on the flat land just above the river had to remove anywhere from four to twenty feet of topsoil before reaching the paydirt and diggings in the hills, farther from the river bed, sometimes went as deep as one or two hundred feet before striking bedrock.[29] In general, it can be concluded that land near the water would have had more gold and could have been mined at a lower cost than land farther from the water.

To further substantiate this conclusion, the brief survey of the technology of placer mining disclosed the fact that the pan, the cradle, the sluice and hydraulic mining all required water as an input in the production process. Easy access to a large supply of water significantly reduced mining costs. Therefore, given this technological constraint and the geological process by which placer deposits were formed, it is possible to divide the mining claims into four categories, similar to those used by the miners, and rank them in order of decreasing *expected* productivity: 1) Claims located by the side of a stream or river which were usually called "wet" or "bar" claims;   2) Claims located in a gulch or ravine which had water flowing through it part of the year;   3) Claims located on a "flat" just above the water level which could obtain water by constructing a ditch or a flume from a nearby river to their mining site; 4) Claims located on a hill where paydirt had to be carted to the water or water pumped up to the claim.

A. Evidence. Restating my hypothesis in light of the preceding observations, the claim size, as stipulated by the district contract, would have increased with the distance from the water. Where the district was located

29. A description of the geological conditions found in hundreds of individual mining districts can be found in Clark (1970), and Browne (1887).

such that all the claims were about the same distance from water, the claim sizes would have been uniform.

The evidence I offer was obtained from an empirical investigation of the provisions found in the contracts governing 106 different placer districts.[30] This represents about 35 percent of the estimated placer districts formed in California between 1848 and 1866.[31] As I indicated above, in many of these contracts the miners chose to categorize claims as follows: wet claims, gulch or ravine claims, flat claims and hill claims.[32] The dimension measured in every placer mining contract was surface area, and in most cases the length and width was explicitly stipulated. Some problems arose, however, in the measurement of gulch and hill claims. Gulch claims were frequently specified in length along the gulch, with the width limited by the banks on either side. This made it difficult to discern from the contract exactly how large a gulch claim was. Based on the reports of early geological surveyors, photographs found in the county histories[33] and the data contained in some of the contracts themselves, it is safe to assume that in most cases these gulches, ravines and creeks rarely exceeded 50 feet in width and were usually narrower. Similarly, there was a problem in measuring hill claims. Many of the districts measured these claims in "feet along the front of the hill and extending into the hill indefinitely" or "to the center of the hill." Again, basing my figures on early geological reports, contracts, photographs and information derived from early accounts,[34] the distance to the center of a hill seldom could have been less than 400 feet. Where the contract provided no specified limit on the length of these hill claims, I assumed they were unbounded and left to the miners' discretion as long as they remained within the boundaries of the district.

The data indicates that out of 106 placer districts, 43 chose to contractually differentiate between claim locations with respect to water. With few exceptions they appear to have followed the predicted pattern. Wet claims are usually the smallest, followed by gulch claims, flat claims and hill claims. A simple Chi Square test shows that the observed alloca-

30. The sources for all of these contracts and charts summarizing the important provisions in each can be found in Umbeck, forthcoming.

31. Because of the "rushing" of the miners from one gold deposit to another it is difficult to determine exactly how many districts were actually formed. Most historians put the figure at around five hundred but this includes nearly two hundred quartz mining districts.

32. There was actually one other category called a "river claim." Such claims were created when the miners diverted a river into a ditch, by means of a dam, and worked the exposed river bed. These beds were often very rich in gold but the high costs of constructing a dam and digging a ditch would have partially offset the gains from the higher gold yield and the proximity to water. As a result, I am unable to rank, ex ante, the expected net yield of "river claims" compared to dryer claims. For this reason they were not included in the study.

33. *The Mining Magazine*, (New York: 1854, p. 185), Browne (1887, p. 239, Clark (1970, pp. 34, 35, 48, 76, 99, 104, 135, 142, 175).

34. Browne (1887, pp. 65, 93, 97, 239), Clark (1970, pp. 67, 76, 77, 100, 197, 134, 144, 145).

tion of land is significantly (at the .01 level) different from a random distribution.

The remaining 63 districts had no contractual provisions for discriminating by location. Judging from descriptions contained in the contracts themselves and information from geological surveys,[35] the land within each of these districts appears to have been roughly homogeneous with respect to the characteristics I have enumerated. For example, the contract for Empire Hill district provided that "the claim allowed each person upon this hill shall be one hundred feet square," indicating that all were hill diggings. Little Humbug Creek provided "that the claims on Little Humbug shall be one hundred yards in length extending up and down the creek, and shall be one hundred and fifty feet in width," indicating that claims in this district were on the creek. Greely Flat allowed "that all claims in this district be 200 feet long by 200 feet wide with a right of way to Robinson Hill, Strawberry Garden Bluffs or to Feather River of 20 feet wide for a cart road to haul pay dirt for the purpose of washing it." This suggests that all the claims were on a flat near several water sources. All of these districts allowed for a uniform claim size.

The hypothesis has not been refuted by the evidence. It appears that the size of the claim, as provided by contract, and the expected productivity of the land were inversely related.

B.   An Alternative Test. A second test of the theory is provided by the observation that 21 of the districts for which I have records allowed for a different claim size on land that had been mined previously.[36] Of these districts, 13 made allowances through a revision of the original contract, while eight districts provided exceptions for reworked land in the original agreement. Because it has been mined once, reworked land would have had a lower expected yield per square foot. The hypothesis implies that claims allowed on reworked land will be larger than on virgin land. This is the case without exception. To further substantiate this, observers during this period have reported that, in general, districts allowed a miner more land on reworked ground than on new ground.[37]

---

35. Browne (1887); Clark (1970).

36. It is difficult to understand why land, once worked, would become vacant so that another miner could claim it by pre-emption. There are three possible explanations. Early districts reportedly prohibited the sale of claims. Therefore, if a miner decided to leave the district, he had to leave the claim open to pre-emption by another miner. Second, it is possible that a claim was found to be so poor that it was not worth searching for a buyer, especially not when rich strikes were being reported elsewhere. Third, miners died. If they had no partner, the claim was open.

37. Bean (1867, p. 30); Coy (1948, p. 56); Shinn (1885, p. 111); Hittell (1898, p. 252); Bancroft (1888, p. 398, note 47).

V. CONCLUSIONS

As I stated in the beginning, the purpose of this paper was to explain the formation and initial distribution of rights to scarce resources. The model, based on the constraint of competition through force, was capable of generating propositions which could be tested under certain, well defined conditions. While I was fortunate enough to find these conditions closely approximated in the California gold rush, the empirical tests are certainly very limited. Any attempt to test the theory on the emergence of private ownership rights in modern countries would be plagued with numerous empirical problems. For example, most rights arose hundreds or even thousands of years ago. Locating reliable data would be most difficult. Also, in many cases these rights were developed slowly over the course of many years. During this time the constraints may have undergone significant changes making any ceteris paribus assumptions questionable. Despite the limited empirical tests available, the hypothesis does suggest some implications which are relevant to the modern world.

First, it implies that all private ownership rights are ultimately founded upon the ability to forcefully exclude potential competitors. Force, not fairness, determines the distribution of wealth in a society. While I could have assumed that each miner in California wanted to divide up the land fairly, such that everyone received a claim to the same amount of wealth, this could not explain why every mining district had provisions for punishing claim "jumpers" and excluding outsiders in their bid for some of the already claimed land. Any individual or group of individuals who wish to maintain their ownership rights to scarce resources must continually be willing and able to forcefully exclude all competitors.

Second, in considering possible income redistribution programs, account must be taken not only of the political problems and the work incentive effects but also the potential use of force as individuals readjust their wealth positions. I suspect that economists have so long assumed that the initial distribution of wealth is given arbitrarily that we have come to think of this process as random. As such, wealth can be easily redistributed since there are no particularly powerful forces working to maintain the initial allocation. To the contrary, this paper suggests that the initial allocation is not a random process and any reallocation program which assigns to individuals less wealth than they could have through the use of their own force will be a costly failure.

As I pointed out earlier, there is one serious shortcoming in this paper. It does not provide a good test for a theory of force, only a more general theory of competition as a constraint on the allocative process. That the potential use of force by an individual is a relevant constraint in determining the initial allocation of wealth is not only intuitively plausible but is also suggested by the theory offered here. And while casual empiricism indicates that force (threatened or actual) was an important factor in the

California gold fields, the actual empirical test in this paper is not a good test of a theory of force. This is because the assumed and observed variance in the ability to use force was insignificant, so all observed distribution patterns were attributable only to differences in land values. To test for the actual importance of force we would need to find a situation where this variance was relatively large. Then we could determine whether or not the most forceful individuals received more wealth than those who were relatively weak. This is a problem for future research.

REFERENCES

Alchian, A.A., and Allen, W.R., *Exchange and Production, Theory in Use,* 1st ed., Wadsworth Publishing Co., Inc. Belmont, 1969.

Bancroft, H.H., *History of the Pacific States,* Vol. 18, The History Company, San Francisco, 1888.

Bean, E., *Bean's History and Directory of Nevada County,* California, Daily Gazette Book and Job Office, Calif., 1867.

Brown, J.R., *Report on the Mineral Resources of the States and Territories West of the Rocky Mountains,* D. Appleton and Co., Washington, 1887.

Bryant, E., *What I Saw in California,* Lewis Osborn, Calif., 1876.

Buffum, E.G., *Six Months in the Gold Mines,* The Ward Ritchie Press, Calif., 1859.

Bush, W., "Individual Welfare in Anarchy," in *Explorations in the Theory of Anarchy,* ed. by Gordon Tullock, Center for the Study of Public Choice, VPI & SU, Virginia, 1972.

Cheung, S.N.S., "A Theory of Price Control," *Journal of Law and Economics,* April 1974.

Clark, W.B., *Gold Districts of California,* Bulletin 193, California Division of Mines and Geology, San Francisco, 1970.

Coy, O.C., *In the Diggings in Forty-Nine,* The California State Historical Association, Los Angeles, 1948.

Hittell, J., *Mining in the Pacific States of North America,* San Francisco, 1861.

_____, *The Resources of California,* A. Roman and Co., Calif., 1863.

Hittell, T., *History of California,* Vol. 4, Stone and Co., Calif., 1898.

Howe, O.T., *Argonauts of '49, History and Adventures of the Emigrant Companies From Massachusetts, 1849-1850,* Harvard University Press, Cambridge, 1923.

Hughes, M., *The Argonaut Mining Companies of 1849-1850,* unpublished thesis, University of California, Berkeley, 1937.

Langley and Mathews, *The State Register and Yearbook of Facts for 1857,* San Francisco, 1859.

Lindley, C., *A Treatise on the American Law Relating to Mines and Mineral Lands,* Vol. 1, Bancroft-Whitney Co., San Francisco, 1903.

Mansfield, G.C., *The History of Butte County,* California, Historic Record Co., Los Angeles, 1918.

Marryat, F., *Mountains and Molehills: or Recollections of a Burnt Journal,* J.B. Lippencott Co., New York, 1855.

Moerenhout, J.R., *The Inside Story of the Gold Rush,* translated by Abraham Naseter, California Historical Society, Special Publications, No. 8, San Francisco, 1885.

Shinn, C., *Land Laws of Mining Districts,* Johns Hopkins University, 1884.

——————, *Mining Camps: A Study in American Frontier Government*, Charles Scribner's Sons, New York, 1885.

Umbeck, J., "The California Gold Rush: A Study of Emerging Property Rights," *Explorations in Economic History*, August, 1977.

——————, *A Theory of Property Rights with Special Application to the California Gold Rush*, forthcoming, Iowa State Univeristy Press.

Williams, M.F., *History of the San Francisco Committee of Vigilance of 1851*, University of California Press, California, 1921.

Yale, G., *Legal Titles to Mining Claims and Water Rights in California, Under the Mining Law of Congress of July 1866*, A. Roman and Co., San Francisco, 1867.

The American Law of Mining, Vol. 1, Cumulative Supplement, ed. by the Rocky Mountain Mineral Law Foundation, Mathew Bender and Co., Inc., New York, 1973.

The Mining Magazine, New York, 1854.

Reproduction of Fariss and Smith's History of Plumas, Lassen and Sierra Counties, California, Howell and North Books, Berkeley, 1971.

PART III

THE ECONOMIC THEORY OF PROPERTY RIGHTS

[10]

Introduction to Chapters 11, 12, 13, 14 and 15

The mark of a capitalist society is that resources are owned and allocated by such nongovernmental organizations as firms, households and markets. (Armen Alchian and Harold Demsetz, 'Production, Information Costs, and Economic Organization', *American Economic Review* 62, December 1972, p. 777.)

To say that we live in a world of uncertainty and incomplete information means that people continuously create and disseminate knowledge about opportunities for exchange and innovation. The subjective perceptions individuals form about their opportunity sets and the cost of trade-offs must differ from one person to another. In order to create testable propositions about the world in which we live, economic analysis must then separate discussion about abstract values from cognition. Karl Brunner wrote:

We observe with rising frequency ... an implicit denial of cognition, or a serious confusion between articulated valuations and substantive knowledge. . . . The contemporary concern for values may have permeated our social fabric sufficiently to assume almost the form of a counter-revolution to the cognitive revolution initiated centuries ago. . . . The sacrifice of cognition is particularly easy to detect in objections to the market system induced by discrepancies between one's desires, usually glorified as social values, and the result of market processes. . . . My moral indignation only reveals that I prefer another state of the world to the state actually observed. . . . But our ability to visualize 'better' states more closely reflecting our preferences yields no evidence that this state can be realized.[1]

The importance of Brunner's message is hard to exaggerate. Members of the intellectual community such as Durkheim, Galbraith and Vanek have been selling their 'social values' to the public as if those values were cognitive statements about our world. By ignoring the only source of valuation: *the individual*, these scholars have, in effect, been supplying public policy makers with the philosophical rationale and social justification for wealth-reducing institutional changes. The relevant choice for a free society is not between two or more frictionless blackboard models, or between a hazy vision of things that would be nice to have and the prevailing system with all of its shortcomings and problems. The relevant choice is between two or more imperfect systems.

In Chapters 11 through 15, Armen Alchian, Benjamin Klein, Yoram Barzel, and Armen Alchian and Susan Woodward internalize into a theoretical framework: (i) the development and creation of property rights, (ii) the effects of alternative property rights on the costs of transactions and incentive structures, (iii) the effects of the costs of transactions and incentives on economic behavior, and (iv) the evidence for refutable implications of those effects. In the process, they contribute to the development of the economic theory of property rights.

By emphasizing the effects of property rights on transaction costs and incentives, the economic theory of property rights has been able to avoid the limitations of neoclassical economics. For example, analytical tools of neoclassical economics such as downward-sloping investment schedules and upward-sloping supply schedules are predictable behavioral consequences of the incentive effects in private-property, free-market economies. The incentive effects of private property rights embodied in those analytical tools are not operative under alternative property rights arrangements.[2] Yet, research has consistently applied neoclassical analytical tools to nonprivate property economies with misleading results.[3] That is why the system of central planning in the former USSR, codetermination in Germany, the labor-managed economy in former Yugoslavia, and the welfare system in Sweden have always performed better in classrooms and academic articles than in real life.

An implication is that with uncertainty and incomplete knowledge, property rights matter. On this point, Ronald Coase has enriched our knowledge. The Coase theorem says that (i) clearly defined private property rights are an essential requirement for resolving the conflict of interest among individuals via market exchange, and (ii) an efficient allocation of resources is independent of the initial assignment of property rights as long as transaction costs are insignificant.

Transaction costs are usually defined as the costs of all resources required to transfer property rights from one economic agent to another. They include the costs of making an exchange (e.g., discovering exchange opportunities, negotiating exchange, monitoring, and enforcement) and the costs of maintaining and protecting the institutional structure (e.g., judiciary, police, armed forces). Obviously, zero transaction costs are exceptions rather than the rule. Thus, the initial assignment of property rights does affect the allocation of resources.

Coase's objective is not to discuss the 'what ifs' as though the costs of transaction were zero. Coase's world is the world in which we live – that is, the world of positive transaction costs affecting the values of other economic variables in the system: 'The reason why economists went wrong', he says, 'was that their theoretical system did not take into account a factor which is essential if one wishes to analyze the effect of a change in the law on the allocation of resources. This missing factor is the existence of transaction costs.'[4]

Coase reserves his sharpest criticism for current trends in economic analysis to substitute mathematical formalism (largely independent from any reality) for the cognitive comprehension of our world. This is what he said about William Baumol's research on taxes and welfare:

> Apparently what Baumol meant by saying that, 'taken on its own grounds, the con-clusions of Pigovian tradition are, in fact, impeccable', was that its logic was impeccable and that, if its taxation proposals were carried out, which they cannot be, the allocation of resources would be optimal. This I have never denied. My point was simply that such tax proposals are the stuff that dreams are made of. In my youth it was said that what was too silly to be said may be sung. In modern economics it may be put into mathematics.[5]

The economics of property rights has developed the theory of the firm as the key organization explaining economic performance under alternative property rights structures. The theory starts from a simple premise that teamwork is an efficient method for organizing production and that firms exist because they are the organizations for teamwork. In Chapter 15 Armen Alchian and Susan Woodward capture the essence of this new theory of the firm as the theory has evolved over the last twenty-five years.

Notes

1. Karl Brunner, 'Knowledge, Values and the Choice of Economic Organization', *Kyklos* 23, 1970, pp. 560–65.
2. For example, Vanek's claim that external financing of investments could make labor-managed firms efficient depends on the assumption that the rate of interest in a labor-managed economy could perform the same function it performs in free-market, private-property economies. He ignores the transaction costs of having the rate of interest express the present prices of capital goods relative to their current costs of production.
3. Bonin, Drèze, Meade, Svejnar, Vanek and others have asserted that the labor managed firm could be an efficient method of organizing production. They got their 'favourable' results by a mechanical extension of neoclassical analytical concepts to the performance of producers' cooperatives, labor-managed firms and codetermining firms, while ignoring the effects of the property and contracting rights specific to those organizations on incentives and transaction costs. Evidence has failed to support the blackboard models of Vanek and like thinkers. Producers' cooperatives, labor-managed firms, codetermining firms, etc. have all failed to appear on a significant scale in free-market, private-property economies. An implication is that the value of labor participation to the employees of business firms is worth less than the costs to their contractual partners of providing it.
4. R. Coase, *The Firm, the Market and the Law*, Chicago: University of Chicago Press, 1988, p. 175.
5. Coase, *ibid.*, p. 185.

[11]

HOW SHOULD PRICES BE SET?

by Armen Alchian (*)

How should prices be set? No one knows. God may know; but not care. One interpretation of this question is « By what *competitive behavior* should scarce resources be allocated among competing claimants and uses? *Who* should have what and for what purpose? » Read this way, the question asks how society should be ordered; and what each person should be allowed to do. In another sense the question can be interpreted very narrowly and incompletely: Should price discrimination be allowed? Should prices be set by decree or by open-market competitive forces? Should collusive action by sellers or buyers be encouraged? But these, if pressed far enough, go back to the broader question asked first.

With that prologue let me pose the question anew. « What are the consequences of setting prices in various ways? » and also, « What conditions must exist if prices are to be set that way? » In this more general form of the question — as a sociologist might put it — « What are the cultural, political and economic consequences of various processes of allocating goods and what are the institutional conditions that must prevail if that allocation or process is to be realised? » In so far as you would prefer one or another kind for the society, would your preferred process depend upon the particular goods and the people involved? Would you want the same system to apply to drugs, books and shoes? For everyone, children, aged, literate, more informed? Do you prefer that the young cannot buy alcohol? That licensed doctors can buy morphine; while we unlicensed doctors can not? Do you think it desirable that Frenchmen and Englishmen have less competitive clash of ideas and options via television and radio than do Americans? That minority groups are less likely to get jobs in public utilities and in strong unions? That liquor store owners are a strong source of political support for politicians? That a strong patronage arm of the politician is the licensing board which issues licenses in various professions; radio and television stations are more likely to be awarded to ex-congressmen than any other class of people; college teachers will discourage weak students from continuing their education whereas a golf teacher will encourage the slow learner to keep trying? And do you prefer that doctors prohibit advertising and open competition for their services; that universities and schools assign students to schools nearest their residence, whereas those who eat out are not so assigned to restaurants; that public employees are less helpful to the public they serve than the employee of a selfish private employer? And that public government or non-profit employers

---

(*) Department of Economics, University of California, Los Angeles.

are more discriminatory in their employment policies than private property employers? And that public services are more likely to be underpriced than are privately provided services? The list could be lengthen-
ed easily. What are your preferences — as if anyone really cared!
More sensible is an understanding of why those phenomena occur. All
are results of the pricing system used. However, the ability to use particular pricing tactics depends upon the property system.

Let me emphasize the fundamental fact that every question of pricing
is a question of property rights. We could have asked « What system
of property rights shall be used? ». For the existing system of property
rights determines the system of price setting in the exchange or allocation
of scarce resources. I am repeatedly impressed with how many apparently
diverse questions come down to the same element — the structure of
property rights to use of scarce resources. In fact, and this is a proposition I should like to emphasize as strongly as I can, Economics
is the study of property rights. Without scarce resources there is no
point to property rights. The allocation of scarce resources in a society
is the assignment of rights to uses of resources in a society. So the
question of economics or of how prices should be set is the question
of how property rights should be defined and exchanged and on what
terms.

I cannot present a theory of all the implications of various forms
of property rights — as a means of deriving the implications of various
ways of setting prices — *i.e.*, of rationing scarce goods among competing
users. But a general outline of the standard elements, with some examples, can be attempted.

Economic theory (which *is* a theory of society) postulates that
behavior conforms to the hypothesis that every person has a convex
utility or preference function with his goals and goods entering as
substitutable variables. Eating, physical comfort, sex, honor, intellectual interchange, and marketable wealth are some of the goods, and
among them substitution or tradeoffs occur. Each person is constrained
to some feasible set — the set composed of all the achievable combinations of those goods. Typically in standard economic theory, the boundary
of the feasible set is defined by one's marketable *private* property and
market prices. Almost the entire development of mathematical economics has used that *very special* constraint and from it has come
much of our current theory.

Goods controlled as private property are more likely to be exchanged
(allocated) via a market clearing money price than goods not so controlled. The reason is simple enough. With private property, two persons
may exchange rights to goods on whatever terms they mutually accept.
The exchange of one good for several other marketable goods or for
friendship or for charity or for whatever other service one wishes to
contemplate is unrestricted. It is unrestricted in the sense that any
person who prefers some other mixture or form of payment for the
goods he sells can offer or ask for it. A seller can sell to pretty women

rather than ordinary women if he prefers. He can accomplish that
mixture by accepting a lower price from « beauties » in order to deal
more with them. Or as a buyer he can pay higher wages or prices and
get a choice of other characteristics in his employees or pay higher
prices and get better quality. He can more fully discriminate. Prices
will reflect the variations in preferences and quality of goods.

This point, I think, bears repetition. In the open-market, property
rights can be privately reshuffled and exchanged for whatever kind of
mixture of other rights or goods that any two people can agree to.
Any kind of mixture of components or goods can be suggested as the
components of price. No one has to sell for money only; he can sell
for very little money and ask the buyers to not smoke or not drink or
to dress well or to perform little dances or to do any of large variety
of other things. The buyer has his own tradeoffs or marginal rates of
substitution among units of the various goods or activities for which
he is asked as a condition of exchange of rights. If the two parties
can agree on some mixture of services or rights to be made available
to one party in exchange for some mixture from the other, we have a
sale. Typically, with private property, one party transfers money and
the other some nonmoney goods. But there is nothing to prevent someone
from asking for less money and a bigger smile, or a pledge not to
smoke — to name but two. The more « side » conditions asked the less
the money price available, with private property, the open-market provides each person the broadest opportunities to find exchanges on the
best terms possibile. The person who wants pleasant employers who will
also provide a more relaxed atmosphere can accept a lower money salary.
That is why more pleasant working conditions are associated with lower
money wages, and riskier, less pleasant work with higher wages. Conversely a less desired type of employee can obtain a job by asking for
a lower money wage.

The old principle of « equalising differences » applies to *all* exchange
— not merely to labor and wage markets. The lower is one desired
component, the larger must be the equalising differential. The lower
is the monetary payment asked by the seller, the more will he be able
to get in non-monetary forms of equalising differentials. This is simply
an implication of the negative sloping iso-utility line in a convex utility preference function.

A private property system seems to be dominated by formal marketable means of payment — money; but, as we have seen, pleasant working
conditions, congenial colleagues often serve as payments in attracting
employees (who are a form of good purchased by the employer). It is
not the case that private property results in the maximum possible
monetary price as the principal rationing criteria. If it did, we would
not see people of the same skills working for less pay in accord with
working conditions. An open-market seems to maximise the permissible
range of feasible mixtures — the variety of behavior from which one can
choose — perhaps to one's regret. My tentative conclusion is that if you

would increase the range of variety of mixtures of goods and exchange conditions — and remember that a society is essentially a means of facilitating exchange of specialised services — then a private property system scores high (est?). I am further tempted to mean by « freedom » that *range* of options (not the *size* of the particular basket selected). This does not imply that freedom is the only goal in my utility function. I trade some of it for more porridge i.e., for a larger sized basket out of a narrower option. I trade options for more of a given good ...else why would I be employed at a state owned and operated university?

Costs of Policing Exchange.

But in speaking of private property I have talked as if there were no costs of obtaining information about exchange options, or of negotiating contracts and of policing their enforcement. Lumping together momentarily the costs of discerning exchange opportunities and of communicating with potential exchangers, and of contracting and enforcement, it can be seen that these costs will, in some instance for some goods, be so large as to preclude market exchange. For example, the cost of policing the occupants of a parking lot and of negotiating payment may be greater than the cost of providing such parking space. At a zero price the parking lot may always be full, with rationing accomplished on a « first-come, first-served » basis. If one desires to accommodate those who feel the cost of making themselves the « first come » is excessive relative to the value of the parking space, more space could be provided, or the parking lot could be policed and the spaces sold via market (i.e., money) exchange. If policing costs exceed the costs of providing enough more spaces to accommodate the desired « second-comers », and if having space for the second comers is worth the extra cost of more spaces, then more spaces will be created and provided « free » until the marginal cost of the land equals the marginal gain — which may or may not be in sufficient quantity to avoid rationing at even a zero price. Free (i.e., non priced) parking spaces near large department stores in suburban areas where land is cheaper but not economically free, are more common than in cities where land is more expensive — they are not priced — i.e., free because the cost of transactions via the market is higher relative to the land value in the suburban areas. So, if one thinks private property should be or is associated with market clearing prices, he must first reckon with the costs of private property systems.

Other resources than land, say water in rivers or underground basins, rights to emanate radio energy, or rights to moving-cocoons of airspace all may be allocated by a non-market pricing system because the costs of policing the market contract exceed the value of using a « superior » rationing system. If radio rights are worth $ 1, but if the costs of recording and negotiating a market sale exceed $ 1.00 it is cheaper to assign in some other way. The exchange price (value to the highest claimant) must exceed the cost of negotiation and contract enforcement by at least the cost of production of the exchanged good (1).

Employee Policing Costs.

Transactions or contracting or enforcement costs are present also in an employee-employer relationship. An employee acts « for » the person vested with private property rights to the goods being allocated. In this case the employee-agent is « supposed » to act as if he were the owner himself. If the proceeds accrue to the employer as his private property, the employer will take some care that the employee charges the market clearing money price, despite the employee's preference for a lower money price so the employee could ration the goods on some nonmonetary price criteria in such a fashion that more of the payment accrues to the employee. For example, at a lower price the employee can be more relaxed in making sales and less solicitous to potential customers; he can induce customers to be « nicer » and even to perform some of the functions of the employee. The customers (in order to enhance their competitive basis — which is no longer completely manifested in money prices) will offer other kinds of appeals pleasing to the employee. We all learned this, at least, from our experience with price controls and government employees. However, the lower are the costs of carefully watching and policing the activity of the employee, the closer will the market price be to the market clearing price.

I believe the costs of policing the activity of employee-agents increases the larger the number of employees and the larger the number of people among whom ownership is divided as in a corporation. Thus I would expect to find more deviations from market clearing money prices in a large firm than a small one, and more deviation in a widely held corporate firm than in a proprietorship or closely held firm. Rules and regulations imposed on employees serve to prevent their straying from the path of maximizing employer wealth. We all know that in some special or unusual circumstances it would be better for the employer if the employee did violate some inflexible rules. At such times, we, as customers or subordinate employees, are annoyed by the « red tape » that prevents managers from acting in a « sensible » way. We complain that if only we could talk to the owner he would make an exception to his « rule » — a rule used because of the conflict of interest between employee and employer. However, if authority to deviate is granted, deviations will occur to further the employees also, to the detriment of the employer. Do not misunderstand; there is also a common area of interest. Nor am I arguing that employees of private employers behave just like employees of governments or nonprivate employers. They do not, as we shall see later.

---

(1)   I wonder what fraction of our total product is devoted to policing property and contracts? Is 10 percent too large an estimate?

This implied kind of deviant behavior by the employee in large enterprises is frequently characterised by the assertion that large corporations are less likely adjust prices to clear the market than the small firm; that the small firm will adapt itself to customer desires more readily than the large firm. The same kind of consequence is evident in the behavior of foremen and supervisors intermediary between owners and employees. Supervisors, foremen and managers will, the greater are the costs of surveillance and enforcement of activities directed at maximising the owners wealth, engage more in favoritism or « arbitrary » employee promotion or firing practices. The subordinate employee feels the supervisor or manager is « taking advantage » of his situation in a larger corporation. But the analysis is incomplete. Competition among present or potential employees and among supervisors has the effect of reducing behavior that departs from employer interests. New employees will offer to take the place of old employees who are inefficient in attending to the interests of the employer. With perfect competition among employees we would eliminate this effect — if by perfect we include information as a free good.

But information is not free. All potential new employees do not know what can be achieved. Circumstances are always changing; opportunities change. Insiders may know more than some outsiders. Which employee is acting inefficiently? Which employer's interests could in fact be better attended to by you? It does not suffice to say that « inefficiency » exists. To eliminate it the person who can do better must know where the « inefficiency » is. This is costly to ascertain and to the extent it is costly, employees can act inefficiently, and competition among employees will not immediately eliminate it. However « inefficiency » will be more viable where the employer himself is not the owner of the enterprise nor a manager agent for some private owner.

Kinds of Property Rights and Rewards of Exchange.

Not all non-money market-clearing prices occur because of high information, policing and transactions costs relative to the marketable value of the rights. The exchange value of the rights may be biassed downward by the kind of property rights in them. If no one owns a peach tree, the value of the ripe peaches is not reflected in any marketable way that anyone can capture. People will pick the peaches before they are ripe for fear that someone will beat them to the peach. If no one possesses the right to the peach, the marketable value will not be as effective. In controlling that resource, private property rights have the characteristic that it is easier (cheaper) to exchange the rights for other forms of marketable (money) than for rights that are less private. In fact one dimension of the concept of private property is this relatively greater ease of converting or exchanging private rights for marketable value. In publicly owned property it is not legally possible for one person to sell his rights to public goods to some other people. The rights are not marketable individually as is corporate stock ownership. It is this feature which I think is the « crucial » distinction between private and public property.

I do not intend to suggest only a bipolar distinction between public and private property: rather I use the terms as the two ends to the spectrum rangers in the marketable transferability of the rights. In passing it is wise to remember that marketability implies *capitalisation* of future effects on to present values. Thus, long range effects are thrust back on to the current owner of the marketable value of the goods. He will heed the long-run effects of current decisions more carefully than if the rights were not transferable. It is this feature which some people forget when they say that all a stock-holder can do in a corporation is sell his stock if he doesn't like the way things are going — as if to say that this has no effect on the way things will be going. There exists a strong temptation to identify *incorrectly* the power of a person with his relative share of voting strength — thus equating the political power and acts of a single person in a society of ten thousand voters with that of an owner of 1 share of stock out of 10,000.

Diffused private property still retains one powerful difference. Rights may be exchanged and may be consolidated into blocs, so that some people do have large interests. This ability to sell an attribute has two features: first is the capitalisation of future effects on to present value — something that is not feasible with public property. A larger span of value effects is imposed on each current rights holder and is more effective on current decisions. Secondly, the ability to sell the rights enables some to specialise and exercise greater control in particular goods. For example the specialisation gives incentives to people to buy up shares of malfunctioning corporations, improve them and capture the capitalised gains. There is a similar incentive on politicians to assemble voting blocs, but these do not possess the same elements of capitalisation and concentration of power. One should avoid the mistake of thinking of a large, dispersed private property business as identical to an equally large (number of owners) publicly owned enterprise.

An implied observable difference is that private firms will be closer to market clearing prices than will the publicly owned agency. Example — water, telephone, power and transportation services. Shortages will be more chronic in publicly owned than in privately owned enterprises — with the consequent change in the weights of competitive factors and behavior in the rationing of the available services.

Suppose that as citizens of the state, we prefer to see public goods used where their value is highest. The costs to each of us of enforcing efficient behavior is higher and the gains lower than in a private, equally large enterprise. The absence of both (a) transferable marketable rights that can have exchange values revealed, and (b) the possibility of concentrating one's rights in particular directions so as to capture more capital value gains of improved marketable value of the resources imply a lower force toward market-clearing money prices for services rendered by publicly owned agencies.

Before illustrating this deviation from market clearing money prices, it is useful to note there is a spectrum of rights from private to public. For example, in between there can be placed non-profit enterprises, public utilities with limited profits, profit sharing cooperatives and labor unions. The protected public utility with a limited profit is an instructive case. Increments of wealth beyond the limit would accrue not to the stockholders but to the customer; if profits exceed the legal limit, prices to customers would be cut to pass the gain to the customer. « Stockholders » will not be willing to incur as much costs to insure wealth maximising behavior in the public utility. Employees will have greater scope for personal non-market sources of utility increments, e.g., easy working conditions, prettier secretaries, more discrimination according to color, sex and age, and easier retirement and weaker discharge policy. Unions will find public utility managers more agreeable to wage rises.

It is safe to say, I believe, although I have not tested this systematically, that the kinds of behavior characterised by Berle and Means in the famous book on corporate behavior applied more to the limited profit, public utility corporation than to the privately owned, unrestricted corporation and even less to the closely held corporation.

In this range we can fit also the not-for-profit corporation, and the publicly operated agency that is *supposed to* dispose of its product via the market, (leaving for the extreme, in the rationing of immigration visas, radio and television broadcast rights and a polyglot host of other goods controlled by the government). In non-profit institutions, there are no private « owners ». Trustees or stokholders exist, but they can not sell the stock or declare dividends for stockholders. Costs are inflated to match receipts, by paying larger salaries, by not firing incompetent people, by hiring more expensive luxurious surroundings in terms of buildings, furnishings and people. Prices of services will be set too low, relative to clearing the market so that the operators can reap more benefits either directly from customers or by an easier management task. As a prime example, I cite the mutually owned cooperatives. They are active in the savings and loan business in the U.S. Yet their record relative to privately owned stock corporations is exactly in accord with the implication mentioned. It is the stock-owned companies that are first to adjust interest rates to clear the market — to cite but one (and for present purposes, the relevant) example of evidence.

Between the diffused ownership of a corporation and the citizen-owned rights to public property there is the labor union or self-licensed profession in which licenses are awarded by the profession itself. In a union in which entry is limited, as in the case in several unions, entry permission constitutes a rationing and allocation of a monopoly rent. The entry controllers do not have private property rights in « entry » permits (and the monopoly rents). They therefore have less reason to

sell them in the market, since marketable payments would redound to
the benefit of the union treasury. Union entry will be underpriced (in
money terms), but the non-money payment price of entry will be higher.
Furthermore, applicants queuing for admission will agree to not advertise, will perform special services to help incumbents (do charity
work for doctors or do the lesser paying jobs), will be relatives of incumbents, and will agree not be critical of their colleagues. Negroes
and other minority groups will find exclusion more common.

Where should we rank government agencies like the Port Authority
of the New York, or the Tennessee Valley Authority, or the Federal Reserve System — agencies that have their own sources of revenue but
which are publicly or governmentally owned? State or public universities,
with which we are better acquainted, serve as better understood examples
of the ability to avoid market clearing prices. We note in passing that
there is an alternative hypothesis — that state universities are employed
in order to avoid market rationing of services, i.e., to avoid full cost
tuition as the rationing criterion.

Before exploring that example more fully, let me review the discussion. The setting of price *is* the setting of standards and criterion for
the allocation of rights to scarce resources. But this *is* the allocation
of property rights. And this affects the kinds of competitive behavior
people manifest in their attempts to improve their utility. The setting
of prices is itself dependent upon the rights possessed by those who can
transfer the rights. In sum the structure of property rights affects the
way prices are set — the way rights are distributed or transferred.
Some classification of rights structures has been attempted and I have
tried to show these affect the pricing system used. By implication these
would then affect the behavior of the people, as they compete for access
to rights or to transfer of rights. That is why it seems that to ask how
prices should be set is to ask what kinds of behavior we want or what
kinds of property rights should be instituted in order to get that kind of
behavior if any of us think that knowledge of such questions would in
fact affect policy.

Applications to Pricing of University Services.

To make the analysis vivid, I shall discuss the allocation of educational services — something we know about. I shall interpret events
as implications of the preceding theory of property rights and behavior.
A public university in typically financed from taxes — not from sales
to customers. Even private schools have similarities; a large portion
of their proceeds come from endowment or sources independent of market sales. What is the rationing system? More generally, what behavior
by students and faculty and administrators is fostered by institutional
arrangement?

I recognize that an alternative interpretation is that university
education should not be rationed at a market clearing price and should

not be controlled by market sales. If I accept that I then ask what institutional system will permit that desired rationing system. If I do not accept that premise — as I do not — then I merely shift emphasis from intent to effect. And since intentions are not sufficient to make behavior viable, we can agree that the issue is one of viable, not of intended or unintended, behavior.

Universities are marked by zero or low tuitions fees. (I shall be extreme and put things in black and white terms and you can interpret to put it in comparative terms). We use grades as conditions of entry and of continuance in school. We impose required courses with examinations. We have faculty control; academic freedom; tenure; and acquiescent students. Students are severely restricted in their ability to transfer from course to course, to drop courses in mid term, to repeat courses until they obtain passing grades; they are policed in the kinds of behavior that will result in dismissal or inability to enter. Compare that with a department store. Do the employees or managers so control or select customers? Of course not, and the reason is not that education is different. Education *is* different, but it is the ownership arrangement that is the explanatory difference and *only* that. Such is the bed I am making for myself; now notice how comfortably I can lie in that bed.

I (a member of the faculty) *can* survive with a market clearing price. But students will insist on better treatment else they will transfer their custom to a competitor, and competitors will exist at market clearing prices. Intentionally, or not, with foresight or not, we keep the fees low in order to accommodate less wealthy, more needy but deserving students. Low fees enable us (faculty) to select students according to non-money criterion. My utility will be enhanced as I select the better learners and smarter people who obviously « deserve » a higher education. How easy to swallow that self-serving contention!

The same reasoning can be applied elsewhere. Concerts should be free and financed by the state so that musicians can select the audience, admitting those who have the keenest ear and are best at making music themselves. Less discerning people can do other things. After all there is no sense in wasting music on those less able to appreciate it. If food were rationed at a zero price, chefs and dieticians who prepare the food could see that only the most deserving got the good food, while those who were less appreciative of food would get standard food without luxurious and expensive deserts. Or if we are couturiers and dress makers, we will let only the most beautiful women have the best clothes. The average woman can wear her shapeless, less expensive dress. How wasteful to spend hundreds of dollars on a woman of hopeless figure, while there are women who, if beautifully dressed, would provide external benefits to the rest of society. Clearly, on the external benefit count alone, clothing should be distributed as is education. That the beautiful and shapeless alike should both have to pay would never cross our minds. After all how could a poor beautiful girl pay. Certainly she could not borrow and pay out of later proceeds, for how could she earn more?

Education could readily be financed by borrowing, but not beautiful clothes. After all education is productive of income — but beauty, no. We must provide zero-priced beautiful clothes to the prettiest women, while education can be sold at market clearing price, with repayments out of later enhanced income. Couturiers have long advocated that the state finance dress-making with zero prices for clothing so that they too can select their clients with the gracious social beneficial care that we teachers employ. But not until the designers get tax supported endowment support or non-profit dress design and manufacturing institutions will they be able to serve society as well as we teachers do.

We tax supported professors ration our entrants according to criteria that increase our utility, and bring in less revenue to the institution, but *we* do it in order to increase the welfare of society. Once a student has arrived with a good scholastic and behavior record, we give him grades, not simply to tell him how he is doing, but to see that he continues to act in ways to support our utility. Of course, if a student offered to pay $ 100 for the privilege of staying in my class a second time after failing it, I would accept, except for my contract with the university which, for not mysterious reasons, prohibits such behavior. Yet my golf teacher, my Berlitz foreign language teacher, my teachers of music, typing, shorthand, driving, dancing, electronic computer programming, all are willing to continue to teach me so long as I pay the admission price. They do not seem to care if I take only part-time schooling, or get drunk periodically. But we teachers at zero tuition schools are less tolerant. Tolerance would be a waste of resources — to us. Once the student has been admitted he is subjected to a battery of tests to satisfy some psychological research worker, he must stand in line for hours to register and pay his bills (can you imagine a department store making you stand in line to buy and to pay your bills!); he must continue to behave in an exemplary manner; he must not belong to fraternities that discriminate among races. Can you imagine a private for-profit store engaging in such customer exclusionary tactics and suffering the loss of monetary wealth?

And the student who seeks advice about courses is ignored. Professors do not advertise their courses in the student newspaper as do the booksellers. Since students are not rationed on a money income basis, we mistreat students with greater success the lower is the tuition. The cost of our doing so is lower, the lower is the tuition relative to costs of education or the value of it to the student.

The land and facilities of the university are internally assigned on a non-price basis. Faculty offices, parking lots, uses of classrooms are not rented. They are distributed so that those in charge of the allocation get a greater utility than if the market-clearing sales proceeds were collected and turned over to the university administration or added to the state or university budget. As Dean of a department I could get parking space under a zero-price market scheme with excess demand. As a faculty I could get space before any student could. But under a market rationing system I would have to pay more for space I get now « free ». The sales proceeds would give less benefit to any administrator than if he were a manager for a privately owned enterprise. Hence parking spaces are more frequently allocated not by pricing but by hierarchical status. My point is that allocation of rights to use of university space are based on a hierarchical system reflecting the avoidance of trouble and obtaining an easier life for the amdinistration — more so than if it were privately owned or market oriented. So we practice the principle of rationing with the squeaking wheel getting the oil.

What means do use students to exert pressures on the administration? Leave? Small effect that would have with queues of new students already « too long ». Taking their business elsewhere is not as effective as it would be in a market place. Protest? Yes, by *staying* and being obnoxious. Protest in the guise of constitutional rights and basic civil freedoms such a free-speech. If students protest by sit-ins and physically taking over the premises in the name of free speech — the faculty, conditioned to respond to the phrase « free speech » like Pavlov's dog to the bell, will lick their chops and rush to the students' aid rather than expelling them. So long as students want space to « talk » we of the faculty mistakenly think they have a constitutional right to the space. So long as students identifiy their demands with free-speech, our faculty colleagues will associate free speech with free resources. Free speech has nothing to do with free resources. We think the students should have the right to take whatever resources they wish — as if were free — in order to engage in « free speech ». How easy it is to confuse « free » (in the sense of governmentally unrestricted rights to say what you want to a willing listener) with « economically free » resources with which to talk. Free speech (in the sense of unrestricted voluntary conversation) does not require « free goods ». One can hire a hall.

Free speech does not involve use of public resources. Until this distinction is understood I fear we shall go on thinking we have given students free speech, when in truth we give them paternalism and economic goods — i.e., qualified rights to use university facilities for certain purposes, (e.g., conversation). For example, they may use the space only so long as they do not express immoral ideas. But in a privately hired hall, filthy obscene words are consistent with free speech... even though many people would regard that as « abuse » of free speech — thereby exposing the fallacy that free speech is something provided by access to *non*-private property. The *public* space is allocated and rationed at a zero price so long as it is used as the rationer thinks appropriate. With private property, the rationers own standards can be bought away and resources more reliable made available for whatever speech is voluntarily agreeable to the two discussants.

So we find that rationing space that is controlled by an agent not responsible to private owners implies less use of market clearing prices and an increase in non-marketable types of goods; to wit, an increase in the ability of the allocator to condition the behavior of applicants, as with students. Furthermore we increase the resort to public demonstration on public property as a means of acquiring control over more of the non-market price rationed goods. Such protests impose costs on the allocators (rather than monetary rewards), and as a condition of being relieved of such costs the claimants are given what they seek. This is known as the inalienable right to protest, though I confess I fail to see the difference between that and the man who sits in my house and prevents my using it until I let him have a room. There appears to be a difference because my house is typically sold or rented at a market clearing monetary price, whereas public property is not. Hence in the latter case, rationing devices that are *typically* used include first-come, first-served and political pressures upon the agent. Pressures run a wide gamut of devices including simple blockage of any use of the resources... now popularly known as sit-ins or public demonstrations blocking use of the streets for travel.

It is not surprising that a « first-come, first-served » method of protest is applied to public streets. Since street use is normally rationed at a zero money price with first come first served, we are accustomed to that system for streets. We often ask why people drive so rudely, when they behave so nicely in other places. The simple fact is that we ration space on the road in accord with the first-come, first-served principle; so we see that kind of « rude » behavior on streets.

That is how prices should be set if you wish to encourage that kind of behavior. And to get prices set that way it is more viable to have the streets (or resources) public owned. One can look at the range of public services and find this principle of rationing widely used: public parks, golf courses, public housing, water, telephones, court room services — to name a few. In some instances I find it preferable — especially if I happen to have the characteristics that increase by being « first come » or if I happen to be the allocator as with university resources. So do not condemn my remarks.

Private property reduces the scope of control authority by politicians, it reduces the scope of wealth available to those rich in the survival traits of political competition for access to political power. Viable behavioral traits depend upon the political system. In some countries it is skill at military tactics. In others it is personality appeal and oratoric ability. We can not imagine Lincoln acquiring political power in a military junta. We can not imagine some dictators acquiring power in a democratic election. Certainly some people are more skilled at political endeavours than the market oriented survival skills. In students of political science and in business administration and in engineering you will see signs of developing differential skills. Small wonder then that politicians will be rewarded by public ownership . Their own power is enhanced, politicians will look more sympathetically upon public ownership and espouse their desire for it to help the public. The man who enters political life to restrain the growth of public ownership, publicly operated agencies and services will enter an office, if elected, in which he must dismantle his major sources of power and wealth once he is in office. His survival traits in political office will diminish compared to one taking the opposite position.

I have tried to show (1) the kind of pricing or rationing criteria used has a significant effect on behavior — socially, culturally as well as economically, and (2) the pricing or rationing system employed depends upon the system of property rights held by the allocators of the goods. A valid theory of the relationship between kinds of property rights and rationing criteria and techniques and generated personal behavior is not completely absent. Economics is social science. Applying it so narrowly to the private property market and to business administration, we have concealed its enormous applicability to sociology, political science and jurisprudence.

ARMEN ALCHIAN

Riassunto — Il livello a cui i prezzi vengono stabiliti nel mercato, riflette la struttura dei diritti di proprietà posseduti dal venditore dei beni. Anche se l'economia non dice in qual modo i prezzi dovrebbero essere determinati, tuttavia essa dice come verranno stabiliti sotto diversi sistemi di proprietà. Per esempio, in regime di proprietà privata, i prezzi si avvicineranno di più a livelli di «clearing», con pagamenti in denaro aventi un ruolo importante nel determinare chi ottiene i beni. Sotto quel sistema il venditore riceve tutti f pagamenti del compratore. In altri sistemi di proprietà esistono forze che fanno sì che i prezzi siano più bassi. Se la persona detentrice dei beni non può reclamare i pagamenti del compratore come propri o se la persona non agisce come agente di un privato possessore di beni, ne risulta per il «venditore» un incentivo a praticare prezzi più bassi e ad ottenere profitti sotto altre forme, da coloro che concorrono nel richiedere i beni. Quanto meno esistono diritti di proprietà, tanto più grande è l'incentivo per le persone detentrici dei beni a richiedere un prezzo monetario più basso ed un pagamento più alto in termini non pecuniari.

Transaction Cost Determinants of "Unfair" Contractual Arrangements

By BENJAMIN KLEIN*

Terms such as "unfair" are foreign to the economic model of voluntary exchange which implies anticipated gains to all transactors. However, much recent statutory, regulatory and antitrust activity has run counter to this economic paradigm of the efficiency properties of "freedom of contract." The growth of "dealer day in court" legislation, FTC franchise regulations, favorable judicial consideration of "unequal bargaining power," and unconscionability arguments, are some examples of the recent legal propensity to "protect" transactors. This is done by declaring unenforceable or illegal particular contractual provisions that, although voluntarily agreed upon in the face of significant competition, appear to be one-sided or unfair. Presentation of the standard abstract economic analysis of the mutual gains from voluntary exchange is unlikely to be an effective counterweight to this recent legal movement without an explicit attempt to provide a positive rationale for the presence of the particular unfair contractual term. This paper considers some transaction costs that might explain the voluntary adoption of contractual provisions such as termination at will and long-term exclusive dealing clauses that have been under legal attack.

I. The "Hold-up" Problem

In attempting to explain the complicated contractual details of actual market exchange, I start by noting that complete, fully

*Professor of economics, University of California-Los Angeles. This paper was written while I was a Law and Economics Fellow at the University of Chicago Law School. Armen Alchian, Roy Kenney, Edmund Kitch, Timothy Muris, Richard Posner, and George Priest provided useful comments on earlier drafts.

contingent, costlessly enforceable contracts are not possible. This is a proposition obvious to even the most casual observer of economic phenomenon. Rather than the impersonal marketplace of costlessly enforceable contracts represented in standard economic analysis, individuals in most real world transactions are concerned with the possibility of breach and hence the identity and reputation of those with whom they deal. Further, even a cursory examination of actual contracts indicates that the relationship between transacting parties often cannot be fully described by a court-enforceable formal document that the parties have signed (see Stewart Macauley). While the common law of contracts supplies a body of rules and principles which are read into each contract, in many cases explicit terms (which include these general unwritten terms) remain somewhat vague and incomplete.

Contracts are incomplete for two main reasons. First, uncertainty implies the existence of a large number of possible contingencies and it may be very costly to know and specify in advance responses to all of these possibilities. Second, particular contractual performance, such as the level of energy an employee devotes to a complex task, may be very costly to measure. Therefore contractual breach may often be difficult to prove to the satisfaction of a third-party enforcer such as a court.

Given the presence of incomplete contractual arrangements, wealth-maximizing transactors have the ability and often the incentive to renege on the transaction by holding up the other party, in the sense of taking advantage of unspecified or unenforceable elements of the contractual relationship. Such behavior is, by definition, unanticipated and not a long-run equilibrium phenomenon. Oliver Williamson has identified and discussed this phenomenon of "opportunistic behavior," and my recent paper with Robert Crawford and Armen Alchian attempted to make operational some of the conditions under which this hold-up potential is likely to be large. In addition to contract costs, and therefore the incompleteness of the explicit contract, we emphasized the presence of appropriable quasi rents due to highly firm-specific investments. After a firm invests in an asset with a low-salvage value and a quasi-rent stream highly dependent upon some other asset, the owner of the other asset has the potential to hold up by appropriating the quasi-rent stream. For example, one would not build a house on land rented for a short term. After the rental agreement expires, the landowner could raise the rental price to reflect the costs of moving the house to another lot.[1]

The solution we emphasized was vertical integration, that is, one party owning both assets (the house and the land). Because the market for land is competitive, the price paid for the land by the homebuilder does not reflect these potentially appropriable quasi rents. However, this solution will not necessarily be observed. The size of the hold-up potential is a multiplicative function of two factors: the presence of specific capital, that is, appropriable quasi rents, and the cost of contractually specifying and enforcing delivery of the service in question —the incentive for contract violation and the ease of contract violation. Even where

[1] This problem is different from the standard monopoly or bilateral monopoly problem for two reasons. First, market power is created only after the house investment is made on a particular piece of land. Such postinvestment power can therefore exist in many situations that are purely competitive preinvestment. Second, the problem we are discussing deals with the difficulties of contract enforcement. Even if some preinvestment monopoly power exists (for example, a union supplier of labor services to harvest a crop), if one can write an enforceable contract preinvestment (i.e., before the planting), the present discounted value of the monopoly return may be significantly less than the one-time postinvestment hold-up potential (which may equal the entire value of a crop ready to be harvested).

there is a large amount of highly specific capital, the performance in question may be cheaply specifiable and measureable and a complete contract legally enforceable at low cost. Therefore, while a short-term rental contract is not feasible, a possible solution may be a long-term lease. In addition, since the cases we will be considering deal with human capital, vertical integration in the sense of outright ownership is not possible.

II. Contractual Solutions

Since the magnitude of the potential holdup may be anticipated, the party to be cheated can merely decrease the initial price he will pay by the amount of the appropriable quasi rents. For example, if an employer knows that an employee will cheat a certain amount each period, it will be reflected in the employee's wage. Contracts can be usefully thought to refer to anticipated rather than stated performance. Therefore the employee's behavior should not even be considered "cheating." A secretary, for example, may miss work one day a week on average. If secretary time is highly substitutable, the employer can cut the secretary's weekly wage 20 percent, hire 20 percent more secretaries and be indifferent. The secretary, on the other hand, presumably values the leisure more than the additional income and therefore is better off. Rather than cheating, we have a voluntarily determined, utility-maximizing contractual relationship.

In many cases, however, letting the party cheat and discounting his wage will not be an economical solution because the gain to the cheater and therefore his acceptable compensating wage discount is less than the cost to the firm from the cheating behavior. For example, it is easy to imagine many cases where a shirking manager will impose costs on the firm much greater than his personal gains. Therefore the stockholders cannot be made indifferent to this behavior by cutting his salary and hiring more lazy managers. The general point is that there may not be perfect substitutability between quantity and quality of particular services. Hence, even if one knew that an unspecified element of quality would be reduced by a certain amount in attempting the holdup, an *ex ante* compensatory discount in the quoted price of the promised high quality service to the cost of providing the anticipated lower-quality supply would not make the demander of the service indifferent. Individuals would be willing to expend real resources to set up contractual arrangements to prevent such opportunism and assure high-quality supply.

The question then becomes how much of the hold-up problem can be avoided by an explicit government-enforced contract, and how much remains to be handled by an implicit self-enforcing contract. This latter type of contract is one where opportunistic behavior is prevented by the threat of termination of the business relationship rather than by the threat of litigation. A transactor will not cheat if the expected present discounted value of quasi rents he is earning from a relationship is greater than the immediate hold-up wealth gain. The capital loss that can be imposed on the potential cheater by the withdrawal of expected future business is then sufficient to deter cheating.

In our forthcoming article, Keith Leffler and I develop this market-enforcement mechanism in detail. It is demonstrated that one way in which the future-promised rewards necessary to prevent cheating can be arranged is by the payment of a sufficiently high-price "premium." This premium stream can usefully be thought of as "protection money" paid to assure noncheating behavior. The magnitude of this price premium will be related to the potential holdup, that is, to the extent of contractual incompleteness and the degree of specific capital present. In equilibrium, the present discounted value of the price-premium stream will be exactly equal to the appropriable quasi rents, making the potential cheater indifferent between cheating and not. But the individual paying the premium will be in a preferable position as long as the differential consumer's surplus from high-quality (noncheating) supply is greater than the premium.

One method by which this equilibrium quasi-rent stream can be achieved without the existence of positive firm profits is by having the potential cheater put up a forfeitable-at-will collateral bond equal to the discounted value of the premium stream. Alternatively, the potential cheater may make a highly firm-specific productive investment which will have only a low-salvage value if he cheats and loses future business. The gap between price and salvageable capital costs is analytically equivalent to a premium stream with the nonsalvageable asset analytically equivalent to a forfeitable collateral bond.

III. "Unfair" Contractual Terms

Most actual contractual arrangements consist of a combination of explicit- and implicit-enforcement mechanisms. Some elements of performance will be specified and enforced by third-party sanctions. The residual elements of performance will be enforced without invoking the power of some outside party to the transaction but merely by the threat of termination of the transactional relationship. The details of any particular contract will consist of forms of these general elements chosen to minimize transaction costs (for example, hiring lawyers to discover contingencies and draft explicit terms, paying quality-assurance premiums, and investing in nonsalvageable "brand name" assets) and may imply the existence of what appears to be unfair contract terms.

Consider, for example, the initial capital requirements and termination provisions common in most franchise contractual arrangements. These apparently one-sided terms may be crucial elements of minimum-cost quality-policing arrangements. Given the difficulty of explicitly specifying and enforcing contractually every element of quality to be supplied by a franchisee, there is an incentive for an individual opportunistic franchisee to cheat the franchisor by supplying a lower quality of product than contracted for. Because the franchisee uses a common trademark, this behavior depreciates the reputation and hence the future profit stream of the franchisor.[2]

The franchisor knows, given his direct policing and monitoring expenditures, the expected profit that a franchisee can obtain by cheating. For example, given the number of inspectors hired, he knows the expected time to detect a cheater; given the costs of low-quality inputs he knows the expected extra short-run cheating profit that can be earned. Therefore the franchisor may require an initial lump sum payment from the franchisee equal to this estimated short-run gain from cheating. This is equivalent to a collateral bond forfeitable at the will of the franchisor. The franchisee will earn a normal rate of return on that bond if he does not cheat, but it will be forfeited if he does cheat and is terminated.

In many cases franchisee noncheating rewards may be increased and short-run cheating profits decreased (and therefore franchisor direct policing costs reduced) by the grant of an exclusive territory or the enforcement of minimum resale price restraints (see my paper with Andrew McLaughlin). Franchisors can also assure quality by requiring franchisee investments in specific (nonfully salvageable) production assets that upon termination imply a capital-cost penalty larger than any short-run wealth gain that can be obtained by the franchisee if he cheats. For example, the franchisor may require franchisees to rent from them short term (rather than own) the land upon which their outlet is located. This lease arrangement creates a situation where termination implies that the franchisor can require the franchisee to move and thereby impose a capital loss on him up to the amount of his initial nonsalvageable invest-

ment. Hence a form of collateral to deter franchisee cheating is created.[3]

It is important to recognize that franchise termination, if it is to assure quality compliance on the part of franchisees, must be unfair in the sense that the capital cost imposed on the franchisee that will optimally prevent cheating must be larger than the gain to the franchisee from cheating. Given that less than infinite resources are spent by the franchisor to monitor quality, there is some probability that franchisee cheating will go undetected. Therefore termination must become equivalent to a criminal-type sanction. Rather than the usually analyzed case of costlessly detected and policed contract breach, where the remedy of making the breaching party pay the cost of the damages of his specific breach makes economic sense, the sanction here must be large enough to make the expected net gain from cheating equal to zero. The transacting parties contractually agree upon a penalty-type sanction for breach as a means of economizing on direct policing costs. Because contract enforcement costs (including litigation costs which generally are not collectable by the innocent party in the United States) are not zero, this analysis provides a rationale against the common law prohibition of penalty clauses.

The obvious concern with such seemingly unfair contractual arrangements is the possibility that the franchisor may engage in opportunistic behavior by terminating a franchisee without cause, claiming the franchise fee and purchasing the initial franchisee investment at a distress price. Such behavior may be prevented by the

---

[2]At locations where this incentive is very large, for example, on superhighways where the probability of repeat sales by particular customers is very low, the franchisor may "vertically integrate" and not compensate their employees on any profit-sharing basis. Such fixed wage compensation schemes reduce the incentive to cheat but at the cost of reducing the incentive for workers to supply any effort that is not explicitly specified and measureable by the employer. It is this latter incentive that is harnessed by franchising arrangements.

[3]The initial franchise investment also serves as a means of establishing an efficient compensation mechanism. Because the franchise investment is a saleable asset it provides a market measure of future profit and hence a precise incentive on franchisee efforts to build up the business. While an employee contract can contain a profit-sharing arrangement, and retirement and stock option provisions to reward employee efforts that yield a return far in the future and protect the employee's heirs, it would be extremely difficult to write ex ante complete, enforceable (i.e., measureable) contract terms that would as accurately reflect the value of marginal employee efforts.

depreciation of the franchisor's brand name and therefore decreased future demand by potential franchisees to join the arrangement. However, this protective mechanism is limited by the relative importance of new franchise sales compared to the continuing franchising operation, that is, by the "maturity" of the franchise chain.

More importantly, what limits reverse cheating by franchisors is the possible increased cost of operating the chain through an employee operation compared to a franchise operation when such cheating is communicated among franchisees. As long as the implicit collateral bond put up by the franchisee is less than the present discounted value of this cost difference, franchisor cheating will be deterred. Although explicit bonds and price premium payments cannot simultaneously be made by both the franchisee and the franchisor, the discounted value of the cost difference has the effect of a collateral bond put up by the franchisor to assure his noncheating behavior. This explains why the franchisor does not increase the initial franchise fee to an arbitrarily high level and correspondingly decrease its direct policing expenditures and the probability of detecting franchisee cheating. While such offsetting changes could continue to optimally deter franchisee cheating and save the real resource cost of direct policing, the profit from and hence the incentive for reverse franchisor cheating would become too great for the arrangement to be stable.

Franchisees voluntarily signing these agreements obviously understand the termination-at-will clause separate from the legal consequences of that term to mean nonopportunistic franchisor termination. But this does not imply that the court should judge each termination on these unwritten but understood contract terms and attempt to determine if franchisor cheating has occurred. Franchisees also must recognize that by signing these agreements they are relying on the implicit market-enforcement mechanism outlined above, and not the court to prevent franchisor cheating. It is costly to use the court to regulate these terminations because elements of perfor-

mance are difficult to contractually specify and to measure. In addition, litigation is costly and time consuming, during which the brand name of the franchisor can be depreciated further. If these costs were not large and the court could cheaply and quickly determine when franchisor cheating had occurred, the competitive process regarding the establishment of contract terms would lead transactors to settle on explicit governmentally enforceable contracts rather than rely on this implicit market-enforcement mechanism.

The potential error here is, after recognizing the importance of transaction costs and the incomplete "relational" nature of most real world contracts, to rely too strongly on the government as a regulator of unspecified terms (see Victor Goldberg). While it is important for economic theory to handle significant contract costs and incomplete explicit contractual arrangements, such complexity does not imply a broad role for government. Rather, all that is implied is a role for brand names and the corresponding implicit market enforcement mechanism I have outlined.

IV. Unequal Bargaining Power

An argument made against contract provisions such as termination-at-will clauses is that they appear to favor one party at the expense of another. Hence it is alleged that the terms of the agreement must have been reached under conditions of "unequal bargaining power" and therefore should be invalid. However, a further implication of the above analysis is that when both parties can cheat, explicit contractual restraints are often placed on the smaller, less well-established party (the franchisee), while an implicit brand name contract-enforcement mechanism is relied on to prevent cheating by the larger, more well-established party (the franchisor).

If information regarding quality of a product supplied by a large firm is communicated among many small buyers who do not all purchase simultaneously, the potential holdup relative to, say, annual sales is reduced substantially compared to the case where each buyer purchased from a separate independent small firm. There are likely to be economies of scale in the supply of a business brand name, because in effect the large firm's total brand name capital is put on the line with each individual sale. This implies a lower cost of using the implicit contract mechanism, that is, a lower-price premium necessary to assure non-breach, for a large firm compared to a small firm. Therefore one side of the contract will be relatively more incomplete.

For example, in a recent English case using the doctrine of inequality of bargaining power to bar contract enforcement, an individual songwriter signed a long-term (ten-year) exclusive service contract with a music publisher for an agreed royalty percentage.[4] Since it would be extremely costly to write a complete explicit contract for the supply of publishing services (including advertising and other promotion activities whose effects are felt over time and are difficult to measure), after a songwriter becomes established he has an incentive to take advantage of any initial investment made by a publishing firm and shift to another publisher. Rather than rely on the brand name of the songwriter or require him to make a specific investment which can serve as collateral, the exclusive services contract prevents this cheating from occurring.

The major cost of such explicit long-term contractual arrangements is the rigidity that is created by the necessity of setting a price or a price formula *ex ante*. In this song publishing case, the royalty formula may turn out *ex post* to imply too low a price to the songwriter (if, say, his cooperative promotional input is greater than originally anticipated.) If the publisher is concerned about his reputation, these royalty terms will be renegotiated, a common occurrence in continuing business relationships.

If an individual songwriter is a small part of a large publisher's total sales, and if the value of an individual songwriter's ability generally depreciates rapidly or does not

persist at peak levels so that signing up new songwriters is an important element of a publisher's continuing business, then cheating an individual songwriter or even all songwriters currently under contract by refusing to renegotiate royalty rates will imply a large capital cost to the publisher. When this behavior is communicated to other actual or potential composers, the publisher's reputation will depreciate and future business will be lost. An individual songwriter, on the other hand, does not generally have large, diversified long-term business concerns and therefore cannot be penalized in that way. It is therefore obvious, independent of any appeal to disparity of bargaining power, why the smaller party would be willing to be bound by an explicit long-term contract while the larger party is bound only implicitly and renegotiates terms that turn out *ex post* to be truly divergent from *ex ante*, but unspecified, anticipations.

However, the possibility of reverse publisher cheating is real. If, for example, the songwriter unexpectedly becomes such a great success that current sales by this one customer represents a large share of the present discounted value of total publisher sales, the implicit contract enforcement mechanism may not work. Individuals knowingly trade off these costs of explicit and implicit-enforcement mechanisms in settling upon transaction cost-minimizing contract terms. Although it would be too costly in a stochastic world to attempt to set up an arrangement where no cheating occurs, it is naive to think that courts can cheaply intervene to discover and "fix up" the few cases of opportunistic behavior that will occur. In any event, my analysis makes it clear that one cannot merely look at the agreed upon, seemingly "unfair" terms to determine if opportunism is occurring.

V. Conclusion

Ronald Coase's fundamental insight defined the problem. With zero transaction costs, the equilibrium form of economic organization is indeterminate. However, rather than distinguishing between the crude alternatives of vertical integration and

---

[4] See *Macaulay v. Schroeder Publishing Co., Ltd.* discussed in M. J. Trebilcock.

market exchange, what we really have to explain are different types of market-determined contractual relationships. I have argued that a particular form of transaction cost based upon the existence of incomplete contracts (due to uncertainty and measurement costs)—a transaction cost I have called the hold-up problem—may be an important reason in many cases for termination-at-will and exclusive-dealing contractual arrangements.

The danger is that a discussion of hold-up-type transaction costs can lead to *ad hoc* theorizing. The discussion here was meant to be suggestive. If economists are to explain satisfactorily the form of particular complex contracts adopted in the marketplace, they must "get their hands dirty" by closely investigating the facts and state of the law to determine hold-up possibilities and contract enforcement difficulties in particular cases. The most useful legal input to obtain knowledge of the institutional constraints on the trading process, is not likely to come from professors of contract law. Rather, we should consider the knowledge accumulated by practicing attorneys familiar with the likely hold-up problems and the contractual solutions commonly adopted in particular industries. When all firms in a particular industry use similar contractual provisions, it is unlikely to be the result of duress or fraud and should not necessarily be considered (as some courts have) as evidence of collusion. Such uniformity suggests the existence of independent attempts

within a competitive environment to solve an important common problem and signals the presence of a prime research prospect.

REFERENCES

R. J. Coase, "The Nature of the Firm," *Economica*, Nov. 1937, *4*, 386–405.

V. P. Goldberg, "Toward an Expanded Economic Theory of Contract," *J. Econ. Issues*, Mar. 1976, *10*, 45–61.

B. Klein, R. G. Crawford, and A. A. Alchian, "Vertical Integration, Appropriable Rents and the Competitive Contracting Process," *J. Law Econ.*, Oct. 1978, *21*, 297–326.

_____and K. Leffler, "Non-Governmental Enforcement of Contracts: The Role of Market Forces in Guaranteeing Quality," *J. Polit. Econ.*, forthcoming.

_____and A. McLaughlin, "Resale Price Maintenance, Exclusive Territories and Franchise Termination: The Coors Case," unpublished manuscript, Univ. California-Los Angeles 1979.

S. Macauley, "Non-Contractual Relations in Business: A Preliminary Study," *Amer. Soc. Rev.*, Feb. 1963, *28*, 55–69.

M. J. Trebilcock, "The Doctrine of Inequality of Bargaining Power: Post-Benthamite Economics in the House of Lords," *Univ. Toronto Law J.*, Fall 1976, *26*, 359–85.

Oliver E. Williamson, *Markets and Hierarchies: Analysis and Antitrust Implications*, New York 1975.

[13]

MEASUREMENT COST AND THE ORGANIZATION OF MARKETS*

YORAM BARZEL

University of Washington and Hoover Institution

Pᴇᴏᴘʟᴇ will exchange only if they perceive what they get to be more valuable than what they give. To form such perceptions, the attributes of the traded items have to be measured. Some measurements are easy to obtain; others pose difficulties. For example, determining the weight of an orange may be a low-cost, accurate operation. Yet what is weighed is seldom what is truly valued. The skin of the orange hides its pulp, making a direct measurement of the desired attributes costly. Thus the taste and the amount of juice it contains are always a bit surprising. The grower, more knowledgeable than the consumer, may gain by making the surprise an unpleasant one. The potential errors in weighing the commodity and in assessing its attributes permit manipulations and therefore require safeguards. The costs incurred by the transactors will exceed those under joint maximization.

A sampling of activities that arise solely because these costs are positive may hint at how costly the measurement of commodity attributes is.[1] Had product information been costless, warranties would disappear since attribute levels and defects could be effortlessly identified at the time of exchange; fancy packaging (unless valued for its own sake) as well as the *Consumer Report* and the Good Housekeeping Seal would be super-

---

* Steven Cheung should be credited with pointing out the importance of the "measurement problem." Thanks are due to Christopher Hall for his penetrating comments. I also received valuable comments from Keith Acheson, Armen Alchian, Steven Cheung, John Hause, Keith Leffler, and John McManus.

[1] A trifling episode dramatically illustrates how costly some measurements might be. In one of Eddie Bauer's sporting goods stores, sneakers were marked down to almost a third of the regular price after a single "defect" was found: their size markings were missing. (Thanks to Dean Worcester for the information.) Presumably, the cost to Eddie Bauer of measuring the sneakers' sizes, and perhaps of convincing consumers that nothing else was faulty, was perceived as more than half the retail price. The inducement required to compensate consumers for undertaking the measurement was obviously smaller than Eddie Bauer's cost, but still very substantial.

[*Journal of Law & Economics*, vol. XXV (April 1982)]

27

fluous, as would professional certification and recruiting efforts; and beautiful but rotten apples would fetch the appropriate price.

Virtually no commodity offered for sale is free from the cost of measuring its attributes; the problem addressed here is pervasive. "Market signaling" and "adverse selection" are seemingly instances of the general case. In both cases, the costs of measuring the attributes of individuals are high, and the resulting errors permit people to transfer wealth to themselves at a resource cost. Costly measurement is a factor common to these and various other instances where individual and joint maximization do not coincide.

The accuracy of measurement differs fundamentally from other valuable attributes. The presence of random errors introduces the opportunity for costly transfers of wealth. Of concern here are the effects of such behavior and the market arrangements that emerge to reduce the losses from the exploitation of the inaccuracies.[2]

THE NATURE OF MEASUREMENT ERROR

Consider a model adopting all but one of the Walrasian assumptions for a competitive economy; the exception is that product information is costly to obtain. Product information is defined as information on the levels of the attributes per unit of the commodity and on the actual amount contained in the nominal quantity. Measurements of these magnitudes are subject to error. The greater the variability of the measurement around the true value, the lesser the information about the commodity.[3]

Had product information been freely available, equally valued units would sell at the same price and, so long as choosing does not damage the commodity, a seller would not be harmed from allowing buyers to pick and choose. The seller then would have no incentive to constrain choice. It will be seen that when product information is costly, the seller may gain from imposing such a constraint.

The purchase of oranges when the desired good is fresh orange juice can illustrate the measurement problem. Suppose that oranges are identical in the quality of their juice, but the amount each yields varies; that the cost of squeezing oranges at the sellers' premises is prohibitive; that buyers and sellers are able to form estimates of the amount of juice any

---

[2] John C. McManus, The Costs of Alternative Economic Organizations, 8 Can. J. Econ. 334 (1976), takes a rather similar approach. Steven Cheung, A Theory of Price Control, 17 J. Law & Econ. 53 (1974), it seems, was the first to introduce the notion that markets are organized to minimize dissipation.

[3] Measurement is the quantification of information, and its use will facilitate in making the model operational.

orange contains and that the cost of greater accuracy is increasing. The amount of the attribute desired by consumers (and its price) then is subject to measurement error.[4]

Suppose further that numerous sellers sell the commodity. Each sorts it to as many classes as he wishes and then posts a price, say, in dollars per pound, for each class, permitting consumers to select any item provided they pay the posted price.

A consumer's periodic demand for the desired good is downward sloping, reflecting substitution within the period and the increasing cost of storage. The selection of a seller to buy from entails a fixed cost assumed to be so large that the entire period's quantity is obtained from a single bin of a single seller. After deciding which seller to patronize, a consumer will meet the period demand from that seller's offerings.

Had the units in the bin been identical and the amount of the desired attribute they contain known, the quantity purchased by a consumer would be determined by his demand for the attribute and by the price of the commodity. Had the units been varied, but not enough to justify *any* selection effort by the buyer, the quantity purchased would depend in part on the buyer's aversion to variability. At the going price for the commodity, the *expected* price for the attribute is determined, but the quantity obtained is subject to error. For now this effect of the error is abstracted from.

The quantity purchased in a particular period depends on the cost of selection in the following way. If, for instance, a buyer plans to buy only units estimated to be at the top quarter of the distribution, it is expected that four units will be inspected for each unit selected. The total cost of a purchased unit then is the sum of the posted price and the cost of inspecting four units. If, relative to its posted price, the commodity seems a better buy, so that the buyer plans to buy units from the top one-third of the distribution, then for every unit bought only three units will be inspected.

Thus, the interaction among the buyer's demand for the attribute, the buyer's cost of measuring the commodity, the posted price, and the estimated distribution of the attribute determines the amount purchased. That amount will increase as the demand for the good rises, as the cost of selection falls, as the posted price of the commodity falls, as the average quality increases, and, most important, as the *variability* of the commod-

---

[4] The assessment of how long a machine will last, the quality of a particular performance of a long-running play, and the cost of preparing a site for construction are a few additional examples of commodities that are difficult to evaluate or to measure, and thus their measurements are subject to error.

ity offered increases. The reason for the last result is that there is no added penalty for inspecting an exceptionally poor item, but there is an added gain to finding an exceptionally good one.

What are the constraints on the seller in posting his price? Buyers, it is assumed, make use of their past experience to predict the relationship between a seller's posted price and the distribution of his commodity. They will stop patronizing a seller who they determine has a high price relative to the distribution offered. This is the route by which competition from other sellers enters the model. Subsequent to a buyer's decision to buy from a particular seller, that seller faces a downward-sloping price function. To survive, however, the relationship between a seller's price and the quality of his offering cannot "exceed" that of other sellers too often.

How finely will a seller sort his commodity? Assuming that the cost of estimation increases with the accuracy of the estimate, suppose first that this cost is the same to the seller and to his buyers and that all buyers are identical in their aversion to variability. When the variability of the commodity offered at a given price is very low, buyers will forgo selecting and will take whatever is handiest. As variability increases, a point will be reached where selection will begin.

Under the assumptions here, sellers will sort the commodity to that break-even point in variability, that is, just finely enough to dissuade buyers from any sorting. When the seller effects such sorting, each item is measured *exactly* once. On the other hand, when buyers effect the measurement, each item will be measured *at least* once; some will be measured twice or more. Thus the net price—that is, price net of the cost of measuring—at which the commodity can be offered is lowest when the seller effects the measurement. Competition will force sellers to effect the measurement.

The conclusion that the seller will be the one to measure does not depend on the level of this cost so long as this cost is the same to buyers and to the seller. Whatever that cost is, the seller will always measure just finely enough to prevent buyers from measuring regardless of how averse to variability they are. The other side of the coin is that even when buyers do not value a better-sorted product, they will gain from measuring by getting the more highly valued units selling at a given price.

Suppose now that the buyers' cost of measuring is higher than the sellers', say, because a tax on measurement by buyers is imposed or because they are constrained in some way. It immediately follows that the sellers' level of sorting will fall to the new level that would just prevent buyers from any sorting. A striking feature of this result is that when the buyers' cost of measuring is increased, the net price they pay for the commodity, or for the desired attribute, will fall.

Buyers perform their measurements in the market in two steps. In the first they estimate the distributions different sellers offer to decide from whom to buy; in the second they determine the properties of individual items. If the increase in buyers' cost applies only to the second step, then the analysis is complete. If, however, it applies to the first step also, a new problem arises.

If buyers' cost of determining what the distribution is is increased, a seller could more easily entice buyers to buy from him even when his merchandise is "overpriced." In that case, buyers must rely more heavily on their past experience or on some other proxy measure and less on assessing what they are offered on a particular shopping trip. The role of a seller's reputation, warranty, and so forth acquires, then, greater prominence. Constraining buyers' choice in that case will generate some gains but will also introduce new problems. Moreover, the imposition of such a constraint is unlikely to eliminate all measurement by buyers since buyers need to convince themselves that they do not receive worthless merchandise.

The earlier assumption that sellers' measurement cost is not higher than that of buyers seems satisfactory for single-attribute commodities. In reality, most commodities have numerous attributes whose levels vary across units. If a commodity is sorted by all its attributes, each unit may occupy a class by itself. If a commodity is not sorted so exhaustively, various buyers will find it worth their while to pick and choose by attributes that they value highly, but not ones by which the seller sorted the commodity. Whereas such sorting will generate a gain, it will be carried "too far" in comparison with the joint-maximization level.[5]

Because of the cost of measurement, the seller cannot capture the entire value of his merchandise had it been costlessly described. This was shown to be the case when the seller sorted to prevent consumers from any choosing. It is also the case when consumers engage in choosing, selecting items valued more than their price. Because of competition among consumers, however, they will be able to obtain the differential in value only by spending resources—those used on measuring the commodity and perhaps on rushing to the top of the line.

In the remainder of the paper, an attempt is made to determine whether particular market practices are designed to cope with the excess-measurement problem, and implications capable of refuting the hypotheses are derived. Some casual empirical observations are made, but no serious tests are conducted. The particular practices considered below are selected on the basis of their apparent "importance" or "interest."

---

[5] The buyer will sort to the point where an extra dollar's worth of sorting effort yields one dollar in value. Whereas the valued attribute is costly to produce, it is obtained by the buyer at a zero marginal charge from the seller.

An examination of some of the earlier considerations may facilitate in the derivation of hypotheses. A consumer who is convinced that he received a random selection from an optimally measured commodity will not use additional resources for measuring. This requires that trust is established, perhaps by acquiring brand names. The seller still has to select a method of selling to avoid excessive sorting. One such method is to raise the buyer's measurement cost. DeBeers's diamond "sights" seem a case in point. The approved dealers have diamonds chosen for them by DeBeers, and they are not allowed to pick and choose from different offerings.

A buyer's incentive for excessive measurement can also be lowered if he is compensated for items ultimately revealed to be of exceptionally low value, which may explain product warranties. The terms of exchange for warranted products depend on subsequent performance rather than relying entirely on measuring the commodity by the time of exchange. The arrangement, however, lowers the buyer's cost of the careless handling of the product. The severity of this problem depends on the nature of the commodity and on the contractual ability to curb abuse. Share contracts rely even more fully on subsequent performance and obviate the need for certain measurements at the time of exchange. Such contracts are expected, then, when the determination of the value of the exchanged property at the time of exchange is exceptionally costly.

The next four sections discuss product warranties, share contracts, brand names, and the suppression of information. Hypotheses are offered to explain these arrangements, and testable implications are derived. Later sections further expand the model and its applications to such diverse issues as vertical integration and futures markets.

Product Warranties

In every exchange, both the seller and the buyer will require some verification of the measurements of the exchanged goods: the seller to assure himself he is not giving up too much, the buyer to assure himself he is not receiving too little. The process of producing a commodity spans a period of time; the costs of measuring the attributes and of verifying the measurements will vary along the way and will be different for the buyer than for the seller. Which quantitites, then, will be measured, when, and by whom? The remainder of this section concerns measurement by the consumer at the time of consumption.

As a rule, measurement is by the seller, whether in advance or at the time of exchange. Quite often, however, measurement is automatic, or its cost is greatly reduced as the commodity is used. Therefore, substantial savings will result if measuring is left to the buyer to be performed at the time of consumption. A prevalent arrangement for vesting in the consumer the responsibility for certain measurements is that of the guarantee. Presumably, it is too costly for the seller to determine which of his products may have defects. The consumer, on the other hand, can obtain this information cheaply at the time of consumption.[6] In the absence of a guarantee, to avoid getting stuck with a bad item, the consumer will examine several to identify the one with the fewest defects. Given the expected cost of selection by buyers, the seller must price the items he sells below the expected valuation of the best unit; otherwise he will not be able to sell any unit. The differential between the price and the valuation of the units offered for sale is effectively left in the public domain, and buyers will spend resources to acquire it. Selling a commodity with a warranty is essentially a promise to provide one *good* unit at the going price. Thus, the warranty reduces the differential in value received by consumers for given payment and reduces correspondingly the attendant resource expenditure.

The fact that some new cars have numerous defects is not necessarily a sign of poor workmanship. The consumer may simply be more efficient than the seller in providing quality control. When no guarantee is offered, however, a buyer would inspect several cars before choosing one. This excessive examination is avoided when the product is guaranteed. A seller who guarantees his product, then, can raise his price not only by an amount equal to the expected cost of repair, but by a premium representing the cost to the consumer of a prior examination.[7] Guarantees are routine for new cars, but not for used ones. The apparent reason is that a new-car seller can relatively cheaply verify the measurement supplied by the buyer, which is not the case for used cars.[8]

When a warranty is too expensive to supply, two types of arrangements can be used to reduce excess measurement. One is a higher degree of

---

[6] The same consideration may explain certain return privileges. For such items as paint, tiles, and wool it may be difficult to match the items if a second purchase is needed. Since the consumer can measure his requirements most economically at the time of consumption, he is promised a refund for excess quantities of these goods he may buy originally.

[7] In his seminal "lemon" paper, George Akerlof discusses this role of warranties. See George Akerlof, The Market for "Lemons": Quality Uncertainty and the Market Mechanism, 84 Q. J. Econ. 488 (1970).

[8] The warranty is warranted only if buyers cannot easily exercise it even though they, rather than the seller, are at fault. The ability of one party or the other to abuse his position seems to correspond to Williamson's notion of "information impactedness," where "circumstances relevant to the transaction, or related set of transactions, are known to one or more parties but cannot be costlessly discerned by or displayed for others." See O. E. Williamson, Markets and Hierarchies 31 (1975).

quality control, which one would expect, for instance, with commodities designed for the tourist trade. The section on brand names continues this discussion. The other arrangement is to get the consumer to act as if his choice were random. The sale of used cars, where dealers often obliterate potential distinctions among cars, is, seemingly, a case in point. This issue is further developed in the section on the suppression of information.

SHARE CONTRACTS

Share contracts are often said to reflect the desire of the risk averse to moderate the effect of risk. Had this been their sole explanation, it would be refuted by the royalty payment to authors. The royalty contract between author and publisher stipulates that the author will receive a given share of the revenue from the sale of the book. Since the success of the book and the total revenue its sale will generate are not known when the contract is drawn, the author's income is uncertain. Had authors been paid a lump sum, their entire risk would have been shifted to publishers. Publishers are often diversified to start with, and thus paying a lump sum would increase the riskiness of their operations only moderately. The desire to reduce risk, then, would have generated the outright purchase of rights to books rather than the common royalty contract.

What else, then, could explain the sharing arrangement? In the royalty contract the share, or share structure, is set in advance, but the absolute amounts the two parties will receive are contingent on consumers' actual demand subsequent to publication. Because of the difficulty in predicting the ultimate success of the venture, the determination of the appropriate lump sum is expensive to reach. If publishers make competitive lump-sum bids, each of them will require some market research. Even the successful bidder's effort is excessive, since subsequently the information will emerge anyhow. Had publishers attempted to lower the cost by spending only a small amount on research, their bids would be subject to large errors, and the winning bidder might turn out to be a big loser.[9] By sharing, the need for market research is reduced and the error is largely limited to the sharing percentage, making the expected value of the royalty contract larger than the lump sum would have been.[10]

Share contracts are subject to incentive problems absent from lump-

[9] Their loss is similar to the loss to speculators in Hirshleifer's model. See Jack Hirshleifer, The Private and Social Value of Information and the Reward to Inventive Activity, 61 Am. Econ. Rev. 561 (1971). In that model, speculation is with respect to price; here, it is with respect to quantity.

[10] Similarly, owners of mineral rights usually do not sell their rights but rather agree to a share of the unknown revenues.

sum contracts and in this regard are more costly. For instance, the publisher will tend to advertise less than when he does not share added revenues with the author. The lesser the information problem, the more attractive the lump-sum arrangement; thus share contracts are expected to be more common with new authors than with established ones,[11] with the first editions than with subsequent ones, and with novels than with "how-to" manuals.

The sharing arrangement, then, makes some search less profitable. Market forces dissuade publishers and authors from acquiring prior information on the value of the traded property.[12] But because such acquisition would have been wasteful, the sharing arrangement is a more efficient solution.[13]

BRAND NAMES

Since consumption yields direct measurement, it is often advantageous to let consumers do the measuring, which may explain warranties and contracts as argued above. Consumers, however, can gain by understanding the value of the good, and it is often difficult to verify their measurements. On the other hand, at the time of transaction, measurement or verification may be rather costly.[14] How can costly measurement be avoided?

Suppose one wants to buy a six-pack of beer. To determine whether the beer is cold enough, he will touch one or two bottles, but not all of them. Similarly, if he looks for a rope of certain strength, he will test just a small segment. In both examples the procedure followed is not as innocuous as it may appear. The beer seller can reduce refrigeration costs if the easiest-to-reach bottles are coolest, and the rope maker can strengthen just the exposed end of the rope. When the buyer does not engage in a

---

[11] The more books an author publishes, the smaller the proportionate effect of risk from variability in the royalty income from any of the books. The risk-aversion model then implies that sharing, or royalties, will become more common as the number of books an author publishes increases, which is the opposite of this paper's prediction.

[12] See Yoram Barzel, Some Fallacies in the Interpretation of Information Costs, 20 J. Law & Econ. 291 (1977).

[13] Hashimoto hypothesizes that the Japanese wage-bonus payment is a sharing arrangement induced by the cost of evaluating a worker's contribution. He finds that the evidence conforms with this hypothesis. See Masanori Hashimoto, Bonus Payments, on-the-Job Training and Lifetime Employment in Japan, 87 J. Pol. Econ. 1086 (1979).

[14] Various contests and calls for bids are subject to a time limit. Presumably, the caller would wish to have all the materials assembled by a given time. The restriction imposed, however, is on the time marked on the posting, since this seems a much cheaper validation method.

more comprehensive test, he is implicitly trusting the integrity of the seller. But convincing others of one's integrity is a costly activity.

If the buyer is to buy without measuring every item, he has to be persuaded to rely on the seller's assertion of the prior measurement. In some instances, the seller will try to convince the buyer that his purchase will actually be "representative" of the lot; in others that the good is quite uniform and would not vary significantly from sample to sample. Uniformity is the subject of the remainder of this section; suppression of information is the subject of the next section.

A canner known to change the quality of peas (e.g., size, tenderness, sweetness) from one season to another will induce buyers to conduct a fresh, costly test every season. If, on the other hand, the canner is known to maintain tight quality control, much less testing is required. The canner's reputation, or brand name, serves here to guarantee that the product is, and will remain, uniformly good.[15]

The canner incurs costs in establishing reputation,[16] both in controlling quality to assure uniformity and in the maintenance of uniformity when external pressures would call for a change,[17] as any change endangers the canner's reputation, reducing the value of his brand name. Even a higher quality offered at the old price will cause problems by reinducing costly sorting. Thus, it is expected that when the seller's reputation is used to back the product, quality will fluctuate less than when the consumer is to measure it.

Product uniformity lowers the cost of measurement to the consumer. It is probable that to provide continuing uniformity, extensive measurement is required by the seller. However, a seller of established reputation can choose to measure at the cheapest point in the production process rather than at the time of exchange, as would be necessary if the buyer were to insist on verification of the measurement.[18]

---

[15] In an article on the growing and canning of peas, Susan Sheehan gives a detailed description of the extraordinary effort by Green Giant to guarantee product uniformity at all grades. See Susan Sheehan, Peas, The New Yorker, September 17, 1973, at 103.

[16] If it is easier to convince a consumer of the uniformity of a widely distributed product than of each of several narrowly distributed ones, horizontal integration is advantageous.

[17] This point was contributed by Levis Kochin. The pursuit of constant quality by Mars, a candy maker, is detailed in an article in Business Week (August 14, 1978, at 291). "One source of that mystique is Mars' fanaticism about the quality and freshness of its products. . . ." "While other manufacturers were . . . reducing the quality of their candy because of the price of sugar and cocoa . . . Mars [did not]." "[Mars] was the first candy manufacturer to date its products and to guarantee to take back and credit merchandise still on the shelf in four months."

[18] Brand name also involves "standards." Had the most desired characteristics of peas been easy to measure, the label of each can could have stated their amounts. A shopper then

When a buyer receives a bad unwarranted item, his money is lost. Thus, to gain the buyer's patronage the seller must persuade him that he himself will suffer a substantial loss if his product is found deficient. By backing the quality of the item with a brand name, a bad item sold under that name will tarnish the entire brand. The more likely the consumer is to encounter the brand in the future, the more severe the penalty he can impose on the seller and thus the less he has to worry about being cheated.[19] It is expected that the more difficult it is to measure commodities at time of exchange or to warrant them, the more extensive would be the brand under which they are sold. It is also expected, paradoxically, that a seller committed to compensate the buyer for defective products will sell relatively more defective units than a seller who makes no such commitment.

THE SUPPRESSION OF INFORMATION

The provision of uniform commodities would some of the time be too costly. A commodity may be defined as heterogenous if, when allowed, its consumers will spend resources on choosing among equally priced units. Thus, patrons line up for preferred seats in a single-price movie theater; produce and meat in a grocery store are routinely subject to selection; and prospective employers spend resources in recruiting among equally paid, but diverse, workers. As already noted, the competition for the high-valued items is a costly activity; spared of the added cost, a consumer would have offered more for the item.[20]

How much is a buyer who is not permitted to inspect and to choose willing to pay for a commodity? This depends on his guess of the quality of the unit handed to him, which, in turn, depends on how much he trusts the seller. He expects to be given an item from the low-quality end from a mistrusted seller. Suppose, however, that the seller is able to persuade the buyer that he is offering a random or a "representative" selection.

---

could choose his exact preference and uniformity would lose value. A consumer seeking uniformity would simply buy units having the same specifications. Thus the capability to measure implies the existence of "standards." These appear to be a substitute for brand name, and the usage of the two will be negatively correlated. It is expected that the fewer the dimensions of a commodity amenable to standardized measurement, the greater the emphasis on the brand name. Even for commodities that can be cheaply measured, however, brand name helps to assure that the measurements are correct.

[19] Klein and Leffler discuss the nature of brand names and particularly the "last-period" problem. Benjamin Klein & Keith Leffler, The Role of Market Forces in Assuring Contractual Performance, 89 J. Pol. Econ. 615 (1981).

[20] Precisely the same reasoning led to the conclusion that consumers will pay a premium (apart from those for risk reduction and for saving on the expected cost of repair) for commodities sold with warranties.

The buyer will have to submit to the choice effected by the seller, but the resource expense of duplicate sorting is bypassed. Thus, abstracting from risk aversion, he will be willing to bid up to his expected valuation.

Operating within the framework of competitive markets, it is argued that information on the quality of goods that inspection would have generated is deliberately suppressed.[21] On occasion, sellers may even offer buyers "a pig in a poke." There is no difficulty in opening the poke to inspect the pig. When trust can be created cheaply enough, trusting consumers will offer a higher average price for the entire batch when inspection is not allowed, and this arrangement will prevail. In some cases inspection might damage the commodity. In other cases, however, the arrangement is deliberately contrived at a cost of resources.

This may explain why apples are often sold in opaque bags filled in advance by the seller. The consumer spends less time per apple on inspection than when choosing them individually. He obviously will not buy the bag unless he believes that on average he gets a better buy; thus the seller's "fairness" becomes a factor in his decision. It is predicted that sellers catering to transient trade will sell a smaller fraction of their apples by the bag and will sort them into more uniform grouping than will sellers whose credentials are well established.[22]

The advantage of suppressing information may explain some of the practices associated with the selection of physicians by patients. As a rule, a physician has an immense edge over a patient in measuring the service delivered because of the complexity of medical problems and because of the great variability in outcome of a given treatment, even for a single person at different times. Since the patient's cost of measuring the service is much higher than the physician's, resources can be saved if physicians rather than patients engage in measuring. But how can patients be stopped from spending resources trying to identify the best buys? One way is to enhance even further the asymmetry in information between physician and patient.

Sellers of medical services, through the AMA, ADA, etc., spend a large amount of resources to persuade buyers to choose among physicians as if the choice were random.[23] Various measures taken by the AMA lower still further the return to measurement by patients. A high uniformity of skill among physicians is attained through the control of training, of qual-

---

[21] This parallels the argument that with the royalty-payment scheme, authors and publishers will abstain from collecting duplicate information on the value of a manuscript.

[22] The hypothesis could be tested by comparing the behavior of shopkeepers in resort areas during the tourist season with that during the off-season.

[23] The assumption of competition through free entry does not hold in this case. As will be shown presently, however, in at least one dimension the restriction on entry may prove to be efficient.

ifying examinations, and of admission to medical schools (where, e.g., large fellowships are less readily available than in other graduate programs). Not surprisingly, then, medical school graduates seem more uniform in ability than those in other professions.[24] Moreover, the gap between the training of nurses and physicians is so wide that only seldom would patients compare the services of the two.

Comparison among physicians also is discouraged. Physicians are constrained from criticizing one another, and until recently were not allowed to advertise and were severely restricted with respect to office signs, yellow-page entries, and the like. Additionally, price information is kept in low profile. Thus, a patient can compare physicians only by expedients such as word of mouth.

If the preceding hypothesis is correct, the following observations are implied: (1) The AMA would resist moves to make comparisons easier. (2) The easier it is for patients to measure a medical service, the looser will be its control by the AMA. (3) Income variability among doctors would be less than in other professions that require a comparable amount of training, such as law. Casual observations on the first two implications are in conformity with the hypothesis. The tenacious fight of the AMA against prepaid medical insurance is consistent with the first implication. The question as to whether to join such an insurance group itself requires comparison, and when a compensation schedule is provided, price comparison becomes easier.

With respect to the second implication, consider the distinction between acute and chronic medical problems. A person afflicted with a chronic problem gains experience which in time increases his ability to measure the service he receives. To that extent, he has a comparative advantage over someone with an acute problem. From this it is predicted that the treatment of chronic problems will be less tightly controlled by the AMA. This seems to be borne out by the fact that chiropractors, whose specialty is treating predominantly chronic ailments, are allowed to compete with physicians.

Vertical Integration

When production is specialized, the product will change hands before reaching the ultimate consumer. In this section, some of the problems associated with measuring the product in its intermediate stages are analyzed.[25] Home production is an extreme form of vertical integration.

---

[24] Medical societies also deny membership, and the right to practice, to physicians who prove "incompetent."

[25] Cohen's discussion of the firm is based, in part, on the difficulties in measurement. L. R. Cohen, The Firm: A Revised Definition, 46 S. Econ. J. 580 (1979).

Since all stages of production are carried out by a single person, the motive for excess measurement is absent but the advantages of specialization are lost. What role does the vertically integrated firm play regarding the problem of measurement?

Consider a production process requiring several workers. A firm employing these workers will incur the costs of contracting with them and policing their activities. These costs would be avoided if the process were divided among firms, each consisting of one worker who would buy the intermediate good from the one preceding him on the production line. He may also buy other needed materials and buy, or rent, the space and equipment he uses. These factors, combined with his own work, would enhance the value of the intermediate good which he subsequently would sell to the next man on the line.[26] If production is so organized, the problem of "shirking" disappears.[27]

At most points, however, the value of the intermediate product may be difficult to assess, and therefore its sale may be accompanied by excess sorting. Thus, costs are incurred also in the exchange among such firms. Sometimes the relationship between input and output is well understood. The change in input may then serve as a satisfactory proxy for the change in output value.[28] As will now be shown, the use of input as a proxy for output does not by itself necessitate exchange within a firm, though it is a condition for this form of organization.

Would separate one-worker firms be formed in a production process spanning the tasks of several workers where output is easily measured at the end points but not at others? If the first step is organized as a separate one-worker firm, its output has to be sold to the firm performing the next task. As asserted, it is more costly to evaluate that output directly than to

[26] During the 1860s, several major industries in Birmingham were composed of numerous one-man firms. See G. C. Allen, The Industrial Development of Birmingham and the Black Country, 1860–1927 (1929; reprinted ed. 1966).

[27] Jensen and Meckling analyze the problem of borrowing and of the associated policing when the amount of capital required for the efficient firm size diverges from what the entrepreneur can supply. For their analysis to hold, firm size has to be independent of what they call "agency cost." This would be the case if optimal firm size were an exogenous "technological" datum. It is suggested here that this size is itself economically determined. See M. C. Jensen & W. H. Meckling, Theory of the Firm: Managerial Behavior, Agency Costs, and Ownership Structure, 3 J. Fin. Econ. 305 (1976).

[28] Alchian and Demsetz state, ". . . Suppose a farmer produces wheat . . . with subtle and difficult quality variations determined by how the farmer grew the wheat. A vertical integration could allow a purchaser to control the farmer's behavior in order to more economically estimate productivity." A. A. Alchian & H. Demsetz, Production, Information Costs, and Economic Organization, 62 Am. Econ. Rev. 785 (1972). This statement comes close to the basic argument here. Alchian and Demsetz, however, do not make the crucial distinction between random and biased errors.

measure the value of the products entering the first step plus its additional inputs. Thus, to determine the value of the product it receives, the second firm will have to monitor the inputs of the first firm. So long as the transition to the third-step output can be measured cheaply, however, there is no clear advantage in integrating the first two steps.[29]

When inputs have to be measured at two successive junctures, a rationale for an integrated firm emerges. If the second firm is also a one-worker enterprise whose output is difficult to measure, the firm performing the third step will have to monitor not only the inputs in the second step but also the value of the product entering the first step and the inputs within the step. Thus, the inputs of the first firm have to be monitored by both the second and the third firm. Although the second firm could provide the third with its own evaluation of the first firm's inputs, it stands to gain from overstating the case. The third firm, then, would need to verify the figures in some way. The problem is obviously compounded as the number of steps increases. If a separate organization performs this function for all steps, the conservation of information is clear: There is no longer a need for each firm to monitor the inputs in all prior steps. It is hypothesized that this is a function of the "firm."[30]

In view of this explanation, the notion of residual payments so commonly associated with the firm obtains an entirely different interpretation. When output is easily measured directly, the contribution of a worker can be assessed by his output, and there is a strong incentive for him to become self-employed. At other times, output can be measured by inputs more cheaply than by measuring it directly. If output is measured by inputs, remuneration of inputs cannot be based on output. Employees of a firm are paid by inputs rather than by output not because of lack of "entrepreneurship," but rather because their input is measured more eco-

---

[29] Indeed, airlines employ engineers to inspect the airplanes assigned to them while they are being built by Boeing. Similarly, in other equipment contracts and in construction it is not uncommon that the buyer retains the right to inspect the production process.

[30] Coase pointed out two forces favoring organizing production by the firm rather than by the market. One is the cost of "discovering what the relevant prices are"; the other is "the costs of negotiating and concluding a separate contract for each exchange transaction which takes place on a market." R. H. Coase, The Nature of the Firm, reprinted in Readings in Price Theory 336 (1952). Suggested here is another force—the cost of measuring intermediate outputs which, it is argued, favors production within a firm. The motive for vertical integration suggested here resembles that offered by Klein et al. See Benjamin Klein, Robert G. Crawford, & Armen A. Alchian, Vertical Integration, Appropriable Rents, and the Competitive Contracting Process, 21 J. Law & Econ. 297 (1978). Their argument, however, hinges on small numbers; at the extreme, one buyer facing one seller. There is no restriction here on the number of either buyers or sellers. In Williamson's view also, small numbers are a necessary condition, since vertical integration "harmonizes interests" and reduces the hazard of cheating between firms (see Williamson, *supra* note 8, at 82).

nomically than their output; otherwise they would have become self-employed. Having employees bear the risk in output value through direct ownership has no desirable incentive effect and thus is of little purpose. When tasks are performed by employed workers, "shirking" becomes a problem and the entrepreneur is remunerated for his monitoring of inputs, which implies that he has to assume the risk of price and other fluctuations.[31]

Distinct firms will form and trade with each other at junctures where output can be readily measured, but where output is difficult to measure the different steps will be performed within the firm. Between the time that a commodity such as canned salmon leaves the manufacturer and the time it reaches the consumer, its physical properties and its value will have changed only slightly. Other goods such as produce and bread may change a great deal. The ownership of a commodity may not change at all between production and consumption, as is the case with home-grown vegetables, or it may change several times. It is predicted that ownership will change more frequently the less the commodity is subject to change. Thus, canned salmon is expected to change ownership more times than fresh salmon, powdered milk more than fresh milk, cookies more than fresh bread, and so on. A comparison, admittedly casual, of cookies and bread is in conformity with the prediction. Grocers buy the cookies they sell, but only rent shelf space to bakeries for bread sold through them.[32]

ERRORS OF PROXY MEASUREMENT

Often, the units by which a commodity is exchanged differ from those for which it is desired. For example, tires are measured by ply, size, and tread, whereas they are valued for strength, road-holding ability, and longevity; oranges are sold by weight, which includes the seldom-wanted skin. In this section, some of the problems that arise from the use of proxies are discussed.

Consider the tastiness of apples. Suppose that taste is extremely costly to measure and that it is correlated with color, which can be measured by the naked eye.[33] Color, then, is used as a measure of taste, and the market price of apples becomes a function of their color—the redder are Red

---

[31] This argument strongly parallels that of Alchian and Demsetz, *supra* note 28. Their "team production" output can be measured cheaply, but because of scale economies the output of a team member cannot. Team members, then, have to be policed and are remunerated according to their inputs.

[32] Coor's beer, which is more difficult to keep fresh because it has no preservatives, is supposedly monitored by that brewery more vigorously than do other breweries.

[33] John Umbect says (personal communication) that in Tangier, tangerines offered for sale are displayed on a branch with a leaf or two. The apparent reason is that a leaf is a better visual indicator of freshness than is the fruit itself.

Delicious apples, the higher is their price. Thus, an orchardist will optimize with respect to color.

When the proxy measure can be manipulated, here, too, people will redistribute income at the expense of resources. Suppose that a chemical fertilizer can enhance apples without affecting their taste. Abstracting from the asesthetic value of apples, if the consumer cannot discern whether the chemical has been used and obtaining that information is too costly, the orchardist will then apply the chemical.[34]

Since consumers ultimately value apples for their taste and not their color, had it been possible effortlessly to stop the use of the fertilizer, the cost of the extra reddening would have been avoided without incurring any other loss.[35] The use of the proxy seems wasteful—the apples are made "excessively" pretty. The proxy, however, is presumably used because the alternative of not using it is still more costly.

The use of the chemical will affect the relationship between color and value. Assuming diminishing marginal valuation, R_0 in Figure 1 is the original relationship between the two attributes. The application of a given amount of the fertilizer will shift the curve to the right to R_1. Apples of any given color are now valued less. Still, the redder an apple is, the tastier and more valuable it is. The shift in the curve, however, is not likely to be uniform. Rather, the redder the apples are to start with, the smaller is the shift. This is due to two factors, each of which is sufficient for the argument here. First, the originally redder apples are likely to gain less in value from a given increase in color. Second, a given dose of the fertilizer is expected to affect them less noticeably.

Thus R_1 is steeper than R_0. Given the cost and the error of measuring redness, the steeper relationship constitutes a reduction in the informational value of the color of apples. This is a force constraining the application of fertilizer, but it also guarantees that some amount will be used. To see this, assume momentarily that the relationships between redness and value and between redness and the amount of fertilizer are both linear. This means that R_0 and R_1 are parallel straight lines. If the return from the application of one unit of the chemical is positive, then a reapplication will yield the same return. Eventually, however, consumers would cease to employ color as a measure of taste. At this point, the return from its use in *any* amount will drop to zero. But as the use of the fertilizer is discon-

---

[34] A grower using the fertilizer need not be aware that his behavior is dissipating. He is informed by the market-price structure that consumers value redness, and that is what he is providing.

[35] Spence's "signal" is also a measurable attribute which is correlated with the "true" one and subject to manipulation. See M. Spence, Job Market Signaling, 87 Q. J. Econ. 355 (1973).

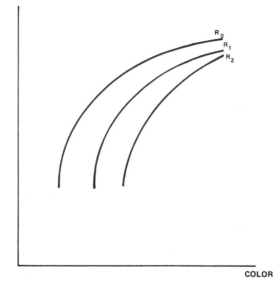

FIGURE 1

tinued, the relationship between color and value will be restored, return-ing us to the starting point of the cycle.[36]

When returns are diminishing, however, the dilemma disappears. In Figure 1, R_2 represents the effect of a second dose of the fertilizer. The return is lower because the effect on color is less than that of the first dose, and also because an extra unit of color increases revenue less than it did before, as R_2 is steeper than R_1. As more fertilizer is used, a point will be reached at which the return from an extra dose is equal to its cost.

If the simplifying assumptions—that the fertilizer does not affect taste and that color is valued only as a proxy for taste—are relaxed, the analy-sis grows more complicated but the logic remains the same. To the extent that taste would be improved by the use of the fertilizer, dissipation is decreased. If taste is affected adversely, but the correlation between taste and color remains positive, dissipation will exceed the cost of the fer-tilizer. If taste is affected more than color, too little of the chemical will be used; indeed, it will not be used at all if it does not alter color even though it improves the taste.

Now, relaxing the second assumption, suppose that the color of apples is valued for its own merit. In this case, the fertilizer will be applied apart from its effect on taste, and it will be used beyond the point that would

[36] Rothschild and Stiglitz present another "no-equilibrium" result. Their setting is com-petitive insurance markets. See Michael Rothschild & Joseph Stiglitz, Equilibrium in Com-petitive Insurance Markets, 90 Q. J. Econ. 629 (1976).

have been dictated if color were merely a proxy for taste. The rest of the analysis remains unchanged.

The color of apples can undoubtedly be affected in other ways, such as the choice of harvest time, of storage temperature, and so on. Each of these methods will be used (and the information content of color function "degraded") to a point where the return equals the cost. The general principle is that maximization occurs with respect to whatever measures consumers use to determine market values. Presumably, the measures in actual use combine a high correlation with the desired ones while possessing high resistance to degradation.

Activities directed toward the market measures will, in general, be off the mark in terms of their effect on the "true" measures. Nevertheless, a grower who applies less of the fertilizer will find his revenue declining more than his cost since, given the assumptions here, he is unable to convince consumers that his less colorful apples are as tasty. This is an instance where the "bad" drives the "good" out of the market. Similarly, a consumer cannot gain by buying apples that are not as red as his own preferences dictate, since the price structure of applies of different shades of red is itself determined by consumers' valuation.

It is tempting to think that if a grocer would mark a bin of apples "ugly but tasty," and if the apples indeed proved flavorful, he could overcome the problem of the spurious measure.[37] The difficulty in convincing buyers that what looks unattractive may nevertheless be good is illustrated by the owner who spends resources to "beautify" the house he plans to sell in a way he did not feel was worthwhile when he was living there. Buyers are well aware of this common practice, but its survival demonstrates that the skin-deep treatment does affect their decisions. In the case of apples, the greatest benefits accrue to those growers able to convince consumers that they avoid the fertilizer while in fact using it. It is difficult to allay consumers' suspicions, since for each type of apple the redder it is the better it tastes.

Still, suppose that to a particular grower the cost of convincing consumers that no fertilizer was used is low enough.[38] It is predicted that on average the grower's apples will look less attractive, or rather, less red, than those grown with the fertilizer; that for given redness, the unfer-

---

[37] Safeway stores seem to harp on this theme when advertising their "Scotch Buy" brand as "It ain't fancy but it sure is good!" This brand, however, is backed by Safeway's own brand name. Two other examples (supplied by Marion Impola) of attempts to dispel mistrust are a seller's sign by his Kiwi fruit, "Ugly, but interesting," and Smucker's ad, "With a name like Smucker's, it's got to be good."

[38] If a growers' association can police its members more cheaply than consumers can police a grower, the association is expected to prohibit the use of the fertilizer. This restrictive practice actually promotes efficiency.

tilized apples will be more expensive; and that the unfertilized apples of a given taste will be cheaper, an implication that is easy to verify subjectively but not objectively.

Given the last implication, the unfertilized apples should drive the other apples out of the market. However, the cost of upholding the no-fertilizer claim will vary among consumers. It is expected, then, that both types of apples will continue to be provided. It seems plausible that the farther consumers are from the grower, the higher the cost of creating "trust." The notion that better Washington apples or California oranges will be shipped to the East Coast then applies to the better-looking, but not to the better-tasting, fruit.

FUTURES MARKETS[39]

The impersonality that characterizes markets in received models does not appear to hold for most actual markets, where the identity or brand name of transactors is essential to functioning. In "futures" markets, however, the trustworthiness of the parties is inconsequential, since apart from the enforcement role of the exchange there is no continuing relationship. The exchange certifies that the traded commodities meet the required specifications and that payment is forthcoming. Thus, the buyer need not worry about receiving defective merchandise and the seller does not have to spend resources to collect his pay. However, far from the accepted view, it appears that such impersonality is attained at high cost.

Suppose that the rate at which a good will deteriorate can be controlled. If the present price decreases as expected deterioration increases, the seller will spend resources to retard that process. Suppose, however, that measurement of the expected deterioration at the time the exchange is agreed upon is so costly that it will not be performed. Now, if the exchange is strictly by specifications, as in the futures trade, the prevention of deterioration will not occur since it will not be remunerated. On the other hand, in the spot market, where sellers operate under a brand name, deterioration will be controlled because a positive return is expected.[40]

This distinction may explain an otherwise puzzling phenomenon: Farm products traded in futures markets tend to be characterized as of "low-quality" or "garbage" grade.[41] How can such a term apply to a commod-

---

[39] An earlier analysis of these markets by Acheson and McManus is not unlike the one presented here. See K. Acheson & J. McManus, The Costs of Transacting in Futures Markets (August 1979) (unpublished paper, Carleton Univ.).

[40] Lindsay draws a similar distinction between government output that is evaluated strictly by specification, and private output, in which unspecified margins are (somehow) adhered to. See Cotton M. Lindsay, A Theory of Government Enterprise, 84 J. Pol. Econ. 1061 (1976).

[41] The costliness of measuring the protein content of wheat and the resulting allocation of

ity that meets all stipulated specifications? The answer may well be that other *non*stipulated attributes will be underproduced when the commodities are destined for futures markets. The levels of the valuable qualities could have been increased at a lower cost than their valuation except for the cost of measurement—which has prevented such action. For this reason, producers are not expected to plan to produce for the futures markets. Only when the commodity is found unsuitable for regular customers would they divert it toward the futures market.

Since commodities sold in futures markets are also sold in spot markets, two testable implications are suggested. First, the price in the spot market is predicted to be higher than that in the futures market for what appears, in terms of specifications, to be the same commodity. Second, specifications are expected to be more comprehensive in futures markets than in spot markets. Since brand name is already established in the spot market, some direct measurements can be dispensed with.

Uncertainty and Dissipating Behavior

Diminishing marginal utility of income implies that the more income varies around a given mean the less it is valued. The presumption that in reality the marginal utility of income is indeed diminishing is the basis for the accepted explanation of insurance, product warranties, and sharing arrangements that are said to reduce the uncertainty facing the individual. It was suggested, however, that warranties and sharing arrangements may be explained by a quite different force: the cost of getting reliable information about a good. This argument is now more generally related to the problem of uncertainty.

Some uncertainty is truly and entirely random; in most situations, however, opportunities abound for the human hand to affect the odds. A person facing an uncertain situation has reason to fear that if the odds are tampered with, they will not be in his favor. A used-car buyer who suspects that the salesman will attempt to saddle him with a worse-than-average car will take some countermeasures. Both the odds tampering by the seller and the protective steps by the buyer consume resources. The buyer, then, would pay a premium independent of any "risk aversion" to convert the uncertain situation into a certain one.

The risk-aversion model predicts that risk will be shifted toward the party for whom risk is less costly. The prediction here is that whoever is in a position to affect the odds will tend to assume the risk, though the two are not mutually exclusive. The payment of royalties rather than a lump

---

high-protein wheat to regular channels and low-protein wheat through impersonal channels is described by Carl L. Alsberg, Protein Content: A Neglected Factor in Wheat Grades, in 2 Wheat Studies of the Food Research Institute 163–76 (1926).

sum to an author, and particularly to a novice, tends to support the latter hypothesis.

The offering of warranties or of some other means to reduce uncertainty is itself costly. It is predicted that the more easily tampering can be detected and the larger the subsequent loss, the less frequently will a warranty be offered. Indeed, people are expected to expose themselves deliberately to detection to reduce the buyer's fear of being cheated.[42] It is predicted, though most tentatively, that well-established law firms will set fixed fees or fixed hourly charges rather than contingent fees more often than will less prestigious law firms. The highly reputable law firm having more of a reputation to protect is expected to monitor its members to provide clients with satisfactory service. To attract business, law firms of lesser reputation in effect offer insurance when they base their fees contingent on good performance.

Concluding Remarks

The problems and costs of measurement pervade and significantly affect all economic transactions. Errors of measurement are too costly to eliminate entirely. The value of equally priced items will differ, then, and people will spend resources to acquire the difference. Such resource expenditure is wasteful, and it is hypothesized that exchange parties will form such contracts and engage in such activities that reduce this kind of resource use. The customer's random selection from an already optimally sorted commodity will avoid the excessive expense. Thus, for example, it is expected that some readily obtainable information will be suppressed to preempt opportunities for excessive measurement.

Because inputs are sometimes the best available proxies for measuring output, vertical integration in the form of organizing output within firms can conserve some measurement costs. Measurement losses also can be lowered by other expedients such as share contracts and warranties. "Trust," "brand name," "repeat purchases," and the like also lower the need for costly measurements, though they are too costly to produce.

The fragments of evidence presented are only illustrative and should not be construed as a test of the model. Even the hypotheses offered are rather tentative; more thorough knowledge of the details of market organization are needed to make firmer predictions. They help to demonstrate, however, that the concept of "measurement" is operational and that the model based on it is capable of generating testable implications.

---

[42] The owner of a race track has less incentive to tamper with the results of a horse race when betting is on a parimutuel basis, which may explain the prevalence of that arrangement. In general, it seems that organizers of games of chance are rewarded not on the basis of their risk but of gross income. Sellers of insurance, on the contrary, subject themselves to substantial risk.

[14]

PROPERTY RIGHTS AND TECHNOLOGICAL INNOVATION*

By Svetozar Pejovich

I. Economic Development, Innovation, and Property Rights

The economist Armen Alchian said once that ever since the fiasco in the Garden of Eden, we have been living in a world in which what we want exceeds what is available. The desire for more satisfaction is a predictable behavioral implication of the fact of scarcity. In fact, it might have helped mankind to survive against competition from other forms of life. Man's desire for more utility gives rise to two interdependent issues that each and every society has to face: (i) how to increase the value of the community's wealth,[1] and (ii) how to allocate the increment in wealth. We generalize those issues as the demand for economic development.[2]

Innovation means doing something that has not been done before. It could be the production of a new good, the opening up of a new market, the discovery of a new source of supply, the development of a new method of production, or changes in the rules of the game. Whichever is the case, by injecting a novelty into the flow of economic life, innovation offers the community a new choice. Innovation is the engine of economic progress.

Most innovations that affect the economy are technological (scientific) innovations.[3] Technology, broadly defined, embodies the prevailing knowledge. The growth of knowledge then creates new technological possi-

---

* An earlier version of this paper was presented at the Conference on the Process of Transition in Eastern Europe in Trento, Italy, in March 1995. I am grateful to the Earhart Foundation for support of my research on the economics of property rights.

[1] Wealth is the value of all pecuniary and nonpecuniary goods that yield income to a person. In addition to assets that yield money (pecuniary) incomes, people derive nonpecuniary income from a number of specific "goods" such as leisure, a pleasant environment, clean air, a good football team in town, friendly neighbors, and so on. The value of satisfaction from nonpecuniary goods is subjective and has its monetary equivalent.

[2] Economic development and economic growth are not identical concepts. Economic development means changes in the value of people's total wealth. Economic growth measures changes in the value of goods and services included in various accounting categories such as gross national product (GNP). The former is all-inclusive and subjective. The latter is easier to quantify. However, it leaves out of the calculation many of the (nonpecuniary) goods that determine the value of people's wealth.

[3] This essay is about technological innovations by business firms. I prefer to use the term "technological innovation"; the term "scientific innovation" might fail to convey a clear distinction between invention and innovation—that is, between creating new knowledge (which is generally but not exclusively done by scientists) and using it (which is done by nonscientists as well). Examples of technological innovation are modern airplanes, computers, the Internet, etc. For all practical purposes, the two terms ("technological innovation" and "scientific innovation") could be used interchangeably.

bilities. Since both the growth and the direction of new knowledge are unpredictable, the flow of innovations is also unpredictable and their impact on the economy uncertain. The innovator translates new technological possibilities into new choices. That is, innovation is a consequence of the *individual's* perceptions about the applicability of technology, willingness to accept the risk and uncertainty associated with doing something new, and ability to see the innovation through. Thus, the innovator must possess traits such as ingenuity, optimism, stubbornness, perseverance, and imagination. Boards of directors, governments, agencies, organizations, and other groups cannot innovate. A member of one of those entities has to perceive an opportunity to innovate and sell it to his colleagues. Potential innovators are difficult to identify *ex ante*, and innovation is not an activity that we can plan for. We cannot decide to have two innovations each month.

Innovation represents an addition to the community's set of opportunity choices. The implementation of a novelty requires that resources be withdrawn from other uses. By implication, innovation is a trade-off between (1) the value of output which the resources used by the innovator were producing before and (2) the use of those resources to make an addition to the community's set of choices. Voluntary acceptance of an innovation by the community means that the community is better off. Otherwise, innovation would have failed.

The innovator is, then, much more than a passive agent who directs production in accordance with the consumers' preferences. He is a mover and shaker of the system, while the consumers get to judge the innovator's entrepreneurial decisions. This means that we have no way of telling whether innovations that are not voluntarily accepted by interacting individuals benefit the community. Consider, for example, the influence of state authorities such as the Food and Drug Administration (FDA), which have the power to impose and *enforce* policies regarding innovation. Such policies, as Karl Brunner notes, can have unexpected and adverse·consequences:

> The traumatic impact on public impressions made by the tragically crippled and deformed babies resulting from the use of thalidomide by pregnant women influenced new legislation and tougher regulatory policies. . . . The measures implemented [to reduce the risk of such a tragedy being repeated] raised the costs of development for new products by a large factor. . . . Innovation consequently declined by a wide margin and the appearance of new drugs sharply contracted. . . . A policy addressed to minimize the probability of bad [pharmaceutical] products maximized at the same time the probability of *not* having useful drugs.[4]

---

[4] Karl Brunner, "The Limits of Economic Policy," in *Socialism: Institutional, Philosophical, and Economic Issues*, ed. Svetozar Pejovich (Dordrecht: Kluwer Academic Publishers, 1987), pp. 41–42.

We can say that technological innovation unfolds the meaning of economic development as the expansion of choices *voluntarily* accepted by the community. That is, economic development is neither about more of the same nor about new choices imposed on the community from without.

Thus, economic analysis of economic development must identify the factors that affect the flow of innovation in the community and the circumstances upon which those factors depend. Research and empirical evidence have shown that property-rights structures are one such critical factor.[5] The purpose of this essay is to analyze the impact of three types of property rights in business firms[6] on the flow of technological innovation. I focus on the three types of firms that have been implemented over a reasonably long period: the privately owned firm under capitalism,[7] the labor-managed firm in a decentralized socialist state (former Yugoslavia and, to a lesser degree, Hungary),[8] and the state-owned firm in a centrally planned economy (former USSR and most Eastern European countries). The last two types of business firms, the only two which were fully implemented in the pre-1989 socialist world, were entirely consistent with the basic philosophical and economic premises of the socialist doctrine as it had evolved since the eighteenth century.

II. Property Rights and the Flow of Innovation

This essay analyzes the effects of alternative types of property rights on the flow of innovation under several subheadings: freedom to innovate, incentives to innovate, the power to innovate, and the integration of innovation into the economy.

---

[5] For example, Douglass North has demonstrated a strong link between different types of property rights and economic development (and has received a Nobel prize for his research).

[6] Most innovations, especially technological innovations, are likely to take place within business organizations. For example, an independent innovator has incentives to create a firm before carrying out his or her innovation, in order to reduce the costs of negotiating contracts across markets, to limit liabilities to creditors, and to exploit tax advantages.

[7] The bundle of property rights that define the privately owned firm includes the owner's right to appropriate the residual after all cooperating inputs are paid their contractual prices, the owner's right to hire and fire cooperating inputs, and the owner's right to sell those two rights in competitive markets.

[8] The bundle of rights that define the labor-managed firm includes the state's ownership of capital assets held by the firm, the employees' right to appropriate (and distribute among themselves) the return from those assets, and the employees' right to govern the firm. The employees' rights specified above are not transferable; they are contingent on their employment by that firm. It is important not to confuse the labor-managed economy with producers' cooperatives in capitalism. In a free-market, private-property society, producers' cooperatives emerge spontaneously and have to survive competition from other types of firms. The fact that producers' cooperatives have not happened on any significant scale in capitalism is evidence of their relative inefficiency. I am always puzzled when some colleagues say that I have tried, in some of my works, to show that the labor-managed firm is inefficient. Nothing could be further from the truth. Competitive markets have done that. All that an economist can do is to try to determine why the labor-managed firm is inefficient.

A. Alternative types of property rights and freedom to innovate

Potential innovators do not emerge from a specific social class. We observe that they come from all social groups. Thus, the larger the number of people who have the freedom to innovate, the higher the probability of increasing the flow of innovation.

In a private-property, free-market economy, everyone has the right to acquire resources and use them to pursue any lawful activity, including innovation. However, private property rights are often attenuated in free societies. For example, codetermination laws[9] raise the cost of equity capital, license requirements reduce the number of people who can pursue specific activities, monopoly privileges (including protectionism) limit one's right choose how to use one's own resources, FDA rules delay and perhaps discourage some innovators.[10] While it would be wrong to argue that restrictions on the right of ownership have no benefits, the attenuation of private property has to affect the flow of innovation by placing restrictions on the freedom to innovate.

In a centrally planned economy, entry into decision making is attained through membership in the ruling elite. Individuals (including members of the ruling group) have no right to acquire productive resources. Members of the ruling group, managers of enterprises, and all other individuals who perceive an opportunity for an innovation must sell the idea to their colleagues or superiors, who in turn have to sell it to their superiors, and so on.

In a labor-managed economy,[11] the pool of those who have the right to acquire and use resources is restricted to the working collective. The term "working collective" is important here. Only a working collective, either directly or through its governing board, can decide to carry out innovations. An employee who perceives an opportunity to innovate must sell the idea to other employees (or to the board). That is, he must sell it to a group of people with limited business experience, diverse attitudes toward risk, and short time horizons.[12]

---

[9] Codetermination means that employees join shareholders on the boards of directors of corporate firms and take an active role in decision making. Germany has been a leader in promoting codetermination in the West. For example, the Codetermination Act of 1976 requires that in business firms employing more than two thousand employees, one-half of the members of the board of directors (in Germany it is called the "supervisory board") must be labor representatives.

[10] See Brunner, "The Limits of Economic Policy."

[11] The labor-managed firm is a socialist version of codetermination: labor participation in decision making without private property rights. Former Yugoslavia is the only socialist country that has tried this type of firm on a large scale and over a long period of time. A major academic advocate of this method for organizing production in the West has been professor Jaroslav Vanek of Cornell University; see, e.g., Jaroslav Vanek, *The General Theory of Labor-Managed Market Economies* (Ithaca, NY: Cornell University Press, 1970). See also note 8 above.

[12] The shortness of time horizons is due to the nontransferability of assets held by the group. In the context of the labor-managed firm, the nontransferability means that workers have the right to use assets held by their firm and to appropriate returns (earnings) from

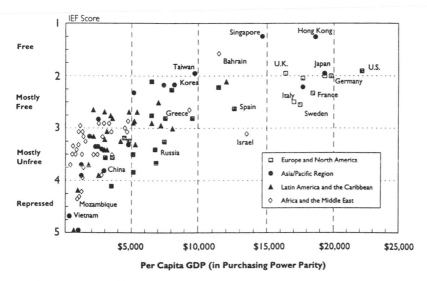

FIGURE 1. A comparison of economic freedom and wealth in various countries.

In a carefully researched study, Bryan Johnson and Thomas Sheehy set out to find a method for measuring the relationship between economic freedom and wealth, as well as the relationship between economic freedom and the rate of growth. To this end they developed an index of economic freedom.[13] The index is based on several factors including private property rights. Using their index, Johnson and Sheehy examined 101 countries and ranked them as *free* (7 countries), *mostly free* (36), *mostly unfree* (50), and *repressed* (8).[14] The study provides compelling evidence of a strong relationship between economic freedom and economic prosperity. Figures 1 and 2 summarize Johnson and Sheehy's major findings.[15]

The study is a rich source of observations about the link between economic freedom and prosperity. Hong Kong and Singapore, classified as free economies, have enjoyed a high rate of economic development over

---

those assets, but not to sell the assets or change their value (i.e., workers must reinvest each year an amount approximately equal to the assets' wear and tear).

[13] Bryan Johnson and Thomas Sheehy, *The Index of Economic Freedom* (Washington, DC: Heritage Foundation, 1995). The study does not discuss political and civic freedoms.

[14] Johnson and Sheehy classify Eastern European countries along with all other countries and do so on the basis of their institutional arrangements prevailing in the early 1990s.

[15] Both tables are reproduced from Johnson and Sheehy, *The Index of Economic Freedom*, by permission of the Heritage Foundation. In Figure 2, the 1965 figures are from the Agency for International Development and first appeared in Edward Hudgins and Bryan Johnson, "Why Asia Grows and Africa Doesn't," Heritage Foundation Backgrounder No. 756 (March 2, 1990); the 1991 figures are from the United Nations Development Programme's *Human Development Report 1994*; the figures for Taiwan are for per-capita GNP.

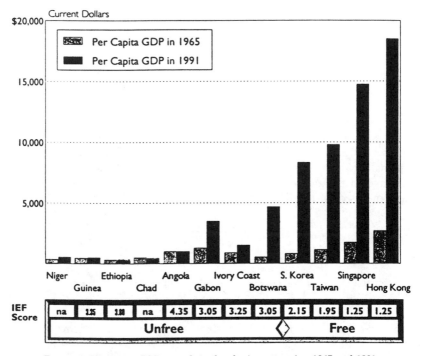

FIGURE 2. Per-capita GDP growth in developing countries: 1965 and 1991.

the last twenty-five years. By contrast, the repressed economies of Vietnam and North Korea are among the world's poorest.

In 1965, mostly unfree Gabon had a per-capita gross domestic product (GDP) of $1,286. Since that year Gabon has been flooded with hundreds of millions of dollars of foreign aid and other nonmarket grants. Yet, by 1991, Gabon's per-capita GDP had risen to only $3,448. By contrast, per-capita GDP in free Taiwan rose from $1,133 in 1965 to $9,805 in 1991. And Taiwan received a relatively insignificant amount of nonmarket funds during that period.

In the early 1970s, Chile was the world's second largest recipient of foreign aid, had a stagnating economy and, under Salvador Allende, had a shrinking GDP. By 1990, Chile's economy had changed dramatically. Augusto Pinochet's market reforms drastically reduced government intervention in the economy, maximized economic freedoms, and helped transform Chile into one of the fastest-growing economies of the world.

Among former communist countries, mostly free Estonia and the Czech Republic have provided credible guarantees of property rights, adopted low rates of taxation, and seriously reduced government regulations. And the economies of these two countries are performing better than any other former socialist state.

In an interesting article, Keith Richburg discusses the issue of why African development has lagged so far behind that of East Asia, which suffered from a similar set of initial obstacles. Why has East Asia become a model of economic success, while Africa, since independence, has seen increasing poverty and hunger? Richburg offers two major explanations for those differences in economic development. First, after independence, which for most of them occurred in the first two decades after the end of World War II, the majority of African countries opted for government ownership of enterprises, due to a distrust of private property rights and foreign investment. Asians chose a brand of capitalism. Second, the prevailing informal institutions in Africa turned out to be less adaptable (relative to the prevailing informal institutions in East Asia) to the requirements of efficiency in production and exchange.[16]

B. Alternative types of property rights and incentives to innovate

A successful innovation yields benefits in excess of what the bundle of resources used by the innovator was earning before. However, innovation is a nonroutine activity, and the level of risk associated with it is not known. The innovator has to choose, in effect, between investing a bundle of resources in a project whose outcome is unpredictable, or in one of the routine activities for which the level of risk is known. The latter is the cost of innovation. The innovator's decision must then depend on his or her incentives (i.e., the penalty-reward system) to accept the uncertainty associated with the outcome of the innovation.

In a private-property capitalist economy, the innovator can capture the present value of the flow of benefits from a successful innovation either in one lump sum (by selling it to another person or company) or as a stream of payments. Also, a private-property, free-market economy provides incentives to innovate even for those who do not own resources. For example, the manager of a privately owned firm benefits from a successful innovation through the labor market for managers, in which the current profitability of the enterprise operated by that manager affects his salary via competing offers by other firms.

The gains from a successful innovation are only temporary, however. In a private-property, free-market economy, the gains attract duplications and imitations. Thus, the present value of the benefits from a successful innovation depends on how long the benefits are expected to last. That is, the innovator's choice between routine investments and

---

[16] Keith Richburg, "Why Is Black Africa Overwhelmed while East Asia Overcomes?" *International Herald Tribune*, July 14, 1992, pp. 1 and 6. Informal institutions in a community are parts of its heritage which have passed the test of time. They stem from the experiences, traditional values, religious beliefs, and all other factors that influence the subjective perceptions that individuals form about survival requirements in the world in which they live. Those informal rules are frequently referred to as the ethos, the hand-of-the-past, or the carriers of history.

innovation has to be influenced by the expected length of the imitation lag.[17] In fact, if all potential rivals were able to imitate successful innovations quickly, incentives to innovate would be seriously impaired. The gap between the novelty and the routine use of resources, which is the source of the innovator's gain, endures because it takes time, effort, and resources for potential rivals to learn, evaluate, and implement new technology.

The prevailing property rights in a labor-managed economy (i.e., in the absence of transferable claims on the returns from capital goods) have two consequences that tend to dampen the collective's incentives to innovate. First, the absence of the right to capitalize the expected future benefits into their present market price means that the working collective cannot appropriate the expected benefits of a successful innovation in one lump sum. Relative to a free-market, private-property economy, the innovator has fewer options for appropriating the benefits of a successful innovation. Second, since the collective can capture the benefits only as they occur, some of its members (e.g., those who expect to retire soon or change jobs) must have a bias against innovations that are expected to yield benefits over a long period of time.

In a planned economy, any individual (e.g., the manager of a firm) is free to propose an innovation to his superiors. However, there is a world of difference between the right to make suggestions and the right to do things. For at least two reasons, a member of the ruling group has reduced incentives to push an innovation through the decision-making channels. First, decisions to innovate are not made by individuals. They are reviewed and debated by layers of various committees, whose members are likely to have incentives not to rock the boat. Second, the private costs of pushing a specific innovation through the channels are substantial.[18] If the innovation is a success, the innovator will share the benefits with colleagues and superiors. If it is a failure, colleagues and superiors will blame the innovator. Socialist states did attempt to alleviate the absence of incentives to innovate via various awards (Lenin prizes, Stakhanovite rewards for performance, free vacations, etc.), but those attempts avoided granting more property rights to potential innovators. Thus, they were not strong enough to offset the effects of the absence of credible and stable incentive structures on the flow of scientific innovation. In a very interesting study, Leszek Balcerowicz, the first Minister of Finance of post-communist Poland, argued that the then-prevailing institutional structures in a Soviet-type economy were totally incapable of either producing scientific innovations or imitating technological developments abroad. Balcerowicz's point was that information about Western

---

[17] The purpose of copyrights, patents, etc., is to extend this lag over a long enough period not to discourage innovations.

[18] In addition to a potential loss of income due to demotion, the innovator's private costs in a Soviet-type economy also include potential loss of nonpecuniary benefits such as better housing, subsidized vacation, access to special stores, etc.

technological innovations, which the Soviets used to steal at high costs, was generally useless to them.[19]

C. Alternative types of property rights and the power to innovate

Having the freedom to acquire and use resources is not the same thing as actually having the power to get them. And not all potential innovators have resources of their own. By evaluating and pricing our perceptions of opportunity choices, financial markets in a capitalist economy match the quantity of venture capital demanded with the quantity supplied to reflect contractual agreements on various issues, including risks. In fact, a major issue facing successful firms in a capitalist economy is how to preserve creativity as they grow in size. Pat Haggerty, a founder of Texas Instruments, has remarked that the firm's top management spent many months trying to find a way to institutionalize the process of proposing, approving, and implementing innovations. We can say that private property rights provide an institutional framework within which new firms with humble beginnings (e.g., Apple, Microsoft, etc.) can acquire the power to innovate, while such rights give mature firms like Texas Instruments an opportunity to regain their initial vigor.

In a labor-managed economy, the nontransferability of the employees' claims on the firm's cash flow, and the fact that those nontransferable claims have to be contingent on people's employment with that firm,[20] reduce the collective ability to acquire the power to innovate. The absence of financial markets leaves the labor-managed firm with two major sources of investable funds: retained earnings and bank credit. The former is not a likely source of funds for innovation. A loss of retained earnings is borne by the entire working collective now, while the benefits of a successful innovation have to be shared with new employees. The power of the labor-managed firm to innovate, then, depends on the banking system. But a study I conducted recently in this area suggests that the incentive effects of the prevailing property rights in a labor-managed economy rule out bank credit as a reliable source of funds to innovate.[21]

In a planned economy, the ability to innovate is limited to those inno-

[19] Leszek Balcerowicz, "The Soviet-Type Economic System and Innovativeness," Institute for Economic Development, Warsaw, 1988, paper no. 19.

[20] To alleviate the effects of these conditions, some writers have proposed various immunizing stratagems (e.g., giving workers who leave the firm some future rights in the residual) which either ignore the costs of those stratagems, or ignore transaction costs *specific* to the labor-managed economy, or tend to privatize labor-managed firms, or all of the above. See Henryk Flakierski, *The Economic System and Income Distribution in Yugoslavia* (New York: M. E. Sharpe, 1989), pp. 67–70.

[21] See Svetozar Pejovich, "Why Has the Labor-Managed Firm Failed?" *Cato Journal*, vol. 6, no. 2 (Fall 1992), pp. 461–73. The study shows that the employees of the labor-managed firm have incentives to make investments that would shift the firm's profits forward (benefiting current employees), and to negotiate investment loans with repayment schedules that are as lengthy as the banks are willing to provide (shifting costs to future workers).

vations that are approved by the ruling group, and it usually requires a miracle to get the state bureaucracy to go along with a risky novelty. A remarkable 1957 book by Vladimir Dudintsev, which has not aged with the passage of time, describes the frustration of an engineer in the USSR who has an idea for an important technical innovation but is faced with an entrenched bureaucracy which would rather destroy him than approve a risky venture.[22]

The importance of the transferability of claims (a critical feature of the private-property economy) for the flow of innovation is difficult to exaggerate. Transferable claims allow for specialization in risk-bearing across individuals with different degrees of risk-aversion. (For example: Being risk-averse I sell an oil field I have inherited and put my money in government bonds. My colleague Maurice, who is a risk-preferrer, cashes in his inheritance of government bonds and invests the proceeds in a Broadway show.) That is, people can choose a portfolio of claims consistent with their attitudes toward risk. Moreover, the absence of transferable claims (that is, the absence of, or restrictions on, private property rights) makes it all but impossible to compare the future consequences of the alternative decisions one is currently faced with.

D. Alternative types of property rights and the integration of innovation into the economy

A novelty does not necessarily make people better off. It has to be voluntarily accepted and integrated into the economy. Once again the question is: How do different types of property rights integrate innovations into the economy?

In a private-property economy, competitive markets evaluate the novelty. As German philosopher Hans Albert writes:

> The power of the consumer ... does not consist of giving orders for the solutions of problems in the sphere of production, but in testing the solutions adopted by the entrepreneurs and in influencing the future activities in the sphere of production indirectly by accepting or refuting these solutions.[23]

Freedom of exchange reveals the costs and benefits of the novelty as perceived by interacting individuals. And those costs and benefits, via relative prices, tell us whether or not the innovation has enriched the community. By internalizing the gains from a successful innovation,[24]

---

[22] Vladimir Dudintsev, *Not by Bread Alone* (New York: E. P. Dutton and Co., 1957).

[23] Hans Albert, "Is Socialism Inevitable? Historical Prophecy and the Possibility of Reason," in Pejovich, ed., *Socialism (supra* note 4), p. 69.

[24] That is, by making the innovator and those who choose to imitate his or her innovation bear the costs and capture the benefits of their actions.

TABLE 1. *Money incomes of families in various income groups in the U.S.*
(as a percentage of total national income).

	1950	1960	1970	1980	1990
Lowest fifth	4.5	4.8	5.4	5.1	4.6
Second fifth	12.0	12.2	12.2	11.6	10.8
Middle fifth	17.4	17.8	17.6	17.5	16.6
Fourth fifth	23.4	24.0	23.8	24.3	23.8
Top fifth	42.7	41.3	40.9	41.6	44.3

private property rights encourage a greater flow of innovation[25] than collective or state property rights under socialism.

A greater flow of innovations has two important consequences. First, it raises the average income in the community.[26] Second, a greater flow of innovations increases the mobility of individuals between income classes without any appreciable effect on the distribution of income. Initially, successful innovators earn more money than before. However, the resulting increase in income inequalities is only a temporary phenomenon. Large incomes of successful innovators are eventually whittled away through market competition via (i) lower prices paid by consumers, and (ii) higher prices of resources (used to imitate innovations) received by their owners. For example, the distribution of income in the United States has remained relatively stable over several decades in spite of different growth rates during those years (see Table 1). The income share of the poorest 20 percent of families (and unattached individuals) in the United States was about 4.5 percent of the total national income in 1950 and 4.6 percent in 1990; the income share of the wealthiest 20 percent was 42.7 percent of the total in 1950 and 44.3 percent in 1990.[27]

In the 1970s, Lowell Gallaway estimated the income shares by quintile in the United States, Sweden, and the former Soviet Union.[28] He found

---

[25] Governments have tried to capture a share of profits from innovations via various devices such as progressive taxes on profit, windfall taxes, etc. The (observable) effect of those profit-sharing schemes is to reduce incentives to innovate.

[26] I am assuming here that a larger flow of innovations tends to produce a larger flow of successful innovations.

[27] Imagine the list of all families and unattached individuals ranked in terms of their income in a given year. Then, separate them into five equal groups, add incomes within each group, and divide them by the total income for the country. The numbers in Table 1 are the percentages of total national income in current prices captured by each of those five groups. The reader should bear in mind that a relative stability of income shares by five income groups does not affect the flow of people between income groups from one period to another. (The figures in Table 1 are from U.S. Bureau of the Census, *Current Population Report*, Series P-60, No. 174, 1993.)

[28] Lowell Gallaway, "The Folklore of Unemployment and Poverty," in *Government Controls and the Free Market*, ed. Svetozar Pejovich (College Station: Texas A&M University Press, 1976), pp. 41-69.

the differences in the degree of inequality in the respective distributions to be minor. Thus, the important factor is the effect of property rights on the average income, as shown in Figure 1 (see Section IIA above).[29]

Integration of innovation in a labor-managed economy has three limitations, all of which can be attributed to the prevailing property rights. First, although a successful innovation creates larger earnings for the collective which implements it, it is less likely to spread to other firms than would be the case under a capitalist system: the absence of financial markets raises the cost of information to potential rivals. Second, when information about larger profits does become available, only existing firms enter into competition with the innovating firm. The entry of new firms in a labor-managed economy has to be slow because it requires a group and/or state decision to create a new firm. Third, suppose that rival firms have to hire additional workers in order to compete with the innovating firm. Given the prevailing property rights, new workers are new policy-makers as well. This means that the current collective has incentives to trade off some pecuniary income that could be had by hiring additional workers in order to ensure the security of its common interests.

Thus, the labor-managed economy provides signals regarding whether the community has or has not accepted an innovation only at a significant cost. First, the labor-managed economy has no built-in incentives to reduce the costs of identifying the mix of outputs reflecting consumers' preferences. Second, the labor-managed economy does not have a built-in mechanism (like a private-property, free-market economy, discussed above) to reestablish the initial distribution of income. An implication of this is that the process of imitating successful technological innovations in a labor-managed economy has a predictable tendency to increase money-income inequalities.

In a planned economy, the absence of private property rights and contractual freedom makes the costs of knowing whether the community has or has not accepted an innovation staggeringly high. Why? The acceptance of an innovation requires its evaluation in terms of the value which resources used by the innovator would have if they were employed differently. But the only source of value can be the individual interacting

---

[29] There is no economic theory that says that more equality in the distribution of money income is better than less equality. All that economists can do is try to identify and analyze the factors that account for income differences between individuals and groups and the circumstances upon which those factors depend. For example, in the early 1990s, median income for Asian Americans, whose work ethic and entrepreneurship are exemplary, was $36,784, and median income for whites was $31,435 (*New York Times*, July 24, 1992, p. A16). Also, any attempt at income redistribution creates at least two problems. First, a society in which incomes are not related to performance is going to be a poor society. This is so because adverse incentives reduce the production of *future* wealth. Second, the administrative costs of redistribution eat up *current* incomes. As Richard Posner writes: "Involuntary redistribution is a coerced transfer not justified by high market-transaction costs; it is, in efficiency terms, a form of theft. Its justification must be sought in ethics rather than in economics" (Richard Posner, *Economic Analysis of Law*, 4th ed. [Boston: Little, Brown, and Company, 1992], p. 461).

with other individuals in free markets. To paraphrase James Buchanan: economic activities can only be conceived in terms of values; but how are values determined? They are determined by prices which emerge in competitive markets. That is, prices have no meaning (other than being accounting devices for the state) in a nonmarket context, where the choice-influenced opportunity costs (the value of goods and services in their best alternative uses) are not identifiable.[30]

III. Conclusion

This essay has two conclusions. First, alternative types of property rights have specific and predictable (i.e., observable) effects on the flow of technological innovation. Second, the rights of ownership and contractual freedom are more conducive to enhancing the flow of technological innovation than other institutional arrangements. I conjecture that the failure of socialist states and the slow rate of economic development in countries of the so-called Third World[31] are predictable consequences of their inability or unwillingness to adopt and enforce the basic institutions of capitalism: the right of private ownership, the freedom of contract, and the constitutional state.

Economics, Texas A&M University

---

[30] James Buchanan, "General Implications of Subjectivism in Economics," paper presented at the Conference on Subjectivism in Economics, Dallas, Texas, 1976, p. 8.

[31] Many countries, especially developing countries, tend to attribute their low rate of economic development to a variety of causes, such as exploitation by former colonial rulers, an inadequate resource base, shortage of capital, and/or poor planning. None of these alleged causes of "poverty" makes much sense. After several decades of political sovereignty, the exploitation argument is increasingly becoming an embarrassing one for developing countries to offer as an excuse for economic stagnation. If an inadequate resource base is responsible for poverty in India, why is a resource-poor country like Japan doing well? If overpopulation is a problem in China, why are people in Hong Kong so much better off? A shortage of capital is not holding back economic development in Eastern Europe, Africa, South America, etc. The flow of capital is held back by political instabilities, currency controls, restrictions on the right of ownership, discriminatory taxes, and corrupt governments. Compare the level of capital flowing into Japan with that flowing into India, or the level in East Asia with that in Africa, or the level in the Czech Republic with that in Romania.

Journal of Economic Literature
Vol. XXVI (March 1988), pp. 65–79

The Firm Is Dead; Long Live the Firm
A Review of Oliver E. Williamson's
*The Economic Institutions of Capitalism**

By ARMEN A. ALCHIAN

University of California, Los Angeles

and

SUSAN WOODWARD

Council of Economic Advisers

*The authors thank unnamed referees for improvement in content
and exposition. The usual caveats apply.*

O NCE UPON A TIME, the organization of cooperative economic activity we call the firm
was a black box. Into this box went labor and
capital, and out came products. The mechanism
was driven by wealth maximization and governed by the laws of returns. Some venturesome economists have wondered what the black
box contained, seeing as how market prices
could guide all gains from specialization. What
more could a firm do?

No one has been more venturesome than
Oliver Williamson in his eminently readable
and imperially titled book, *The Economic Institutions of Capitalism*, essentially a compen-
dium, elaboration, and revision of certain of
his publications in this decade. It summarizes
his many significant insights that gave substance
to Coase's suggestion that firms reduce transactions costs, and presages a research agenda for
himself and others. For those seeking a more
accessible presentation of the transactions approach, the new book is both a more general

and at the same time more precise exposition
of Williamson's contributions.

Because the book is a summary of Williamson's contributions to the analysis of the firm,
this review will of necessity, and deservedly,
become a sort of analytic review of both (a)
the prevailing transaction cost interpretation of
agreements among owners of cooperatively
used resources and (b) some important implications that are being derived from that
model.

The emphasis in Williamson's book is not on
capitalism's "free markets," but on the constraints that are voluntarily arrived at when
transactors are free to impose restrictions upon
themselves. The restrictions that interest Williamson are not "anticompetitive" (though some
used to be presumed so by some economists)
but rather those crafted in competitive markets
and that minimize transactions costs both across
markets and within firms.

I. The Puzzle

The traditional price-theoretic paradigm in
which gains from trade depend on a comparative advantage in production (i.e., by marginal

* Oliver E. Williamson. *The Economic Institutions of Capitalism: Firms, Markets, Relational Contracting*. NY: The Free Press; London: Collier Macmillan Publishers, 1985. Pp. xiv, 450. ISBN 0–02–
934820–X.

The Economic Foundations of Property Rights 207

cost equalization across producers) is distinguished by two features: First, no one relies on someone else for directions about what to do; market prices alone direct production and exchange. Second, production results from cooperative teamwork or cooperative production, leaving no role for contracts or any other constraints (such as rigid prices) on the options of cooperating parties. Yet in a wide array of economic activities people rely on and follow the administrative directions of other people, and both explicit and implicit agreements restrict options. In other words, "firms" or organized and managed "coalitions" exist. Why?

An answer—transactions costs—has been developed in two complementary, but different, directions. One emphasizes the administering, directing, negotiating, and monitoring of the joint productive teamwork in a firm. The other emphasizes assuring the quality or performance of contractual agreements. Both activities prevail across markets and within firms, but to different degrees and with different opportunities for containment. Where these costs are high, market transactions tend to be replaced with internal production and direction and common ownership of more of the jointly used resources so that quality is controlled (managed) and monitored through and during the production process.

A. *Bounded Rationality and Opportunism*

The first three chapters concern how Williamson views bounded rationality and opportunism as a source of many transactions costs, both across markets and within firms. By "bounded rationality," Williamson means that people have limited information and limited ability to process it. This implies incomplete information about market opportunities, limited ability to predict the future and derive implications from predictions, and limited ability to prespecify responses to future events. People don't know everything and so they make mistakes; moreover each person may know different things.

Opportunism follows from bounded rationality plus self-interest. When a conflict arises between what people want and what they have agreed to do for others, they will act in their own interest insofar as it is costly for others to know their behavior (others face costly informa-

tion). Opportunism, not merely self-interest, is the original and deadly sin recognized by Williamson.

Opportunism covers more than the propensity for mutually reliant parties to mislead, distort, disguise, obfuscate, or otherwise confuse (p. 47) in order to expropriate wealth from one another. It includes honest disagreements. Even when both parties recognize the genuine goodwill of the other, different but honest perceptions can lead to disputes that are costly to resolve. The point is important because many business arrangements interpreted as responses to potential "dishonest" opportunism are equally appropriate for avoiding costly disputes between honest, ethical people who disagree about what event transpired and what adjustment would have been agreed to initially had the event been anticipated.

B. *Transactions, Exchanges, and Contracts*

The notion of a "transaction" includes both exchanges and contracts. An exchange is a transfer of property rights to resources that involves no promises or latent future responsibility. In contrast, a contract promises future performance, typically because one party makes an investment, the profitability of which depends on the other party's future behavior. The transactions that are the focus of Williamson's approach are contractual, not just spot exchanges or even a long-lasting series of spot exchanges. In a contract a promise of future performance is exchanged, and investments are made, the value of which becomes dependent on the fulfillment of the other party's promises.

For Williamson, transaction cost is more than the cost of finding other people, inspecting goods, seeking agreeable terms, and writing exchange agreements; it includes, almost to the extent of ignoring the former, the costs incurred in making contracts enforceable by law or by self-enforcement, and extends to the precautions against potential expropriation of the value of investments relying on contractual performance as well as costs of informing and administering terms of contractual relations. These costs are associated with the containment of opportunism.

Williamson defines ex ante costs as the costs of actions and tasks involved in establishing a contract. Ex post costs are those incurred in subsequently administering, informing, monitoring, and enforcing the contractually promised performance—features that dominate the transaction cost approach. Williamson labels the transition from precontract to postcontract the Fundamental Transformation. Options available in the former stage are lost in the latter; as a result, the value of some resources becomes dependent on particular unique other parties because of loss of significant substitutability by equivalent resources. Other terms used for this dependence are *asset specificity, interspecificity, reliance,* and Williamson's previously used term *idiosyncratic.*

The contract terms that make possible the Fundamental Transfomation include both promises of performance and agreements on price. If price (or a price formula) were to be changed or renegotiated whenever either party proposed, no effective commitment of performance would be present. Precommitments to a price by both parties constrain the options and restrict future renegotiability, which is precisely the point of a contract—to protect dependent, reliant resources from malperformance, and to guarantee them a prespecified compensation.

Although this is called a "transaction cost" approach, it involves identifying factors that make spot market transactions less viable, and transactions governed by contracts more viable. It also involves identifying the factors that shape contractual restraints. But we know what the behavioral factors are—bounded rationality and opportunism. Evidently, these can occur in various ways and circumstances, which calls for different institutions for their management. Indeed, we submit that by drawing some distinctions among kinds of opportunism, Williamson's analysis can be made more powerful.

II. *Moral Hazard and Holdup*

Paradoxically Williamson's exposition and, in part the analysis, does not distinguish analytically between the two kinds of opportunism: moral hazard and holdup. Fortunately, it only rarely leads Williamson to errors. But the distinction will help the reader get to many of Williamson's conclusions. In this section we set out the distinction.

A. *Holdup and Specificity*

Uncertainty about price or compensation arises when the value of a collection of resources dependent on continued association for their maximum product exceeds their summed market values. Resources dependent upon one another in this way are referred to by Williamson as "specific" or "interspecific," and those making investments specific to other assets will seek protection against reneging or "holdup" by the other parties. This view gives us insight into contracts, pricing policies, and agreements that constrain markets, and also gives us a theory of the types of assets the firm will own.

Alfred Marshall, in his *Principles* ([1890] 1936, pp. 453–54 and 626) was the first to identify these elements in the context of what he called "composite quasi-rent." A quasi-rent is the excess above the return necessary to maintain a resource's current service flow, which can be the means to recover sunk costs. Composite quasi-rent is that portion of the quasi-rent of resources that depends on continued association with some other specific, currently associated resources. Thus, composite quasi-rent is the amount those other currently associated resources could attempt to expropriate by refusing to pay or serve, that is, by holdup.

Marshall offered the example of a steel mill that locates near a public utility and makes an investment, the profitability of which depends on being able to buy power at some given price. Once the steel mill incurs costs that become sunk, the power company could raise power prices. The steel mill would continue to operate so long as the new marginal cost did not exceed marginal revenue, even though the sunk costs are not being recovered. Marshall recognized the danger of parties with sunk costs relying on those in a position to expropriate composite quasi-rents. But he assumed the threat was resolved by "doing what is right" or by "haggling." So far as we can ascertain, Marshall did not develop the importance of quasi-rent for understanding the organization of the firm.

Composite quasi-rent has been recently rediscovered by others in discussion of "time-irreversibility," "asymmetric information with uncertainty," "bilateral monopoly," "opportunism," "self-enforcing contracts," and "principal-agent relationships" to name a few.

If a resource can leave a team without cost or loss of its value, Williamson would say it is independent or is not team-specific, or is "redeployable." But if the remaining resources would lose by its departure, they are dependent (*reliant* is the term in legal proceedings) on it, and to them, the departing resource is unique because they cannot replace it with no loss. Resources that are mutually dependent are also mutually unique, and vice versa.

A landowner renting land as a site for a skyscraper is an owner of a resource that is unique, but impotent. The landowner cannot cheaply alter the services of the land as a means of extracting some of the quasi-rent of the building from the building owner. But the owner of the building could refuse to pay all of the promised rent, nevertheless secure in the knowledge that the landowner has no feasible alternative use of the land. The landowner's remedies by law limit the expropriation the building owner could extract, but the expense of the remedies limit the protection afforded the landowner through such remedies. An owner of a unique resource will be more tempted to exploit the situation as the composite quasi-rent grows large and as the unique resource's flow of services become more controlled (for example, by failing to pay the rent, or to show up for work). The more likely and foreseeable is this temptation, the greater is the likelihood that precautionary contractual terms will be sought. Obviously, dependency motivates a desire for reliable services from the unique resource that is relied upon. Services can be obtained by (1) buying the services, or (2a) owning or (2b) renting the unique resource for self-service. Buying *services* exposes the purchaser to a holdup threat. Hence, the unique resources are more likely to be controlled by (2a) ownership or (2b) rental for self-use. The choice will depend on the ability of the owner to detect abuse or effects on the resource consequent to the way it is used by a renter. With cheap detection, the unique resource is likely to be rented rather than owned by the dependent party. The two features (a) dependency and (b) monitorability of use are important in determining whether the relied upon services will be obtained by ownership or by rental, and hence the degree of integration of ownership of resources in a firm.

B. *Moral Hazard and Plasticity*

Moral hazard, a form of opportunism, arises in agreements in which at least one party relies on the behavior of another and information about that behavior is costly. The owner of a firm hires a manager and wants the manager to maximize profits. The manager hires employees and want them to follow directions. An investor lends money to a firm and wants the firm to act in that debt holder's interest. Because it is costly for the principal to know exactly what the agent did or will do, the agent has an opportunity to bias his actions more in his own interest, to some degree inconsistent with the interests of the principal.

The term *moral hazard* has been unjustly maligned for its moralistic overtones. In the finance literature, especially, it is often called *post-contractual opportunism*. We resist. First, as we argue here, the events that can give trouble ex post of the contract are not just those associated with moral hazard but also those of holdup, which we believe are neglected compared to moral hazard in most of the principal-agent literature. Second, the term *moral hazard* correctly implies that if everyone would simply agree to undertake a given standard of effort and abide by the promise, a more efficient outcome would result. The term suggests that people cannot be counted on to do what they say they are going to do, and that failure manifests itself in prices and in contractual arrangements. It also indicates correctly that among the devices used to control such behavior are moralistic aggression and contempt.

Though moral hazard is involved in many transactions, it does not follow that they are regretted. For example, both the insurance market and the labor market experience moral hazard, but all parties are better off having made the transactions than not. The insured pay the full expected losses plus administration to the insurer, so all costs are compensated. The laborers earn their expected marginal product. The moral hazard loss simply measures what could be gained if magically either the cost of monitoring behavior by the insurer/employer were zero, or if people could be counted on to do as they promise.

Though criticizing Williamson for not analytically distinguishing between two types of opportunism, we note that the literatures on holdup and moral hazard are almost entirely unintegrated.

The degree to which resources are vulnerable to morally hazardous exploitation depends on what can be called their "plasticity" and on monitoring costs. We call resources or investment "plastic" to indicate that there is a wide range of discretionary, legitimate decisions within which the user may choose. For example, compare a drug research laboratory with a steel manufacturer. There are fewer options for discretionary behavior in steel manufacturing. The technology is largely determined by the nature of the plant. Absentee owners and debt holders have little cause to worry about the managers' turning the resources of the plant into personal consumption, or increasing the riskiness of prospective outcomes. In contrast, a drug research firm could be working on some mundane project with a modest but sure payoff, or on some long shot with a slight change of a high payoff. Research and development firms are plastic.

We conjecture as further illustrations that enterprises with intellectual research and capital, for example, fashion designers, professional service firms such as engineering, law and architecture, and computer software creation, are especially plastic and susceptible to moral hazard. In contrast, industries with less plasticity are railroads, utility services, airlines, petroleum refining (but not exploration), and other activities involving much in the way of "hard" resources. Interestingly, physical resources requiring large sunk costs, and consequently that are vulnerable to holdup, can be implastic and immune to moral hazard.

Cash is among the most plastic of resources, because it can be hastily exchanged for nearly anything. But this example serves well the point that plasticity must be combined with high monitoring costs to result in opportunities for moral hazard. Cash is plastic, but very easy to track as it is used (once the records establish that it is there). Thus, we expect managers handling large cash balances to be subject to considerable controls and review by principals, but we observe that there are many large financial institutions operated by nonowner managers.

By "plastic" we do not simply mean risky. Oil that has only to be pumped and sold is highly implastic. The optimal rate at which to pump the oil depends on the pattern of prices over time, and there is little in the way of possibilities for exploiting an oil well either by increasing the riskiness of its value or by changing its product into personal consumption. But an oil well is a risky asset if the price of oil fluctuates.

C. *Two Expeditions Reunited*

The early explorers of transctions costs set out on two very different expeditions. One party, guided by the notion of moral hazard and adverse selection, headed off in the direction of insurance and risk, and ventured successfully into generalized principal-agent conflicts. The implications of informational asymmetries and impactedness for behavior and market viability explained various aspects of insurance markets, the assignment of liability, the use of the firm for teamwork, some firm financing decisions, and conflicts of interest between owners and managers, between inside owners and outside owners, and between debt holders and equity holders. In particular, monitoring costs associated with moral hazard became a basis for explaining two different aspects of firms. The first aspect is the role of "management." Some firm members are managers while others are managed, because the party with comparative advantage in deciding what a particular worker should do is not necessarily the worker himself. This relationship is subject to moral hazard, and the desire to control the costs associated with it explains some aspects of firm organization. Second, monitoring costs will also motivate ownership of assets by their user. If the user of an asset is also its owner, the full consequences of how the asset is used falls on the user. When the owner and user are separate parties, the owner bears the costs of the user's behavior, even if the user is careless. Costly detection of care, moral hazard, is thus a source of asset specificity and will drive ownership of an asset by the user. Once the asset is owned by the firm (used by the owner), informational asymmetries regarding that user's effect on the resource keep it in the firm, that is, make it firm-specific.

The other party studying the firm headed off from industrial organization to look for explanations as to why firms vertically integrate. Chapters 4–10 recount Williamson's earlier vehicle for exploring beyond that territory: holdup and its prevention. Holdup could explain not only common ownership of assets and aspects of contracts, but also contractural constraints on markets such as posted or otherwise inflexible prices, pay or take, first negotiation, and rights of refusal.

From these two different explorations the question arose: Does the essence of the "firm" lie in teamwork or in the nexus of long-term contracts (i.e., agreements restraining the behavior of transactors)? Williamson writes as if he believes teamwork always involves such contracts. We agree, because we can think of neither significant nor interesting cases where teamwork does not create dependencies calling for contractual restraints. The durability of the team-specific investments, especially accumulated team-specific information involved in teamwork, connects teamwork to contracts.

We observe that in most cooperative production (teamwork), people show up for work at the same place every day. (As a matter of fact, people often show up for play in the same locations, too, though less reliably, but for many of the same reasons.) Team members are more productive working together than working separately, and this differential at least partly depends on knowledge of one another's personal talents. This specific knowledge has lasting value, and consequently departure of part of the team can threaten the team's value. This special, lasting knowledge makes the members of the team mutually team-specific. They will want assurance of performance and compensation before they will be willing to make any self-financed investments in the team's efforts—hence, long-term contracts. Teamwork and long-term contracts seldom appear without the other.

III. *The Firm*

To help explain Williamson's conception of the firm, we offer a provisional characterization. The classic, paradigmatic private property firm is a coalition among owners of separately owned resources whose value as a team exceeds the sum of the market values each could get separately. Some of this value derives from the durable and costly specialized knowledge they possess about each other. That value depends on continued association; the departure of any of the mutually dependent resources would diminish the value of the team. The desire to protect this value and secure a share of it will motivate contracts among inputs for the continuing services of the resources of the team.

It follows that the team members who own resources (human as well) whose values depend most heavily on the performance of the team (i.e., are the most team-specific) will be willing to pay the most for the right to control the team. By definitional consequence of being owners of such resources, they own the residual value. They are the ones who are called the owners of the firm, though no one literally owns all the resources used in the firm. The owners, or equity holders, as a precaution against moral hazard and holdup, will be common to all contracts with input owners, will possess the right to sell their contractual status, and will bear the residual value of team-specific resources. The more general, less specific, more substitutable resources (some of which are called employees) will be rented, because their value and reward are independent of the fortunes and behavior of the team. They must be, and are, paid no more or less than their opportunity value.

The differences between the value of the team and the summed values all the resources could command outside the team is a return to the entrepreneur's investment in the search for a successful team. It is, as such, much like the *expectational* return to investments in search for oil. Absent any team-specific investment on their own part, the other members will earn just their value elsewhere, unless they are able to collude to extract a successful team-assembling entrepreneur's quasi-rent and profit.

A. *Ownership Integration*

One form of protection from opportunism is common ownership of the dependent resources as one bundle, that is, ownership integration, sometimes misleadingly called "vertical" or "horizontal" integration, although these adjectives are unnecessarily restrictive. This is obvious enough when all the firm-specific resources are owned by one person. Problems develop if either (a) those resources are owned in common by several people (as in corporations and partnerships), or (b) the firm-specific resources are not all owned in common (as in joint ventures or cooperatives).

B. *Joint and Several Ownership in Common*

Chapters 11 and 12 apply Williamson's schema to the corporation. In corporations, stockholders jointly own the firm-specific unique resources. While predetermined shares of ownership preclude disputes over the division of the resulting value (at least in the idealized corporation), the shareholders may have different beliefs about the best choice of action, when dividends ought to be taken, or how much risk to take on. One way to get around this difficulty is to make the shares transferable. Then changes in beliefs and personal consumption plans can be accommodated through buying and selling, without affecting the operation of the firm itself.

Williamson sees the anonymity of stockholders as something of a problem. He describes stockholders as having "investments that are not associated with particular assets" (p. 305) and as "the only voluntary constituency whose relation with the corporation does not come up for periodic renewal" (p. 304). He argues that the "diffuse character of their investments puts shareholders at an enormous disadvantage" with respect to protection from opportunistic exploitation. "The board of directors thus arises endogenously, as a means by which to safeguard the investments of those who face a diffuse but significant risk of expropriation because the assets in question are numerous and ill-defined and cannot be protected in a well-focused, transaction specific way" (p. 306).

Anonymity is derived from limited liability and lowers the transaction costs associated with transferable shares. If shareholders were liable for debts of the firm, both creditors and shareholders would find it in their interest to investigate the wealth of each shareholder. They would also find it in their interest to inhibit sales by rich shareholders to poor ones, for such transactions would leave the remaining shareholders with enlarged liability and creditors with less security. Limited liability insulates both shareholders and creditors from differences in wealth among shareholders. The shareholders become a true *société anonyme*. These considerations explain why virtually all corporations with publicly traded shares limit share-

holders' liability, and why closely held, non-traded firms often extend the liability of one or more shareholders through personal loan guarantees.

The flexibility and liquidity that enable diffuse ownership and anonymity of shareholders are surely among the great virtues of the modern corporation. But these desirable qualities come at a cost because when ownership is diffuse, the shareholders must delegate operation of the firm. Delegation requires monitoring. The problem is not an absence of firm-specific capital on the part of any stockholder, but simply the fact that the stockholders are numerous. But the potential for "political market failure" due to numerous stockholders is substantially abated by the opportunity for some shareholders to control blocks of shares.

If shareholders opt for concentrated ownership another cost arises: Because shareholders have limited wealth, substantial ownership of wealth in one firm implies that the shareholder with a large block has a less well diversified portfolio with an inferior risk-return trade-off and in some way must be compensated for this by the "outside" shareholders. Other things being equal, people prefer to diversify. Compensation may be in the form of higher salaries for owner-managers, or profits from trading on insider information (Harold Demsetz and Kenneth Lehn 1985). The monitoring costs of different activities should thus explain why some firms are organized with substantial owners being managers (aligning the incentives of management and owners) and others with none. Personal, firm-specific investments made by managers result in both the desire of managers to own stock to protect their firm-specific investments and for various other forms of protection, such as golden parachutes.

We wish Williamson had seized this opportunity explicitly (rather than implicitly) to refute the myth that firms are owned, controlled, and administered by "capital" rather than "labor." He could have cited labor-owned firms: law, architecture, accounting, engineering, economic consulting, advertising, restaurants, computer software creators—the list is long. These are firms in which the human resources are firm-specific, and "labor" is the owner. To believe that "capital" is in some sense the "boss" and hires "labor" is to fail to understand the most basic forces that shape the firm: First, the leader of a team (management) is the member with the comparative advantage in deciding what the team and its members should do, and this manager need not be an owner or even part owner in the firm; second, ownership of the team *is* the residual claimancy on the most team-specific resources, which may be labor or capital. To start an analysis of firms by assuming the presence of "capital" or that capital hires labor is to beg the question of the basis for the existence of a firm.

C. *Financing*

The partitioning of income to assets owned in common may also take the form of separate debt and equity claims. In a brief but provocative and important paragraph (p. 307), Williamson suggests that the manner in which resources are financed will depend on the attributes of the resources. In other words, debt and equity financing will vary directly with the degree of firm-specificity and redeployability—a view in sharp contrast to theorems of the irrelevance of capital structure. We argue and here attempt to elaborate on that important contention. But the *type* of firm-specificity is at least as important as the degree. In particular, the distinction between holdup and moral hazard illuminates the issue considerably. Assets that are firm-specific and vulnerable to holdup will affect firm financing very differently from those that are firm-specific and also vulnerable to moral hazard. Moreover, there will be different effects on the degree of inside ownership, the potential for being publicly traded, and the optimal incentives for managers.

If a firm's assets are plastic and costly to monitor, moral hazard costs arise with debt (which, incidentally, limits the degree to which the tax advantages of debt can be exploited). Once indebted, the equity holders do not bear the full downside losses on projects. Their incentive is to increase risk taking, because the bondholders will bear part of the risks of downside losses, but the equity holders get all of the gains. Bondholders, aware of this incentive, design contracts between themselves and equity holders to control it. Debt contracts usually aim at controlling two potential forms of moral hazard opportunism. First, they often constrain the size of dividends that equity holders can pay to themselves, limiting the ability of equity holders to carry away some of the assets (in the form of a dividend) that secure the debt. Second, debt contracts constrain the degree to which the riskiness of the assets can be increased. For example, they might restrict sales of some assets and purchase of others. But the contracts are not perfect. Bondholders charge equity holders for the expected uncontrollable losses imposed on them. In choosing debt financing, equity holders are trading off the moral hazard costs of debt against the attraction of creditors who are risk averse as well as the tax advantages.

The theory of debt financing rests on the degree of asset plasticity as an explanation of the debt-equity ratio. Compare the opportunities for debt financing for a drug company versus a public utility. The drug company has a much wider range of legitimate choices than does the public utility. The drug company's activities are more difficult to monitor. This implies that it will be difficult for the debt holders to write a contract with the equity holders to keep from being exploited. The drug company will find debt expensive. But with the public utility, the assets are cheaper to monitor and assess (and the returns to equity are regulated), so the public utility will find that the moral hazard consequences of debt are low.

It is not the riskiness, but the plasticity of the firm's assets that drives the cost of debt financing. What matters is the degree to which the equity holders can exploit the bondholders ex post by altering the returns to assets. We predict that firms with more plastic assets will have lower debt/equity ratios than firms with less plastic assets. Our earlier example, the oil well, serves well the point that the issue is not risk. The oil well is very implastic but very risky; we deduce that oil recovery will be a highly debt financed business, but that drilling and exploration will not.

Another view is that debt is a device to prevent holdups and to restrain moral hazard. There are two versions of this story. First, Richard Ippolito (1985) suggests that committing income to debt holders keeps strong unions from expropriating it. Second, Michael Jensen (1986) argues that if income is committed to bondholders, the managers cannot spend it, because they have less discretion over interest payments than over dividends. The important point in both views is that when a quasi-rent is present, because of large sunk costs or a windfall gain, the quasi-rent is vulnerable to expropriation. Managers of a firm with exceptionally large quasi-rents or profits could invest the proceeds toward self-aggrandizing but unprofitable investments. Or the union could strike for higher wages. If, instead, the firm had committed to large interest and debt repayments, these cash flows would have to be channeled to outsiders.

The debt/equity decision can also be seen as a "flow" response to fluctuating financing needs (rather than as an optimal "stock") which seeks to avoid the suspicion of opportunism. If a firm's managers sold equity every time it sought additional financing, and bought stock back when it had cash balances, stockholders would find it difficult to distinguish between a true financing strategy and "insider trading." How can stockholders be certain that managers are not simply selling stock when on the basis of inside information they think the price is too high, and buying when it is too low? Only transacting stockholders would be harmed by this, but knowing this, investors who valued liquidity would be reluctant to buy. Perhaps this is a clue as to why nearly all transient fluctuations in financing of public traded firms are in debt and retained earnings, and almost none with equity issues.

D. *Incomplete Integration of Ownership*

In Chapter 12 Williamson explores corporate governance, in particular where integration of ownership of firm-specific resources is incomplete. Resources cannot be classified as purely firm-specific and dependent or not, and an absolutely nonoverlapping distinction cannot be made among (a) stockholders, (b) creditors, and (c) employees. If some stockholders own firm-specific resources not shared in common by all other stockholders, or if some nonstockholders have some firm-specific resources in which ownership is not shared with stockholders, conflicts of interest among the otherwise homogeneous interests will arise.

Employees can be both dependent and depended upon. They may have agreed to make self-financed investments with firm-specific value; to develop skills or knowledge with firm-specific value; to purchase homes whose values

depend on the firm's success; to accumulate rights to subsequent benefits, like pensions; to receive payment later for earlier underpayment when the employee's actual productivity was difficult to predict. Or, employees may have high transfer or mobility costs to the next best work. If so, they will demand some protection from employer opportunism. And they may seek representation on the board of directors, or at least some control with respect to certain decisions affecting the probability of fulfillment of their contracts, though this incomplete and disproportionate sharing in equity relative to fixed payments will create divisiveness on other issues. Williamson concludes that whether labor serves on the board of directors depends on whether employees have made firm-specific investments.

Dependence does not typically stop at the boundaries of groups of cooperating people in what is conventionally called a "firm." Not to be ignored are some customers of the firm's products. A consumer who buys a product, the future performance of which depends on the firm's continued activity, will have become an owner of a firm-specific resource—much like Marshall's steel mill, or like a buyer of computers or automobiles for which future spare parts are valuable. When customer dependence becomes dominant, the firm will tend to be organized as a mutual, and the customers will own the firm. A subcontractor whose resource values depend on the prime contractor is a dependent part of a coalition, possibly one involving strong mutual interdependence. Though the resources of a subcontractor and a prime contractor may be separately owned, mutual dependence creates a coalition with contractual relationships similar to those "within" a conventional "firm." Owners of such firm-specific, but separately owned, resources would want representation or influence on the board, even though, again, this will create divisiveness and conflicts of interest.

Although firm-specificity can extend beyond the traditional boundaries of the firm, this does not imply that it is efficient for all, even slightly, firm-specific parties to be represented on the board of directors. As more parties are added, the commonality of objectives diminishes and the cost of making decisions goes up; the cost of negotiating decisions must be traded off against the costs of a decision unfavorable to some parties. From an ex ante perspective, negotiating for control and representation should protect all parties willing to pay for protection before becoming dependent. If parties with repeated transactions unexpectedly find themselves mutually dependent, they will be without a contract to contain opportunism. They will have no choice but to negotiate, and to appeal to social institutions larger than the firm (for example, the law) to determine appropriate protection. But the practice of putting ex ante disinterested parties on the board is insidious. Advocates of membership on the board of directors by ex post interested, or firm-independent resource owners, are, possibly unwittingly, undermining the viability of the corporate form by making it easier for owners of non-firm-specific assets to expropriate quasi-rents from firm-specific assets, thereby reducing the willingness to invest in assets organized as a corporation.

IV. Credible Commitments

Absent integration of ownership of all the interdependent resources, investments can sometimes be protected from opportunism by credible commitments. Williamson emphasizes the important role of credible commitments, as distinct from credible threats, in the entire transaction cost analysis. Indeed it is the major implication and message of this book. These commitments can take several forms with varying degrees of credibility and effectiveness, several of which Williamson explores. At the simplest level, a unique (relied upon) party can post a hostage or a bond forfeitable upon malperformance. Less commonly recognized forms of credible commitments are often misinterpreted as monopolizing, or competitor-obstructing, devices. Some of the following examples are illuminated in Williamson's two chapters on credible commitments: reciprocity, take-or-pay, duplicative suppliers, product exchanges, posted prices, inflexible prices, most-favored-customer clauses, block-booking, blind-selling, blind-buying, buy-sell agreements, stock options, patent pools, joint ventures, premium profit streams supported by exclusive territories and resale price maintenance, franchise-specific investments,

exhibition clearances, athlete trades among teams, and reserve and waiver clauses. All these can serve as means of creating competitive, economical mutual reliance and self-enforcing contracts.

We digress a bit to elaborate on one. Price stability can restrain opportunistic behavior by a resource owner who otherwise could alter the price of its services to extract composite quasi-rent from a reliant party. The resource owner, say a buyer from a dependent supplier (e.g., the only oil field pipeline gathering system buying from several oil well owners, or a tuna or salmon canner buying from fishermen who serve only that canner) would desire to assure those dependent suppliers that the buyer would not engage in opportunistic alteration of prices to expropriate quasi-rents of canner- or pipeline-dependent investments by suppliers for whom there were no other economically readily available buyers.

By publicly posting a price and holding it constant, a buyer can assure suppliers of no last-minute price opportunism. Such posted prices tend to be unresponsive to transient changes in demand and supply, and are changed only when the underlying demand and supply conditions have remained changed for some time. Otherwise, adjustments of price to *alleged* momentary shifts in demand or supply could mask extensive opportunistic expropriation of dependent supplier's quasi-rents. This implies that posted or stable prices would prevail where suppliers are in a position of substantial dependence with respect to a buyer. Casual observation seems to support that implication, for example, in pipelines for gathering oil and gas, for fishing boats selling to a cannery, and in restaurants. Even restaurants that print or post menus daily seldom change the price of their offerings in the middle of the evening. Williamson correctly emphasized that a clearer perception and appreciation of the problems that arise when two parties separately own interdependent resources would help redirect the inhospitable gaze of economists and lawyers away from the restraints-of-trade paradigm to one in which reliability of future performance is the focus (Alchian and Woodward 1987).

Williamson's Chapter 10 on the organization of work contains a withering examination and critique exposing the emptiness of the so-called radical economics interpretation of power and hierarchy in business firms. It is, however, a very constructive chapter with focus on the organization of employees and on the means whereby people who become reliant on other people, whether on their personal services or capital equipment, protect their investments from holdup. This allows a double purpose of employee unions: to cartelize employees to restrict competition, but also to protect employees' human firm-specific investments. Tenure, seniority, company "unions," company towns, layoffs and shutdowns, rigid wage rates, and golden parachutes are some examples of devices or contractural clauses to protect firm-dependent human capital (see Alchian and Woodward 1987).

V. *Hierarchical Governance Patterns*

Administration, direction, or management involves a flow of information through a chain of decisions, suggestions, orders, and so on, which Williamson calls the *governance hierarchy*. It takes on many forms, for example, putting-out, inside and outside contracting, federated groups, peer groups, employer-employee authority, and the unitary, multidivisional, or holding company forms of governance which he calls U, M, and H forms. His attempts (in Chapter 11) to bring the U (unitary), H (holding company), and M (multidivisional profit center) organizational forms into line with his main argument are, in our opinion, novel and plausible, but as yet a less successful portion of his published work. He associates them with the extent of firm-specific, nonredeployable resources and the extent of other safeguards against opportunism.

The stereotype U form has a unitary chief over subordinate functional divisions (production, sales, finance, engineering, etc.), of a single product firm, so Williamson associates the U form (unitary control) with greater viability where there is no major complex integration.

Williamson suggests that safeguards against opportunism (reflecting degree of specificity of resources) across firms are provided by integrating and using the M form, rather than the U form. The U (unitary) form suffered from inability to collect and utilize all pertinent information at one central headquarters. The M form separated the firm into separate profit centers to reduce the need for information flows across divisions and to permit a more independent ability to use information where it existed (in the divisions). This restrains opportunism of information and physical services across the divisions. The distinctive elements are (*a*) feasibility of decentralizing the flow of information while providing incentives to use the information to make better decisions and (*b*) safeguards against opportunistic use or concealment of information. As enterprises increased in complexity and integrated complementary activities to avoid potential opportunistic behavior by outside suppliers, the more integrated firm (whether vertical or horizontal) became more complex and difficult to administer by a central office.

The incentive to use information more effectively is sharpened if responsibilities are separated into semiautonomous profit centers which, in turn, are overseen by managers who monitor and evaluate division performance (instead of managing and administering the divisions), reward or punish division managers, and allocate investable funds among them. Thus, the argument goes, the M form evolved precisely for the same reason the "firm" evolved: to restrain opportunism among controllers of interdependent resources.

The H form (holding company) also divides the group into profit centers, and limits control by the top officer primarily to the amount of reinvestment of each center's income. The manager of each subordinate division controls its own reinvestment selections. The top holding group primarily retains dividend-like returns. Williamson seems to suggest that an H form is more likely among firms that have less operational and informational interdependence among the several divisions; however, a clearer identification of the resource, product, or production conditions that make one form rather than another the more viable seems to be the next item on the research agenda.

VI. *External Government Controls*

Government regulatory agencies can help not only to avoid "monopolistic prices," but also to prevent opportunistic holdups of the type illustrated by Marshall. Chapter 13 contains Williamson's critical review of regulatory experiences in some TV cable franchise bidding for natural monopolies. Though precontract award bidding is competitive, the Fundamental Transformation occurs in passing to the post-award stage. Williamson argues convincingly, at least to us, that post-award regulatory authority to restrain opportunism is not effectively or totally displaceable by bidding for franchises with long-term contractual commitments.

Chapter 14 opens with this statement: "Antitrust enforcement has been massively reshaped in the past twenty years" (p. 365). That reshaping is concisely reviewed with respect to merger policy, nonstandard contracting, and strategic behavior, a reshaping in which Williamson's analysis has had a part, and which is very briefly evaluated in Chapter 14. That chapter is convincing evidence that media pundits and politicians who believe that the policies of the Antitrust Division of the Department of Justice and the Federal Trade Commission have been altered by the Reagan administration, and who long for a return to the old antitrust policies, are wrong and are bound to be disappointed. Not the current administration, but instead the advancing understanding of transactions issues is responsible because it is now the intellectual apparatus of economists. Regardless of the administration, economists will use the best economic understanding available and that, rather than some administration's biases, will guide future antitrust actions. To believe otherwise is to insult economists in those agencies and, worse, to believe economic understanding has no effect on government.

VII. Definitions and Boundaries of "Firms"?

A. Future Forays into Terra Incognita

The view of organizations arising from the concept of resource interdependence or firm specificity makes the boundary of the firm fuzzy; a bright line distinguishing "inside" and "outside" is missing. The interpretation of the firm as a nexus of long-term contracts among interspecific resources weakens the "firm" as a useful basic unit of analysis. Though we have used the word *firm*, we believe a better and more useful concept is a coalition: a set of resource owners bound by contractual relations that depend on the degrees of dependence and

uniqueness. But definitions are for the taking; none is standard.

The old notion led to an intrafirm versus an interfirm conception of agreements in which "interfirm" relations were viewed inhospitably and with suspicion. An egregious example of the pitfalls of this line of thinking was the procedures in a 1982 antitrust suit within the National Football League. The disputants forced the judge to "determine" whether the 24 teams in the league were "one firm" or separate firms, presuming a clear distinction could be made. As the foregoing emphasizes, this approach ignores the nature and degree of dependence among the involved resource owners and the reasons for contractual arrangements to control free-riding on investments and to restrain opportunistic expropriation of dependent quasirents. The court "found" the league to be 24 separate firms, and inferred they were therefore subject to court review as to legality of joint action. Instead the court could have ruled they were one firm, with 24 subordinate divisions.

This does not mean that economists could have provided an analysis for the NFL case, or reliably ascertained the effects of different rulings. So far as we are aware, economists have not adequately analyzed many mysterious arrangements in interteam sports, for example, trades rather than sale, or players' employment contracts. Moreover, the mysteries are not limited to team sports: trades or exchanges of products among members of an industry (e.g., exchanges of petroleum and its products, electricity, aluminum, gypsum, corrugated cardboard, and new automobiles) are not rare. We suspect the explanation for these arrangements lies in avoiding potential expropriative behavior where spot supplies are small, but we are not sure.

The institutions of capitalism are more than just firms, markets, and relational contracting. Dependence occurs in complex ways and motivates a large variety of precautionary arrangements. Joint ventures, mutuals, social clubs, cooperatives, and families, to suggest a few "capitalist" institutions, are, as we understand them, basically similar contractual arrangements in which (a) the joint venturers will be interreliant but the assets, especially human capital will not be owned in common, and (b) the joint venturers will be dependent on the services of the venture (e.g., research, sociability, pipeline transportation), and (c) alienability of a member's interest is restricted. Without a joint, restrictive arrangement, one venturer could otherwise hold up the other dependent nonowner user of the services.

The country club is a complex and rich example of a cooperative firm. The customers (members) of the country club own the firm—the club. They are also the producers of the firm's product—sociability. The most important assets of the firm are not the grounds and building, but the members themselves, who are now "owned by the firm." The members are mutually reliant on one another to produce the sociability that makes membership in the club worthwhile. Sale of membership is restricted to prevent entry of "undesirables," those whose sociability is not regarded as sufficient to exchange for reciprocal sociability. Members can sell their membership only back to the club, and new memberships can be admitted only upon consent of the group. Outside ownership of such a firm is not viable. The outside owner could admit, for a high price, new members who would destroy the composite quasi-rent created by the members themselves, or could raise the price to existing members to extract the quasi-rent.

VIII. *Social Restraints*

That contracts are not sufficiently well enforced by resort to the law is emphasized by Williamson. Unique parties who could expropriate dependent quasi-rents resist the temptation, in part, because "it isn't right." Social opprobrium and the feeling of guilt may operate. Actions regarded as "unconscionable" or "unfair" can result in social ostracism or moralistic aggression. We believe it is important to recognize the forces of ethics, etiquette, and "proper, correct, reasonable, moral, etc." standards of conduct in controlling business relationships. We do not believe contracts are observed (e.g., self-enforcing) only so long as the personal economic costs of contract violation exceed expropriable rents obtainable by violations. People do not always violate contracts whenever their own costs are less than their own gains from violation. Temptations of free-riding or stealing

are resisted even when the net gains of free-riding or stealing are great. We don't know enough about how such "moral" forces operate to say more than that they exist and should not be ignored in seeking an understanding of how the economic institutions of capitalism, or any other -ism, evolve and operate.

One can see how morally aggressive, pejorative terms like "gouging" with reference to prices make economic sense. A remote auto repair shop servicing an unlucky traveler whose car's fanbelt has unexpectedly failed might charge far more than the full costs of replacing the belt, in order to extract almost the total value of an emergency repair to the unfortunate driver—the value of the service to a customer in dire straits. Or, imagine an ambulance operator or a doctor charging a price reflecting the value of emergency service to a critically injured person. Not without reason is such behavior condemned. It is wicked and reprobate, and it's inefficient.

If such opportunistic expropriation were expected by travelers, they would travel less, or take expensive safety precautions to avoid expropriation. The avoidance costs would exceed the true cost of providing the emergency service, so that society would incur greater costs if people did not act "responsibly, fairly, conscientiously and ethically." Whatever the emotive language, "decent" behavior saves resources and enables greater welfare. (It is another question how such "responsible, nonopportunistic" behavior is induced in society, or why people "waste" their own scarce resources berating gougers.) This is consistent with the usual explanation for why professions (i.e., sellers of services whose buyers are in a position of trust and substantial dependence) typically promote and enforce professional codes of ethics to protect the clients or principals from "expropriative" unethical tactics.

IX. *Evaluation*

It is hard to decide whether the title or the content of Williamson's book is the more general. Williamson describes explicitly only some of capitalism's institutions. But the forces Williamson describes surely operate in all systems. Regardless, the analysis in Williamson's book will enable a broader, more profound understanding of coalitions, institutions, and contract structure, including the allocations and partitioning of property rights, as well as a variety of "institutions" that lack contracts but establish and maintain behavior of a contractual type. A central message of the book bears repeating in Williamson's words:

> Upon observing that humans have a propensity to behave opportunistically, Machiavelli advised his prince that "a prudent ruler ought not to keep faith when by so doing it would be against his interest, and when the reasons which made him bind himself no longer exist . . . [L]egitimate grounds [have never] failed a prince who wished to show colourable excuse for the promise." But . . . preemptive opportunism is . . . a very primitive response. . . . The more important lesson, for the purposes of studying economic organizations, is this: Transactions that are subject to *ex post* opportunism will benefit if appropriate safeguards can be devised *ex ante*. Rather than reply to opportunism in kind the wise prince is one who seeks both to give and to receive "credible" commitments. (p. 48)

The message of Machiavelli is to be reversed: Instead of opportunism, offer and seek credible commitments. It is clear Williamson's view is that the main purpose served by economic organization is not monopoly, efficient risk bearing, power or the like but is transaction cost economizing, in no small part by use of credible commitments.

Even economists who have read the original articles will find Williamson's *The Economic Institutions of Capitalism* provocative, informative, edifying, and very much worth reading.

REFERENCES

Because Williamson's book contains an extensive bibliography through 1984, we have merely added some other and more recent citations.

ALCHIAN, ARMEN A. AND WOODWARD, SUSAN. "Reflections on the Theory of the Firm," *J. Institutional Theoretical Econ.* (Z. ges. Staatswiss.), 1987, *143*(1) pp. 110–37.

ALLEN, FRANKLIN. "On the Fixed Nature of Sharecropping Contracts," *Econ. J.*, Mar. 1985, *95*(377), pp. 30–48.

BARZEL, YORAM. "Transaction Costs: Are They Just Costs?" *J. Institutional Theoretical Econ.*, Mar. 1985, *141*(1), pp. 4–16.

BAYSINGER, BARRY D. AND BUTLER, HENRY N. "The Role of Corporate Law in the Theory of the Firm," *J. Law Econ.*, Apr. 1985, *28*(1), pp. 179–91.

BEHRENS, PETER. "The Firm as a Complex Institution," *J. Institutional Theoretical Econ.*, Mar. 1985, *141*(1), pp. 62–75.

BONUS, HOLGER. "The Cooperative Association as a Business Enterprise: A Study in the Economics of Transactions," *J. Institutional Theoretical Econ.*, June 1986, *142*(2), pp. 310–39.

BRICKLEY, JAMES; BHAGAT, SANJAI AND LEASE, RON. "The Impact of Long-Range Managerial Compensation Plans on Shareholder Wealth," *J. Acc. Econ.*, 1985, *7*(1–3), pp. 119–29.

CARLTON, DENNIS W. "The Rigidity of Prices," *Amer. Econ. Rev.*, Sept. 1986, *76*(4), pp. 637–58.

CECCHETTI, STEPHEN G. "Staggered Contracts and the Frequency of Price Adjustment," *Quart. J. Econ., Supplement, 100,* 1985, pp. 935–59.

CREW, MICHAEL A. AND CROCKER, KEITH J. "Vertically Integrated Governance Structures and Optimal Institutional Arrangements for Co-generation," *J. Institutional Theoretical Econ.*, 1986, *142*(2), pp. 340–59.

DEMSETZ, HAROLD AND LEHN, KENNETH. "The Structure of Corporate Ownership: Causes and Consequences," *J. Polit. Econ.*, 1985, *93*(6), pp. 1155–77.

DRÈZE, JACQUES, "(Uncertainty and) the Firm in General Equilibrium Theory," *Econ. J.*, Supplement, 1985, *95*, pp. 1–20.

FRECH, H. E. III, "The Property Rights Theory of the Firm: Some Evidence From the U.S. Nursing Home Industry," *J. Institutional Theoretical Econ.*, Mar. 1985, *141*(1), pp. 146–66.

GILLEY, OTIS W.; KARELS, GORDON AND LYON, RANDOLPH M. "Joint Ventures and Offshore Oil Lease Sales," *Econ. Inquiry,* Apr. 1985, *24*(2), pp. 321–40.

HOLMSTROM, BENGT AND WEISS, LAURENCE. "Managerial Incentives, Investment and Aggregate Implications—Scale Effects," *Rev. Econ. Stud.*, July 1985, *52*(3), pp. 403–25.

IPPOLITO, RICHARD A. "The Labor Contract and True Economic Pension Liabilities," *Amer. Econ. Rev.*, Dec. 1985, *75*(5), pp. 1031–43.

JENSEN, MICHAEL C. "Agency Costs of Free Cash Flow, Corporate Finance, and Takeovers," *Amer. Econ. Rev.*, May 1986, *76*(2), pp. 323–29.

KAHNEMAN, DANIEL; KNETSCH, JACK L. AND THALER, RICHARD. "Fairness as a Constraint on Profit Seeking: Entitlements in the Market," *Amer. Econ. Rev.*, Sept. 1986, *76*(4), pp. 728–41.

LEVY, DAVID. "The Transactions Cost Approach to Vertical Integration," *Rev. Econ. Statist.*, Aug. 1985, *67*(3), pp. 438–45.

MACDONALD, JAMES M. "Market Exchange or Vertical Integration," *Rev. Econ. Statist.*, May 1985, *67*(2), pp. 327–31.

MARSHALL, ALFRED. *Principles of economics.* 8th ed. London: Macmillan, [1890] 1936.

MASTEN, SCOTT E. AND CROCKER, KEITH J. "Efficient Adaptation in Long-Term Contracts," *Amer. Econ. Rev.*, Dec. 1985, *75*(5) pp. 1083–93.

MATHEWSON, G. FRANK AND WINTER, RALPH A. "The Economics of Franchise Contracts," *J. Law Econ.*, Oct. 1985, *28*(3), pp. 503–26.

OLMSTEAD, ALAN L. AND RHODE, PAUL. "Rationing Without Government: The West Coast Gas Famine of 1920," *Amer. Econ. Rev.*, Dec. 1985, *75*(5), pp. 1044–55.

PORTER, PHILIP K.; SCULLY, GERALD W. AND SLOTTJE, DANIEL J. "Industrial Policy and the Nature of the Firm," *J. Institutional Theoretical Econ.*, Mar. 1986, *142*(1), pp. 79–100.

ROGERSON, WILLIAM. "The First-Order Approach to Principal-Agent Problems," *Econometrica*, Nov. 1985, *53*(6), pp. 1357–68.

RUBIN, PAUL H. "The Theory of the Firm and the Structure of the Franchise Contract," *J. Law. Econ.*, Apr. 1978, *21*(1), pp. 223–34.

SCHULTZE, CHARLES L. "Microeconomic Efficiency and Nominal Wage Stickiness," *Amer. Econ. Rev.*, Mar. 1985, *75*(1), pp. 1–15.

SINGH, NIRVIKAR. "Monitoring and Hierarchies: The Marginal Value of Information in the Principal-Agent Model," *J. Polit. Econ.*, June 1985, *93*(3), pp. 599–609.

TELSER, LESTER G. "Cooperation, Competition, and Efficiency," *J. Law Econ.*, May 1985, *28*(2), pp. 271–95.

TITMAN, SHERIDAN. "The Effect of Forward Markets on the Debt-Equity Mix of Investor Portfolios and the Optimal Capital Structure of Firms," *J. Financial Quant. Anal.*, Mar. 1985, *20*(1), pp. 19–27.

VICKERS, JOHN. "Delegation and the Theory of the Firm," *Econ. J.*, Supplement, 1985, *95*, pp. 138–47.

WILLIAMSON, OLIVER. "Reflection on the New Institutional Economics," *J. Institutional Theoretical Econ.*, Mar. 1985, *141*(1), pp. 187–95.

WOODWARD, SUSAN. "The Economics of Limited Liability," *J. Econ. Theory and Inst.*, 1985, *141*(3), pp. 601–11.

PART IV

PROPERTY RIGHTS AND ECONOMIC PERFORMANCE

[16]

Introduction to Chapters 17, 18, 19, 20 and 21

> It is not true that administration of an economy is simply a technical problem devolving from the basic 'given' conditions. (G.W. Nutter, *Political Economy and Freedom*, Indianapolis: Liberty Press, p. 102.)

We observe the growth of institutional arrangements that enhance the growth of wealth. We also observe the growth of rules that restrict exchange and production. How do we explain the fact that more efficient institutions have failed to drive less efficient ones out of existence? Why do less efficient institutions manage to survive? And why do less efficient institutions survive in democratic societies? This is, what has happened to the median voter's preference for more wealth?

Changes in property rights are a critical factor affecting economic performance. The efficiency outcome of new or modified property rights hinges on whether they create incentives for transaction costs to be reduced (or increased). We observe two major avenues for changes in property rights.

First, suppose that there is an event that creates either new exchange opportunities for individuals or new issues that need to be resolved or both. If the prevailing property relations are poorly attuned to these opportunities, the transaction costs of pursuing them will increase. People will then generate pressure for legislators, judges and/or bureaucrats to adjust the prevailing property rights to new requirements of the economic game. The expected effect of endogenous changes in property rights is to create incentives to reduce transaction costs.

Second, new property rights are often passed by governments in order to change the economic game. However, changes in property rights that are imposed from without (exogenously) may be in conflict with the prevailing informal rules (e.g., rules on gun controls in southwestern United States) with unfavorable effect on transaction costs.[1] Exogenous changes in property rights are favored by legislators, bureaucrats, political coalitions, ideologues, and pressure groups who are acting in the pursuit of their own values and private ends, while hiding behind the facade of the public interest. Given their objectives, ruling elite (i.e., opinion makers and decision makers) in various countries must then discover the rules of the game that are specific to their intended outcomes, sell those rules to the median voter in democratic societies or implement them by fiat in less democratic ones, and protect them from competition by alternative rules of the game.

An implication is that the ruling elite in any society has incentives to increase the demand for knowledge specific to its objectives. Indeed, we observe public investments in think tanks, research grants to scholars, and various subsidies for universities. And scientists and educators have incentives to respond to this derived demand for knowledge in their respective countries by extolling the efficiency or welfare virtues of the rules that promise to produce intended outcomes. A good recent example is enormous investments that are being made all over Europe in seminars, stipends, research projects, and other efforts to promote the idea of European integration from above.

Chapters 17 to 21 cover the effects of exogenous changes in the rules of the game on the production of wealth in a number of countries and regions. Peter Bauer discusses the effects of the absence of credible property rights in Africa; Enrico Colombatto and Jonathan Macey analyse the transition to capitalism in Eastern Europe from the public choice perspective. My contribution emphasizes the importance of the old ethos in the transition process in Eastern Europe. James Dorn looks at the role of property rights in China. Karl Brunner's article provides an important overall analysis of why the actual results of social engineering *have to diverge* from those it was intended to produce.

Note
1. Informal rules are customs, traditional values, religions, and all other factors that influence the subjective perceptions individuals form about the world in which they live. They are part of the heritage which has passed the test of time. That is why informal rules are referred to as the old ethos, the hand of the past, or the carriers of history.

[17]

Black Africa: Free or Oppressed?

Lord Bauer

The Price of Freedom

Liberty, what crimes are committed in thy name.[1]

Post colonial Africa is termed liberated, free. Yet millions in Black Africa live under mass coercion and lawlessness undreamt of in the 1920s and '30s, indeed under conditions harsher than at any time since slavery. Since the 1960s, hundreds of thousands, possibly millions, perished through government action or in civil wars, or amidst the collapse of order brought about by government policies, and millions have been forcibly uprooted.

I shall examine this tragic and paradoxical situation and its background, largely with reference to British Colonial Africa, primarily West Africa. Somewhat similar developments took place elsewhere in Africa, though the change was less abrupt because before the war personal freedom, especially economic freedom, was greater in British Colonial Africa than elsewhere.

Restrictions of Colonial Rule

The people of a colony are politically unfree in a clearly defined sense. They do not have a say in government. They do not participate directly in the political process beyond the municipal, village or tribal level, though they may have a large measure of freedom of speech and information. How objectionable the population regards such alien rule depends on such factors as the characteristics and activities of the government, on the ethnic and cultural homogeneity of the population, and on the expectations of different groups about successor governments.

For various reasons the great majority of the population did not find the British colonial rule in Africa particularly irksome. For the first time in centuries, perhaps in history, their lives and property were safe. Slave trading and tribal warfare had been suppressed. Taxation was light. The population of most colonies was heterogeneous. In Nigeria, for instance, there were, as there still are, some four or five major tribal groups and at least sixty different tribes, a diversity which dilutes the concept of alien rule. The vast majority of ordinary people knew little of politics beyond the village or tribal level and had never known elective government. Their concerns were with their families, with raising and marketing their crops, and with tending their animals. Like most people, they were much more interested in not being misgoverned than they were in self-government. For these reasons the population at large did not much question colonial rule. Adverse economic changes, such as a fall in export prices or higher taxes, elicited outbreaks of discontent with little or no political thrust.

There did, however, emerge in the 1930s numerically small but articulate groups resentful of colonial rule and hostile to it. They were Western educated or westernised people, some of whom began to be heard in politics, in schools and colleges, the media, and in commerce. They were vocal, and they also had contacts with their opposite numbers in the West.

They resented colonial rule, partly because it was alien but also because it denied them the power, status and money they hoped for under an independent government.

Reversal of the Principles of Colonial Rule

Until the late 1930s, modern British colonial rule in Africa was guided by clearly recognised principles. These were: limited government, especially in economic life; acceptance of traditional leaders and local councils as representatives of African opinion and interests; and their gradual evolution and reform towards independence.

Limited government, open economies, and maintenance of traditional authorities made colonial rule widely acceptable, which in turn made government relatively easy and inexpensive. In such conditions public affairs vex no man, as Dr. Johnson observed.

Between the 1930s and decolonisation in the 1950s and '60s, the guiding principles of British colonial rule were abruptly reversed. In both the political and the economic spheres, one set of principles was replaced by their exact opposite.

As heirs designate of British rule, traditional rulers and councils were replaced by recently urbanised, articulate, literate or partly literate westernised people, notably politicians, teachers, journalists, lawyers and their allies in commerce. Gradual modernisation and reform of traditional authorities and institutions was to be replaced by early introduction of mass democracy interpreted as universal suffrage, a concept previously wholly unknown in Black Africa.

This abrupt reversal of political direction took place in the 1940s and '50s under the impact of such forces as the emergence of U.S. interest in Africa and the influence of Fabian socialism in the British Civil Service, as well as in politics, academia and the media.

The mass of the population in the African colonies did not press for these political changes and was indeed largely unaware of them. And those who were aware of them did not like what they saw. This was recognised with unexpected candour by Obafemi Awolowo, a prominent Nigerian politician of the early post-war period:

> Given a choice from among white officials, Chiefs and educated Nigerians as the principal rulers of the country, the illiterate man today would exercise his preference for the three in the order in which they are named. He is convinced, and he has reasons to be, that he can always get better treatment from the white man than he could hope to get from the Chiefs and the educated elements.[2]

The illiterate man, in the context synonymous with the ordinary man, was, however, not given a choice.

Introduction of Economic Controls

The other main guiding principle of colonial rule, limited government, especially in economic life, was similarly reversed at about the same time. It was replaced by a system of close economic controls; without these the political changes may not have issued in the far-reaching and lasting consequences which I shall note later.

Over most of British Africa the establishment and extension of such economic controls began in the late 1930s and gained momentum in the war and early post-war years, a momentum which continued until independence and beyond. By the eve of independence, these economies were largely state-controlled. The controls and their instruments included state monopoly of major branches of industry and commerce, notably in the import and export trade, including comprehensive monopoly over agricultural exports; numerous state-owned and operated enterprises, often with monopoly power; licensing of commercial and industrial activity; comprehensive control over international transactions; ethnic quotas in employment and in the allocation of licences; price controls and prescription of minimum wages; large-scale support for co-operative societies, in effect, extensions of government departments.

Such controls place the economic opportunities and even the livelihood of people, outside subsistence agriculture, at the mercy of the government and its agents. This was particularly evident in the operation of agricultural export monopolies (marketing boards), which, by virtue of their sole right to purchase and ship these products, could impose a ceiling on producer incomes.

The war and its immediate aftermath did much to promote these controls by lending spurious plausibility to the need for them, even when they were quite irrelevant to the war or were even contrary to their declared purposes. This applied notably to the most far-reaching of these measures, state export monopoly over all major crops.

The principal controls were introduced because they appealed to dirigiste civil servants whose power and status they enhanced; to some British politicians; and to some influential commercial interests, both expatriate and African. They also accorded with the ideology of the terminal period of colonialism in Africa.

The departing colonialists thus bequeathed to their successors the ready-made framework of economic totalitarianism. The incoming African rulers welcomed the controls because these gave them a close grip over their subjects which enabled the rulers to pursue more effectively their personal and political purposes. They extended the controls whenever they could. As we shall see, the West has helped them to do so.

Economic Controls Increase the Power of African Governments

Some results of the controls which I have recited are familiar: divorce of output from demand; raising of costs through quotas and restriction of entry; creation of contrived scarcities with the resulting divorce of prices from the opportunity cost of resources; and emergence of privileged incomes and windfalls unrelated to productive performance.

Certain characteristics of the African scene reinforce or compound these results. The pronounced ethnic, tribal and geographical differences in human, physical and financial resources increase the economic costs of controls. Again, the controls obstruct emergence from subsistence agriculture and keep many people in poverty and backwardness. The absence of effective price control at the retail level both increases the windfalls and privileged incomes and makes them evident and even measurable.

The controls bequeathed to the independent African governments, and extended and reinforced by them, have endowed the rulers with pervasive power over the economic and even physical survival of their subjects. In these conditions the stakes in the struggle for power increase very greatly. People's energies and resources, especially those of alert and ambitious people, are diverted from productive economic activity to the political arena, sometimes from choice, but often from necessity. Who has the government becomes a matter of overriding concern. This sequence promotes and exacerbates political tension and conflict, especially so in the multi-racial and multi-tribal countries of Black Africa. One of the results is the emergence of centrifugal forces and of armed conflict which in turn invites forcible suppression.

The rulers in Black Africa are largely articulate, recently urbanised people as are their allies in the politicised military. There are wide differences in political and military effectiveness between these rulers and the unorganised, inarticulate and illiterate rural people. This difference affects the way political power is exercised, including the operation of controls, the method of taxation, and the pattern of public spending.

The primary interest of the rulers is to maintain themselves in power and to extend it as much as possible. For this purpose they reward their supporters and enfeeble their actual or potential rivals and opponents. Therefore, they try to reduce their subjects to an undifferentiated malleable mass by removing all social and economic distinctions among them.

In the pursuit of their overriding objectives, the rulers are unconcerned with the hardships they inflict. Recurrent examples include large-scale maltreatment of their subjects, often but by no means always ethnic or tribal minorities, maltreatment extending to officially perpetrated, encouraged or tolerated killings and massacres; coercive transfer of population, including enforced herding of people into so-called socialist villages, often mere sites; suppression of private trade; forced collectivisation and other forms of confiscation. These policies have often been reported in the Western press, including newspapers notably sympathetic to the new African governments, such as the *Washington Post, The New York Times, The Times* (London), and the *Financial Times*.

In recent decades in Africa, despotism and lawlessness have gone hand in hand. Economic controls have provoked and exacerbated conflict. Preoccupation with these controls has diverted the resources and attentions of governments from the basic task of protecting lives and legitimate property. Indeed, over wide areas of Black Africa, the governments themselves have destroyed public security. Large-scale maltreatment of their subjects by the rulers extending to massacres, killings and forcible removement of people from their homes to distant regions and the breakdown of public security have inflicted massive hardship on millions of Black Africans. Persistent fear for their lives and property has become the lot of millions.

It is sometimes thought that the situation in Black Africa represents a reversion to pre-colonial tribal conflicts. The analogy is incomplete. The traditional chiefs often ruled capriciously and brutally. But within the confines of their tribes, at any rate, they were usually constrained by tribal councils, by custom and by fear of deposition. They were much closer to their people than are the contemporary rulers. Nor did they possess such physical and financial resources as do the contemporary despots. These resources have all too often been augmented by the West, a matter to which I shall shortly return.

Nor are the African governments elective. Governments change not through elections, but through coup, civil war, or the death of the ruler. (Dr. Nyerere has resigned as President of Tanzania but remains President of its sole party in which power is vested.)

Some Results of Economic Controls

The oft-noted pervasive corruption in Black Africa does not inhere in the African character. Nor does it inhere in the extended family, though this system facilitates the spread of corruption which originates in other government involvement in the economy which underwent a rapid and large-scale extension in Africa after World War II. Under some of the controls, corruption became practically inescapable. Two major economic controls, state monopoly over agricultural exports and import licensing, throw into relief the operation of economic control in Africa.

State monopoly over agricultural exports in British Africa was introduced first in British West Africa (the marketing boards) and subsequently extended to East Africa and elsewhere. Restrictive licensing of traders and processors, on the other hand, was first introduced in the 1930s in East Africa and subsequently spread to West Africa. Such spread of control was the result of centralised decision making in a dirigiste climate at high echelons both in London and in the colonies. This was accompanied by the diminution of the status and influence of provincial commissioners and district officers closer to the grass roots.

The West African marketing boards were established during the war and put on a permanent footing in the early post-war years. The British government documents announcing these measures incorporated categoric assurances that the boards would on no account serve as instruments of taxation. They would act as agents and trustees for producers by means of short-term, intra-seasonal, price stabilisation. These assurances were promptly broken.

From their inception to the early 1960s (when some of the boards ceased to publish accounts), many hundreds of millions of pounds were withheld from West African producers by the boards directly and through other taxes made possible by this system. This extremely heavy taxation operated both in the terminal years of colonial rule and continued after independence. It represented taxation at rates far higher than those borne by other groups with comparable incomes in West Africa.

As a result of the operation of the marketing boards, hundreds of millions of pounds came to be handled by people who previously had thought in terms of only very modest sums. They had little experience of government or sympathy for the majority of the people. The marketing board system was also inherently corrupt in that its operation was unrelated to its declared purposes and also clearly violated formal official undertakings. In any case, the primary loyalties of the politicians and civil servants who controlled the boards were to their families, relatives, friends and political allies, not to the abstract concept of the public welfare of large and heterogeneous countries. Understandably, and even inescapably, they used the system in their own political and personal interests and those of their families and allies.

The funds which accrued to the boards and the governments through the operation of the state export monopolies were spent in accordance with the priorities of the rulers. Large-scale political and personal favours, military spending, prestige projects, expensive government buildings, heavily subsidised industrial or commercial ventures (many of them complete failures), and loss-making co-operatives had been prominent among these priorities, to some extent already in the late colonial period and more so since independence. In Ghana, for instance, the Nkrumah Government rapidly dissipated the large reserves of the export monopolies inherited from the Colonial Government, spent the cocoa revenues and was bankrupt after several years of acute shortage of consumer goods in the country.

In their early years the operation of the marketing boards reflected the personal and political interests and inclinations first of the British civil servants and to some extent also the influence of the trading firms. Subsequently, they served the purposes of African politicians and administrators and those of their agents and allies. Neither the British civil servants, nor the politicians and administrators in control of the boards, ever had to pay much heed to their unorganised and largely inarticulate constituents or subjects.

In Black Africa there is generally no effective price control at the retail level. In its absence the allocation of an import licence or of a controlled commodity at a price below the market clearing level produces a windfall the size of which is readily ascertainable. This generates a scramble for licences and controlled supplies. Extensive corruption becomes inescapable: the bribe serves as a rationing device and as a partial return of a gift. The windfalls which accompany specific controls also set up and exacerbate political conflict, especially in multi-ethnic societies.

Such results of the controls are examples of the interaction of the familiar variables of economic theory, such as prices and quantities, with factors treated as parameters, such as the political climate or the extent of the exchange economy. This type of interaction deserves closer attention in economics, especially in development economics, than it often receives.

Western Aid Reinforces Totalitarian Rule

Western politicians, civil servants, academics, people in the media and businessmen bear a distinct responsibility for the widely prevalent despotism, lawlessness and corruption in Black Africa.

The controls introduced in the last years of colonial rule politicised economic life and intensified the struggle for political power. This result was much reinforced and extended by massive official aid to the new governments. This aid has enabled them to pursue, for years on end, barbarous policies which also entailed extremely damaging economic results. Thus it was Western aid which enabled Dr. Nyerere to continue so long with forcible collectivisation, with the forcing of millions of people into socialist villages, with suppression of trade. Dr. Nyerere not only received massive Western aid, but was held up by Western spokesmen, notably including Mr. McNamara, as an example to be followed by other African rulers. The critical role of Western aid in the political survival of Dr. Nyerere has been freely acknowledged by his Western admirers.

The totalitarian rule of a number of other African despots, including Nkrumah, among others, was for long shored up by Western economic aid. Sustained large-scale Western aid to the Government of Ethiopia has certainly been of great assistance to that Marxist-Leninist dictatorship and may well have been indispensable for its survival. Official Western aid to that government has been in place since the mid-seventies and it still continues on a large scale. Over this period the government pursued all the damaging policies listed in section 4 above, which in turn were largely behind the several civil wars still (as of June 1986) being waged in Ethiopia.

The West also provided military assistance to despotic rulers. British military and financial aid enabled Obote of Uganda in 1966 to destroy the widely popular Kabaka and his many supporters and to establish his dictatorship. When the Tanzanian army mutinied in the 1960s, Britain provided the troops requested by Dr. Nyerere to enable him to stay in power. President Mobutu of Zaire also owes his survival to Western military and economic support.

Without aid, African rulers might well have decided to rely on less economic control and on less large-scale brutality. They might have had to rely more on market forces. African experience contradicts rather than supports the currently much canvassed idea that official aid could be used to bribe the recipients into more market-oriented policies. The opposite outcome is much more probable. Closely controlled economies serve the purpose of the new rulers in Africa; they will abandon close economic control only if they are forced to do so by the danger of a breakdown. If they are rescued, they will not abandon it even though they may pay lip service to private initiative. It is therefore not surprising that advocates of so-called policy-oriented aid have already begun to warn that it would be politically unwise to ask recipients to liberalise more than a small part of their economies.

Western academics, media men and businessmen have also helped along the politicisation of life in Africa. The special interest groups behind the marketing board system and the import controls included both civil servants and merchants. State economic monopoly was welcomed by academics who also provided the stream of insubstantial and inconsistent rationalisations for the special taxation of the producers. Western academics have persistently supported both so-called development planning in Africa and official aid, and the linking of aid to the adoption of comprehensive planning. Comprehensive planning, i.e., extensive state economic control and official aid, have been the two principal policy proposals of modern mainstream development economics.

Since the war, both academics and the media in the West have widely supported African governments, however coercive and brutal, as long as they could be labelled progressive. This label has come to carry a set of distinct connotations: distrust of the market system, personal freedom, private enterprise, private property and individual farming; pursuit of politically organised egalitarianism; and rejection of traditional rulers, even if freely accepted by the population. Hostility to the West is also often part of this syndrome.

Both academics and people in the media have often rationalised or excused totalitarian policies as necessary for economic progress and for nation building. These policies have patently obstructed economic advance and emergence from poverty. The advocates of nation building regard people as bricks rather than as human beings, bricks to be manipulated at will for the purposes of the rulers. Far from building nations, throughout Africa such policies have engendered large-scale violent conflict and generated centrifugal forces.

Nkrumah enjoined African politicians first to seek the political kingdom because, if they attained that, all else would be added unto them. The support of the West has been indispensable for the success of this quest. The results and rewards of attaining the political kingdom have much exceeded expectations. For this outcome too, the West is largely responsible.

Misconceptions and Misuse of Language

Liberty, Sir Isaiah Berlin wrote in 1958, was a concept so porous that there was practically no interpretation it was capable of resisting. The confused identification of the sovereignty of African governments with the freedom of Africans is an example.

Discourse on African matters has come to be vitiated by misconceptions and misuse of language. Blacks in South Africa are supposed to be enslaved. Yet large numbers of Blacks from all over Africa travel long distances to get there.

Indeed, public discourse on African freedom confirms that the world language of the late 20th century is not English. It is Newspeak.

NOTES

1. Mme Roland, quoted by Lamartine, *Histoire des Girondins*, Oxford Dictionary of Quotations, 1964, p. 408.

2. Obafemi Awolowo: Path to Nigerian freedom, quoted in Frederick Pedler, *Currents of West African History, 1940-78*, London, 1979, p. 265.

[18]

Enrico Colombatto
Università di Torino and ICER

Jonathan Macey
Cornell University Law School

A Public Choice View
of Transition in Eastern Europe

1. – Introduction

The most important economic challenge of the last twenty years has probably been the beginning of the transition process in Eastern Europe. Some five years have now elapsed since the political events which started the process; and in a very limited number of countries – the Czech Republic, Slovenia and perhaps Poland – transition seems to be heading towards success; in others prospects remain uncertain or worrisome (Russia is typical, in this light). Indeed, as has been observed for the Russian situation in Ulam [1994], the plausible possible futures for Russia «range from an enticing vision of society à la Milton Friedman to one more in the style of Stalin. [...] There is no end to incongruous data about the main remnant of what used to be the fatherland of socialism» (p. 40).

The existence of a fairly wide spectrum of transition attempts and results is well supported by plenty of evidence; but economists still have to come out with convincing explanations of the differences. For instance, according to the neoclassical view transition towards a market economy comes to a standstill because of the reluctance to liberalize prices and the slow pace adopted in the privatization process; agents are left without adequate signals, for central planning is dead, but the efficient relative-price system has not yet seen the light. On the other hand, gradualists maintain that slow transition is inevitable and that success is by no means guaranteed; the present situation was thus to be expected and foreign support is now crucial to keep the process going.

Nevertheless, it still remains unclear why price liberalization in some countries has been easier than in others; why some economies have been able to meet the transition problems through shock therapy, whereas policy makers who have taken a gradualist stance are still stuck.

As a matter of fact, all real «orthodox» explanations, including those derived from the «new political economy» [1] are tied up with the behaviour of exogenous

---

[1] See, for instance, the survey by Asilis and Milesi-Ferretti [1994]: «this literature clearly cannot provide firm conclusions and a set of policy recommendations guaranteed to ensure the sustainability and success of reforms» (pp. 2-3).

Economia delle scelte pubbliche, 2-3, 1994.

114

and unpredictable variables: foreign aid, higher aggregate demand in the so-called «West», the evolution of the political situation, including the resurgence of nationalist sentiments and of Cold War hostilities. It is now becoming clear that the three pillars of transition – privatization, price liberalization and currency convertibility – are extremely fragile, if not meaningless, unless they are realized within a suitable institutional/constitutional framework[2].

This is surely persuasive; but it is also far from satisfactory on two accounts. For it fails to rationalize what is now happening in Eastern Europe and does not shed any light on what may happen in the future.

The present paper tries to develop a different approach to transition, by elaborating on public choice modelling, that is by applying the principles of economic theory to the production of law and legislation. Application of the principles of public choice to the experience of the recent past in Eastern Europe has important practical and theoretical implications. Contrary to the traditional view taken in the literature, we shall try to investigate (1) the origin of the agents' behaviour, which cause the speed in transition, (2) the nature of such behaviour around the critical points in the transition process, (3) the role possibly played by the exogenous variables mentioned above.

From a broader theoretical perspective, analysis of events in Eastern Europe also holds the promise of contributing to an important, albeit nascent, theoretical debate at the heart of the public choice movement. There is indeed a widespread consensus among public choice scholars (a) that rent-seeking[3] is a negative-sum game for society, since resources are wasted in non-productive activities and it leads to production and consumption inefficiencies[4]; (b) that special interest groups have an interest to form pressure groups to influence both politicians and bureaucrats[5], so as to subtract rents to the rest of the community; (c) that the interaction between rent-seeking pressure groups

---

[2] The case of Russia, where privatization is a success only on paper, is typical in this context. See, for instance, Daviddi [1994] and also Boycko, Shleifer and Vishny [1994].

[3] Rent seeking refers to the process of attempting to obtain economic rents, which are payments for the use of economic capital (both human and fixed) through government intervention in the market. A classic example of rent-seeking is an attempt by a single firm or subset of firms to obtain a government monopoly in a particular market niche. Such monopolies enable the firm or firms to raise prices above competitive levels. The increased income from monopoly pricing is economic rent from government regulation.

[4] An important exception to this is when the initial situation is already characterized by distortions and the activity of the rent-seekers is such that the final (second-best) outcome is closer to that typical of a distortion-free economy. See Bhagwati, Brecher and Srinivasan [1984], and also Vousden [1990, ch. 3] for a formal analysis of exogenous DUP (Directly Unproductive Profit-Seeking Activities).

In this paper, the analysis will however be limited to endogenous DUP; in other words, it is assumed that interest groups aim at creating new rents, rather than at seizing the benefit of existing rents.

[5] The former are in charge of setting the rules of the game, and are subject to periodical evaluation-elections; the latter are in charge of enforcing such rules, but are appointed for much longer periods.

with politicians and bureaucrats dominates the process of day-to-day political life[6]. As a consequence, although society as a whole has an incentive to develop a constitutional order in which rent is banned, agreement on this order is guaranteed only if information were perfect, majority voting and lump-sum transfers costless.

The theoretical deficiency in the public choice literature results from the fact that the consensus about the *desirability* of curbing rent-seeking is not matched by a concomitant consensus about the bargaining conditions under which it will be possible to do so when the qualifications which guarantee a pressure-group-free constitutional order are violated. In other words, under what «soft» conditions, if any, will it be possible to overcome the strangle-hold of politicians, bureaucrats and special interests, and design rules for the political game that will serve the common interests[7]? Implicit in the work of important scholars [EPSTEIN, 1982, 1984, 1985a, 1985b, 1986; MASHAW, 1980; SUNSTEIN, 1984], is the core assumption that it is possible for citizens to find themselves in a bargaining position in which a constitution that reduces rent-seeking can be crafted. By contrast, others [LANDES and POSNER, 1975; CRAIN and TOLLISON, 1979a, 1979b; TOLLISON, 1988] claim that the process of constitution-making inevitably will be dominated by special-interest groups, and that this process merely presents additional opportunities for politicians, bureaucrats and special interests to obtain wealth transfers at the expenses of the public-at-large.

The general argument made here is that the understanding of events in Eastern Europe can be considerably improved by the application of public choice principles; and that the future of the area is path-dependent; that is, it has been determined by the bargaining dynamics that initially caused the demise of the old regime and the emergence of the new state.

We begin in section 2 by examining the public choice literature to determine what, if anything, the public choice model can predict about the behaviour of the relevant players and the likely outcomes generated by their actions. In section 3 we analyze the means by which organic institutional change can evolve in economies where rent-seeking is widely perceived as a significant welfare-reducing phenomenon, even by successful rent-seekers. The discussion is developed further in section 4, where three different bargaining configurations are discussed. The results obtained are then applied to the case of Russia (section 5), where the crucial role played by the nomenclature in the transition process is emphasised. The conclusions are drawn in section 6, where the future is shown to depend on whether the constitutional moment

---

[6] The size of the phenomenon is significant and ranges from about 3% of GNP in developed countries (*e.g.* the USA) to well above 10% in LDCs (*e.g.* in Turkey). See Posner [1975] and Krueger [1974].

[7] Buchanan [1988, p. 113] has described the task of the constitutional political economist as «to assist individuals, as citizens who ultimately control their own social order, in their continuing search for those rules of the political game that will best serve their purposes, whatever these might be».

is effectively under way, or just a prospect; in the former case – contrary to common beliefs – hopes for rapid and sound improvement are probably misplaced.

2. – *The economic theory of law*

In this section we first provide a straightforward description of the economic theory of law as applied to ordinary, day-to-day, political activities. We then turn our attention to organic, constitutional change.

A. – Economics and the Production of Legal Rules

The economic (or «interest group») theory of law «asserts that legislation is a good demanded and supplied much as other goods, so that legislative protection flows to those groups that derive the greatest value from it, regardless of overall social welfare» [POSNER, 1982, p. 265]. In other words, the economic theory of regulation applies generally accepted principles of rational economic behavior to decisions made by politicians, bureaucrats, and interest groups.

The economic theory of law-making has predictive implications that are starkly different from the traditional, public-interest theory of regulation, which holds that regulation is designed to benefit the public by solving collective-action problems and other sorts of market failures. By contrast, the economic theory of regulation holds that political decision-makers – that is politicians and bureaucrats – behave just like private-sector consumers and businesses; they attempt to maximize their own self-interest, generally at the expense of overall societal welfare.

Under the economic theory of law-making, interested parties form coalitions, which trade power, money and political support in exchange for legislation and «preference»[8], that provides private benefits for the members of the coalitions. Efficiency considerations indicate that a group forms into an effective political coalition when the benefits from achieving wealth transfers from the legislature outweigh the costs of organizing. Benefits are of course net of the costs associated to the purchase of legislation and/or preference; furthermore, the term «organization» refers to the cost of collecting the resources required to make the coalition powerful and credible enough. For a number of reasons, some groups will be able to organize into distributional coalitions more cheaply than others [McCORMICK and TOLLISON, 1981, pp. 16-18; OLSON, 1982, p. 18].

In the end, the law-making process is viewed as a market in which legal rules

---

[8] The term «preference» refers to the trade relations between the bureaucrats and the interest groups and applies to two kinds of deal. On the one hand, it refers to the way legislation is interpreted and implemented; on the other to the role of the bureaucracy in getting pieces of legislation approved.

go to the individual or group that values them most, as measured by its willingness and ability to pay.

Thus, while qualifications sometimes are in order, a useful generalization is that the economic theory of regulation posits that legislation will be characterized by concentrated benefits for discrete groups and widely dispersed social costs. This is because legislatures pass laws to benefit those groups that are able to trade political support and/or money in exchange for obtaining passage of such laws[9]. The costs of legislation are of course borne by those who are in the worst position to object to them – the amorphous and disaggregated public. The losers pay for legislation that benefits special interest groups with higher taxes, increased regulatory burdens at all levels, and higher prices for goods and service [MACEY, 1988] and are considered incapable of fighting back: either because «clever» losers guess that the «new» politicians would behave in the same way as the others (even if the favoured coalition may no longer be the same)[10]; or because «ignorant» losers don't realize that their welfare is falling (this is often the case with protectionism); or – finally – because decision makers at the center cannot be easily removed (this is the case with the bureaucracy almost everywhere, or with the politicians in many countries of the world).

Thus, the outcome of the political market is usually a negative sum game because it wastes economic resources as groups devote efforts to organizing into effective political coalitions, providing political support to sympathetic politicians, providing political opponents of unsympathetic politicians, imposing sanctions on non-cooperative group members, fighting against the rent-seeking activities of rival groups. If successful, rent-seeking leads to distortions (*e.g.* monopoly power). If the outcome is uncertain, the probability of successful rent-seeking reduces economic incentives to engage in productive economic activity for fear that investments be hit by government regulation.

The above discussion is a straightforward account of the process of rent-seeking by interest groups during times of ordinary politics. The following discussion examines public choice theory during times of organic, constitutional change

---

[9] Macey [1986] argues that «market forces provide strong incentives for politicians to enact laws that serve private rather than public interests and hence statutes are supplied by law-makers to the political groups or coalitions that outbid competing groups» (p. 223).

See also Stigler [1971], where the theory of regulation is presented as the result of the interaction of various coalitions, each of them evaluating the costs and benefits of their lobbying operations. The analysis has been further enriched by Peltzman [1976], where politicians take into account the losers explicitly.

[10] A clever loser understands that no politician is ever going to pay attention to him, because of the negligible voting power of the group the loser belongs to, or because of the modest resources the politician expects to extract from the loser's rent-seeking activities. Thus, the loser takes successful rent-seeking by strong interest groups for granted, and aims at keeping the «ruling class» in office. By pursuing this strategy the amount of unproductive, rent-seeking activities is likely to be smaller, since they tend to be an increasing function of the turnover in the bureaucracy and in the political class. See also Shleifer and Vishny [1993].

within a society of the kind that has been taking place in Eastern Europe for the past several years. Unfortunately, here the public choice model becomes less a paradigm than a pair of competing hypotheses.

One hypothesis is that constitution-making is no different from ordinary law-making. This hypothesis posits that rent-seeking dominates both types of law-making, so that constitutional change is simply a sort of high stakes variant of ordinary law-making.

The competing hypothesis is that the incentives facing the interest groups and individuals drafting constitutional rules are fundamentally different from the incentives facing such groups and individuals during times of ordinary law-making. As a result of these new incentives, constitutions can be expected to be far more restrictive than ordinary laws in the degrees of freedom afforded to interest-group politics.

Our argument is that both of these hypotheses are possible. Sometimes constitution-making is indistinguishable from ordinary law-making. Where this happens, the ultimate political equilibrium that emerges from the constitution-making process will enhance rather than inhibit rent-seeking, because the process of constitution-making will be designed to increase returns to the politicians who control the process. Alternatively, the ultimate political equilibrium that emerges from constitution-making may inhibit rent-seeking. Determining what sort of constitutional framework will emerge from any particular constitutional debate will depend on whose voices are heard at the bargaining table.

B. – The Economics of Constitutional Change

As has been mentioned, according to the first school of thought «constitutional provisions are worth more than normal legislation to interest groups because they are more durable (*i.e.*, harder to repeal), but they are also more costly to obtain because of stricter procedures required for passage» [TOLLISON, 1988, p. 346]. According to this view, contrary to ordinary law-making, constitutional rules address the severe bargaining problem resulting from non-simultaneity of performance between politicians and interest groups attempting to strike mutually beneficial deals[11].

For example the executive veto, by making it more difficult to repeal a law once it is enacted, increases the durability of legislation, and thereby helps to solve the non-simultaneity of performance problem. Similarly, Landes and Posner [1975, p. 875] argue that an independent judiciary facilitates interest-group interactions with politicians because it prevents special interest group bargains from being thwarted by subsequent legislatures:

---

[11] The non-simultaneity-of-performance problem is particularly acute because the passage of the legislation in period 1 gives rival interest groups harmed by the initial passage the incentive to galvanize into effective political coalitions to fight for repeal in period 2. The specter of an escalating cycle of rent-seeking due to the inability of politicians and bureaucrats to «stay bought» may affect the willingness to pay them in order to obtain wealth transfers in the first place.

«The element of stability or continuity necessary to enable interest-groups politics to operate in the legislative arena is supplied in the first instance, by the procedural rules of the legislature, and in the second instance, by the existence of an independent judiciary[12]».

In other words, under this variant, major organic changes in constitutional structure will occur in order to improve contracting problems that exist between politicians and interest groups. This we will call the «politics as usual» theory of constitutional change. This theory strongly predicts that life will be worse for ordinary citizens after a period of constitutional change because interest groups and politicians will find it less costly, at the margin, to make agreements that transfer wealth to themselves.

At the same time, however, the price of the deal struck by politicians and interest groups is likely to be higher within a constitutional-change framework. As Buchanan and Tullock [1962] have observed, change in the constitution implies a higher number of entities (judges, presidents, as well as legislators) that must be «bought off» in order to achieve passage of an interest-group wealth transfer. In addition, politicians and – to a lesser extent – bureaucrats know that constitutional law making is a constraint on their subsequent decision-making power. Therefore they are likely to give up this power at a higher price than in a politics-as-usual framework.

The role of bureaucrats needs careful examination in this context. As such, constitutional change is not particularly important from the bureaucrat's point of view, but the nature of the change surely is. For example, if constitutional change favours the centralization of the policy-making process, then the civil service will be monitored by some kind of central authority, which is more likely to focus on the administrative issues, rather than on the substance of its activity. On the other hand, decentralization would make the civil service more responsible towards the local community, and thus deprive it of some latitude.

In general, however, while constitutional change weakens the bargaining power of the politician in a politics-as-usual context, it does not affect that of the bureaucrat, who actually becomes the only relevant counterpart *vis-à-vis* the coalitions. One should therefore expect support for constitutional change from the bureaucracy; more so if such a change leads to centralized decision making and if the country is large[13]. On the other hand, serious objections to constitutional change could be raised by the bureaucracy in a relatively large country where decentralization is the name of the game.

In short, the most likely constitutional change according to a politics-as-usual

---

[12] Actually, if the judiciary is also efficient (in the sense of fast and able to detect biased implementation by the civil service), then the role of the bureaucracy in the rent-seeking game is reduced considerably.
[13] Of course, below a given threshold, the smaller the size of the country, the less relevant is the centralization-decentralization dichotomy.

theory is one characterized by a move to a constitutional regime of separated powers with an independent judiciary and an independently elected executive with veto powers. It tends to be expensive, but finds support in the bureaucracy; as for its consequences, the cost of subsequent politics-as-usual bargains is reduced, and the balance of power shifts from the politicians to the bureaucrats.

Another view of the nature of constitutional change draws on the fact that rent-seeking by one interest group calls for rent-seeking also by other interest groups, with likely welfare losses for all groups, as all fight for a larger share of a shrinking pie. In the absence of a credible, enforceable agreement to prevent rent-seeking, individual interest groups can make themselves better off if they engage in rent-seeking, provided that nobody else does; on the other hand, the worst possible outcome for any individual or group would be to refrain from engaging in rent-seeking while other groups are rent-seeking. In the end, this situation leads to a high level of DUP, in spite of the fact that no rent-seeking would be far superior.

Thus, as long as the relevant individuals and groups within a society recognize that rent-seeking is a negative-sum game which dissipates opportunities for growth, they will have incentives to solve the prisoner's dilemma outlined above by drafting credible, sustainable constitutional rules that restrict the level of rent-seeking during times of ordinary politics:

«Clearly, people have an incentive to develop a constitutional order whereby they agree to abide by the rules of trade and to refrain from plunder. A constitutional contract provides a possible escape from the prisoners' dilemma in which the members of society are otherwise caught. In effect, constitutional order is a mutually advantageous treaty among what would otherwise be warring factions – a treaty which promotes the substitution of wealth-creating trade from wealth-reducing (i.e. rent-seeking plunders)» [WAGNER and GWARTNEY, 1988, p. 33].

The above discussion has referred to a bargaining model to describe the way constitutions are likely to be shaped during times of constitutional change. Bargaining, of course, is most likely to occur when the gains from trade are highest, which is the case in countries where low or stagnant economic growth is coupled with high potential for growth. The case of Eastern Europe in the late 80s may actually match this situation.

Therefore, if this view is accepted, the critical question is not whether people have *incentives* to design constitutional barriers to rent-seeking; but whether people can overcome the contracting problems that make it difficult to do so.

4. – *Some bargaining configurations*

Still, the assumptions presented in the previous section do not guarantee that the relevant parties will agree to a constitutional regime that curbs rent-seeking. A host of bargaining problems may prevent the parties from reaching an agreement despite the existence of significant potential gains from trade.

In particular, critical to this analysis is the possibility that some groups expect to be net winners in a rent-seeking society. This is due to the fact that, even though rent-seeking is a negative sum game overall, for some individuals and groups (politicians, bureaucrats, lawyers, lobbyists, the nomenclature) rent-seeking is clearly a positive-sum exercise. The ability of successful rent-seekers to peek behind the constitutional-stage bargaining veil to get a view of their role in the post-constitutional order will cause them vigorously to resist efforts to forge constitutional rules that eliminate the demand for their services by reducing aggregate levels of rent-seeking.

Thus, the identity of the groups actively involved in deciding on governmental structure and allocations of power during times of organic constitutional change will be critical to the outcomes generated by the bargaining process. There are three possible bargaining configurations, each of which leads to varying results in terms of overall social welfare.

A. – Consumer Control of the Process: the Constitutional Moment

One possibility is that the net losers from rent-seeking (for ease of exposition let us call them «consumers»), somehow will be able simply to exclude the net winners from the bargaining table, or else to eliminate their influence once they are there. Rational ignorance usually deprives consumers of the incentive to galvanize into effective political coalitions to oppose statutes passed during the course of every-day politics because the transaction costs of forming such coalitions outweighs the benefits in the form of savings from wealth transfers. However, this cost-benefit calculation changes when organic, constitutional rules are being considered, since the impact of constitutional rules is much higher than the impact of ordinary laws. Thus, following McCormick and Tollison [1981, p. 127]:

«We would expect the citizen-consumer-taxpayer to play a larger role in constitutional processes than in normal political processes [...] [because] the individual voter's stake is [...] larger when considering constitutional issues. At the relevant margins of behavior, then, we expect more voter impact on constitutions than on regular elections».

Thus, consumers may be able to galvanize into an effective political coalition and freeze rent-seekers out of the process. The period in which consumers overcome the free-rider and rational ignorance problems that result in the prisoner's dilemma of ordinary politics in order to craft constitutional rules that impede rent-seeking has been called «constitutional moment»: typically, it represents an agreement among people to restrict their rent-seeking activities in exchange for an agreement by others to do the same.

B. – Bureaucratic Control of the Process: Politics as Usual

Just as consumers have incentives to initiate and gain control of the process of constitutional formation in order to make themselves better off at the expense of bureaucrats, so too do bureaucrats have incentives to initiate and gain control of the process of constitutional formation in order to make themselves better off at the expense of consumers.

The bureaucrats can benefit from constitutional change to the extent that they are able to design organizational rules that enhance their (monopolistic) decision-making power – getting things done. By doing this the bureaucrats can increase the demand for their services and fill the void left by the politicians in the rent-seeking game. Bureaucrats act as brokers among consumers and various groups of producers. They *establish an equilibrium* by efficiently pairing these demanders and suppliers of legislation [McCORMICK and TOLLISON, 1981, p. 62].

Thus, politicians will have to choose between pressing for constitutional changes that increase the durability of special interest legislation and thus the value of their once-and-for-all services [CRAIN and TOLLISON, 1979]; or press for «politics as usual», which is associated with lower returns for rent-seekers and bureaucrats, but with the need for repeated services by politicians (to prevent changes in the ordinary legislation). In both cases, of course, bureaucrats will attempt to exclude the consumers from the bargaining table, or else to ignore their interests once they are there.

C. – The Bargaining Game

The final possibility is that neither the bureaucrats nor the consumers are able to exclude each other or to ignore their influence. Each group will have to take the interests of the other into account. In particular, the bureaucrats who expect to lose from reductions in rent-seeking may be able to form a blocking coalition to impede the consumers from reaching a walfare-increasing (on aggregate) constitutional change. This is because organic societal changes often require the support of a super-majority. Side payments (from consumers to bureaucrats) are of course a possible solution, the feasibility of which is however greatly reduced by their likely size, as well as by the existence of non-simultaneity and social problems: the gains from setting constitutional rules to impede rent-seeking are *future gains* to be realized from increases in productivity and aggregate social wealth. Consequently, bureaucrats will be asked to make immediate sacrifices by accepting constitutional impediments to rent-seeking and power cuts, in exchange for promises of future compensation from consumers, which would however become more difficult to enforce in the new post-constitutional order.

In addition, side payments to the bureaucrats would be illegal: in principle, civil servants are supposed to be acting in the best interests of society; bureaucrats would actually endanger their power base by accepting explicit payments.

The likely mechanism for solving both of these contracting problems will be to keep the bureaucrats in office, in exchange for their agreement to refrain from interfering with the consumers' activities in the market. Keeping the bureaucrats in office allows them to keep politicians at bay in ordinary decision-making, so as to compensate them for acquiescing in the consumers' proposed changes.

In other words, the key is to compensate the bureaucrats for the smaller rent-seeking pie by allowing them access to a larger share (at the expense of the politicians)[17].

D. – Beyond bargaining

A non-bargaining alternative mechanism by which a society can wrest itself from the shackles of welfare-reducing distributional coalitions is suggested by Olson [1982, pp. 75-76], who is indeed aware of the fact that interest groups' rent-seeking *reduces an economy's dynamism and rate of growth*, whereas constitutional rules can be an effective impediment to passage of special-interest legislation. But in his view the dominant distributional coalitions that are frustrat-

---

[17] It is true that life employment for bureaucrats is usually passed by «ordinary politics», rather than by constitutional amendments; as such, compensation offered to the bureaucrats is less reliable than the gains acquired by consumers. Consumers, however, can organize into coalitions at a high cost, which is endured during constitutional moments, but not under politics as usual; this should guarantee bureaucrats from repeals of life-employment legislation.

ing their society's potential for growth can only be *emasculated or abolished by totalitarian government or foreign occupation*; after that, countries «should grow relatively quickly after a free and stable legal order is established. This can explain the postwar economic «miracles» in the nations that were defeated in World War II, particularly those in Japan and West Germany. The everyday use of the word *miracle* to describe the rapid economic growth in these countries testifies that this growth is not only unexpected but outside the range of known laws and experience».

5. – Russia: the bargaining model alternatives

Unfortunately, it is not possible to apply Mancur Olson's paradigm to the Russian experience, because there has been no abolition of that country's distributional coalitions by totalitarian government or foreign occupation. Olson's approach has indeed been at the basis of the attempts to run shock-therapy privatization in the Czech Republic and in Poland [LIPTON and SACHS, 1990, pp. 296-299]; but the very need to emasculate or brain-wash the bureaucracy – as was to some extent the case, say, in Poland[18] – explains why gradualism is still the *leit motiv* in the former USSR, where most, if not all of the country's basic distributional coalitions remain in place and where «enterprises escaped from central planning into an endless series of negotiations with the bureaucracy over subsidies, prices and output, rather than into a true market environment» [LIPTON and SACHS, 1990, p. 304].

Ironically, Russia's problem is precisely that it has not suffered a major military defeat (or an equivalent shock). The dominant interest groups, particularly the apparatchiks and members of the economic bureaucracy remain in place[19]. They are unwilling to carry out the transition process so long as transition threatens the loss of their power and privileges [COLOMBATTO, 1992, pp. 273-275]. The actions of the Russian parliament, which has consistently opposed and obstructed economic reform whenever possible, provide ample evidence of the problems for meaningful reform.

Thus, in Russia, even though the ideology of the communists was discredited, the interest groups and bureaucrats that thrived under communists rule continue to control the country's resources. These bureaucrats and interest groups are holding reform hostage.

---

[18] Lipton and Sachs [1990, p. 305] report that «after the collapse of Poland's communist regime, [...] the nomenclature system collapsed, as did the direct intervention on the enterprise matters».

[19] Historically, an apparatchik works within the bureaucratic apparatus of the communist party. A member of the nomenclature is an appointee of the communist party apparatus.

A. – A Constitutional Moment for Eastern Europe?

In terms of the bargaining model presented above, clearly the first possibility which posits consumer control of the process with bureaucrats and interest groups agreeing to rules that curb rent-seeking has not taken place. Privatization has been a sort of cruel joke, as the former bureaucrats remain in control of industry, and have relatively easy access to government subsidies (provided by the nomenclature). Central planning has been cancelled; but the centralized bureaucratic system is well alive. Many large entities that have been privatized enjoy state subsidies and monopoly power; and there is no reason why they should operate efficiently, since they can more easily devote resources to rent-seeking. In countries such as the U.S., which have constitutional structures designed to curb rent-seeking by raising the decision costs of government, the idea that wealth transfers could be obtained simply by making a phone call to a government bureaucrat would be unthinkable. Clearly, many East European bureaucrats – Russia is again typical in this respect – enjoy this degree of power and autonomy and will not willingly relinquish it for the sake of greater efficiency.

B. – Bureaucratic Control of the Process: Politics as Usual

The question, then, is which of the other two possibilities, complete bureaucratic control of the process, or bargaining between bureaucrats and consumers, best describes the ongoing situation in many East European countries. It does not appear that the bureaucrats have gained control of the process of constitutional formation and are making themselves better off at the expense of consumers. For the bureaucrats have not succeeded in excluding the consumers from the bargaining table entirely, and thus have been unable to ignore consumer interests completely.

Actually, there are reasons to believe that bureaucrats have been unwilling to promote constitutional change, because of the role consumers could have played during the constitutional moment. Indeed, bureaucrats may have been encouraged in doing so by the confused political situation: lack of constitutional change deprives politicians of their bargaining power (based on personal credibility and expected length of stay in office), and favours the role of the bureaucrat which would appear as the only solid rock in the storm.

On the other hand, the possibility of a constitutional moment leads bureaucrats to act in order to increase the efficiency of the present system, so as to reduce the perceived gap between potential income and actual income, and delay a constitutional moment which could be dominated by consumers. The real issue to discuss in this light, is then whether the bureaucracy is able to improve economic performance; doubts seem justified.

C. – The Bargaining Game in Russia

It is most likely, though, that once the constitutional process is launched, neither the bureaucrats nor the consumers are able completely to exclude each other from the bargaining table or to ignore each others' influence.

Still consumers may be unable to strike a bargain with the bureaucrats that would result in constitutional change to reduce aggregate levels of bureaucratic waste caused by rent-seeking. The problems caused by the bargain trap – as discussed in this paper – may not be easy to remove.

One possible means of avoiding it is through «innovative» Western aid[20]. But, Western tax payers do not appear to be willing to permit their funds to be used to pay bureaucrats to refrain from interfering and to subsidize the organization of consumers into effective pressure groups. What is needed is a means of packaging aid from the West to accomplish this objective without appearing to do so. As Winiecki [1990] has observed in his path-breaking article on the problems of reforming Soviet-style economies, there are two principal types of rents enjoyed by the existing élites. First, and most obviously, are the kickbacks, by which managers and other members of the ruling élite divert the resources of the enterprise to others in exchange for private gains for themselves. Second, and perhaps more importantly, are the payments that members of the bureaucracy receive in exchange for making appointments.

As Winiecki rightly emphasizes, the expected losses of rent by people in power is the major obstacle to reform. When an enterprise is privatized, the bureaucrats lose their powers of appointment, and the people running the enterprise, even if they remain in control, lose the ability to obtain funds from kickbacks. Thus both sorts of rents disappear in the event of privatization.

Consistent with the bargaining framework advanced in this article, one means of resolving this dilemma is to have entrepreneurs pay the apparatchiks in exchange for the rights to set up a private firm[21]. Unfortunately, the existing legal structures strongly discourage this. Receiving a payment in exchange for permission to set up a private firm would constitute a bribe under Russian law, and be considered a criminal act. By contrast, rent extraction in appointments is either perfectly legal, or at worst, in the «grey area» between the improper and the criminal [WINIECKI, 1990, p. 206]. It would be far better, of course, if bribes to accomplish privatization were decriminalized, and even encouraged, while appointments to managerial posts within industrial firms by bureaucrats were criminalized. But it is not clear how such a change could be accomplished. And it is also not clear why the new-entrepreneur coalitions should stop from carrying out their own rent-seeking activities.

Once the constitutional moment has started, the only viable means for solving

---

[20] See Eichengreen and Uzan [1992] against «traditional» aid programmes: «The institutional infrastructure that is a prerequisite for an aid-instigated acceleration of economic growth is not yet in place. Not even the outlines of a social contract are evident. These considerations militate against a Marshall plan for the East» (p. 16).

[21] The amount of the bribe paid by the would-be private entrepreneur should also be enough to make sure that the other firms do not get subsidies, that the new firm will not be stopped by administrative difficulties/ interference in the future, that the exchange rate will not be arbitrarily manipulated in such a way that imports will flood the market, etc.

All this would of course be too much for a single entrepreneur, but might be within the reach of some kind of «Entrepreneurs' Association», *i.e.* a coalition.

the contracting problems that stand in the way of reform is to keep the bureaucrats in office, and to obtain an agreement from them to refrain from interfering with the operation of markets. Unfortunately the bureaucrats have incentives to act opportunistically to enhance their power by creating crises, so as to convey the impression that they are only capable of being resolved by the work of a powerful state, which would of course be based on a powerful and centralized civil service. Thus, the dramatic rise of criminal activities in general, and mafia-related violence in particular, is consistent with the self-interests of Russia's bureaucrats because these events increase the public demand for a powerful state.

The demise of Gorbachev and Yeltsin's subsequent rise to power can be seen as a textbook example of the bargaining model described in this paper. As Tatyana Tolstaya [1994, p. 3] has observed, as long as Gorbachev was in power as head of the Communist party, Yeltsin's role as President of Russia was symbolic at best and meaningless at worst. Until Gorbachev's demise, Yeltsin was just another «toy 'president'» of all the other republics within the former Soviet Union. These presidents realized significant gains from overthrowing Gorbachev. In doing so, they obtained real power for the first time:

«They finally had the prospect of unlimited rule at home. They wouldn't have to account to 'Moscow' or crawl on their bellies to send tithes: rugs, diamonds, cognac, money, porcelain vases of human height with portraits of the Great Russian Boss. [...] Yeltsin would have to share with his fellow bandits, especially since this would allow him to seem a great democrat, and pronounce those sweet words, sovereignty, independence, equal rights» [p. 4].

Thus the demise of the former Soviet Union can be attributed to Yeltsin's quest for power. He traded an empire in exchange for greater power to the local rulers in their own country. The twin promises of economic reform and democracy were mere smoke screens to disguise the power-grab. Once Yeltsin achieved his goal of becoming President of Russia, the ability of the apparatchiks and bureaucrats responded to their powerful incentives to resist change[22].

These apparatchiks and bureaucrats, however, are now a significant restraint on Yeltsin, for they are likely to revolt if he places their dominance in jeopardy by changing the command and control nature of the economic system. That includes the current system of side payments and of kickbacks from managers of industrial firms to bureaucrats and apparatchiks; the private benefits obtained by the managers of inefficient, state-supported enterprises, when they delegate

«workers from auxiliary factory divisions to build country houses at sharply reduced prices, to build one-of-a-kind furniture for the apartment of a superior on the same basis,

---

[22] The reason why all this occurred when it did, and not earlier, is due to the fact that before Gorbachev there had never been a serious threat of constitutional change; and thus no need for previous leaders to trade formal imperial power for substantial local power.

In turn, Gorbachev gave up to pressures for constitutional change both because he hoped to trade an increasingly shaky absolute power (due to the economic crisis and to the increasingly authoritative nomenclature) in exchange for greater power in a less totalitarian empire; and because of the severe financial-economic crisis the USSR was suffering.

etc.. The relative unimportance of efficiency allows managers to absorb, without being held accountable, the costs of these kickback activities. Leakage of wealth thus takes place not only through the losses incurred and gains foregone by incompetent managers, but also because of the time and effort spent on rent-seeking activities [WINIECKI, 1990, p. 200].

Last, but no least, Winiecki rightly points out that existing bureaucrats also have strong incentives to resist changes because reform might eliminate layers of bureaucracy. This in turn would not only harm the bureaucrats whose employment is terminated, but also the higher level apparatchiks, since they will be able to command fewer rents in exchange for making such appointments. More generally, the apparatchiks would most strongly resist attempts to move the society towards a market-based meritocracy, since this would undermine the power of the apparatchiks to make appointments. This is why the nomenclature has never been abolished for managerial posts in the Russian economy. Ironically, since it is in industry that there are the best opportunities for kickbacks, it is in industry that the existing élites most strongly resist moving to a market-based system that would threaten the nomenclature. By contrast, in agriculture, where there are fewer opportunities for the apparatchiks to obtain rents from the nomenclature they appoint, the resistance to market forces has been less intense. Thus, the history of Russia (and other former Soviet-style economics) «shows some partly successful reforms of state agriculture while to date no reforms of state industry, based on general parameters, accountability, or merit, have been successful» [WINIECKI, 1990, p. 202].

6. – *Conclusion*

As North [1979, p. 253] has observed, the persistent tension between the organizational structure of a government that maximizes the income of its ruler (and his supporters) and an efficient system that reduces transaction costs and encourages economic growth is the «root cause of the failure of societies to experience sustained economic growth». The way that this tension between the interests of the ruler and the interests of the governed is resolved in Eastern Europe over the next few years will determine the economic future of the area. Of particular importance will be whether the leaders are able to reach a bargaining solution with consumers that will allow both sides to enjoy the gains from trade that accrue from reducing aggregate levels of rent-seeking. It is by no means clear that they will be able to do this.

Consistent with basic principles of path-dependence, it is inevitable that the future of reform in Russia will be determined by the initial conditions under which the collapse of the Soviet Union took place. In particular, the lack of a meaningful external force to remove the strangle-hold of pre-existing interest groups strongly suggests that the dramatic economic reforms that took place in post-War Germany and Japan will not be seen – say – in Moscow. The open question is whether things will get a little better, or a lot worse. If the bureaucrats feel threatened and are not successfully bought off either by outside powers or by internal interests, economic performance may improve a little, so as to avoid the constitutional moment. On the other hand, if is thought that constitutional change is already under way, then things may easily get a lot worse. But, if a mechanism can be designed for paying off the bureaucrats, things may get a lot better. Just how much better will depend on the nature of the bargain struck with the bureaucrats, and the price at which it is reached.

Thus, until some means can be devised for paying off the bureaucrats, or for getting them out of power entirely (an unlikely prospect) real reform will be impossible.

REFERENCES

ASILIS, C. and MILESI-FERRETTI, G. M., «On the Political Sustainability of Economic Reform», *IMF Paper on Policy Analysis and Assessment*, IMF, 1994.

BHAGWATI, J. N., BRECHER, R. A. and SRINIVASAN, T. N., «DUP Activities and Economic Theory», *European Economic Review*, 24, 1984, pp. 291-307.

BOYCKO, M., SHLEIFER, A. and VISHNY, R., *Privatizing Russia*, Brookings Institutions, Washington, 1994.

BUCHANAN, J., «The Constitution as Economic Policy», in J. D. GWARTNEY and R. E. WAGNER (eds.), *Public Choice and Constitutional Economics*, Greenwich, CT, JAI Press, 1988.

BUCHANAN, J. and TULLOCK, G., *The Calculus of Consent*, Ann Arbor, Michigan Press, 1962.

COLOMBATTO, E., «The Integration of the East and the Options for the West», *Journal des Economistes et des Etudes Humaines*, 2/3, 1992, pp. 273-288

CRAIN, M. and TOLLISON, R. D., «The Executive Branch in the Interest-Group Theory of Government», *Journal of Legal Studies*, 8, 1979a, pp. 555-567.

CRAIN, M. and TOLLISON, R. D., «Constitutional Change in an Interest-Group Perspective», *Journal of Legal Studies*, 8, 1979b, pp. 165-175.

DAVIDDI, R., «Property Rights and Privatization in the Transition to a Market Economy. A Comparative Review», unpublished, European Institute of Public Administration, Maastricht, 1994.

EICHENGREEN, B. and UZAN, M., «The Marshall Plan», *Economic Policy*, 14, 1992, pp. 14-75.

EPSTEIN, R. A., «Taxation, Regulation, and Confiscation», *Hall Law Journal*, 20, 1982, pp. 433-453.

EPSTEIN, R. A., «Toward a Revitalization of the Contract Clause», *University of Chicago Law Review*, 51, 1984, pp. 703-751.

EPSTEIN, R. A., *Takings: Private Property and the Power of Eminent Domain*, Cambridge, Harvard University Press, 1985a.

EPSTEIN, R. A., «Needed: Activist Judges for Economic Rights», *Wall Street Journal*, Nov. 14, 1985b, p. 32.

EPSTEIN, R. A., «An Outline of Takings», *Miami Law Review*, 41, 1986, p. 3-19.

GWARTNEY, J. D. and WAGNER, R. E., «Public Choice and Constitutional Order», in J. D. GWARTNEY and R. E. WAGNER (eds.), *Public Choice and Constitutional Economics*, Greenwich, CT, JAI Press, 1988.

KRUEGER, A. O., «The Political Economy of the Rent-Seeking Society», *American Economic Review*, 64, 1974, pp. 291-303.

LANDES, W. and POSNER, R., «The Independent Judiciary in an Interest-Group Perspective», *Journal of Law and Economics*, 18, 1975, pp. 875-901.

LIPTON, D. and SACHS, J., «Privatization in Eastern Europe», *Brookings Papers on Economic Activity*, 2, 1990, pp. 293-333.

MACEY, J., «Promoting Public-Regarding Legislation through Statutory Interpretation: an Interest-Group Model», *Columbia Law Review*, 86, 1986, pp. 223-268.

MACEY, J. «Transaction Costs and the Normative Elements of the Public Choice Model: An Application to Constitutional Theory», *Virginia Law Review*, 74, 1988, pp. 471-518.

MASHAW, J., «Constitutional Deregulation: Notes Toward a Public, Public Law», *Tulane Law Review*, 54, 1980, pp. 849-876.

McCORMICK, R. and TOLLISON, R.D., *Politicians, Legislation and the Economy: An Inquiry into the Interest Group Theory of Government*, Boston, M. Nijhoff, 1981.

NORTH, D., «A Framework for Analyzing the State in Economic History», *Explorations in Economic History*, 16, 1979, pp. 249-259.

OLSON, M., *The Rise and Decline of Nations: Economic Growth, Stagflation and Social Rigidities*, New Haven, Yale University Press, 1982.

PELTZMAN, S., «Toward a More General Theory of Regulation», *Journal of Law and Economics*, 19, 1976, pp. 211-240.

POSNER, R., «The Social Costs of Monopoly and Regulation», *Journal of Political Economy*, 83, 1975, pp. 807-827.

POSNER, R., «Economics, Politics, and the Reading of Statutes and the Constitution», *University of Chicago Law Review*, 49, 1982, pp. 263-291.

SHLEIFER, A. and VISHNY, R., «Corruption», *Quarterly Journal of Economics*, 108, 3, 1993, pp. 599-617.

STIGLER, G. J., «The Theory of Economic Regulation», *Bell Journal of Economics and Management Science*, 2, 1971, pp. 3-21.

SUNSTEIN, C., «Naked Preferences and the Constitution», *Columbia Law Review*, 84, 1984, pp. 1689-1732.

TOLLISON, R.D., «Public Choice and Legislation, Transactions Costs and the Normative Elements of the Public Choice Model: An Application to Constitutional Theory», *Virginia Law Review*, 74, 1988, pp. 339-371.

TOLSTAYA, T., «Boris the First», *The New York Review of Books*, 23, 1994, pp. 3-7.

ULAM, A., «The Vision Thing», reviewing D. YERGIN and T. GUSTAFSON, «Russia 2010: And What it Means for the World», *The New Republic*, 20, 1994, p. 40.

VOUSDEN, N., *The Economics of Trade Protection*, Cambridge, Cambridge University Press, 1990.

WINIECKI, J., «Why Economic Reforms Fail in the Soviet System - A Property Rights Based Approach», *Economic Inquiry*, 28, 1990, pp. 195-205.

[19]

INSTITUTIONS, NATIONALISM, AND THE TRANSITION PROCESS IN EASTERN EUROPE*

By Svetozar Pejovich

I. Introduction

In the late 1980s, the actual accomplishments of capitalism finally made a convincing case against socialism. After several decades of experimentation with human beings, socialism in the former Soviet Union and Eastern European countries (hereafter, Eastern Europe) died an inglorious death. To an economist, the present value of the expected future benefits from socialism fell relative to their current production costs. And Marx was finally dead and, hopefully, buried.

Short of risking a social breakdown, new leaders in Eastern Europe could not and did not immediately put an end to all the institutions and legacies of socialism. Instead, they were confronted with two critical issues: (1) how to choose new institutions, and (2) at what rate the new rules of the game should replace the old ones. Evidence shows a significant disparity among Eastern European countries in dealing with those two issues. It has become quite clear that, in a heterogeneous region like Eastern Europe, the transition paths and the rate of institutional change have to differ. Whenever we get impatient with the rate of transformation to capitalism in Eastern Europe, we should remind ourselves that, notwithstanding our free-market institutions, political freedoms, and stock of human capital, the transition to capitalism has not been completed in the West either.

The end of totalitarian socialist rule in Eastern Europe has indeed opened a highway to liberty along which there are many incentives to take detours. The detours are set by the ideas and perceptions that Eastern Europeans have of the Western world. They have also been created by the ideas that the West has about what the East ought to do. In fact, the transition process in the East has been a gift from heaven for social engineers from the West. They have responded to this gift by flooding the economic and political markets with all sorts of models, proposals, and schemes for the development of new institutional arrangements in the

* An earlier version of this essay was presented at the Einaudi Foundation seminar in Rome on June 25, 1992. I would like to thank the Earhart Foundation and the Lynde and Harry Bradley Foundation for support of my research on the economics of property rights in Eastern Europe. I also wish to thank professors E. Colombatto, H. Kliemt, A. Petroni, and especially E. Paul for many useful suggestions.

region. The problem with most of those models is that they are not likely to be implemented spontaneously; that is, they would have to be introduced by fiat.

The purpose of this essay is to discuss the causes of the resurgence of nationalism in the multi-ethnic states of Eastern Europe and the effects of nationalism on the direction and rate of institutional change in the region.

II. SOME EVIDENCE OF RISING NATIONALISM IN EASTERN EUROPE

Nationalism is not a monopoly of Eastern Europe. We observe a strong dose of nationalism in Ireland, Canada, Israel, Palestine, Italy, Germany, and many other countries. "In the historical perspective, nationalism is neither returning, rising nor reappearing. It never left Eastern Europe. Marxism-Leninism was supposed to make it irrelevant, and the Soviet power was calculated to suppress it. But it was always more durable than either."[1] An important characteristic of nationalism in the multi-ethnic states of Eastern Europe lies in the effect it has on the transition path in those countries.

Nationalism could become a serious problem in Bulgaria and Romania. It is a serious problem in Czechoslovakia. Serious fighting has already occurred in Georgia, Armenia, Moldova, and Azerbaijan. It is clear that numerous national groups within Russia are getting restless. And nationalism has taken the most violent turn in Croatia, Bosnia, and Serbia.

The main minority ethnic groups in Bulgaria are the Turks and the Macedonians. They account for 8.5 percent and 2.5 percent, respectively, of the population in that country. After five centuries of Ottoman rule, the Turks are not the Bulgarians' favorite people. The last Communist ruler of Bulgaria, Todor Zhivkov, even hoped to save the regime by actively "encouraging" the Turks to leave the country. The new (non-Communist) government of Bulgaria has abandoned Zhivkov's anti-Turk policies. However, the Bulgarian people have not. Clashes between Turks and Bulgarians, some of them serious, are happening often enough to be noticed. As for Macedonia, Bulgaria and Serbia fought a short but bitter war over Macedonia in 1913. Bulgaria has yet to recognize the Macedonians as a national group.

In June 1991, Romania asked for Bessarabia and Bukovina to be returned to Romania, because the majority of people in that region are Romanians. The government of Ukraine responded by saying that parts of the area are ancient Ukrainian lands which Romanians acquired by force after the October Revolution of 1917. Of course, the problem with

---

[1] J. Brown, "The Resurgence of Nationalism," *Report on Eastern Europe*, no. 2 (June 1991), p. 35.

"historical" rights in Eastern Europe is that they are quite confusing. In this case, Romania was never a sovereign state until the end of World War I. Thus, Bessarabia and Bukovina were part of the state of Romania only from 1918 until 1939. In 1939, the Molotov-Ribbentrop Treaty gave this area to the USSR, and part of it ended up in Ukraine. The issue between Romania and Ukraine is the same as that between Serbia and Croatia: the former favor ethnic borders, while the latter argue for current administrative borders.

After several centuries of Hapsburg rule, Czechoslovakia became a sovereign state in 1918. The country quickly became a showcase of political democracy, civil liberties, and economic progress. Today, Czechoslovakia is a major testing ground for the transition from socialism to capitalism. Unfortunately, the country's political stability is threatened by a conflict between the two major national groups: the Czechs and the Slovaks. These groups account for 63 percent and 32 percent, respectively, of the population in Czechoslovakia. While the Czechs seem indifferent to ethnic issues, the Slovaks are not. Slowly but ceaselessly, former Communists in Slovakia have turned to nationalism as a vehicle to retain some of their old power. Under their influence, the Slovaks have come to believe that the economic reform taking place is anti-Slovak, that privatization is proceeding too fast, and that the role of the state in the economy has been reduced too much. In June 1992, the Czechs elected Vaclav Klaus, a strong anti-Communist, whose major interest seems to lie in returning the country as quickly as possible to its pre-Communist prosperity. The Slovaks elected Vladimir Meciar, a former member of the Communist Party, and a "born-again" nationalist. As of this writing, Meciar and his cohorts have taken Czechoslovakia dangerously close to a breakup into two sovereign states (and as I revise this essay for publication, in the fall of 1992, they have just about taken the country apart).

The former Soviet Union has over one hundred national groups within its borders. These groups have their own languages, traditions, customs, and cultures. They also have ethnic problems with each other. The Armenians are fighting for their ethnic independence; the Islamic Renaissance Party is fighting against the perceived Slavic influence in former Soviet Asia; Moldova, Georgia, and the three Baltic states (Latvia, Lithuania, and Estonia) seem to be as interested in settling their accounts with Russia as with the former USSR. Within the Slavic family (75 percent of the population in the former USSR), the Ukrainians have historically felt threatened by the Russian state. In Russia proper, nationalism is becoming a major political and social force and is creating a powerful coalition which includes a variety of political groups, ranging from the Communist left to the "holy" Russian right. The sentiments the leaders of this coalition promote sound exactly like those we have been hearing from Franju Tudjman in Croatia and Slobodan Milosevic in Serbia: "Russian nationalism pure and simple. . . . Blame the communists, blame the democrats, blame the West. Blame everyone, in fact, apart from the great and long-suffering Russian people themselves."[2]

Alexis de Tocqueville once said that the most dangerous time for a bad government is when it starts to reform itself. His statement is certainly applicable to Milosevic's government in Serbia and Tudjman's in Croatia in the early 1990s.

Serbia became a sovereign state in the early twelfth century. Toward the end of the fourteenth century, the country was conquered by the Ottoman Empire. Independence was regained in 1878. Croatia was a sovereign state for only a brief period in the eleventh century and during World War II (1941–1945). Otherwise, it was a province of the Austro-Hungarian Empire. Bosnia is a region inhabited by three peoples who have lived together for centuries: Moslems (40 percent), Serbs (32 percent), and Croats (18 percent). Kosovo is a region in southern Serbia where the first Serbian state was formed. As late as the sixteenth century, the Serbs accounted for 97 percent of the total population in Kosovo. After many wars and several migrations—brought on, in part, by Turkish terror—Albanians now account for about 90 percent of the population in Kosovo. I believe that the Kosovo problem is likely to be potentially more explosive than those we have witnessed in Croatia and Bosnia. Finally, the Serbs account for about 14 percent of the population in Croatia, and are concentrated in a few areas that are ethnically Serbian. During World War II, the state of Croatia carried out a massacre of the Serbs. The Serbs took to the mountains, and a terrible civil war ensued. According to Dr. Drago Roksandic of the University of Zagreb, the number of Serbs from Croatia who died during the war was 131,000, or 22 percent of their total number in Croatia. The conflict between the Serbs and the Croats, which triggered an all-out war in 1991, was over borders: the Serbs wanted borders drawn on ethnic lines; the Croats preferred those drawn by Tito in 1945.

III. The Transition Process and Nationalism in Eastern Europe

There are three main causes of post-Communist nationalism in Eastern Europe: institutional instability, the region's philosophical heritage, and its nomenklatura. These factors are having profound effects on the transition paths taken by the multi-ethnic states in the region.

Post-socialist institutional instability

The end of totalitarian socialist rule in Eastern Europe has destabilized institutional arrangements that have been in place for nearly five decades. What we refer to as the transformation of former socialist states is, in effect, their search for a new set of institutions.

[2] "The Nationalist with a Dash of Paranoia," *The European*, May 28, 1992, p. 11.

Institutions are usually defined as the legal, regulatory, and customary arrangements for repeated human interactions—or, what comes to the same thing, as the rules of the game. They provide members of the community with some specific benefits and impose on them some specific costs. From an individual's standpoint, rules yield a flow of *benefits*: the predictability of other people's behavior. The *costs* borne by an individual are the satisfactions forgone due to his inability to engage in some specific activities. The flow of benefits from a set of rules depends on their stability. As time goes by, people learn how to adjust to the prevailing set of institutions, identify exchange opportunities, and exploit the most preferred ones.

Most human interactions have future value consequences (e.g., buying a car, getting married, joining a religious community, and even eating out). With uncertainty and incomplete information, any person's evaluation of the expected future consequences of his current decisions has to be subject to large errors. Yet these are decisions that we have to make each day. A stable set of rules reduces uncertainties involved in making all decisions, but especially in those that have long-term consequences. South Americans prefer the lower expected returns on their investments in the United States to the much higher rates that are often available in their homelands; an investor in Guatemala seeks a shorter payoff period than an investor in North Dakota; and a Croatian guest worker in Switzerland prefers a deposit in a Swiss bank at zero interest to a two-digit interest rate promised by a bank in Croatia.

Frequent changes or expectations of frequent changes in the rules of the game reduce the time horizon over which individuals make their decisions. Consequently, the most beneficial rules are those that are self-sustaining and produced spontaneously within the system itself. Such rules eliminate the time-horizon problem and create a sense of social stability, because they provide incentives for individuals in the community to maximize the extent of voluntary human interactions. The critical function of institutional arrangements is, then, to foster the predictability of behavior.

Socialist rule in Eastern Europe subverted the rule of law to the will of the ruling elite and seriously undermined the people's confidence in enforcement mechanisms. During the immediate post-Communist years, the prevailing socialist institutions themselves have been destabilized. Although most socialist institutions were not immediately jettisoned, it was clear that they were not going to last. Theory tells us that when the rules of the game are seriously compromised, the extent of exchange among individuals is reduced, and this is precisely what has happened.[3]

---

[3] The reason for this reduction in exchange has to do with the nature of interactions. Voluntary interactions among individuals are vehicles by which they seek to increase their well-being (utility). However, interactions are frequently not simultaneous (e.g., *A* pays *B* a sum of $1,000 for the right to use water from *B*'s well over a period of five years), and most interactions have consequences that occur after the agreement is concluded (e.g., *X* mar-

Perceiving an institutional vacuum, Eastern Europeans needed a stable set of rules for carrying out transactions among themselves and with the rest of the world. In the multi-ethnic states, members of various groups began to fall back on their traditional, pre-Communist norms of behavior, the old ethos, which links them together through shared values, shared traditions, shared culture, shared language, and shared historical experiences. The predictability of behavior fostered by those rules is, however, limited to a group of people that share the same traditions and values. In Eastern Europe, those groups of people are usually members of the same ethnic groups. Interactions within any specific ethnic group are then subject to rules of behavior that do not necessarily hold in exchanges across ethnic lines. In fact, the general ethos in Eastern Europe is a repository of the old unsettled scores among the region's ethnic groups. It follows that the old ethos creates incentives for members of each ethnic group to interact primarily with other group members and to be cautious in dealing with "aliens."

The post-Communist era has given the dark hand of the past an opportunity to influence the present. Unfortunately, the old ethos has not been adaptable enough to prevent old feuds from being translated into the rise of nationalism throughout the region and the proliferation of ethnic wars in Croatia, Serbia, Bosnia, and a growing number of former Soviet republics.

The region's philosophical heritage

The intellectual tradition of Eastern Europe has remained largely free of such Western European ideas as classical liberalism and methodological individualism.[4] Instead, the ethos in Eastern Europe has a strong bias toward communalism. The prevailing concept of the community in the region is not the classical-liberal one of a voluntary association of individuals who, in the pursuit of their private ends, join and leave the

---

ries Y believing that Y is a good person). The problem with these interactions is that their future consequences might and often do differ from those expected at the time of the agreement. Some of those unintended consequences are inevitable, but many are man-made (e.g., B could decide to build a fence around his well). A major purpose of the rules of the game is to protect interactions among individuals by alleviating risks and uncertainties associated with those problems.

[4] It is frequently said that there was more of a Western tradition in Czechoslovakia, Slovenia, and perhaps Hungary, than in other Eastern European countries. That is certainly true. However, classical liberalism, which is only a part of the Western tradition, does not have deep roots in the region. *Classical liberalism* usually is taken to mean individual liberty, openness to new ideas, tolerance of all views, and a government under law. The liberal community does not have a preordained set of outcomes: a common good. *Methodological individualism* is a method for understanding social phenomena. Its main postulate is that the individual is the only decision maker. That is, governments, universities, corporations, and other entities do not and cannot make decisions, only individuals can and do. To understand the behavior of any social, economic, or political entity, it is necessary to identify incentive structures under which individuals operate.

community by free choice. Instead, the community is seen as an organic whole to which individuals are expected to subordinate their private ends and in which all cooperate to pursue their common values. The communities in Eastern Europe have developed their customs and common values along ethnic lines. This has strengthened mutual understanding within each ethnic group, but it has done so at the cost of reducing their ability to communicate with outsiders. The Serbs in Croatia, the Albanians in Serbia, the Turks in Bulgaria, and the Hungarians in Romania are examples of this spontaneous cultural autonomy.

This tradition in Eastern Europe has survived more than four decades of Communist rule (more than seven in the former USSR). With its emphasis on ethnicity, the extended family (clan), and shared values, the old ethos was a powerful fortress behind whose walls most people were able to hide and learn to live with Communist institutions without ever accepting them. However, Communist rule had an unintended effect on the mentality of Eastern Europeans. It helped to reinforce the communalism of the old ethos, which is now responsible for much of the military, social, and political conflict in the multi-ethnic regions of Eastern Europe.[5] Even though the Communist ideal of the "new socialist man" died long before the system met its end, Eastern Europeans have yet to appreciate that the decision maker, the responsible agent, in all social systems is the individual, and that the individual always has pursued and always will pursue his self-interest.

Given their historical and cultural background, Eastern Europeans are predictably confused about capitalist institutions and their effects on the quality of life. In 1989, the prevailing mode of thinking about capitalism in Eastern Europe was to identify it with a life style based on bountiful supplies of goods and equally large incomes to buy those goods. The benefits of capitalism were somehow to be added to the prevailing socialist welfare programs. After a half-century of Marxist indoctrination, Eastern Europeans did not and could not see capitalism as *a way of life* based on (1) the constitutional guarantees of individual liberty, (2) the right of private ownership and contractual freedom, (3) the exchange culture in which each and every individual bears the value consequences of his decisions, and (4) the behavioral principles of self-interest, self-determination, and self-responsibility. The term "capitalism" was used by Marxists in a tone of ethical and social denigration. A much better term is Adam Smith's: the "natural system of economic liberty."

The ethos in Eastern Europe, the region's intellectual tradition, and the people's perceptions of capitalism explain why, in the search for new

---

[5] It is probably an oversimplification to blame Communist rule for the current turmoil in the multi-ethnic states. It is like blaming labor unions for inflation. Inflation happened before labor unions were organized, and ethnic wars happened before Marx was born. Former Communists trying to cling to their positions of power are only exploiting the opportunity provided by the old unsettled scores.

institutions, "fairness" and "justice" are emphasized over values more suitable to a free-market society. The concern ought to be in creating institutions that reward performance, cultivate tenacity for overcoming risk, promote the development of individual liberties, and place high value on the keeping of promises. The problem with fairness and justice is two-fold. First, they are at best a hazy vision of values that it would be nice for social institutions to promote: something for the intellectuals to shout about and the bureaucrats to shoot at. Second, they require an activist government, as a means of imposing and maintaining them. With their implications for the redistribution of wealth, the objectives of fairness and justice are particularly vulnerable to disagreements, conflicts, and divisions along ethnic lines.

In contrast, government in a free-market, private-property society is supposed to restrict itself to a passive role of monitoring and enforcing the rules of the game. The rules of the game in capitalism are developed to grant individuals a range of freedom to pursue their own ends, make their own decisions, and bear the consequences of those decisions.[6] If I love disco music or football, or prefer emulating Mother Theresa, the system allows me to pursue my own ends. Patterns of social behavior derive from these diverse motivations: driven by their self-interest, individuals seek the most valuable partners, reward those who are industrious and perform well, and give repeat business to those who keep promises. Abundant evidence confirms this proposition about the penalty/reward system in capitalism. For example, the median income of Asian-American households, whose culture instills a strong work ethic, exceeds the median income of white Americans.[7] Much of East Asia has prospered by encouraging these sorts of capitalist transactions and behavior, while Africa has languished under the rule of antithetical principles.[8]

Capitalist society—that is, a society of free and responsible individuals—would mute ethnic animosities in Eastern Europe's multi-ethnic

---

[6] The system also provides people with a right to give up some of their freedoms. For example, when a person joins a religious community, he or she freely chooses to give up the right to make decisions over a range of issues.

[7] "Two Measures of Household Income," *New York Times*, July 24, 1992, p. A10. Median household income for Asian Americans is $36,784 and for whites is $31,435.

[8] In a long and interesting article, Keith Richburg discusses the issue of why African development has lagged so far behind that of East Asia, which suffered from a similar set of obstacles: "Why has East Asia . . . become a model of economic success, while Africa, since independence, has seen increasing poverty and hunger . . . ?" Richburg offers several possible explanations for those differences in economic development. Two of them are related to my discussion in this essay: the economic choices and the ethos. First, after independence, most countries in Africa opted for government ownership of enterprises, due to a distrust of private-sector initiative and foreign investment. Asians chose a brand of capitalism. Second, the ethos in Africa turned out to be less adaptable (relative to the ethos in East Asia) to the requirements of efficiency in production and exchange. Keith Richburg, "Why is Black Africa Overwhelmed While East Asia Overcomes?" *International Herald Tribune*, July 14, 1992, pp. 1 and 6.

states by providing incentives for people to seek exchange opportunities across ethnic lines. Driven by their self-interest, people would, sooner or later, learn to judge others on merit and performance rather than on ethnic origin. Thus, the institutions that promote and strengthen a society of free and responsible individuals could spontaneously curb the rise of nationalism in Eastern Europe and reduce nationalism's menace to the transition process.

Nationalism and the regional nomenklatura

As Communist rule ended in Eastern Europe, the ruling elite had incentives to seek ways to preserve its power and privileges. In the face of significant opportunities for the economic advancement of private individuals, and thus their liberation from elite control, former leaders in the multi-ethnic regions of Eastern Europe realized that creating the perception of an external threat to their respective ethnic groups would give them their best chance to retain power and authority. Most former Communists quickly transformed themselves into virulent nationalists. It was an easy thing for them to do because nationalism and Communism have two important traits in common: (1) the collectivist mode of looking at the world, and (2) the recruitment of political leaders on the basis of their loyalty to the cause or group rather than merit. Thus, the transition of former "internationalists" into newly minted nationalists did not require much of a change of their normal habits. Indeed, most leaders in the multi-ethnic states of Eastern Europe are former Communists. Milosevic in Serbia, Tudjman in Croatia, Meciar in Slovakia, Kravchuk in Ukraine, and Yeltsin in Russia are only the most conspicuous examples. Their human capital — their skills and knowledge — qualify them only for seeking advantages for themselves in a bureaucratic environment; therefore, a free-market, private-property system is a threat to these former Communists' well-being. To preserve the value of their human capital, they have to create a state-centered system. A way of doing this is to convince their people that other ethnic groups are either threatening their political independence, or trying to steal their resources, or both. With many unsettled scores from centuries gone by, these arguments are not too difficult to sell. In the process, the former "internationalists" have become the most zealous defenders of the ethos of their ethnic groups.

The conversion of many former Communist leaders into present-day nationalists was the most efficient way for them to retain some power and influence. It also turned out to have two important implications for the transition paths in the multi-ethnic states. First, the old ethos, with its memories of unsettled scores, translates rather easily into ethnic conflicts, which necessarily result in economic losses. Second, the artificial creation of external threats has deterred the development of individual liberty and the growth of individual responsibility in the multi-ethnic states. Evidence for this is the difference in the transition paths between Eastern European countries that have been able to avoid ethnic conflicts and those that have not. The case of Czechoslovakia is quite important. As I pointed out earlier in the essay, former Communists in Slovakia have, in their quest to retain power and influence, adroitly exploited Slovak nationalism, bringing the country to the point of dissolution into two sovereign states. In contrast, the Czechs, with virtually no former Communists in positions of power, are treating ethnic issues as a nuisance that is interfering with getting the country on the road to economic recovery.

IV. In Lieu of a Conclusion:
Big Bang Versus Gradual Changes

The basic premise of a free society is to let people make their own choices. Yet the end of totalitarian socialist rule in Eastern Europe has resulted in an avalanche of studies by Western scholars on what should be done in the region. Even some free-market-oriented individuals and groups have been advising new leaders in Eastern Europe on how to use the strong hand of the state — the method of institutional change that they consistently condemn at home — to build free-market, private-property economies.

The real problem is that we have scant evidence of what Eastern Europeans themselves want. Political parties that seek to implement free-market reforms have done better in some countries than in others, but their overall strength in the region is not too encouraging. There is even less evidence that ordinary people in Eastern Europe[9] are able to appreciate the consequences of alternative institutional arrangements. What is happening in Eastern European countries is that new institutions are being introduced by fiat[10] and that the direction and rate of institutional changes are largely controlled by their bureaucracies.

---

[9] There is a tendency among intellectuals, especially those inclined toward social engineering, to deprecate the ability of "ordinary" people to make their own survival choices (an economist would say "to maximize their utility"). One has to wonder how ordinary people — and there were only ordinary people around some million years ago — managed to survive against competition from other forms of life. They must have somehow managed to make some right choices. Survival of any species is based on its adaptive behavior rather than on someone's foresight. With uncertainty and incomplete information, people make choices which are, in effect, their best bets. It is from those behaviors that are actually tried that "success" is selected and copied by others. Some Eastern Europeans will eventually try new types of behavior, which others will copy if and when they decide that those behaviors have strong survival potentials. Ordinary people might then choose capitalism when the time is right for them to make that decision, *provided* they have freedom of choice.

[10] Legal changes can be of two sorts: adjustments in the rules to the new requirements of the game that social and economic developments have made possible; or changes in the rules that are imposed from above by those in political power. The term "fiat" in this essay means the latter.

It is a mistake to identify Eastern Europeans' success in throwing the Communists out of power with the median voter's preference for free-market economies. The forty years of socialism (seventy for the former USSR), the old ethos, and the intellectual heritage of the region are conducive to nationalism, hierarchy, and welfarism, but not to "instant" capitalism. Like a good medicine that could either save your life or kill you, depending on how you use it, economic reforms that promise to improve efficiency in production and exchange could cause more harm than good if implemented too hastily. Lifting price controls and privatization are two such problematic reforms.

In Russia, on January 2, 1992, the government decreed a comprehensive price liberalization which (supposedly) freed about 80 percent of wholesale and 90 percent of retail prices (basic food items remained under price controls).[11] Prices perform two functions in a world in which goods are scarce. In the short run, they allocate the goods and services that have already been produced to their highest-valued uses. In the long run, prices generate a flow of goods that conforms to consumers' preferences. Freeing prices in Eastern European countries *would not* accomplish the latter function. For that, Eastern European governments need to (1) guarantee free entry for all potential producers of goods and services, (2) provide incentives for those who determine the use of resources to respond to consumers' preferences, and (3) provide incentives to discover the value of resources in alternative uses. Guaranteeing the right of private ownership and contractual freedom would do the job specified by these three points quite well.

Privatization of state factories is bound to have a negative effect on the people's appreciation of the benefits and essentials of free enterprise.[12] Most factories in Eastern Europe were built without any regard for prices. Their technology is inferior, and the management skills that were prized under socialism have no comparative advantage in a free-market economy. The ability of those firms to survive in competitive markets is quite low. Yet it is very likely that Eastern Europeans will fail to attribute the

[11] The term "supposedly" is used to suggest a few doubts about the real extent of price liberalization. The distribution sector in Russia has a markup ceiling of 25 percent, which is a form of price control. Local governments are issuing regulations that often contradict or ignore price liberalization decrees issued by Moscow. Prices of basic foods are still controlled by the state.

[12] It appears, from time to time, that economists working for the International Monetary Fund (IMF) and the World Bank have a monopoly on economic nonsense. In one of the IMF's recent publications we read: "A mass privatization of the state enterprise sector is the centerpiece of the transition to a market economy" (J. Odling-Smee et al., "Russian Federation," *Economic Review*, IMF, April 1992, p. 35). Some people think that the freedom to choose the methods of organizing production is the centerpiece of a free society. Also, at the Hayek Symposium in Freiburg in June 1992, when Professor Jermakowicz, a leading "expert" on privatization, presented a paper on the aims and methods of privatization in Poland, V. Naishul, a free-market economist from Russia, remarked that the language the Polish bureaucrats use today is exactly the same as the language Soviet planners used yesterday.

dismal performance of these firms (layoffs, bankruptcies) to the decades of economic mismanagement under Communism. Instead, they are likely to "observe" that the free-market, private-property economy is not working either. For example, Zbigniew Janas, a leader of the market-oriented wing of the old Solidarity coalition in Poland has said: "The laissez-faire theory has not proven right. We have got to have state intervention. The question is how deep it should be."[13]

It seems important to identify two basic misunderstandings, one in the East and one in the West, about the transition process in Eastern Europe. The first is related to the image of capitalism among the ordinary people in Eastern Europe. When they voice their disappointments in capitalism, Eastern Europeans are merely revealing their own perceptions of the system. It will take time for them to understand that capitalism is not about getting rich — that the system is about individual liberty, self-responsibility, and self-determination in a world where the role of government is to enforce and maintain a stable set of rules. The second misunderstanding relates to the attitude of many free-market-oriented intellectuals in the West toward the transition to capitalism in Eastern Europe. They seem to ignore the importance of the region's "carriers of history." Western economists, especially neoclassical economists, are trained to think in terms of instantaneous adjustments to new equilibria. Thus, they tend to ignore the role of history and traditional values in shaping people's reactions to various social problems. It could easily turn out to be self-defeating to the cause of freedom in Eastern Europe to impose capitalism by fiat.

To attribute a slow rate of transition to capitalism in Eastern Europe solely to the resistance of socialist institutions and the "old roaders," as former Communists and bureaucrats are called, is a mistake. I believe that the major obstacle to the transition is the "hand of the past." Former Communists and bureaucrats are simply exploiting the old ethos to their advantage. The problem lies with this old ethos and with the philosophical heritage of the region; they are not well attuned to the exchange culture of capitalism and its emphasis on individual liberty. But Western "experts" are not taking this into account. For example, Jeffrey Sachs, a free-market-oriented Harvard professor of economics, has sold himself to a number of Eastern European (and Third World) countries as a transition expert. While Sachs's technical knowledge of economics is undoubtedly sound, his transition models make no allowances for cultural and historical differences between the countries and ethnic groups that he has been advising. The "big bang"[14] approach to the transition, promoted by Sachs and other Western scholars, envisions institutional changes that are

---

[13] Quoted in *Dallas Morning News*, August 4, 1991, p. 28.

[14] The term "big bang" means a quick change in the system. It is hard to find a better example of a big bang than the October Revolution of 1917. Yet it took Lenin and his cohorts quite a few years to implement changes — and they were willing to spill blood in order to get things done.

exogenous to the system.[15] Thus, these changes will confront the difficult task of overcoming beliefs and behaviors that are firmly embedded in the fabric of community life in the countries of Eastern Europe, with consequences unanticipated by any economist's models.

An alternative approach to the problem of the transition to capitalism in Eastern Europe is to let the preferences of the median voter play an important role in choosing both the direction and the rate of institutional change, and hope that capitalist institutions will win support through their performance in the marketplace. Instead of building capitalism by fiat, Eastern European governments could try to create a framework for competitive markets for institutions. That would require a credible guarantee of (1) equal legal protection of all property rights, (2) equal fiscal treatment of all sources of income, (3) efficient financial markets, (4) open entry and exit in all markets, and (5) free access to foreign goods and capital. Instead of imposing capitalist enterprise by fiat, Eastern European states should provide—admittedly by fiat—a legal environment that would allow people to choose among alternative institutional arrangements, including even socialist ones. The existing enterprises held over from the Communist era would then have to compete with newly emerging cooperative, corporate, joint stock, private, or other sorts of voluntarily formed enterprises.[16]

Points (1) through (5) are a normative alternative to what is now going on in most Eastern European states—save, perhaps, Hungary, where spontaneous changes seem to be playing a larger role than they are elsewhere. The implementation of this framework, and even more its en-

---

[15] An explanation of the difference between endogenous and exogenous change is in order. Suppose there is an event that creates new opportunities for individuals to interact. If the prevailing institutional structures are poorly attuned to those opportunities and fail to enforce new interactions, utility-seeking individuals will generate spontaneous pressure to modify the rules of the game to embrace the novelty. For example, technological developments made mass production of goods relatively cheap. However, exploiting new opportunities required a large initial investment in capital assets. But the rule of unlimited liability made contractual agreements for raising large sums of capital difficult. A new rule eventually emerged: limited liability. This was an *endogenous* change that adjusted the rules of the game to the new requirements of the game.

Instead of adapting the rules to the changing requirements of the game, *exogenous* changes force the game to adjust to the rules. For example, codetermination (labor participation in the management of business firms) in Germany was introduced by law. However, prior to this law there was no law in Germany that prohibited codetermination. Managers, workers, and the owners of resources were free to write any contract they chose. Indeed, we observe a large number of different types of business firms in the West, including Germany. All those firms have emerged voluntarily and survived competition from other types of firms. The fact that the German government had to *impose* codetermination by fiat is evidence that the value to the employees of their participation in management was less than the costs to the owners and managers of providing it. Most exogenous changes in institutional arrangements are brought about by ideologists, pressure groups, and bureaucrats in pursuit of their own private ends, while hiding behind the facade of the public interest.

[16] In order to give capitalist institutions enough time to tell their story, a stable social environment is a necessity. This means that the government might have to subsidize a number of large state enterprises over a limited number of years.

forcement, could be quite difficult, but that certainly should not be a reason to give up on it. It could be especially difficult for Eastern European governments to give credible constitutional guarantees within an environment in which the tradition of the rule of law and independent constitutional courts either was never established or was decimated by the Communists. However, the difficulty of implementing this kind of institutional framework is certainly not a good reason for accepting exogenous bureaucratic control of the transition path.

The existing institutions would then have to compete with new ones that people freely choose. Some new institutions will survive, while some old ones will also, but many more will expire. Even before legal guarantees, a large number of small private firms have emerged throughout Eastern Europe. These are mostly kiosks or miniature shops. Many of them will not last, but some have already passed the market test. Currently, these firms represent a small percentage of GNP in Eastern European countries, although their significance has grown in Poland. However, they represent something that is much more important than their current contribution to the aggregate output. These small firms are the breeding grounds for entrepreneurs, a work ethic, a capitalist exchange culture, and constructive attitudes toward individual liberty.

Endogenous institutional changes discussed in this section of the essay suggest neither a specific transition path in Eastern Europe nor the rate of institutional change. In fact, they cannot even guarantee that Eastern Europeans will choose the institutions of capitalism. However, if new governments in Eastern Europe were able and willing to limit the role of the state in the transition process to creating and enforcing the environment in which alternative forms of economic organization could compete with each other, I believe that the institutions of capitalism would eventually and spontaneously emerge, survive competition from other types of institutions, and become dominant in the region.

Economics, Texas A&M University

[20]

PRICING AND PROPERTY: THE CHINESE PUZZLE

James A. Dorn

A Problem of Constitutional Economics

The idea that property rights matter in shaping incentives and behavior is central to understanding economic reform in China. Ownership rights in land, labor, and capital and the status of the entrepreneur's claim to residual income are important determinants of economic development. At the root of any economic reform, however, is a certain conception of policy, that is, a certain ideology. If the prevailing ideology clashes with the economic and social institutions necessary for promoting wealth creation and satisfying consumers' preferences, then political considerations may well dominate any rational attempt to decentralize a socialist economy.

China's leaders have mistakenly perceived their problem as how to introduce markets without establishing effective ownership rights.

The author is Vice President for Academic Affairs at the Cato Institute and Professor of Economics at Towson State University.

CHINA IN TRANSITION

Their deeper conceptual problem is how to achieve economic and social order without central planning. The clue to solving the puzzle as a whole is to recognize that markets cannot exist without private ownership rights and that once such rights are established, a spontaneous economic order can emerge. Thus, at the heart of any effective reform in China is the necessity of understanding what James Buchanan (1979, pp. 81–82) has called the "most important central principle in economics," namely, "the principle of spontaneous order"—and recognizing that this order critically depends on what Friedrich Hayek (1960) has called a "constitution of liberty." By limiting the influence of politics over economics, self-interest can be directed toward realizing mutual gains from market exchange. In this sense, then, the problem of economic reform under socialism is a problem of constitutional economics, that is, a problem of how to change the rules of the game (the effective economic constitution) to increase freedom and wealth.

Stable government by law, private ownership, and freedom of contract—all of which are necessary for establishing a viable market price system in which individual plans can be coordinated without central direction—have yet to gain widespread support among China's ruling elite. Communist party bureaucrats recognize the dangers that a free-market system and a rule of law pose to their privileged position, and they have little incentive to depart from the status quo. But the institutional inertia that is characteristic of all socialist regimes also stems from a lack of vision. The eyes of socialist leaders are typically focused on distributive justice and ignore the commutative justice inherent in a free-market process. Moreover, socialist leaders have not fully appreciated the information and incentive functions of prices and profits in solving society's economic problem, "a problem of the utilization of knowledge which is not given to anyone in its totality" (Hayek [1945] 1948, p. 78).

The impossibility of centralizing the vast array of information spread throughout society and the continual changes in the information available to different individuals point to the necessity of relying on markets and prices to efficiently utilize existing information and to rapidly disseminate new information.[1] To think that central plan-

[1]On the so-called Hayekian knowledge problem, see Hayek ([1945] 1948, pp. 83–84), where he states:
> If we can agree that the economic problem of society is mainly one of rapid adaptation to changes in the particular circumstances of time and place, it would seem to follow that the ultimate decisions must be left to the people who are familiar with these circumstances, who know directly of the relevant changes and of the resources immediately available to meet them.

See also Hayek ([1937] 1948).

40

ners, in China or elsewhere, can duplicate the competitive market process without allowing for private ownership and price competition is a fatal conceit, as Hayek puts it.[2]

A legal system that effectively protects economic and civil liberties is a necessary condition for a spontaneous market order within which individuals will be able to pursue their own interests while also serving the interests of others. When the rule of law is eroded by catering to special interests, the market process will become politicized. The information and incentive functions of market prices will then be weakened as "rent seekers" attentuate private property rights and redistribute national wealth.

Although the modern redistributive state is recognizable in democratic governments in the West, it is pervasive in all socialist countries including China, where there are no effective constitutional limits on governmental takings. Nevertheless, China's experience with social engineering is widely regarded as a dismal failure, and over the past decade China's leaders have demonstrated a willingness to move toward a more open society and a more market-oriented economic system. Since 1978, the search has been under way to discover a new set of rules that provide greater economic stability, make individual decisionmakers more responsible for their use of scarce resources, and set the basis for long-run economic growth. It is generally understood that unless allowance is made for the possibility of loss whenever individuals or firms fail the market test, the redirection of resources required for increased efficiency and wealth will not take place.

Rational economic calculation requires competitive markets and prices supported by a system of private property rights providing individuals with exclusive rights to use their property, to sell it, and to capture the increase in value from prudent use or to bear the loss from mismanagement.[3] The problem of rational economic calculation under socialism and the difficulty of piecemeal reform are clearly recognized in China. The recognition of these problems, in turn, has led to the call for price reform, intended to make prices more fully reflect the underlying forces of demand and supply. Reporting on an article by Wang Guiwu, the *China Daily* stated: "Reasonable prices, reasonable price parities and a rational price composition are formed in the course of market exchanges in line with the requirements of

---

[2]Hayek (1988) uses the phrase "fatal conceit" in a comprehensive way to undermine all of socialism, but the expression seems particularly appropriate to characterize the fallacy of economic calculation under socialism and the knowledge problem.

[3]On the requirements for rational economic calculation, see Hayek ([1935] 1975) and Mises ([1936] 1974).

CHINA IN TRANSITION

the law governing supply and demand. . . . Intense market competition and changes in the supply-demand relationship and prices are not subject to the subjective will of government officials."[4] The *China Daily* went on to quote Wang as saying, " 'The more the government controls, the more it is likely to depart from the requirements of the law governing supply and demand.' " The article concluded by noting that "it is imperative to apply that law [of supply and demand] to the formulation of China's price policies and the introduction of a price managerial system."

The efficient use of resources stemming from competitive markets requires that individuals bear responsibility for their actions. As Hayek ([1940] 1974, p. 156) observed, "to assume that it is possible to create conditions of full competition without making those who are responsible for the decisions pay for their mistakes seems to be pure illusion." This fact too is gaining attention in China. Reporting on an article by Ruan Bin, the *China Daily* noted: "The private economy is the most economical in China. . . . In private businesses, both owners and workers pay the closest attention to thrift and saving, because waste means their own loss."[5] The newspaper cited Ruan as saying, " 'Private businesses regard the customer as king.' " And the major finding of the study, according to the *China Daily*, was that "market-led decisions force private businesses to operate in a pioneering spirit, which is the powerful driving force for the expansion of the private economy."

The problem of ownership has also been openly acknowledged in China as one of the fundamental difficulties in moving toward a market system. Changing the ownership system in China to allow for rational price calculation and responsible decisionmaking at all levels is a problem that China's future leaders cannot afford to ignore. Although China has some 225,000 private enterprises that employ nearly four million people,[6] state-owned enterprises continue to dominate the economic landscape. In September 1988, however, Zhao Ziyang announced a major plan to convert state enterprises into publicly owned enterprises under a "shareholding system," designed to help reduce the nearly $11 billion that the government pays in subsidies to support state-owned enterprises (Southerland 1988b). Unfortunately, the abrupt policy shift following the May-

---

[4]"Lift of Price Controls in Focus," *China Daily*, 13 July 1988, p. 4. (The *China Daily* is an English language summary of key articles in the Chinese press.)
[5]"Private Economy Praised," *China Daily*, 16 July 1988, p. 4.
[6]Ibid.

PRICING AND PROPERTY

June 1989 demonstrations has forestalled any further ownership reform.

As the events surrounding Tiananmen Square illustrate, the major difficulty in reforming the Chinese economy is that under the present system economic questions are necessarily political questions.[7] The widespread corruption in state enterprises attests to the politicization of economic life in China and to the consequent failure of the "contract system," which was supposed to allow managers of state-owned enterprises greater autonomy after satisfying a governmentally determined profitability target. As Julia Leung (1989) observed, many state enterprises remained unprofitable under the contract system and the monies used to prop up inefficient state enterprises were often "squandered on grandiose construction projects, inappropriate equipment and fancy state housing" or found their way into the pockets of "corrupt officials." Again, the basic problem, writes Leung, is "the failure of the contract system to distance government from the running of enterprises."[8]

The politicization of economic life is nowhere more evident than in the sphere of finance and banking, where the state controls the bulk of investment resources. The lack of a private capital market has handicapped economic development in China and hampered rational investment decisionmaking. Moreover, the extension of bank credits to cover the losses of inefficient state enterprises has led to serious inflation. The austerity program, initiated in September 1988, dampened state investment spending and slowed the growth of bank credit. As a result, inflation has been reduced from a peak of 27 percent in 1989 (an official estimate; the actual inflation was reportedly much higher) to about 4 percent for the first half of 1990 (again an official estimate; see Leung 1990). But the program did nothing to change the basic structure of China's economic system—a system characterized by state monopoly of trade and industry, a rigid material-supply system, and state control over prices and property. Indeed, Zheng Hongqing, an adviser to the State Commission for Restructuring the Economy, recently observed that after more than 10 years of attempted reform, the "traditional economic

---

[7]Cf. Hayek ([1940] 1974, p. 158): "In a planned system all economic questions become political questions."

[8]In commenting on the failure to stabilize the Chinese economy and prevent corruption, Hua Sheng, Zhang Xuejun, and Luo Xiaopeng contend that "the root cause lies in our failure to separate political power from economic management. The Chinese economy today is, to a significant extent, manipulated by political power." Quoted in "China Reforms Said Snarled by Politics," *Washington Times*, 11 January 1989, p. A9.

CHINA IN TRANSITION

framework has remained essentially intact" (*China Daily* 26 July 1990; cited in Ellingsen 1990, p. 3).

If anything has been learned from China's experience with reform over the last decade, it is that effective economic reform requires constitutional change to protect persons and property against political opportunism by those who control government. In short, economic decisionmaking must be insulated from political decisionmaking as much as possible if a *private* market system is to develop and prosper. To accomplish this objective, a sound legal system will have to be developed—one that limits the massive state bureaucracy and the ruling elite who will lose their power and privilege as China's economic and political systems are opened to the forces of competition. In this vein, Nien Cheng (1988, p. 543) wrote: "Unless and until a political system rooted in law, rather than personal power, is firmly established in China, the road to the future will always be full of twists and turns."

References

Buchanan, James M. "General Implications of Subjectivism in Economics." In Buchanan, *What Should Economists Do?* pp. 81-91. Indianapolis: Liberty Press, 1979.

Cheng, Nien. *Life and Death in Shanghai.* New York: Penguin Books, 1988.

"China Reforms Said Snarled by Politics." *Washington Times,* 11 January 1989, p. A9.

Ellingsen, Peter. "Chinese Economic Reform 'a Sham.'" *Financial Times,* 27 July 1990, p. 3.

Hayek, Friedrich A., ed. *Collectivist Economic Planning.* 1935. Reprint. Clifton, N.J.: Augustus M. Kelley, 1975.

Hayek, Friedrich A. "Economics and Knowledge." *Economica* 4 (n.s., 1937). Reprinted in Hayek, *Individualism and Economic Order,* pp. 33-56. South Bend, Ind.: Gateway Editions (by arrangement with University of Chicago Press), 1948.

Hayek, Friedrich A. "Socialist Calculation: The Competitive 'Solution.'" *Economica* 7 (n.s., May 1940). Reprinted in *Comparative Economic Systems: Models and Cases,* pp. 140-59. 3rd ed. Edited by Morris Bornstein. Homewood, Ill.: Richard D. Irwin, 1974.

Hayek, Friedrich A. "The Use of Knowledge in Society." *American Economic Review* 35 (September 1945). Reprinted in Hayek, *Individualism and Economic Order,* pp.77-91. South Bend, Ind.: Gateway Editions (by arrangement with University of Chicago Press), 1948.

Hayek, Friedrich A. *The Constitution of Liberty.* Chicago: University of Chicago Press, 1960.

Hayek, Friedrich A. *The Fatal Conceit: The Errors of Socialism.* London: Routledge & Kegan Paul, 1988.

Leung, Julia. "China Faces Huge Ideological Hurdles in Plan to Sell Shares in State Concerns." *Wall Street Journal,* 2 March 1989, p. A12.

Leung, Julia. "China Eases Harsh Austerity Plan to Avert Potential Worker Unrest." *Wall Street Journal,* 27 July 1990, p. A8.

"Lift of Price Controls in Focus." *China Daily,* 13 July 1988, p. 4.

Mises, Ludwig von. "Economic Calculation in Socialism." 1936. Reprinted in *Comparative Economic Systems: Models and Cases,* pp. 120-26. 3rd ed. Edited by Morris Bornstein. Homewood, Ill.: Richard D. Irwin, 1974.

"Private Economy Praised." *China Daily,* 16 July 1988, p. 4.

Sutherland, Daniel. "China Plans to Sell Stock in State-Owned Enterprises." *Washington Post,* 21 September 1988b, pp. F1, F5.

[21]

The limits of economic policy*

Alternative approaches to economic policy

Academic analysis of economic policy and associated normative conclusions exhibits two distinct traditions. The historical evolution of policy and policy conceptions reflects over the past 200 years shifting influences from both traditions. One addresses an open-ended field of specific actions potentially available to government and explores the consequences of these measures. More importantly, this tradition justifies an action-oriented approach aimed at a wide range of specific results over a loosely limited or practically unlimited range. This policy conception envisions government as an active agent at least approximately concerned with the optimization of some social welfare function. This concern would require a wide array of policy instruments in order to allow the policy-makers unobstructed play in the policy game. The analysis of economic policy examines under the circumstances the relation between instruments and goals expressed by a social welfare function and the useful range of possible instruments. It investigates in particular the dependence of the choice of instruments and their setting on the prevailing state of affairs in view of the desired goals of policy-makers. A substantial literature followed this line exemplified by Tinbergen's *Theory of Economic Policy* (1952) and the work on optimal control (Chow, 1975). Most of the discussions directed by academicians to the public arena address the policy problem in a similar vein. They concentrate on specific actions, choices of instruments or their setting in the past, at the present or in the future. Notes are assigned to policy-makers for the adequacy of their choices or alternative specific suggestions are submitted for urgent attention.

The second tradition is more attuned to classical political philosophy and classical economics. It rejects the action-oriented approach with its characteristic desire to mould the world in some detail and its emphasis on choices of specific instruments or their level of application. The classical tradition emphasizes by contrast the proper choice of rules governing the socio-political or socio-economic game. The difference between the two approaches may be usefully explained with the metaphor of a football game. The policy-makers would be represented by the commissioner of the football league and the players represent agents in the socio-economic game. The classical tradition with its constitutionalist thrust limits policy-makers to formulate, monitor

* Originally published in *Schweizerische Zeitschrift für Volkswirtschaft und Statistik*, 3, 1985, 213–235.

and enforce the general rules controlling the detailed plays of the game. The choice of strategies, tactical procedures and all the varied details of play are left to the players. The other tradition empowers the commissioner to shape both the general rules and much detail of play in a shifting pattern in accordance with the state of play. The classic approach to policy analysis thus understands policy not as a choice of specific actions but as a choice of general rules usually embedded in a set of institutions. We may juxtapose it under the circumstances as an 'institutional policy' to 'specific action policies'. Analysis of economic policy means in this case an examination of alternative sets of rules. Variations in the rules yield in general different patterns in the socio-economic game. Any normative concern requires thus some careful analysis of the consequences associated with different sets of rules. Opportunities and incentives are in general affected by the choice of rules. The resulting modification of behaviour influences unavoidably the broad pattern of the outcome produced by the social process. An evaluation of this outcome guides the analysts choice of rules.

Theorists, pragmatists and understanding policy

The discussion of policy is ultimately guided by a desire to provide an understanding of its role and consequences. It should contribute in particular to a reliable assessment of the alternative traditions. Academic contributions, whether made in academia or offered to the public arena, do not exhaust however the public discussions. We also encounter the comments, views and proposals made by the media, suggested by officials or politicians and advanced by policy-makers. Some components in this second strand of the discussion interact quite closely with the academic discussion. But major components evolve according o their own 'logic' and with their own momentum. The discussion surrounding the US budget deficit demonstrates this aspect with remarkable force. The media and other participants in the political process recognize this state and typically reflect it by juxtaposing the pragmatist or practical men of affairs to the academic 'theoreticians'. This juxtaposition involves more than a simple description of facts. It occurs with a peculiar epistemological thrust. It conveys a subtle sense about a difference in the state of knowledge. Practical men of affairs directly immersed in the reality of the policy problem experience somehow an immediate absorption of the relevant knowledge. The academic by contrast approaches reality indirectly via the construction of theories. The underlying message suggests moreover that the epistemological quality of such theories hardly compares with the acquisition of knowledge based on 'direct exposure to reality'. This more or less implicit theme embedded in the cliché represented by the juxtaposition suffers however under a fatal illusion. It thoroughly misconceives the nature of human knowledge. All potential knowledge appears in the form of theories or hypotheses about various aspects of our physical or social environment. This holds for academics and equally for 'practical men of affairs'. The latter are full of theories about matters concerning them. They are however rarely aware of the essentially theoretical nature of their perceptions of reality. They fail consequently to appreciate that perceptions about reality occurring in the form of some general conceptions (i.e. theories) are not automatically true simply because they were motivated somehow by 'exposure to reality'. They still need to be critically assessed against observations. Most of these ideas would hardly survive this process. An analysis of the remainder reveals moreover that they yield almost no information about the range of important consequences to be expected under different sets of policy actions or under various policy institutions. We encounter here the crucial focus of a minimal understanding of economic policy. A rational evaluation and choice of policy actions or institutions requires some more reliable knowledge of the probable consequences. This knowledge defines in an important sense the relevant limits of economic policy. But such knowledge can only be supplied in the form of theories which survived some first rounds of critical assessment. The 'practical men of affairs', geared for other and quite important functions in life, frequently demanding high levels of intelligence, are in general, with remarkable exceptions however, not equipped for this task. They are by contrast often well equipped to provide us with detailed and useful descriptions of the political decision process with suggestively insightful *theoretical fragments* bearing on the general nature of this process. This state of affairs probably contributes to the prevalent belief in the public arena that practical men of affairs possess superior knowledge about economic policy. This belief confounds descriptive knowledge about the decision process with knowledge about the consequences and meaning of policies. My comment neither implies nor suggests that academic economists can be relied upon to possess such knowledge. An academic position is neither a necessary nor a sufficient condition for this state to occur. The verbal supplies of any economist are not our concern. The crucial point which needs to be made on occasion is the existence of a professional core expressed by economic analysis and represented by the best accumulated work of the profession. This core guides our exploration of 'the limits of economic policy'.

Limits of economic policy

General remarks
This exploration does not represent the basic purpose of this paper. It is motivated by our ultimate interest in the alternative traditions of economic policy. The notion of limits associated with economic policy requires,

however, some careful attention. Any metaphor or usual analogy suggesting a limit would in general blur the real issues posed by policy choices. A sense of the relevant limitation on policy-making emerges once we examine the consequences of policies and the nature of the policy-making process. The implications of the constraints imposed by the social opportunity set and the prevalence of perennially incomplete information about the detailed working of the private and public sector determine the range of issues to be examined in this context. One more comment needs to be made here. The term 'economic policy' is used here in a very inclusive way. It subsumes social policy, regional policy, housing policies, labour market policies, etc. It subsumes in a sense all governmental actions conditioning the use and development of (human and non-human) resources.

Implications of constraints characterizing the social opportunity set

The notion of a social opportunity set   The range of possible states of affairs is not unlimited. Physical nature and the patterns of social interaction constrain the feasible set of states potentially realizable. This limitation has been recognized and analysed for a long time by economic analysis under the label of a set of social production possibilities or a social opportunity set. The general properties of this opportunity set have been examined and belong to the standard material of textbooks. The general idea is simple and straightforward (see Figure 13.1). Suppose for convenience that an economy consists of two activities each one with a specific product (*x* and *y*). On the basis of a given endowment of resources existing at a time, the social opportunity set can be represented by a simple graph. The two axes express the output of *y* and *x*, the two goods in the economy. The concave line describes the production possibility frontier. The set of points defined by this frontier and the two axes constitutes the social opportunity set. Any combination (*y*, *x*) within this set is achievable. Interior combinations of the set are however inefficient. This means that one output could be raised without sacrificing any amount of

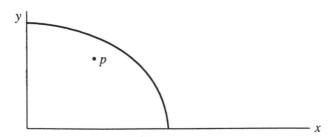

Figure 13.1

the other. The point p reveals this fact. It also reveals that both outputs could be raised simultaneously. It should be noted for our subsequent discussion that the concept of the social opportunity set is not confined to standard goods and services. It can usefully include any dimension of our environment valued positively or negatively.

The social opportunities, whatever the dimensions subsumed, remain limited and the frontier imposes trade-offs with unavoidable choices or associates social costs with all actions. Policy-makers can only move the economy (in the longer run) along the frontier trading off one good for another good. The opportunity set is moreover not just the reflection of a physical environment. It is crucially determined by socio-economic and socio-political institutions. Changes in admissible forms of organizing activities or changes in the admissible range of contractual arrangements modify in general the social opportunity set. We also learned over the past 15 years that variations in policy regime also influence this set. This means that some social costs imposed by policies appear as a contraction of the social opportunity set. This contraction occurs however relative to the expansion produced by economic growths and possible social benefits of policy. Other welfare losses occur as so-called distortions in the use of resources expressed by deviations between marginal social and private costs or deviations between marginal social costs and private relative evaluations (marginal rates of substitutions) expressing the agent's preference system.

The recognition or acknowledgement of such limitations is frequently difficult for 'political entrepreneurs', policy-makers or a politically committed intelligentsia. They will resent an analysis emphasizing inherent limitations and the reality of trade-offs or of social costs. The pursuit of policies which disregard inherent limitations produces unavoidably new problems not expected by the policy-maker and wrongly attributed to a variety of irrelevant conditions. A further round of policies is then introduced to cope with the new problems. They will be quite ineffectual however. They do not, in general, address the crucial conditions and further problems result.

The reality of trade-offs   The general characterization needs some illustrative exemplifications. Two sets of policies based on recent experience and discussions will be adduced. The first set refers to monetary problems. Central Bank officials and politicians attempt (or profess to attempt) on occasion to pursue simultaneously a policy of exchange rate control and a monetary control policy. But this combination is not within the feasible set of possible combinations. An exchange rate policy implies that monetary growth reflects all the random shocks operating on exchange markets. 'Sterilization' or 'desterilization' operations may for a short period appear to reconcile the two goals. This reconciliation cannot persist over the longer run. A monetary control policy on the other hand is consistent with interventions in exchange markets. It is however inconsistent with interventions guided by longer-run exchange rate targeting. The experiences of the past 15 years and most particularly the experience of the Swiss National Bank confirm this point. Monetary authorities and politicians need to recognize the basic facts. They are confronted with a trade-off and they must choose between controlling exchange rates or controlling monetary growth. It is noteworthy that this issue determined Dr Schiller's resignation as Minister of Economic Affairs from the German Government in 1972. The German Government chose to disregard Dr Schiller's warning about a trade-off and was subsequently confronted with the hard facts. We note in passing that the same limitation extends to any attempt to combine a monetary control policy with a policy of controlling some real variables (say, e.g., interest rates). This means also that the constraints imposed by reality exclude the simultaneous realization of a policy avoiding persistent inflationary or deflationary episodes and a monetary policy addressed to control some real variables.

The policy debates of the European Parliament in Strasbourg erupted on occasion with demands for a persistently expansionary monetary policy (*'eine monetäre Vorwärtspolitik'*) substantially raising monetary growth. It seems that advocates of this policy expect with its aid to lower permanently unemployment and to revive permanently the growth or level of output. The reality of the social opportunity set precludes however this option. Its pursuit beyond a deep depression actually reflecting a contraction in aggregate nominal demand involves a serious illusion. Such a policy would under the present circumstances yield at best a very temporary effect on output and ultimately produce a pattern of rising inflation. The same impossibility obstructs the wishful dreams of many politicians who propose to lower interest rates by an accelerated monetary growth.

The US administration's budget forecasts made in past years suffered from politically appealing illusions about feasible achievements on a related issue. The forecasts were based on assumptions bearing on future inflation and interest rates. These assumptions were required to determine the course of revenues and expenditures. But the assumptions were quite inconsistent. No feasible state in the opportunity set could produce the comparatively high inflation jointly with the relatively low interest rates assumed as a basis for the forecasts.

Other examples drawn from agricultural policy, housing policy, tenancy protection, risk regulation, etc., abound. A survey of the range addressed by policy in any country offers a rich menu of possible cases.

Labour market policies pursued in Europe over the past decades yield some particularly important examples. The goal of job security or economic security in a more general sense found increasing favour over the past 20 years in the political arena. The goal was pursued with little recognition of, or concern for, inherent limitations. Such limitations do exist, however, and we can easily appreciate that committed advocates of more (and more) economic security resent being confronted with the reality of such limitations. The limitations impose trade-offs involving economic security, employment, real wages and real fringe benefits. They also impose a trade-off between economic security and economic growth with rising standards of living. The policies addressed to job security or to economic security in general varied between countries. Their gradually expanding implementation within each country proceeded, moreover, with a variety of measures. All these measures, whatever their detail, directly or indirectly raised the real cost of employment. This implies that either employment, real wages or real fringe benefits fall. The inherent nature of the social process thus imposes a trade-off. Its reality exists irrespective of ideological commitments or theological dreams and this reality ultimately confronts us with a choice. Employment will fall or stagnate with an insistent maintenance of real wages. Employment levels can be maintained, on the other hand, with trading-off of real wages. It might appear that these unpleasant choices can be avoided with subsidies to business firms offsetting the increase in the real cost of employment. But such subsidies must be financed, either with taxes or money creation. In the first case, net real wages or net real income from investment will be lowered. And the latter effect discourages investment and lowers growth. The recourse to money creation generates inflation. The political reality of inflation determines moreover a highly erratic inflation with pervasive uncertainty lowering investment and growth. Similarly, an increasingly rigid or demanding policy of economic security impedes economic growth. It obstructs adjustments in the pattern of resource use and lowers incentives to explore new possibilities or opportunities. It contributes to a state of ossification or petrification of society. Most European nations moved along a course trading off employment and stagnation for economic security. But this implicit choice is not recognized in the political arena. The loss in employment imposed by the political choice is insistently attributed by the media and most politicians to the evolution of modern technologies. Any politician who dares to recognize the crucial issue is usually ridiculed and vilified in the public arena. But the professional core of economics informs us that 'technology' is an opportunity for rising general welfare and not the problem asserted. It does become a problem within the institutional arrangements characterizing an ossified or petrified society.

The reality of social costs   The reality of the social opportunity set with the economy's inherent drive to settle in the neighbourhood of the production frontier confronts policy-making with another important dimension. This dimension involves a significant limitation almost systematically neglected in the politics of economic policy. This neglect substantially distorts the balance of social benefits and social costs associated with policy decisions. It encourages economic policies with social benefits less than their social costs. These costs may involve a decline in welfare expressed by a relative compression of the social opportunity set whenever resources are allocated to socially non-productive investments in the political process encouraged by distributional gains associated with the policy-making process. The costs may also reflect larger inputs ('rent-seeking') in the production process required per output unit. But welfare losses also occur whenever policies distort the pattern of resource uses relative to the prevailing preference system within a given opportunity set. In either case, social costs reflect a sacrifice in some dimensions of the social process positively valued by some members of society. Social costs are not an abstract entity beyond human concerns. They ultimately represent underlying human valuations by the only source of human values, i.e. the individual persons in a society.

The regulation of pharmaceutical products initiated in the USA in the early 1960s offers a remarkable example of the consequences associated with the neglect of this particular limitation. The traumatic impact on public impressions made by the tragically crippled and deformed babies resulting from the use of thalidomide by pregnant women influenced new legislation and tougher regulatory policies. Public attention became fixed on a single goal: to lower the risk to zero of admitting new pharmaceutical products with potentially dangerous side-effects. The measures implemented for this purpose substantially raised the costs of development for new products by a large factor. Other measures shortened at the same time the expected pay-off period of new drugs and thus lowered the potential return. Regulatory policies quite generally obstructed the flow of inventions and innovations. Innovation consequently declined by a wide margin and the appearance of new drugs sharply contracted. It would be difficult to dispute that new legislation and regulatory policy provided no benefits. They most probably offered some useful effects. But they also imposed some heavy burdens on the members of society. They obstructed the creation and use of new and effective drugs for a wide array of health problems. Avoidable illness and death due to unavailable but potentially producible drugs increased. Illness and death unrecognized by legislators and regulators forms the social cost of a well-meant endeavour. A detailed research of this problem concluded that the social cost of the new policy vastly exceeded the social benefits it provided to the public. The single-minded obsession with the minimization of risk attached to new drugs failed to recognize the unavoidable alternative risk associated with a lower innovation of useful and health- or life-preserving drugs. A policy addressed to minimize the probability of bad pharma products maximized at the same time the probability of *not* having useful drugs.

The 'obsessive approach' increasingly dominated regulatory policy during the 1970s. This trend was most particularly visible in environmental, health and safety politics. This approach recognized only a single dimension, the desired benefits. The occurrence of social costs were simply neglected. The result was a seriously unbalanced policy process ultimately lowering welfare. Absolutist standards of environmental purity were envisioned. But any serious attempts to realize such standards lower the dimension of the opportunity set and push the production frontier nearer to the origin. The same consequences follow from an obsessive health policy seriously pursuing an absolutist standard. Commitment to such a standard always involves a neglect of social cost in the decision process. Alternatively, a concern for the social cost imposed on the public prohibits an absolutist standard. It forces policymakers to ponder a more balanced approach. Recognition of social costs would not prevent social benefits from environmental and health policies. But the policies would be constrained by the recognition of social costs. The incentives in the political process to recognize social costs remain however weak and uncertain. The emergence of an approximately balanced approach is, under the circumstances, not the result of a recognition of social costs. It emerges usually from a decentralized implementation involving all major interests. A single and central regulatory agency is much more likely to follow an absolutist standard.

Protectionism, cartel legislation and regional policies exhibit a similar pattern. The Swiss Federal Council's report on regional policy presenting arguments for a proposed legislation is quite indicative. It diligently lists the benefits, and here especially the number of jobs saved or created in some regions as a result of the policy. The reader finds however no allusions to any potential social cost. Legislators are not warned that regional policy also means ossification of inherited inefficient structures. It also means that more efficient jobs in other regions are destroyed or thwarted. And it means, lastly, that some non-human resources will be used less efficiently in a social sense. All this implies that the social opportunity set is contracted for the benefit of some 'regional balance or restoration'.

The same argument extends to protectionism and cartel legislation. Benefits and beneficiaries are easily recognized. But these benefits are hardly ever *social* benefits. They usually involve redistributions of income and are matched by corresponding losses elsewhere. These losses, as the gains, are however private. Occurrence of private gain or even of social benefits establishes no social case for such policies. The professional literature determined a long time ago the 'deadweight welfare losses' produced by protectionism and monopolies. These losses are produced by the distortions in the use of resources resulting from such policies. The welfare losses are actually substantially raised by the 'rent-seeking behaviour' of potential beneficiaries. The evolution of public choice theory in the past 20 years directed our attention to this important aspect. The establishment of a privileged position by means of protectionist measures, cartel legislation and its implementation, or on the basis of other monopolizing actions requires substantial investment of resources in the political process. These investments also contract the social opportunity set. 'Rent-seeking behaviour' thus absorbs socially valuable resources and imposes a welfare cost on society. The *social* cost of these policies is usually overlooked in the political process whereas some *private* benefits are much touted as *social* gains. The net effect of these policies involves, however, essentially a redistribution of income and jobs accompanied by a welfare loss due to the dead-weight burden and the rent-seeking behaviour. Dubious benefits are often claimed most particularly for cartel legislation. But these claims need be understood as an ideological fog covering the reality of this economic policy.

The variety of illustrative cases could be multiplied in many directions. Transfer policies (i.e. 'social policies') create incentives in the political process and disincentives for socially productive activities which yield the same general consequences as the measures discussed in the previous paragraph. We note however a crucial difference. In the prior case the redistributional consequences are hidden. On this issue, by contrast, they are the explicit purpose of the policy. Some measure of redistribution expresses probably the political consensus of western democracies. But we also need to recognize that they impose a social cost on society and those costs rise with the extent and complexity of the policies.

The central proposition of this section emphasizes the comparative blindness of the political process to social costs typically associated with economic policy. Political debate centres on the private gains and losses, i.e. on redistributional aspects, and rarely considers the significant limitation expressed by relevant social costs. It is noteworthy that academia suffers under a similar blindness. The standard discussion of market failure resolves the associated welfare problem with suitable interventions by the government. These interventions are moreover supposed to involve no social costs. This is particularly remarkable as many cases of alleged 'market failure' are attributable to the operation of neglected social costs also affecting governmental interventions. It follows that this analysis offers little guidance for rational policy-making.

The problem of information
Legislation and regulatory rules and ordinances encounter a compliance problem. There is no automatic compliance. The norms established by policy-

making must be monitored and enforced. The investment in the apparatus required for this purpose imposes also a social cost on society. Compliance is however linked with another problem involving limitations on economic policy. We need to recognize that the mode of operation of both private and public sector produces a substantial uncertainty about the *detailed* pattern of outcomes. The nature of this problem will be explored in the following two sub-sections.

Uncertainty in the private sector   Government interventions confront members of society with a challenge. These measures modify private opportunity sets and thus induce various responses. Many of these responses address an imaginative search to lower the impact of government intervention. This search by many smart operators eventually produces an array of devices, arrangements and procedures which more or less legally at least partly circumvent the government's intervention. The extent of these activities depends on private costs imposed by intervention and search relative to expected private gains. The very nature of these activities implies moreover that many detailed adjustments made in response to an intervention are quite unpredictable. Important longer-run consequences to complex policies remain thus essentially unknown at the time the policies are under consideration. Even the most rational legislator or policy-maker fully devoted to the mythical entity called the 'public interest' suffers under very incomplete information about the *detailed* ramification of policies. Every intervention tends to produce unintended and unexpected consequences which eventually affect the evaluation and usefulness of the intervention. This uncertainty confronts economic policy with another dimension of possible limitations which need to be considered in rational policy-making.

It may be useful to develop the argument in a more general context. The social process governed by spontaneous interaction between agents in market economies operates as a vast system continuously creating and disseminating new information. Acquisition and interpretation of these flows of new information modifies private opportunity sets and expectations of future market conditions. These revisions induce pervasive adjustments in behaviour. The detailed nature of outcome patterns produced by the social process continuously changes as a result. By the very nature of the process conditioned by the dissemination of *new* information (i.e. essentially *unanticipated*), the evolving outcome patterns are unpredictable in their *full detail*. Economic analysis thus explains quite successfully the nature and characterization of the social process. But this understanding of the spontaneous order created by the social process also implies that no analysis can predict beyond the broad contours the *detailed* outcome of the uncertainty. This uncertainty confronts policy-makers with a serious problem. The correlation between actions or policies and intended outcome or desired results is burdened with shadows of doubt. Some components of the total outcome may be quite predictable but many other evolving effects remain unpredictable. The *full* consequences of policies are thus hidden behind the veils of an uncertain future.

Some examples may elaborate the nature of the issue involved. The public's response to radar traffic control in the USA offers a small but intriguing example. The explosive use of radar detection devices and CB radios to circumvent the measure was hardly predicted. The adjustments produced by tax legislation are both more pervasive and important. These adjustments abound with unexpected and unintended consequences, affecting the use and development of resources. These consequences lower the correlation between motivating intention and actual outcome. This modified correlation confronts any ambitious and complex policy programme with a subtle but effective limitation. We may single out at this stage in particular the corporate income tax. We possess no reliable information about who really pays the tax. The public's vision that the 'corporations' pay the taxes is simply an impressionistic illusion. Taxes are ultimately always borne by persons, in this case the recipients of salaries, wages, income on capital invested or consumers via the real price charged on the corporation's product. The corporation forms just the organizational vehicle for the collection of taxes from the persons associated with it. We can specify a variety of conditions which affect the distribution of the corporate tax among ultimate tax payers. But we lack the detailed empirical knowledge necessary for any reliable information in this respect. This uncertainty explains both the political appeal of the tax and its basic problem. When legislators impose a tax on corporations or change their tax rates they do not know who they really tax. Employees may bear the burden in the form of lower real wages and lower fringe benefits or owners suffer the burden as a result of lower returns on their investments. In either case there would be further repercussions on non-human and human capital formation. Equity and efficiency thus suggest the abolition of the corporate tax and its replacement by a personal income tax. This clashes however with the political appeal of corporation taxes. This appeal is crucially conditioned by the uncertainty described. This uncertainty obscures the true limitations of the tax determined by its social costs. The neglect of the social cost by the political process occurs here in the context of a choice favouring a measure with an inherent information problem.

This theme emerges in the range of stabilization policies with particular force. A wide gulf separates the reality of stabilization policy from the official claims and academic rhetoric. The latter proceed as if we possessed detailed and reliable information about the economy's response structure. Once again this information is not available and the information problem confronts any ambitious stabilization policy with a severe and fundamental limitation. Incomplete information about the economy's detailed response structure lowers the correlation between desired or intended and actual performance level produced by 'stabilization policies'. The unknown detail of the response structure conditions ultimately the outcome of the best-meant policy. Attempts at 'stabilization' proceed under the circumstances in contrast to a general belief without any guarantee of stabilization.

The operation of the public sector   Policies emerge from a political process which contributes to a last dimension of the limitations encountered by economic policy. The inherent nature of the process conditions policy-making into patterns poorly correlated with well-meant and sensible proposals measured in terms of general welfare. Politics is not dominated by consideration of public interest or vague feelings of good-will. Self-interested political entrepreneurship affects the resulting pattern of legislation and executive actions. An examination of environmental or regional policy in Switzerland reveals, for instance, that proposals for efficient (i.e. welfare-raising) solutions to underlying problems do not survive successfully in the political process. The outcome is usually controlled by a redistributional conflict associated with any measure to cope with the problem.

The crucial aspect to be emphasized in this context addresses the pervasive uncertainty about the detailed pattern of legislation, executive actions and court decisions unleashed by some intentions or proposals. The previous section considered the uncertainty produced by the searching and coping responses of agents to policy measures. A similar phenomenon occurs within the political process. Legislation passed influences but does not determine the outcome. The implementation of the legislation by the state's apparatus with the aid of rules, ordinances or regulatory actions frequently enjoys a wide field for the crucial detail of policies. The US experience with a pattern of legislation appearing more and more in the form of general mandates offers some important examples. The independent power of implementing agencies tends to rise with the complexity of the material addressed by the legislators' intentions and the generality of the mandate legislated. Implementing agencies acquire thus some range of operative opportunities. They will exploit this range according to their own political interests and perceptions, searching and coping with their own opportunities. It follows under the circumstances that the translation of legislation into specific actions conditioning socio-economic evolution is a highly uncertain process. This uncertainty is heightened by the fact that implementing agencies often change their interpretations and rules guiding their actions. Various sections of the same agency often proceed moreover according to different interpretations of the same rules. The result is a pervasive uncertainty built into the policy-making process. The ramifications and consequences of policy at the original plane of intention, planning and proposals remain somewhat obscure. This is quite consistent with the fact that immediate beneficiaries suffer little doubt, and correctly so, about their *private* advantage in the matter. Not the least among the beneficiaries are the implementing agencies themselves.

Alternative policy conceptions, once more

The reality of the political process

My lecture opened with the juxtaposition of two basically different policy conceptions. An institutional policy was distinguished from an open-ended action-oriented policy. We may also characterize the alternatives as the choice of a set of general rules monitored and enforced by the government on the one side and an activist intervention over an open-ended range on the other side. The two traditions involve thus an essentially limited, or constitutionalist policy conception and an unlimited, open-ended policy. The issues associated with these two policies still need to be clarified. The discussion of the limits confronting economic policy provides the basis for my assessment. The reality of the social opportunity set imposes trade-offs and social costs associated with policy actions frequently disregarded in the political process. An analysis of this process explains some reasons for this neglect and the role of incomplete information in this context. I refer at this stage to my lecture on 'Reflections on the Political Economy of Government' [Chapter 12 in this volume] presented to this Society in 1978 at the annual meeting in Basel. My account exploited important contributions appearing in the evolution of public choice theory. I suggested in particular that the political arena may be understood in analogy to markets in the private sector as a 'political market'.

> Bureaux (more appropriately bureaucrats) and politicians (incumbent and aspiring legislators, persons holding or seeking appointments, functionaries of political organizations) correspond to producers on the market place sampling the consumer preferences and adjusting competitively their supplies. Both politicians and bureaux thus respond to the preferences of the citizen. But this response proceeds in the context of information patterns and organizational arrangements which open opportunities for the self-interested behaviour of politicians and bureaux. They operate under the circumstances not just as mere or passive vehicles executing the median voter groups' preferred transfer of funds. Their operation implies that a portion of the total funds collected are absorbed by the 'governmental apparatus'. This absorption corresponds to the normal profit in the competitive market place. The voter benefiting from redistribution cedes this portion of the tax revenues to the political and administrative entrepreneurs organizing the benefits. The nature of the political institutions determines extent and form of the competition between politicians and bureaux, or, seen from the 'other side', the extent and form of monopoly achievable by politicians or bureaux and their potential for

collusive behaviour. It seems useful for our purposes in order to focus attention on the major strands of the argument to introduce seven 'postulates':

1. Politicians are entrepreneurs competing in a market for votes and influence. They compete with proposals, programmes and the systematic exploitation of non-cognitive aspects of language. The politicians prefer more votes and influence to less votes and influence. They also share with other men a preference for higher permanent real income.
2. Bureaux sample the political market with proposals, reinterpretations of their mandate, and the detailed manner of administering the tasks developed. This entrepreneurial behaviour is designed to maintain or increase the budget.
3. Costs and benefits associated with *general* programmes are more evenly distributed than the costs and benefits of *specific* programmes.
4. Information costs about costs and benefits of *general* programmes are *large* relative to benefits.
5. Information costs about costs and benefits of *specific* programmes are relatively *small* to the 'positively affected group' and comparatively *large* to the 'negatively affected group'.
6. The marginal cost of political operation (for example, lobbying in various forms) is much smaller for *established* than for *potential* organizations.
7. Potential voters weigh expected costs and benefits associated with the bureaux potential offers and with the alternative packages represented by different politicians.

The crucial information patterns are formulated under assumptions 3 to 5. The distribution of information costs, recognized here, emphasizes a highly uneven incidence depending on the relation between voter groups and types of programmes. This distribution of information costs reflects important aspects of our reality. Rational adjustment by voters to such costs should not be interpreted to express some 'flaws in awareness' or 'ineradicable illusions'. There is no illusion in staying less than fully informed. It is an illusion on the other hand to expect voters to invest in information at a cost substantially beyond the expected return from such investment.

The major consequences of the patterns summarized by the 'postulates' may be developed as follows: 'Entrepreneurial competition thrives on a continued search for *new* proposals, *new* programs, *new* twists, modifications, or *extensions* of existing programs. It encourages a continuous search for suitable means to focus public attention. This is a necessary strategy for politicians to establish themselves in the competitive political market. Continuous market research and sampling of the public market with the aid of an expanding staff is therefore a competitive necessity for the politician.

'There are no rewards in attempts to abolish existing laws or programs. This strategy has no competitive market value. According to proposition 5 above, the beneficiaries of a program know the significance of its curtailment with respect to their wealth or political power. "Outside groups" bearing the cost of an existing program will barely appreciate their own welfare gain resulting from the cut in a program. Insiders' opposition to a proposed reduction tends to override consequently the feeble support of "outsiders" for the change. The basic postulates also imply that "outside groups" can reasonably expect larger returns for any given costs by investing efforts in lobbying for *new specific* programs adjusted to their special benefits. The returns from political investment in organizing opposition to the other groups' specific programs are comparatively small relative to the cost of investment. It follows that proposals to cut programs are neither frequently offered by politicians (with a few exceptions immediately ridiculed by the media) nor frequently advanced by "investors in the political market place". A political entrepreneur finds thus in general that offering "new programs" or "variations on existing themes" assures a higher survival value in the political market. A recent article in *The Banker* noted with interest that in the budget debates proceeding in the British Parliament over ten years not a single MP ever proposed a single time to cut expenditures.

'The politicians' appraisal is reinforced by the media. An examination of commentators in the press and on television demonstrates a preference for "fresh ideas", a *new* rhetoric or a *new* fad. The media rhetoric prefers a *new* word to almost any thoughtful proposal to abolish or reduce an obsolete or dangerous program. The media themselves find a higher market value with new words in the mass college education market. Attention to old programs, inherited legislation or institutions may infrequently have some market value. But such occurrences form usually the initial preparations for "more, better, new and larger programs". Political entrepreneurs find it more advantageous to propose new legislation favoring this or that other group as a way of "offsetting" the negative effect of previous legislation. But the global welfare effects are not offset. Total welfare is further reduced, government programs increase, the budget balloons and the range of influence open to a bureaucracy expands.

'The asymmetry in the distribution of costs and benefits and also the asymmetry in the distribution of information costs summarized above establishes that the emergence of new programs dominates the removal of old programs. They also determine that *specific* programs dominate *general* programs. The capital value expected by organizers proposing *general* and *undifferentiated* tax reductions or expenditure increases is quite small compared to the return achievable for the same efforts invested to effect *specific* and *highly differential* programs. Complex and differentiated programs concentrate benefits on a smaller (interested) group with comparatively low information costs and impose diffuse costs on the "outsiders" who suffer high costs of information and organization. It will in general not be worth much effort for members of an outside group to organize opposition to a specific and specialized program before or after its imposition. The capital value of investing political activity in specific new programs, differentiated for specific purposes with suitable complexity, tends to be much higher. This pattern of asymmetry in the distribution of costs and benefits explains the entrepreneurial choices of the prevalent types of programs and proposals offered by politicians. This analysis also reveals the unavoidable emergence and increasing range of complexity in tax laws or regulatory arrangements. "Tax loopholes" should be understood as a necessary result of the process. The indignant rhetoric attacking and condemning "loopholes" reflects on the other hand the entrepreneurial opportunities politicians acquire from their own previous endeavors. This analysis suggests furthermore the fundamental irrelevance of most chapters in the theory of economic macropolicy and implies that systematic and deliberate macro-policies are somewhat improbable' [Brunner, 1975].

The bias for the new programs and extensions of existing programs inherent in the political process and the associated redistributional mechanism contributes a major strand to the incremental growth of government. We also note that the concentration on specific and relatively complex programs emerges directly from the entrepreneurial behavior of bureaux. The relative success of the bureaux' sampling by the political market determines simultaneously magnitude of budget and government, and also the allocation of the apparatus.

The classic policy conception as a co-operative solution to a prisoner's dilemma problem

The reality of the political process explains the systematic neglect of objectively existing 'limitations of economic policy'. The bias is inherent in any loosely limited or essentially unlimited policy process. The incentives embedded in a more or less open-ended policy process unavoidably produce a pattern with a low feedback from social costs of policy programmes. The political process provides no incentives and no mechanisms for a realistic representation and assessment of the *social* trade-offs and *social* costs associated with economic policy-making. No incentives operate, moreover, to foster a recognition bearing on the consequences occurring over a *longer* horizon. The immanent characteristics of the political process produce an externality problem usually overlooked in 'market failure' and welfare discussions. The parties involved assess their strategies in terms of their *perceived private* gains and costs related to the redistributional consequences of the policy game. These perceived private gains and costs are quite generally poorly correlated with the relevant social benefits and social costs. The latter involve aspects beyond the direct redistributional consequences perceived as the relevant costs and gains by agents in the social process. Social costs are thus not sufficiently 'internalized' by political operators. We encounter here a sort of prisoners' dilemma problem. The activist and open-ended policy game contracts the social opportunity set and lowers general welfare. The members of society as a group are worse off as a result of their prevalent behaviour. The game promises, however, to individuals and subgroups separately substantial advantages. These advantages are acquired of course at the expense of other members of society. Our previous discussion indicates, moreover, that this game is not a zero-sum game with little effect on *general* welfare. The crucial problem goes beyond the redistribution of wealth produced by the game. The reality of social costs associated with the game reminds us that we encounter here a *negative*-sum game compressing the social opportunity set. The costs imposed by active rent-seeking behaviour form in this context a major portion of the relevant social burden of the game.

This analysis of the policy process provides the basis for the classic policy programme. It should be understood as an attempt to break out of the prisoners' dilemma. It offers essentially a *co-operative* solution to this dilemma. A constitutionalist approach expressed by a set of general rules severely constraining the government's admissible range of actions would moderate the game by a large margin. But such a set of rules is not unique and its choice would have to be carefully examined. The accumulated discussion in various fields of economics indicates quite clearly the nature and thrust of rules extending the social opportunity set. The choice of rules proceeds however not beyond the political process. It would appear that the conflict bearing on the choice of general rules is less intense and protracted than the conflict surrounding the redistributional schemes proceeding under any label (cartel legislation, agricultural policy, trade policy, housing policies, export risk guarantees, etc.) The detailed implications of general rules with respect to the specific position of individual members or sub-groups are somewhat obscure and uncertain. The consequences of specific actions and proposals with respect to the specific position of interested parties are much more visible and reliably assessable. The discussion of general rules is moreover more likely to direct attention to their effect on the social opportunity set than the conflict-loaded dispute generated by specific schemes of wealth redistribution.

Objections to the classic programme
The classic programme is often characterized by academic critique as a 'retreat from potential opportunities to raise welfare'. Tinbergen's *Theory of Economic Policy* developed formal arguments representing this vision. The traditional argument on behalf of an activist stabilization policy may illustrate the prevalent attitude. This argument emphasizes that a pattern of discretionary interventions offers opportunities to offset a range of exogenous shocks and produce consequently a much better performance of the economy. Such a policy pattern, not confined by general rules, can sensitively adjust to all contingencies. Such adjustments are bound to raise the economy's overall performance level. But this means that the social opportunity set is actually expanded under the circumstances.

The fallacy of this argument has been demonstrated at another occasion (Brunner, 1981). It is based on two conditions which deny the two dimensions of the information problem confronting any adequate analysis of the policy problem. This problem seems rarely recognized by advocates and is implicitly discarded with the assumptions built into their analytic demonstration of the activist case. The first condition invokes full and reliable information by the policy-maker about the economy's dynamic response structure. The possession of such knowledge would certainly guarantee the possibility for an effective application of activist policy sensitively adjusted to evolving contingencies. But a survey of our state of knowledge denies the existence of this condition. The detail required for the rational guidance of an activist policy is not available. It is moreover inherently impossible ever to acquire this information level. We noted before that market processes also function as mechanisms perennially producing new information to agents. This implies a persistent evolution in a random pattern of an economy's detailed response structure. It follows that this detailed response structure is not constant over time to be approximated even more closely by clever econometric estimation. The information problem destroys the case for an activist and contingent policy pattern. The execution of such policies in spite of inadequate and unreliable information contributes with substantial probability to the opposite of the desired stabilization.

The other condition of the activist case pertains to the political economy of policy-making. The activist argument implicitly assumes a public-interest or goodwill theory of government. Government is supposed to pursue policies only guided by a general interest summarized by some social welfare function. But this (romantic) vision hardly describes the reality of policymaking. This reality was described above and is closely associated with the operation of the political sector under a severe information problem. Politicians, policy-makers and bureaucracies interact with constituencies in a context of incomplete and non-uniform information. They are moreover motivated in the light of an essentially self-interested appraisal of their opportunities. The characterization of policy-makers as optimizers of a social welfare function expressing a social consensus is thus remarkably irrelevant. The policy process actually produces, under the circumstances described above, a pattern of uncertain drift reinforcing the pervasive information problem. The reader is reminded in particular that under the incentives controlling the political process 'stabilization policies' usually appear as a camouflage for redistributional activities with minor, if any, real concern for aggregate stabilization. Examples supporting this point may be observed in any country.

The irrelevance of academic objections and the actual driving forces of the political process

Neomercantilist interests The academic argument supporting an open-ended and activist policy, however seductive it may appear, does not explain the prevalent reality of these policy patterns. The political process may at most exploit these arguments as a rationale to support and cover the really motivating forces at work. The crucial driving forces are found beyond these arguments in neo-mercantilist interests and ideological beliefs. Neo-mercantilist interests systematically exploit opportunities to create and expand some privileged or protected position under any label. Imaginative inventiveness is the only limit to the forms of policies which evolve over time. They may each from import quotes, the subtleties of the 'new protectionism', to housing subsidies, tenant protection, cartel laws, privileged access to banks, etc.

Once the barrier of the classic conception, for reasons not further examined here, has effectively broken down, neo-mercantilist interests experience an open field for their activities. They permeate under the circumstances the reality of the political process summarized above. The essentially unlimited range for potential economic policy offers entrepreneurship on the political market, pursued by politicians, bureaucracies and neo-mercantilist interest groups, a wide and open-ended field. This pattern raises the expected private return from investments in political organization or economic policy organization. There emerge under the circumstances expanding opportunities to use the state and its policy institutions for purposes of wealth redistribution, executed via one or the other of the thousand forms given to 'economic policy'. The range and level of political conflict unavoidably rises over time under the circumstances and 'trade policies' are more bitterly contested between nations. The rising burden of social costs imposed by this evolution lowers the growth of real income and the expansion of opportunities. The search for private wealth derives in this case increasing returns from opportunities associated with investments in the political process at the expense of investments raising the social opportunity set via accumulation of human and non-human resources.

Ideological beliefs   But the complex of neo-mercantilist interests engaged in the exploitation of the political process cannot provide a full explanation of the driving forces at work in contemporary western democracies. We need to recognize more fully the role of ideology and ideological beliefs in this context. My earlier account is thus quite incomplete. We encounter first an extensive use of ideology in the neo-mercantilist struggle for wealth advantages. The ideological component operates here as a camouflage of the underlying relevant interests. The 'Helvetian ideology' surrounding the ongoing efforts for a cartel legislation in Switzerland offers in this respect a particularly interesting example. But ideological beliefs enter the policy process also in a radically different manner. They may still be associated with schemes involving some wealth redistribution. But their crucial aspect for our purposes reaches beyond the political acquisition of wealth fully characterizing the neo-mercantilist interests. Their motivation contains a component which is separate and independent from wealth. This motivation involves basic and radical restructuring of society. The ideological beliefs express a commitment to 'a new socio-economic order' requiring foremost a complete political control over the socio-economic process. The realization of the 'new order' does not rely on revolutionary strategies. It is approached via an 'incrementalist tactic'. Active participation in the policy process is the essential instrument in this game. An unlimited economic policy-making offers thus the necessary field of operation for ideological beliefs. Any potential issue and any measure can be exploited for the purpose of an expanded political control. This 'incrementalist tactic' yields moreover some important benefits. The measures adopted by the political process or executed by policy agencies under the combined influence of neo-mercantilist interests and ideological beliefs frequently create a new pattern of social conditions which can be problematized. The evolution of labour market institutions in Europe exemplifies the point. The various measures of 'job security' raised the real cost of employment. Unyielding real wages impose adjustments on employment and unemployment. Thus emerges a new opportunity for further tactical exploitation. Work-sharing forms the next claim to 'solve the problem'. But once again it will impose a new problem. It will lower the social opportunity set and thus strengthen the incentives for politically engineered wealth redistribution. The more problems the policy process generates along a road influenced by the interaction of neo-mercantilist interests and ideological beliefs the more attractive become the opportunities for 'the incrementalist tactics'.

The experiences with environmental and health policies in the USA offer a wide range of illustrative material for this theme. Environmental and health problems assuredly deserve our careful attention. But they can be approached in very different ways. This field of concern suffers most particularly from the illusion that no deviation from some imagined ideal can be tolerated. Any consideration of social costs imposed by the realization of the absolutist goal is scorned. This implicit refusal to recognize social costs reflects ignorance of either an elitist or an authoritarian attitude. The social costs associated with a given course shaping the use of resources mirror the values attached by members of society to goods and services sacrificed by using resources in this particular manner. A deliberate unwillingness to consider such costs reveals thus a refusal to recognize other people's values. This pattern is unavoidably associated with the role of ideological beliefs in the policy process. The deliberate disregard of social costs in the ideological approach to economic policy is typically supplemented by another pattern. The proposals emanating and issues raised are hardly addressed to the *substance* of a genuine problem requiring serious attention. The proposals and issues formulated are dominated by the ideological motivation directed to an encompassing socio-political vision.

The behaviour of the Ralph Nader group in matters of environmental policy is quite instructive in this context. It seems clearly motivated by a deep hostility towards a society relying on a social co-ordination based on markets and private property. Health policy in the USA, shaped by influential science groups, shows a similar development. A remarkable intellectual establishment effectively suggested that technology and modern industry is responsible for an incipient cancer epidemic. This suggestion crucially shaped important legislation in the USA. A careful examination of the state of scientific

268   Economic analysis and political ideology

knowledge reveals, however, a remarkable absence of supporting evidence for the asserted link between technology and 'cancer epidemic' (Efron, 1984). A further examination shows moreover that these intellectual and scientist groups distorted the scientific evidence in order to serve an essentially ideological socio-political purpose. An absolutist legislation setting almost impossible standards frequently emerges from such operations in the policy process. Such legislation provides a basis for potentially arbitrary and unlimited actions by regulatory bodies 'in the public interest' naturally interpreted by interested groups.

The operation of the so-called 'Hunger Lobby' in the USA offers another interesting example. A remarkable coalition of political agencies, private political organizations and activist groups of scientists justifies a large allocation of government funds to alleviate an allegedly massive hunger syndrome in the USA. The (massive) interests of the various groups in the potential redistribution of income is easily discernible. A deeper examination reveals also the ideological motivation of some important participating groups. Most revealing in this context is the absence of substantial evidence and relevant analysis supporting the strong assertions peddled in the public arena. Independent scholars demonstrated that the reports offered by the 'Hunger Lobby' are unreliable and offer little relevant information bearing on the issue. Ideological camouflage and commitment merge in this case to protect both interests and socio-political goals.

Concluding remarks
Economic policy does not occur in a socio-political vacuum. It forms an essential component of an ongoing fundamental conflict about the future social order of western democracies. Questions bearing on the possible 'limits of economic policy' thus ultimately involve decisions about alternative policy conceptions with substantially different institutional approaches. These differences imply over the longer run divergent social, economic and political evolutions. But the implicit denial of any 'limits of economic policy' expressed by one of the alternative policy conceptions does not suspend their reality. Their neglected operations will increasingly burden societies and moderate our opportunities.

References
Brunner, Karl (1975) 'Comments', *Journal of Law and Economics*, December 1975.
Brunner, Karl (1981) *The Control of Monetary Aggregates: Patrolling Monetary Aggregates III*, Boston, Mass.: Federal Reserve Bank of Boston.
Chow, Gregory C. (1975) *Analysis and Control of Dynamic Economic Systems*, New York: John Wiley.
Efron, Edith (1984) *The Apocalyptics: Cancer and the Big Lie*, New York: Simon & Schuster.
Tinbergen, Jan (1952) *On the Theory of Economic Policy*, Amsterdam: North-Holland.

Name Index